BLACK RHETORIC:

A Guide to
Afro-American Communication

by

ROBERT W. GLENN

The Scarecrow Press, Inc.
Metuchen, N.J.   1976

Library of Congress Cataloging in Publication Data

Glenn, Robert W   1944-
    Black rhetoric.

    Includes indexes.
    1.   Negroes--Bibliography.   I.   Title.
Z1361. N39G55   [185]   016. 8085   75-38912
ISBN 0-8108-0889-7

to

MY PARENTS

PREFACE

This book began in 1969 as a survey of primary and secondary materials that might be useful in a course on Afro-American oratory at Dartmouth College. My goal during the preparation of the book has been to compile a guide to available sources that would simplify the work of an instructor or a student interested in the content and communication of speeches and essays by Afro-Americans. In particular, I wanted ready answers to such questions as: Where can one find good texts by Delany, Garnet, Turner, Crummell? What speeches and essays are available from critical years like 1808, 1831, 1865, 1877, 1883, 1895? What should one read to learn how Afro-American writing and speaking changed from 1890-1895 to 1895-1900? What secondary materials discuss Afro-American abolitionists, the rhetoric of the Civil Rights movement, "Black English"? The present book should provide initial answers to these and similar questions.

The text of the book is divided into four sections. The first section lists 40 bibliographies that I have found useful, and that are intended to supplement the listings in the next three categories. I do not, for example, repeat all of the entries from Hite's excellent bibliography (B10) on contemporary speakers and issues.

The second section lists 182 anthologies, most of which will be available in college and university libraries or accessible through interlibrary loan. The contents of the anthologies are described as to type of material, dates, and, for some anthologies, the precise items included.

The third section lists more than 1,270 books and essays arranged topically, with cross-listings where relevant to an anthology which includes the item, or to a speaker whom the item concerns and who appears in the fourth section.

The fourth section lists over 2,400 speeches and essays arranged alphabetically by author and chronologically within each

v

author-category. Journals such as The Messenger, the Southern Workman and others are not indexed here, for reasons of space and the desirability of separate, exhaustive indices for each. The following entry may serve as an illustration of form:

SE1063 Grimké, Archibald H. "Modern Industrialism and
        the Negroes of the United States." 1908. Ameri-
        can Negro Academy, Occasional Papers No. 12.
        Washington: The Academy, 1908. Rpt. in
        Brotz, A27:464-480.

The entry is no. 1063 in the speeches and essays (SE) section. The speaker is Archibald H. Grimké, whose title in this case is his own; for several entries a new title has been supplied by myself or another editor. The date following the title, 1908, is the date of delivery of the speech; for other entries the date may refer to initial publication or to a terminus ad quem when a more precise date has not been determined. Following the date is the citation of the most authoritative text, the original publication by the American Negro Academy. And finally there is a citation of a reprint of the address in anthology no. 27, Negro Social and Political Thought, 1850-1920: Representative Texts, ed. Howart Brotz (New York: Basic, 1966), pp. 464-480.

Following the section on speeches and essays is a chronological index of all SE items, the arrangement within each year-category being strictly numerical. This is followed by an author index to the first three sections of the bibliography. The speakers and writers of Section IV (SE) are omitted from the author index, since their materials are already arranged alphabetically by author.

A note on accuracy: The present book contains well over 20,000 separate numbers alone, and Tartakover's observation about chess is only too pertinent: "The mistakes are all there, waiting to be made." Against the inevitable errors, however, may be balanced some corrections of previous publications. Woodson, for example, regularly gives as the date of delivery of a speech the date of its appearance in print (e. g., SE1962), or gives no date when one is readily available (e.g., SE1985), or through typographical or other error often assigns a wrong date (e. g., SE1040). Woodson's errors are frequently repeated by later anthologists, and new mistakes are made as well; for instance, one editor reports that the speech after which Malcolm X made his "chickens coming home to roost" remark about President Kennedy's

vi

assassination (SE1582) was delivered November 22, 1963. Whenever such errors have been detected, they have been corrected, sometimes silently.

Work on this project has been generously assisted by the Office of Graduate Studies of The University of Tennessee, Knoxville, which provided Faculty Research Fund Awards for the 1973-74 and 1974-75 academic years. I also wish to thank Danuta Nitecki and her Interlibrary Loan staff, who will be pleased to learn that this book is finished at last, and my colleagues at The University of Tennessee and Dartmouth College for their encouragement. My principal debt is to my friend and former teacher and colleague, John Lee Jellicorse, who is involved in all aspects of this book except its blunders. And to my family, my gratitude: to Daran, for his help in rearranging the index cards; to Alana, for her gentle conversation; and to Wanda, for her patience and support.

Robert W. Glenn
Knoxville, Tenn.
January 8, 1975

ABBREVIATIONS

CSSJ   Central States Speech Journal

JNE   Journal of Negro Education

JNH   Journal of Negro History

NHB   Negro History Bulletin

QJS   Quarterly Journal of Speech

SM   Speech Monographs

SSCJ   Southern Speech Communication Journal

SSJ   Southern Speech Journal

ST   Speech Teacher

TS   Today's Speech

WS   Western Speech

CONTENTS

SECTION I

BIBLIOGRAPHIES (B)

B1   Aptheker, Herbert, comp. Annotated Bibliography of
     the Published Writings of W. E. B. Du Bois. Mill-
     wood, N. Y.: Kraus-Thomson, 1973.

B2   Baxandall, Lee, comp. "African and Afro-American."
     Marxism and Aesthetics: A Selective Annotated Bib-
     liography. New York: Humanities Press, 1968.
     Pages 8-16.

B3   Bergman, Peter M. "Bibliography of Bibliographies."
     The Chronological History of the Negro in America.
     In Bergman, HC438:617-624.

B4   Cole, Johnneta B. "Black Women in America: An An-
     notated Bibliography." Black Scholar, 3 (Dec. 1971),
     41-53.

     [Dickinson, Donald C. A Bio-Bibliography of Langston
     Hughes, 1902-1967. See HC37.]

B5   Du Bois, W. E. B., ed. A Select Bibliography of the
     Negro American: A Compilation Made under the Di-
     rection of Atlanta University, Together with the Pro-
     ceedings of the Tenth Conference for the Study of the
     Negro Problems, Held at Atlanta University, on May
     30, 1905. 1905; rpt. New York: Octagon, 1968.

B6   _____, and Guy B. Johnson. Encyclopedia of the
     Negro: Preparatory Volume with Reference Lists
     and Reports. New York: Phelps-Stokes Fund, 1945.

B7   Dumond, Dwight L., ed. A Bibliography of Antislavery
     in America. Ann Arbor: Univ. of Michigan Press,
     1961.

B8   Edwards, G. Franklin. "The Bibliography of E. Frank-

1

lin Frazier." E. Franklin Frazier on Race Relations. Ed. G. Franklin Edwards. Chicago: Univ.
of Chicago Press, 1968. Pages 325-331.

B9   Graham, James D. "Negro Protest in America, 1900-
      1955: A Bibliographical Guide." South Atlantic
      Quarterly, 67 (Winter 1968), 94-107.

B10   Hite, Roger. "Racial Rhetoric: A Bibliography."
      Proceedings: Speech Association of America Sum-
      mer Conference V. Ed. James E. Roever. New
      York: Speech Association of America, [1969].
      Pages 88-124.

B11   Howe, Mentor A., and Roscoe E. Lewis, comps. A
      Classified Catalogue of the Negro Collection in the
      Collis P. Huntington Library, Hampton Institute.
      1940; rpt. Detroit: Negro History Press, 1971.

B12   Jahn, Janheinz. A Bibliography of Neo-African Litera-
      ture from Africa, America, and the Caribbean. New
      York: Praeger, 1965.

B13   Kaiser, Ernest. "A Bibliography By and About Paul
      Robeson." Freedomways, 11 (1st Qrtr 1971), 125-
      133.

B14   Kennicott, Patrick. "The Black Revolution in America:
      A Selected Bibliography." Proceedings: Speech
      Association of America Summer Conference V. Ed.
      James E. Roever. New York: Speech Association
      of America, [1969]. Pages 125-150.

B15   Kennicott, Patrick C. "The Study of Black American
      Rhetoric: An Annotated Bibliography" [4 pp.]. Dis-
      tributed free by the Speech Communication Module,
      ERIC Clearinghouse on Reading and Communication
      Skills, Statler Hilton Hotel, New York, New York
      10001.

B16   McPherson, Dorothy. "Black Power in Print." Cali-
      fornia Librarian, 31 (April 1969), 93-103.

B17   McPherson, James M., et al. Blacks in America:
      Bibliographical Essays. Garden City, N.Y.: Double-
      day, 1971.

B18   Massey, James Earl. "Bibliographical Essay: Howard
      Thurman and Rufus M. Jones, Two Mystics." JNH,
      57 (April 1972), 190-195.

B19   Miller, Elizabeth W., comp. The Negro in America:
      A Bibliography. Cambridge: Harvard Univ. Press,
      1966.

B20   Morris, Milton D., comp. The Politics of Black Amer-
      ica: An Annotated Bibliography. Carbondale: Pub-
      lic Affairs Research Bureau, Southern Illinois Univ.,
      1971.

B21   O'Quinlivan, Michael, and Benjamin F. Speller, Jr.
      "An Index to Obituary Sketches in the Journal of
      Negro History, 1926-1958." JNH, 57 (Oct. 1972),
      447-454.

B22   Porter, Dorothy B. "Early American Negro Writings:
      A Bibliographical Study." Papers of the Bibliograph-
      ical Society of America, 39 (3rd Qrtr 1945), 192-
      268.

B23   _____, comp. The Negro in the United States: A
      Selected Bibliography. Washington: Library of Con-
      gress, 1970.

B24   Ralph, George, comp. The American Theater, The
      Negro, and the Freedom Movement: A Bibliography.
      Chicago: Community Renewal Society, 116 South
      Michigan Avenue, Chicago, Illinois 60603, n. d.

B25   Smith, Dwight L., ed. Afro-American History: A
      Bibliography. New edn. Santa Barbara, Cal.:
      ABC-Clio, 1974.

B26   Smith, Holly, comp. "A Selected Annotated Bibliogra-
      phy on Regional and Social Dialects." ERIC/Reading
      and Communication Skills, NCTE, 1111 Kenyon Road,
      Urbana, Illinois 61801. Oct. 1972.

B27   Thompson, Edgar T., and Alma Macy Thompson,
      comps. Race and Region: A Descriptive Bibliogra-
      phy Compiled with Special Reference to the Relations
      Between Whites and Negroes in the United States.
      Chapel Hill: Univ. of North Carolina Press, 1949.

B28   Turner, Darwin T., comp. Afro-American Writers.
       New York: Appleton, 1970.

B29   Walters, Mary Dawson, comp. Afro Americana: A
       Comprehensive Bibliography of Resource Materials
       in the Ohio State University Libraries By or About
       Black Americans. Columbus: Office of Educational
       Services, Ohio State Univ. Libraries, 1969.

B30   Whitney, Philip B., comp. America's Third World:
       A Guide to Bibliographic Resources in the Library
       of the University of California, Berkeley. Rev.,
       Aug. 1970. Addendum, 30 Sept. 1970. Berkeley:
       General Library, Univ. of California, 1970.

B31   Williams, Daniel T., comp. "The Awesome Thunder
       of Booker T. Washington: A Bio-Bibliographical
       Listing, 1969." Eight Negro Bibliographies. New
       York: Kraus, 1970.

B32   _____. "The Black Muslims in the United States:
       A Selected Bibliography, 1964." Eight Negro Bibli-
       ographies. New York: Kraus, 1970.

B33   _____. "The Freedom Rides: A Bibliography, 1961."
       Eight Negro Bibliographies. New York: Kraus, 1970.

B34   _____. "The Lynching Records at Tuskegee Institute;
       with Lynching in America: A Bibliography, 1969."
       Eight Negro Bibliographies. New York: Kraus, 1970.

B35   _____. "Martin Luther King, Jr. 1929-1968: A
       Bibliography, 1968." Eight Negro Bibliographies.
       New York: Kraus, 1970.

B36   _____. "The Perilous Road of Marcus M. Garvey:
       A Bibliography, and some correspondence with Book-
       er T. Washington, Emmet J. Scott, and Robert Rus-
       sa Moton, 1969." Eight Negro Bibliographies. New
       York: Kraus, 1970.

B37   _____. "The Southern Students' Protest Movement:
       A Bibliography, 1961." Eight Negro Bibliographies.
       'ew York: Kraus, 1970.

B38   _____. "The University of Mississippi and James
       H. Meredith: A Bibliography, 1963." Eight Negro

Bibliographies. New York: Kraus, 1970.

B39 Williams, Ora. "A Bibliography of Works Written by American Black Women." CLA Journal, 15 (March 1972), 354-377.

B40 Work, Monroe N., comp. A Bibliography of the Negro in Africa and America. 1928; rpt. New York: Octagon, 1965.

[Work, Monroe N. See Guzman, HC70.]

SECTION II

ANTHOLOGIES (A)

A1   Aptheker, Herbert, ed.   A Documentary History of the
     Negro People in the United States.   New York: Cit-
     adel, 1951.
        Contains SE items dated 1661 to 1910.

A2   _____.   A Documentary History of the Negro People
     in the United States, 1910-1932.   Secaucus, N. J.:
     Citadel, 1973.
        Contains SE items dated 1910 to 1932.

A3   _____.   A Documentary History of the Negro People
     in the United States, 1933-1945.   Secaucus, N. J.:
     Citadel, 1974.

A4   Auer, J. Jeffery, ed.   Antislavery and Disunion, 1858-
     1861:   Studies in the Rhetoric of Compromise and
     Conflict.   New York: Harper, 1963.
        Contains HC1077, HC1088, and other studies.

A5   _____.   The Rhetoric of Our Times.   New York:
     Appleton, 1969.
        Contains HC1036, HC1067, HC1093, HC1102,
        HC1134, HC1146, HC1163, and other studies.

A6   Baldwin, James.   Nobody Knows My Name: More
     Notes of a Native Son.   New York: Dial, 1961.
        Contains 15 SE items by Baldwin, dated 1954 to
        1960.

A7   _____.   Notes of a Native Son.   1955; rpt.   New
     York: Dial, 1963.
        Contains 10 SE items by Baldwin, dated 1948 to
        1955.

A8   Barbour, Floyd B., ed.   The Black Power Revolt: A
     Collection of Essays.   Boston: Sargent, 1968.

Contains SE items dated 1791 to 1968.

A9 _____. The Black Seventies. Boston: Sargent, 1970.
Contains SE items dated 1970.

A10 Bell, Howard Holman, ed. Minutes of the Proceedings of the National Negro Conventions, 1830-1864. New York: Arno, 1969.
Contains SE items dated 1830 to 1864.

A11 Bennett, Lerone, Jr. The Negro Mood and Other Essays. Chicago: Johnson, 1964.
Contains HC890, HC1230, and other studies.

A12 The Black Revolution: An "Ebony" Special Issue. Chicago: Johnson, 1970.
Contains 5 HC items and 4 SE items dated 1969.

A13 Blyden, Edward Wilmot. Black Spokesman: Selected Published Writings of Edward Wilmot Blyden. Ed. Hollis R. Lynch. New York: Humanities, 1971.
Contains 24 SE items by Blyden, dated 1857 to 1908, and others.

A14 _____. Christianity, Islam and the Negro Race [1887]. Edinburgh: Edinburgh Univ. Press, 1967.
Contains 15 SE items by Blyden, dated 1871 to 1887.

A15 _____. Liberia's Offering: Being Addresses, Sermons, Etc. New York: J. A. Gray, 1862.
Contains 6 SE items by Blyden, dated 1857 to 1862.

A16 Boggs, James. Racism and the Class Struggle: Further Pages from a Black Worker's Notebook. New York: Monthly Review, 1970.
Contains 16 SE items by Boggs, dated 1963 to 1970.

A17 Bond, Julian. A Time To Speak, A Time To Act: The Movement in Politics. New York: Simon, 1972.
Contains 17 SE items by Bond, dated 1969 to 1972.

A18 Bormann, Ernest G., ed. Forerunners of Black Power:

The Rhetoric of Abolition. Englewood Cliffs, N.J.:
Prentice-Hall, 1971.
Contains SE562, SE945, SE1961, SE2140, and oth-
ers.

A19   Bosmajian, Haig A., and Hamida Bosmajian, eds. The
Rhetoric of the Civil-Rights Movement. New York:
Random, 1969.
Contains SE284, SE288, SE880, SE1438, SE1566,
and SE2347.

A20   Bowen, J. W. E., ed. Africa and the American Negro:
Addresses and Proceedings of the Congress on Africa.
1896; rpt. Miami: Mnemosyne, 1969.
Contains SE items dated 1895.

A21   Bracey, John H., Jr., August Meier, and Elliott Rudwick, eds. The Afro-Americans: Selected Docu-
ments. Boston: Allyn, 1972.
Contains HC1192 and SE items dated 1705 to 1969.

A22   _____. Black Nationalism in America. Indianapolis:
Bobbs-Merrill, 1970.
Contains HC1232 and SE items dated 1787 to 1969.

A23   Braden, Waldo W., ed. Oratory in the Old South,
1828-1860. Baton Rouge: Louisiana State Univ.
Press, 1970.

A24   Brawley, Benjamin, ed. Early Negro American Writers: Selections with Biographical and Critical Introductions. 1935; rpt. New York: Dover, 1970.
Contains SE items dated 1761 to 1870.

A25   Brawley, E. M., ed. The Negro Baptist Pulpit: A
Collection of Sermons and Papers on Baptist Doctrine
and Missionary and Educational Work. 1890; rpt.
Freeport, N.Y.: Books for Libraries, 1971.
Contains SE items dated 1890.

A26   Broderick, Francis L., and August Meier, eds. Negro
Protest Thought in the Twentieth Century. Indi-
anapolis: Bobbs-Merrill, 1965.
Contains HC1231 and SE items dated 1895 to 1966.

A27   Brotz, Howard, ed. Negro Social and Political Thought,
1850-1920: Representative Texts. New York: Basic,

1966.
Contains SE items dated 1848 to 1924.

A28   Brown, Sterling A., Arthur P. Davis, and Ulysses Lee,
      eds. The Negro Caravan: Writings by American
      Negroes. 1941; rpt. New York: Arno, 1969.
         Contains HC68 and SE items dated 1834 to 1937.

A29   Bruce, John Edward. The Selected Writings of John
      Edward Bruce: Militant Black Journalist. Comp.
      Peter Gilbert. New York: Arno, 1971.
         Contains 18 SE items by Bruce, dated 1883 to
      1922, and others.

A30   Calverton, V. F., ed. Anthology of American Negro
      Literature. New York: Modern Library, 1929.
         Contains HC811, SE1679, SE2078, SE2329,
      SE2365, and others.

A31   Carmichael, Stokely. Stokely Speaks: Black Power
      Back to Pan-Africanism. New York: Random, 1971.
         Contains HC356 and 14 SE items by Carmichael
      dated 1966 to 1970.

A32   Chapman, Abraham, ed. Black Voices: An Anthology
      of Afro-American Literature. New York: St. Mar-
      tin's, 1970.
         Contains SE43, SE515, SE1338, SE1954, SE2387,
      SE2388, and others.

A33   Chisholm, Shirley. The Good Fight. New York:
      Harper, 1973.
         Contains 6 SE items by Chisholm, dated 1971 to
      1972.

A34   Clark, Kenneth B. The Negro Protest. Boston: Bea-
      con, 1963.
         Contains SE64, SE1440, and SE1579.

A35   Clarke, John Henrik, ed. Malcolm X: The Man and
      His Times. New York: Macmillan, 1969.
         Contains SE522, 6 SE items by Malcolm X dated
      1963 to 1965, and others.

A36   _____, with the assistance of Amy Jaques [sic] Gar-
      vey. Marcus Garvey and the Vision of Africa. New
      York: Random, 1974.

Contains SE788, SE789, SE792, 30 SE items by
Garvey dated 1913 to 1938, and others.

A37 _____, et al., eds. Black Titan: W. E. B. Du Bois.
Boston: Beacon, 1970.

A38 Cleage, Albert B., Jr. The Black Messiah. New
York: Sheed, 1968.
Contains 20 SE items by Cleage, dated 1967 to
1968.

A39 Cleaver, Eldridge. Post-Prison Writings and Speeches.
Ed. Robert Scheer. New York: Random, 1969.
Contains 15 SE items by Cleaver, dated 1967 to
1968.

A40 _____. Soul on Ice. New York: McGraw-Hill,
1968.
Contains 12 SE items by Cleaver, dated 1965 to
1968.

A41 Cox, LaWanda, and John H. Cox, eds. Reconstruction,
the Negro, and the New South. Columbia, S.C.:
Univ. of South Carolina Press, 1973.
Contains SE681, SE706, SE738, SE739, SE913,
SE2148, SE2189, and others.

A42 Cromwell, Otelia, Lorenzo Dow Turner, and Eva B.
Dykes, eds. Readings from Negro Authors, for
Schools and Colleges, with a Bibliography of Negro
Literature. New York: Harcourt, 1931.
Contains SE19, SE498, SE506, SE701, SE759,
SE1534, SE1680, SE1825, SE2073, SE2259,
SE2366, and others.

A43 Crummell, Alex[ander]. Africa and America: Addresses and Discourses. 1891; rpt. New York:
Negro Universities Press, 1969.
Contains 16 SE items by Crummell, dated 1846 to
1890.

A44 _____. The Future of Africa, Being Addresses,
Sermons, Etc., Etc., Delivered in the Republic of
Liberia. 1862; rpt. New York: Negro Universi-
ties Press, 1969.
Contains 10 SE items by Crummell, dated 1852
to 1861.

A45 _____. The Greatness of Christ, and Other Sermons. New York: Whittaker, 1882.
Contains SE465, SE467, SE468, and 17 SE items
by Crummell dated 1882.

A46 Culp, D.W., ed. Twentieth Century Negro Literature, or
A Cyclopedia of Thought on the Vital Topics Relating to
the American Negro. 1902; rpt. N.Y.: Arno, 1969.
Contains SE items dated 1902.

A47 Current, Richard N., ed. Reconstruction in Retro-
spect: Views from the Turn of the Century. Baton
Rouge: Louisiana State Univ. Press, 1969.
Contains HC636, HC639, HC650, HC655, HC675,
HC691, HC704, and HC738.

A48 Daniel, Bradford, ed. Black, White and Gray: Twen-
ty-One Points of View on the Race Question. New
York: Sheed, 1964.
Contains SE1438, SE1626, and others.

A49 Daniel, Jack L., ed. Black Communication: Dimen-
sions of Research and Instruction. New York:
Speech Communication Association, 1974.
Contains HC328, HC359, HC389, HC391, HC961,
HC990, HC1032, HC1051, HC1083, and HC1147.

A50 Davis, Angela, et al. If They Come in the Morning:
Voices of Resistance. New York: Okpaku, 1971.
Contains HC136, SE72, SE1348, SE1349, SE1772,
and 3 SE items by Davis dated 1971.

A51 Douglass, Frederick. The Life and Writings of Frederick Douglass. Ed. Philip Foner. Vol. I. New
York: International, 1950.
Contains 19 SE items by Douglass, dated 1841 to
1849, and others.

A52 _____. The Life and Writings of Frederick Douglass. Ed. Philip Foner. Vol. II. New York: International, 1950.
Contains 47 SE items by Douglass, dated 1850 to
1860, and others.

A53 _____. The Life and Writings of Frederick Douglass. Ed. Philip Foner. Vol. III. New York: International, 1952.

Contains 35 SE items by Douglass, dated 1861 to
1864, and others.

A54   _____. The Life and Writings of Frederick Douglass. Ed. Philip Foner. Vol. IV. New York: International, 1955.
Contains 35 SE items by Douglass, dated 1865 to
1894, and others.

A55   Douglass, William. Sermons Preached in the African
Protestant Episcopal Church of St. Thomas', Philadelphia. 1854; rpt. Freeport, N.Y.: Books for Libraries, 1971.
Contains 12 SE items by Douglass, dated 1854.

A56   Drimmer, Melvin, ed. Black History: A Reappraisal.
Garden City, N.Y.: Doubleday, 1969.

A57   Duberman, Martin, ed. The Antislavery Vanguard:
New Essays on the Abolitionists. Princeton: Prince-
ton Univ. Press, 1965.
Contains HC493, HC501, HC512, HC586, HC592,
HC1253, and other studies.

A58   Du Bois, W. E. B. An ABC of Color. New York:
International, 1969.
Contains SE items by Du Bois, dated 1896 to 1958.

A59   _____. Darkwater: Voices from Within the Veil.
1920; rpt. New York: Schocken, 1969.
Contains SE items by Du Bois, dated 1904 to 1919.

A60   _____. The Education of Black People: Ten Crit-
iques, 1906-1960. Ed. Herbert Aptheker. Amherst:
Univ. of Massachusetts Press, 1973.
Contains SE items by Du Bois, dated 1906 to 1960.

A61   _____. The Emerging Thought of W. E. B. Du
Bois: Essays and Editorials from "The Crisis." Ed.
Henry Lee Moon. New York: Simon, 1972.
Contains SE items by Du Bois, dated 1910 to 1934.

A62   _____. The Selected Writings of W. E. B. Du Bois.
Ed. Walter Wilson. New York: New American Library, 1970.
Contains SE items by Du Bois, dated 1899 to
c. 1963.

A63 _____. The Seventh Son: The Thought and Writings
of W. E. B. Du Bois. Ed. Julius Lester. Vol. I.
New York: Random, 1971.
Contains SE items by Du Bois, dated 1883 to
1930.

A64 _____. The Seventh Son: The Thought and Writings
of W. E. B. Du Bois. Ed. Julius Lester. Vol. II.
New York: Random, 1971.
Contains SE items by Du Bois, dated 1910 to
1960.

A65 _____. The Souls of Black Folk: Essays and
Sketches. 1903; rpt. New York: Johnson Reprint,
1968.
Contains SE items by Du Bois, dated 1897 to
1903.

A66 _____. W. E. B. Du Bois: A Reader. Ed. Meyer
Weinberg. New York: Harper, 1970.
Contains SE items by Du Bois, dated 1892 to
1954.

A67 _____. A W. E. B. Du Bois Reader. Ed. Andrew
G. Paschal. New York: Macmillan, 1971.
Contains SE items by Du Bois, dated 1897 to
1961.

A68 _____. W. E. B. Du Bois Speaks: Speeches and
Addresses, 1890-1919. Ed. Philip S. Foner. New
York: Pathfinder, 1970.
Contains HC46, SE1470, and SE items by Du
Bois dated 1897 to 1919.

A69 _____. W. E. B. Du Bois Speaks: Speeches and
Addresses, 1920-1963. Ed. Philip S. Foner. New
York: Pathfinder, 1970.
Contains SE items by Du Bois dated 1920 to 1962.

A70 Dunbar, Alice Moore, ed. Masterpieces of Negro Eloquence: The Best Speeches Delivered by the Negro
from the Days of Slavery to the Present Time.
1914; rpt. New York: Johnson Reprint, 1970.
Contains SE items dated 1818 to 1913.

A71 Ellison, Ralph. Shadow and Act. New York: Random, 1964.

Contains SE items by Ellison, dated 1942 to 1964.

A72   Fishel, Leslie H. , Jr. , and Benjamin Quarles, eds.
      The Black American: A Documentary History. New
      York: Morrow, 1970.
      Contains HC867, SE items dated 1817 to 1969, and
      others.

A73   Foner, Philip S. , ed. The Black Panthers Speak.
      Philadelphia: Lippincott, 1970.
      Contains SE items dated 1966 to 1970.

A74   _____. The Voice of Black America: Major
      Speeches by Negroes in the United States, 1797-
      1971. New York: Simon, 1972.
      Contains SE items dated 1797 to 1971.

A75   From Servitude to Service: Being the Old South Lec-
      tures on the History and Work of Southern Institu-
      tions for the Education of the Negro. 1905; rpt.
      New York: Negro Universities Press, 1969.
      Contains SE250, SE758, SE1651, and others.

A76   Fulkerson, Raymond Gerald. "Frederick Douglass and
      the Anti-Slavery Crusade: His Career and Speeches,
      1817-1861." Diss. , Univ. of Illinois, 1971.
      Contains 47 SE items by Douglass, dated 1841 to 1860.

A77   Garrison, Wm. Lloyd. Thoughts on African Coloniza-
      tion. Part II, Sentiments of the People of Color.
      1832; rpt. New York: Arno, 1968.
      Contains SE items dated 1817 to 1832.

A78a Garvey, Marcus. Philosophy and Opinions of Marcus
      Garvey. Comp. Amy Jacques Garvey. [Vol. I.]
      1923; rpt. New York: Atheneum, 1969.
      Contains 9 SE items by Garvey, dated 1921 to
      1922, and others.

A78b _____. Philosophy and Opinions of Marcus Garvey,
      or Africa for the Africans. Comp. Amy Jacques
      Garvey. [Vol. I, 1923, bound with A79.] London:
      Cass, 1967.
      '   Contains 9 SE items by Garvey, dated 1921 to
      1922, and others.

A79   _____. Philosophy and Opinions of Marcus Garvey,

  or Africa for the Africans. Comp. Amy Jacques.
  Garvey. [Vol. II.] 1925; rpt. London: Cass,
  1967, and New York: Atheneum, 1969. [Cass reprint bound with A78b.]
    Contains 33 SE items by Garvey, dated 1920 to
    1925, and others.

A80 Gayle, Addison, Jr. The Black Situation. New York:
  Horizon, 1970.
    Contains HC406, HC926, HC978, and other stud-
    ies.

A81 Geschwender, James A., ed. The Black Revolt.
  Englewood Cliffs, N.J.: Prentice-Hall, 1971.
    Contains HC892, HC1104, HC1210, HC1211,
    HC1228, HC1241, HC1243, and HC1252.

A82 Golden, James L., and Richard D. Rieke. The Rhetoric of Black Americans. Columbus: Merrill,
  1971.
    Contains SE items dated 1829 to 1969.

A83 Goodman, Paul, ed. Seeds of Liberation. New York:
  Braziller, 1964.
    Contains SE63, SE65, SE882, SE1429, SE1434,
    SE2011, SE2012, SE2358, and others.

A84 Grant, Joanne, ed. Black Protest: History, Docu-
  ments, and Analyses, 1619 to the Present. New
  York: St. Martin's, 1970.
    Contains SE items dated 1829 to 1967, and others.

A85 Gregory, Dick. The Shadow that Scares Me. Ed.
  James R. McGraw. Garden City, N.Y.: Doubleday,
  1968.
    Contains HC109 and 10 SE items by Gregory,
    dated 1968.

A86 Griffiths, Julia, ed. Autographs for Freedom. 1853;
  rpt. Miami: Mnemosyne, 1969.
    Contains SE21, SE604, SE1783, SE2104, and oth-
    ers.

A87 _____. Autographs for Freedom. 1854; rpt. Miami: Mnemosyne, 1969.
    Contains SE220, SE602, SE1480, SE1953, SE2105,
    SE2291, SE2292, and others.

A88 Grimké, Francis J. The Works of Francis J. Grimké.
     Ed. Carter G. Woodson. Vol. I, Addresses Mainly
     Personal and Racial. Washington: Associated, 1942.
        Contains 50 SE items by Grimké, dated 1892 to
        1936.

A89 _____. The Works of Francis J. Grimké. Ed.
     Carter G. Woodson. Vol. II, Special Sermons.
     Washington: Associated, 1942.
        Contains 54 SE items by Grimké, dated 1888 to
        1934.

A90 Hale, Frank W., Jr., ed. The Cry for Freedom: An
     Anthology of the Best that Has Been Said and Writ-
     ten on Civil Rights Since 1954. South Brunswick,
     N.J.: A. S. Barnes, 1969.
        Contains SE items dated 1954 to 1968.

A91 Herbert, Hilary A., ed. Why the Solid South? or, Re-
     construction and Its Results. 1890; rpt. New York:
     Negro Universities Press, 1969.
        Contains 15 HC-Reconstruction items.

A92a Hill, Adelaide Cromwell, and Martin Kilson, eds.
     Apropos of Africa: Sentiments of Negro American
     Leaders on Africa from the 1800s to the 1950s.
     London: Cass, 1969.
        Contains SE items dated 1812 to 1961, and others.

A92b _____. Apropos of Africa: Afro-American Leaders
     and the Romance of Africa. Garden City, N.Y.:
     Doubleday, 1971.
        Contains SE items dated 1812 to 1961, and others.

A93 Hill, Roy L., ed. Rhetoric of Racial Revolt. Den-
     ver: Golden Bell, 1964.
        Contains SE items dated 1849 to 1963.

A94 Holsey, L. H. Autobiography, Sermons, Addresses,
     and Essays. Atlanta: Franklin, 1898.
        Contains HC85 and 28 SE items by Holsey dated
        1898.

A95 Hood, J. W. The Negro in the Christian Pulpit; or,
     The Two Characters and Two Destinies, as Deline-
     ated in Twenty-One Practical Sermons. Raleigh:
     Edwards, Broughton, 1884.

Contains SE1416, SE1417, SE1543, SE1724,
SE2173, and 21 SE items by Hood dated 1884.

A96   Hughes, Langston. Good Morning Revolution: Uncol-
      lected Social Protest Writings. Ed. Faith Berry.
      New York: L. Hill, 1973.
      Contains 22 SE items by Hughes, dated 1931 to
      1953, and others.

A97   _____. The Langston Hughes Reader. New York:
      Braziller, 1958.
      Contains SE1321, SE1334, SE1335, SE1336,
      SE1337, and others.

A98   Hyman, Harold M., and Leonard W. Levy, eds.
      Freedom and Reform: Essays in Honor of Henry
      Steele Commager. New York: Harper, 1967.
      Contains HC253 and other studies.

A99   Jacobs, Paul, and Saul Landau. The New Radicals:
      A Report with Documents. New York: Vintage,
      1966.
      Contains HC356, HC897, HC1237, SE1786,
      SE2015, and others.

A100 Johnson, Charles S., ed. Ebony and Topaz: A Col-
      lectanea. New York: National Urban League, 1927.
      Contains SE879, SE934, SE1207, SE1244, SE1398,
      SE1534, SE1839, SE1965, SE2078, and others.

A101 [Jones, LeRoi] Imamu Amiri Baraka, ed. African
      Congress: A Documentary of the First Modern Pan-
      African Congress. New York: Morrow, 1972.
      Contains 26 SE items dated 1970, and others.

A102 Jones, LeRoi. Home: Social Essays. New York:
      Morrow, 1966.
      Contains 9 SE items by Jones, dated 1962 to
      1965.

A103 _____, and Larry Neal. Black Fire: An Anthology
      of Afro-American Writing. New York: Morrow,
      1968.
      Contains HC996, HC1006, SE138, SE285, SE500,
      SE1199, SE1234, SE1475, SE1532, SE2135,
      SE2361, and others.

A104 Jones, Singleton Thomas. Sermons and Addresses.
York, Pa.: Anstadt, 1892.
[Note: This volume is cited by Work, B40:409,
and by Jahn, B12:282, but I have been unable to
locate a copy.]

A105 Katope, Christopher, and Paul Zolbrod, eds. The
Rhetoric of Revolution. New York: Macmillan,
1970.
Contains HC933, HC988, HC1131, SE373, SE570,
SE2359, and others.

A106 King, Martin Luther, Jr. Strength to Love. New
York: Harper, 1963.
Contains 17 SE items by King, dated 1963.

A107 _____. The Trumpet of Conscience. New York:
Harper, 1968.
Contains SE1465, SE1466, SE1467, SE1468, and
SE1469.

A108 Kochman, Thomas, ed. Rappin' and Stylin' Out: Communication in Urban Black America. Urbana: Univ.
of Illinois Press, 1972.
Contains HC345, HC372, HC380, HC1191, and other studies.

A109 Langston, John Mercer. Freedom and Citizenship: Selected Lectures and Addresses. 1883; rpt. Miami:
Mnemosyne, 1969.
Contains 11 SE items by Langston, dated 1858 to
1879.

A110 Lecky, Robert S., and H. Elliott Wright, eds. Black
Manifesto: Religion, Racism, and Reparations.
New York: Sheed, 1969.
Contains SE225, SE904, SE905, SE1054, SE1499,
and others.

A111 Lincoln, C. Eric. Sounds of the Struggle: Persons and
Perspectives in Civil Rights. New York: Morrow,
1967.
Contains HC1175, HC1212, HC1214, HC1216, and
13 SE items by Lincoln dated 1960 to 1967.

A112 Littleton, Arthur C., and Mary W. Burger, eds.
Black Viewpoints. New York: New American

Library, 1971.
Contains SE items dated 1853 to 1970.

A113 Locke, Alain, ed. The New Negro: An Interpretation.
1925; rpt. with a new introduction by Allan H. Spear,
New York: Johnson Reprint, 1968.
Contains SE545, SE799, SE932, SE1363, SE1375,
SE1705, SE1737, SE2328, and others.

A114 Logan, Rayford W., ed. W. E. B. Du Bois: A Profile. New York: Hill, 1971.

A115 _____. What the Negro Wants. Chapel Hill: Univ.
of North Carolina Press, 1944.
Contains SE items dated 1944.

A116 Lomas, Charles W., ed. The Agitator in American
Society. Englewood Cliffs, N.J.: Prentice-Hall,
1968.
Contains SE286b, SE1540, and others.

A117 Long, Richard A., and Eugenia W. Collier, eds.
Afro-American Writing: An Anthology of Prose and
Poetry. Vol. I. New York: New York Univ.
Press, 1972.
Contains SE497, SE562, SE945, SE2180, and oth-
ers.

A118 _____. Afro-American Writing: An Anthology of
Prose and Poetry. Vol. II. New York: New York
Univ. Press, 1972.
Contains SE54, SE371, SE871, SE960, SE986,
SE999, SE1431, SE1533, and others.

A119 Malcolm X. By Any Means Necessary: Speeches, Interviews and a Letter by Malcolm X. Ed. George
Breitman. New York: Pathfinder, 1970.
Contains 5 SE items by Malcolm X, dated 1964 to
1965, and others.

A120 _____. The End of White World Supremacy: Four
Speeches by Malcolm X. Ed. Benjamin Goodman.
New York: Merlin House, 1971.
Contains SE1576, SE1578, SE1580, and SE1582.

A121 _____. Malcolm X Speaks. Ed. George Breitman.
New York: Merit, 1965.

Contains 12 SE items by Malcolm X, dated 1963
to 1965, and others.

A122 _____. The Speeches of Malcolm X at Harvard.
Ed. Archie Epps. New York: Morrow, 1968.
Contains HC1065, SE1574, SE1584, and SE1597.

A123 _____. Two Speeches by Malcolm X. New York:
Merit, 1965.
Contains SE1583, SE1586, SE1589, SE1601, and
others.

A124 Meier, August, and Elliott Rudwick, eds. Black Pro-
test in the Sixties. Chicago: Quadrangle, 1970.
Contains HC208, HC212, HC231, HC232, HC262,
HC274, HC944, HC951, HC1223, SE337, SE1181,
SE1846, and others.

A125 _____. The Making of Black America: Essays in
Negro Life & History. Vol. I, The Origins of
Black Americans. New York: Atheneum, 1969.
Contains HC11, HC282, HC298, HC420, HC562,
HC580, and other studies.

A126 _____. The Making of Black America: Essays in
Negro Life & History. Vol. II, The Black Commu-
nity in Modern America. New York: Atheneum,
1969.
Contains HC254, HC256, HC772, HC790, HC793,
HC795, HC807, HC830, HC849, HC904, HC923,
HC1081, HC1231, SE1648, and other studies.

A127 Miller, Kelly. The Everlasting Stain. 1924; rpt.,
bound with Miller, A129, New York: Arno, 1968.
Contains 26 SE items by Miller, dated 1915 to
1922.

A128 _____. Out of the House of Bondage. New York:
Neale, 1914.
Contains 11 SE items by Miller, dated 1909 to
1913.

A129 _____. Race Adjustment: Essays on the Negro in
America. 1908; rpt., bound with Miller, A127, New
York: Arno, 1968.
Contains 19 SE items by Miller, dated 1895 to
1907.

A130 Moss, James A., ed.   The Black Man in America:
Integration and Separation.   New York: Dell, 1971.
Contains HC415, HC936, HC957, HC1264, 10 SE
items dated 1968 to 1969, and others.

A131 [National Association for the Advancement of Colored
People.]   Speeches By the Leaders: The March on
Washington for Jobs and Freedom, August 28, 1963.
New York: N.A.A.C.P., n.d.
Contains SE881, SE1439, SE1510, SE1913, SE2345,
SE2401, and others.

A132 The Negro and the Elective Franchise.   American Negro Academy, Occasional Papers No. 11.   Washington: The Academy, 1905.
Contains SE422, SE1062, SE1115, SE1303, SE1547,
and SE1654.

A133 The Negro Problem: A Series of Articles by Represent-
ative American Negroes of To-Day.   1903; rpt. New
York: AMS, 1970.
Contains SE315, SE749, SE861, SE921, SE1424,
SE2111, and SE2267.

A134 O'Neill, Daniel J., ed.   Speeches by Black Americans.
Encino, Cal.:   Dickenson, 1971.
Contains SE items dated 1817 to 1969.

A135 Osofsky, Gilbert, ed.   The Burden of Race: A Documentary History of Negro-White Relations in America.   New York: Harper, 1967.
Contains SE items dated 1837 to 1966 and others.

A136 Papers of the American Negro Academy.   American
Negro Academy, Occasional Papers Nos. 18-19.
[Washington: The Academy, 1916.]
Contains SE447, SE1068, SE1237, SE1821, SE2075,
and SE2133.

A137 Payne, Daniel A.   Sermons and Addresses, 1853-1891.
Ed. Charles Killian.   New York: Arno, 1972.
Contains SE1889 and 13 SE items by Payne, dated
1845 to 1890.

A138 _____.   Sermons Delivered by Bishop Daniel A.
Payne, D.D., LL.D.   Ed. C. S. Smith.   Nashville:
Publishing House, A.M.E. Sunday School Union,

1888. [Rpt. in Payne, A137:orig. pag.]
Contains SE1808 and SE1809.

A139 Penn, I. Garland. The Afro-American Press, and Its
Editors. 1891; rpt. New York: Arno, 1969.
Contains SE items dated 1890 and others.

A140 Pickens, William. The New Negro: His Political,
Civil and Mental Status and Related Essays. 1916;
rpt. New York: AMS, 1969.
Contains 14 SE items by Pickens, dated 1910 to
1916.

A141 Porter, Dorothy, ed. Early Negro Writing, 1760-1837.
Boston: Beacon, 1971.
Contains SE items dated 1760 to 1837 and others.

A142 [_____, ed.] Negro Protest Pamphlets: A Com-
pendium. New York: Arno, 1969.
Contains SE409, SE867, SE1186, SE1395, SE1792,
and SE2290.

A143 Powell, Adam Clayton. Keep the Faith, Baby! New
York: Trident, 1967.
Contains 11 SE items by Powell, dated 1950 to
1963, and others.

A144 Powell, A. Clayton, Sr. Palestine and Saints in
Caesar's Household. New York: Richard R. Smith,
1939.
Contains 10 SE items by Powell, dated 1924 to
1939, and others.

A145 Proceedings of the National Negro Conference, 1909.
[1909?;] rpt. New York: Arno, 1969.
Contains SE253, SE768, SE769, SE2213, SE2220,
SE2300, and others.

A146 Ransom, Reverdy C. The Negro: The Hope or the
Despair of Christianity. Boston: Hill, 1935.
Contains 10 SE items by Ransom, dated 1930 to
1935.

A147 _____. The Spirit of Freedom and Justice: Orations and Speeches. Nashville: A. M. E. Sunday
School Union, 1926.
Contains 23 SE items by Ransom, dated 1893 to
1925.

A148 Robinson, William H., Jr., ed. Early Black Ameri-
       can Poets. Dubuque, Iowa: Brown, 1969.
       Contains HC1000 and others.

A149 _____. Early Black American Prose. Dubuque,
       Iowa: Brown, 1971.
       Contains HC134, SE items dated 1760 to 1895,
       and others.

A150 Roman, Charles Victor. A Knowledge of History Is
       Conducive to Racial Solidarity, and Other Writings.
       Nashville: Sunday School Union, 1911.
       Contains SE1983, SE1984, SE1985, SE1986, and
       SE1987.

A151 Rose, Peter I., ed. Americans from Africa: Old
       Memories, New Moods. New York: Atherton, 1970.
       Contains HC932, HC933, HC956, HC958, HC1105,
       HC1249, HC1258, SE284, and others.

A152 _____. Americans from Africa: Slavery and Its
       Aftermath. New York: Atherton, 1970.
       Contains HC1081 and other studies.

A153 Rustin, Bayard. Down the Line: The Collected Writ-
       ings of Bayard Rustin. Ed. C. Vann Woodward.
       Chicago: Quadrangle, 1971.
       Contains 52 SE items by Rustin, dated 1942 to
       1971.

A154 Scott, Robert L., and Wayne Brockriede, eds. The
       Rhetoric of Black Power. New York: Harper,
       1969.
       Contains HC1048, HC1126, HC1127, HC1129,
       HC1130, SE283, SE289, SE1181, and SE1462.

A155 Smith, Arthur L., ed. Language, Communication, and
       Rhetoric in Black America. New York: Harper,
       1972.
       Contains HC331, HC334, HC337, HC339, HC342,
       HC345, HC349, HC364, HC977, HC1042, HC1048,
       HC1050, HC1055, HC1056, HC1063, HC1065,
       HC1075, HC1081, HC1082, HC1091, HC1101,
       HC1121, HC1135, HC1136, HC1137, HC1138,
       HC1139, HC1141, and SE1403.

A156 _____, and Stephen Robb, eds. The Voice of Black

Rhetoric: Selections. Boston: Allyn, 1971.
Contains SE items dated 1828 to 1969.

A157 Spiller, Gustav, ed. Papers on Inter-Racial Problems
Communicated to the First Universal Races Con-
gress. . . . 1911; rpt., with an introduction by
Herbert Aptheker, New York: Citadel, [1971].
Contains SE773 and others.

A158 Sternsher, Bernard, ed. The Negro in Depression and
War: Prelude to Revolution, 1930-1945. Chicago:
Quadrangle, 1969.
Contains HC809, HC867, HC871, SE90, SE835,
and others.

A159 Stewart, Maria W. Productions of Maria W. Stewart.
Boston: Friends of Freedom and Virtue, 1835.
Contains SE2139, SE2140, and others.

A160 Stuckey, Sterling, ed. The Ideological Origins of
Black Nationalism. Boston: Beacon, 1972.
Contains SE items dated 1829 to 1859.

A161 Szwed, John F., ed. Black America. New York:
Basic, 1970.
Contains HC305, HC330, HC358, and other stud-
ies.

A162 Turner, Henry McNeal. Respect Black: The Writings
and Speeches of Henry McNeal Turner. Ed. Edwin
S. Redkey. New York: Arno, 1971.
Contains 6 SE items by Turner, dated 1866 to
1895, and others.

A163 Wallerstein, Immanuel, and Paul Starr, eds. The University Crisis Reader. Vol. I, The Liberal University Under Attack. New York: Random, 1971.
Contains HC422, SE items dated 1967 to 1970,
and others.

A164 _____. The University Crisis Reader. Vol. II,
Confrontation and Counterattack. New York: Ran-
dom, 1971.
Contains SE items dated 1968 and others.

A165 Washington, Booker T. Black Belt Diamonds: Gems
from the Speeches, Addresses, and Talks to Students

of Booker T. Washington.   New York: Fortune,
1898.

A166 _____.   The Booker T. Washington Papers.   Ed.
Louis R. Harlan and John W. Blassingame.   Vol. I,
The Autobiographical Writings.   Urbana: Univ. of
Illinois Press, 1972.
Contains HC189, HC191, and others.

A167 _____.   The Booker T. Washington Papers.   Ed.
Louis R. Harlan et al.   Vol. II, 1860-1889.   Urbana: Univ. of Illinois Press, 1972.
Contains 7 SE items by Washington, dated 1882
to 1888, and others.

A168 _____.   The Booker T. Washington Papers.   Ed.
Louis R. Harlan, Stuart B. Kaufman, and Raymond
W. Smock.   Vol. III, 1889-1895.   Urbana: Univ. of
Illinois Press, 1974.
Contains 23 SE items by Washington, dated 1890
to 1895, and others.

A169 _____.   Character Building, Being Addresses Delivered on Sunday Evening to the Students of Tuskegee Institute.   New York: Doubleday, 1902.

A170 _____.   Selected Speeches of Booker T. Washington.
Ed. E. Davidson Washington.   Garden City, N.Y.:
Doubleday, 1932.
Contains 29 SE items by Washington, dated 1884
to 1915.

A171 _____, and W. E. Burghardt Du Bois.   The Negro
in the South: His Economic Progress in Relation to
His Moral and Religious Development.   1907; rpt.,
with an introduction by Herbert Aptheker, New York:
Citadel, 1970.
Contains SE765, SE766, SE2271, and SE2272.

A172 Weiss, Robert O., and Bernard L. Brock, eds.   Cur-
rent Criticism: Essays from Speaker and Gavel.
[Slippery Rock, Pa.:]   Delta Sigma Rho-Tau Kappa
Alpha, 1971.
Contains HC1095, HC1097, HC1099, HC1119,
HC1126, HC1129, and others.

A173 The White Problem in America.   Chicago: Johnson,
1966.

A174 Whitten, Norman E., Jr., and John F. Szwed, eds.
Afro-American Anthropology: Contemporary Per-
spectives. New York: Free Press, 1970.
Contains HC927 and other studies.

A175 Williams, Jamye Coleman, and McDonald Williams,
eds. The Negro Speaks: The Rhetoric of Contemporary Black Leaders. New York: Noble, 1970.
Contains SE items dated 1945 to 1967.

A176 Woodson, Carter G., ed. The Mind of the Negro as
Reflected in Letters Written during the Crisis,
1800-1860. 1926; rpt. New York: Russell, 1969.
Contains SE items dated 1786 to 1853 and others.

A177 _____. Negro Orators and Their Orations. 1925;
rpt. New York: Russell, 1969.
Contains SE items dated 1788 to 1924.

A178 Wright, Nathan, Jr. Black Power and Urban Unrest:
Creative Possibilities. New York: Hawthorn, 1967.
Contains SE1755 and 11 SE items by Wright,
dated 1966 to 1967.

A179 _____. What Black Educators Are Saying. New
York: Hawthorn, 1970.
Contains SE items dated 1968 to 1970.

A180 _____. What Black Politicians Are Saying. New
York: Hawthorn. 1972.
Contains SE items dated 1972.

A181 Wright, Richard. White Man, Listen! Garden City,
N.Y.: Doubleday, 1957.
Contains HC1011, SE2390, SE2391, and SE2392.

A182 Young, Alfred F., ed. Dissent: Explorations in the
History of American Radicalism. DeKalb, Ill.:
Northern Illinois Univ. Press, 1968.
Contains HC510, HC895, HC923, and other stud-
ies.

SECTION III

HISTORY AND CRITICISM (HC)

BIOGRAPHY AND AUTOBIOGRAPHY

HC1 Adelman, Lynn. "A Study of James Weldon Johnson."
     JNH, 52 (April 1967), 128-145.

HC2 Allen, Richard. The Life, Experience and Gospel La-
     bors of the Rt. Rev. Richard Allen [1833]. New
     York: Abingdon, 1960.

HC3 _____. Journal of Richard Allen. [Excerpt in
     Payne, HC1180:71-83.]

HC4 Anderson, Jervis. A. Philip Randolph: A Biographi-
     cal Portrait. New York: Harcourt, 1973.

HC5 Bacote, Clarence A. "William Finch, Negro Council-
     man and Political Activities in Atlanta During Early
     Reconstruction." JNH, 40 (Oct. 1955), 341-364.

HC6 Batten, J. Minton. "Henry M. Turner, Negro Bishop
     Extraordinary." Church History, 7 (Sept. 1938),
     231-246.

HC7 Bennett, Lerone, Jr. What Manner of Man: A Biog-
     raphy of Martin Luther King, Jr. 3rd edn. Chi-
     cago: Johnson, 1968.

HC8 Bernard, Jacqueline. Journey Toward Freedom: The
     Story of Sojourner Truth. New York: Norton, 1967.

HC9 Berry, Jason. Amazing Grace: With Charles Evers
     in Mississippi. New York: Saturday Review, 1973.

HC10 Billingsley, Andrew. "Edward Blyden: Apostle of
     Blackness." Black Scholar, 2 (Dec. 1970), 3-12.

HC11 Billington, Ray Allen. "James Forten: Forgotten Abo-
     litionist." NHB, 13 (Nov. 1949), 31-36, 45. Rpt.
     in Meier and Rudwick, A125:289-301.

HC12 Brawley, Benjamin. Negro Builders and Heroes.
     Chapel Hill: Univ. of North Carolina Press, 1937.

HC13 _____. The Negro Genius: A New Appraisal of the
     Achievement of the American Negro in Literature and
     the Fine Arts. 1937; rpt. New York: Biblo and
     Tannen, 1966. [Rev. and enl. edn. of Brawley,
     HC966.]

HC14 Brewer, W. M. "Henry Highland Garnet." JNH, 13
     (Jan. 1928), 36-52.

HC15 _____. "John B. Russwurm." JNH, 13 (Oct. 1928).
     413-422.

HC16 Broderick, Francis L. W. E. B. Du Bois: Negro
     Leader in a Time of Crisis. Stanford: Stanford
     Univ. Press, 1959.

HC17 Brown, William Wells. "Memoir of the Author." In
     Brown, SE221:9-34.

HC18 _____. "Representative Men and Women." In
     Brown, HC445:418-552.

HC19 Bullock, Ralph W. In Spite of Handicaps: Brief Bio-
     graphical Sketches ... of Outstanding Negroes....
     1927; rpt. Freeport, N.Y.: Books for Libraries,
     1968.

HC20 Chapman, Gil, and Ann Chapman. Adam Clayton Pow-
     ell: Saint or Sinner? San Diego: Publishers Ex-
     port, 1967.

HC21 Cheek, William F. "John Mercer Langston: Black
     Protest Leader and Abolitionist." Civil War History,
     16 (June 1970), 101-120.

HC22 Chesnutt, Charles W. Frederick Douglass. 1899; rpt.
     New York: Johnson Reprint, 1970.

HC23 Chisholm, Shirley. Unbought and Unbossed. Boston:
     Houghton, 1970.

HC24 Christopher, Maurine. America's Black Congressmen.
      New York: Crowell, 1971.

HC25 Clarke, John Henrik. "The Early Years of Adam Powell."
      Freedomways, 7 (3rd Qrtr 1967), 199-213.

HC26 Clement, Rufus E. "Phylon Profile VII: Alexander
      Walters." Phylon, 7 (1st Qrtr 1946), 15-19.

HC27 Coan, Josephus Roosevelt. Daniel Alexander Payne,
      Christian Educator. Philadelphia: A. M. E. Book
      Concern, 1935.

HC28 Cohen, Robert Carl. Black Crusader: A Biography
      of Robert Franklin Williams. Secaucus, N.J.:
      Stuart, 1972.

HC29 Cooley, Timothy Mather. Sketches of the Life and
      Characer of the Rev. Lemuel Haynes. New York:
      Taylor, 1837.

HC30 Coppin, Levi J. Unwritten History: An Autobiography.
      Philadelphia: A. M. E. Book Concern, 1919.

HC31 Coulter, E. Merton. "Henry M. Turner: Georgia Ne-
      gro Preacher-Politician During the Reconstruction
      Era." Georgia Historical Quarterly, 48 (Dec. 1964),
      371-410. Rpt. in Coulter, HC753:1-36.

HC32 Cronon, Edmund David. Black Moses: The Story of
      Marcus Garvey and the Universal Negro Improve-
      ment Association. Madison: Univ. of Wisconsin
      Press, 1955.

HC33 Cutler, John Henry. Ed Brooke: Biography of a Sen-
      ator. Indianapolis: Bobbs-Merrill, 1972.

HC34 Dancy, John C. Sand Against the Wind: The Memoirs
      of John C. Dancy. Detroit: Wayne State Univ.
      Press, 1966.

HC35 Davis, Daniels. Marcus Garvey. New York: Watts,
      1972.

HC36 Davis, John W. "George Liele and Andrew Bryan,
      Pioneer Negro Baptist Preachers." JNH, 3 (April
      1918), 119-127.

HC37 Dickinson, Donald C. A Bio-Bibliography of Langston
Hughes, 1902-1967. [Hamden, Conn.]: Archon [Shoe
String Press], 1967.

HC38 Douglass, Frederick. Life and Times of Frederick
Douglass [rev. edn., 1892]. Ed. Rayford W. Logan.
New York: Macmillan, 1962.

HC39a _____. My Bondage and My Freedom. 1855; rpt.
New York: Arno, 1968.

HC39b _____. My Bondage and My Freedom [1855].
Chicago: Johnson, 1970.

HC40 _____. Narrative of the Life of Frederick Doug-
lass, An American Slave [1845]. Ed. Benjamin
Quarles. Cambridge: Belknap Press of Harvard
Univ. Press, 1960.

HC41 Draper, Theodore. "The Father of American Black
Nationalism." New York Review of Books, 12 March
1970, pp. 33-41. Rpt. in Draper, HC1256:21-41.
[On Delany.]

HC42 Drinker, Frederick E. Booker T. Washington: The
Master Mind of a Child of Slavery. 1915; rpt. New
York: Negro Universities Press, 1970.

HC43 Du Bois, Shirley Graham. His Day Is Marching On:
A Memoir of W. E. B. Du Bois. Philadelphia: Lippincott, 1971.

HC44 Du Bois, W. E. B. The Autobiography of W. E. B. Du
Bois: A Soliloquy on Viewing My Life from the Last
Decade of Its First Century. [Ed. Herbert Apthe-
ker.] New York: International, 1968.

HC45 _____. Dusk of Dawn: An Essay Toward an Autobiography of a Race Concept. 1940; rpt. New York:
Schocken, 1968.

HC46 _____. "A Pageant in Seven Decades, 1878-1938"
[1938]. In Du Bois, A68:21-72.

HC47 [Du Bois, W. E. B.] "The Ruling Passion: An Esti-
mate of Joseph Charles Price." Crisis, 23 (March
1922), 224-225.

HC48 Edwards, Adolph. Marcus Garvey, 1887-1940. London: New Beacon Publications, 1967.

HC49 Evers, Charles. Evers. Ed. Grace Halsell. New York: World, 1971.

HC50 Farrison, William Edward. William Wells Brown: Author and Reformer. Chicago: Univ. of Chicago Press, 1969.

HC51 Fauset, Arthur Huff. Sojourner Truth: God's Faithful Pilgrim. 1938; rpt. New York: Russell, 1971.

HC52 Fax, Elton C. Garvey: The Story of a Pioneer Black Nationalist. New York: Dodd, 1972.

HC53 Feldman, Eugene Pieter Romayn. Black Power in Old Alabama: The Life and Stirring Times of James T. Rapier, Afro-American Congressman from Alabama, 1839-1883. Chicago: Museum of African American History, 1968. [Rev. version of "James T. Rapier, Negro Congressman from Alabama." Phylon, 19 (4th Qrtr 1958), 417-423.]

HC54 Foner, Philip S. Frederick Douglass, a Biography. New York: Citadel, 1964. [Also available as the introductions to Douglass, A51-A54.]

HC55 Forten, Charlotte L. The Journal of Charlotte L. Forten. Ed. Ray Allen Billington. New York: Dryden, 1953. [Excerpts publ. by Billington as "A Social Experiment: The Port Royal Journal of Charlotte L. Forten, 1862-1863." JNH, 35 (July 1950), 233-264.]

HC56 Fox, Stephen R. The Guardian of Boston: William Monroe Trotter. New York: Atheneum, 1970.

HC57 Franklin, John Hope. "George Washington Williams, Historian." JNH, 31 (Jan. 1946), 60-90.

HC58 Frazier, E. Franklin. "Garvey: A Mass Leader." Nation, 18 Aug. 1926, pp. 147-148. Rpt. in Clarke, A36:236-241.

HC59 Fuller, T. O. Twenty Years in Public Life. Memphis: The Author, 1913.

HC60 Garvey, Amy Jacques. Garvey and Garveyism. King-
      ston, Jamaica: United Printers, 1963.

HC61 Gatewood, Willard B. "William D. Crum: A Negro
      in Politics." JNH, 53 (Oct. 1968), 301-320.

HC62 Goldman, Peter. The Death and Life of Malcolm X.
      New York: Harper, 1973.

HC63 Graham, Shirley. Paul Robeson: Citizen of the
      World. New York: Messner, 1946.

HC64 _____. There Was Once a Slave ... : The Heroic
      Story of Frederick Douglass. New York: Messner,
      1947.

HC65 Greene, Lorenzo J. "Prince Hall: Massachusetts
      Leader in Crisis." Freedomways, 1 (Fall 1961),
      238-258.

HC66 Gregory, Dick. Nigger: An Autobiography. New
      York: Dutton, 1964.

HC67 Gregory, James M. Frederick Douglass the Orator.
      1893; rpt. Chicago: Afro-Am Press, 1969.

HC68 Grimké, Angelina W. "A Biographical Sketch of Archi-
      bald H. Grimké." In Brown, A28:804-808.

HC69 Gutman, Herbert G. "Peter H. Clark: Pioneer Negro
      Socialist, 1877." JNE, 34 (Fall 1965), 413-418.

HC70 Guzman, Jessie P. "Monroe Nathan Work and His
      Contributions." JNH, 34 (Oct. 1949), 428-461.

HC71 Harlan, Louis R. Booker T. Washington: The Mak-
      ing of a Black Leader, 1856-1901. New York: Ox-
      ford Univ. Press, 1972.

HC72 Harlin, Howard H. John Jasper--A Case History in
      Leadership. Publications of the University of Vir-
      ginia, Phelp-Stokes Fellowship Papers, No. 14.
      [Charlottesville]: Univ. of Virginia, 1936.

HC73 Harris, Robert. Black Glory in the Life and Times of
      Marcus Garvey. New York: African Nationalist
      Pioneer Movement, 1961.

HC74 Harris, Sheldon H. Paul Cuffe: Black America and the African Return. New York: Simon, 1972.

HC75 Harrison, William. "Phylon Profile IX: William Monroe Trotter--Fighter." Phylon, 7 (3rd Qrtr 1946), 237-245.

HC76 Hartgrove, W. B. "The Story of Josiah Henson." JNH, 3 (Jan. 1918), 1-21.

HC77 Hatcher, William E. John Jasper: The Unmatched Negro Philosopher and Preacher. 1908; rpt. New York: Negro Universities Press, 1969.

HC78 Haynes, Lemuel. Diary, 26 July 1785 to 6 Aug. 1785. In Fishel and Quarles, A72:71-72.

HC79 Herndon, Angelo. Let Me Live. 1937; rpt. New York: Arno, 1969.

HC80 Hickey, Neil, and Ed Edwin. Adam Clayton Powell and the Politics of Race. New York: Fleet, 1965.

HC81 Hicks, Nancy. The Honorable Shirley Chisholm, Congresswoman from Brooklyn. New York: Lion, 1971.

HC82 Holden, Edith. Blyden of Liberia: An Account of the Life and Labors of Edward Wilmot Blyden, LL.D., as Recorded in Letters and in Print. New York: Vantage, 1966.

HC83 Holland, Frederic May. Frederick Douglass: The Colored Orator. Rev. edn. 1895; rpt. New York: Haskell, 1969.

HC84 Holmes, D. O. W. "Phylon Profile IV: Kelly Miller." Phylon, 6 (2d Qrtr 1945), 121-125.

HC85 Holsey, L. H. "Autobiography." In Holsey, A94:9-30.

HC86 Holt, Rackham. Mary McLeod Bethune: A Biography. Garden City, N.Y.: Doubleday, 1964.

HC87 Holtzclaw, William H. The Black Man's Burden. 1915; rpt. New York: Negro Universities Press, 1970.

HC88 Houston, G. David. "A Negro Senator" [Bruce].
      JNH, 7 (July 1922), 243-256.

HC89 Hoyt, Edwin P. Paul Robeson: The American Othello.
      Cleveland: World, 1967.

HC90 Hughes, Langston. The Big Sea: An Autobiography.
      1940; rpt. New York: Hill, 1963.

HC91 _____. I Wonder as I Wander: An Autobiographi-
      cal Journey. 1956; rpt. New York: Hill, 1964.

HC92 Hughes, William Hardin, and Frederick D. Patterson,
      eds. Robert Russa Moton of Hampton and Tuskegee.
      Chapel Hill: Univ. of North Carolina Press, 1956.

HC93 Jamal, Hakim A. From the Dead Level: Malcolm X
      and Me. New York: Random, 1972.

HC94 "Jesse Jackson: One Leader Among Many." Time, 6
      April 1970, pp. 14-16, 21-23.

HC95 Johnson, James Weldon. Along This Way: The Auto-
      biography of James Weldon Johnson. 1933; rpt.
      New York: Da Capo, 1973.

HC96 King, Coretta Scott. My Life with Martin Luther King,
      Jr. New York: Holt, 1969.

HC97 Langston, John Mercer. From the Virginia Plantation
      to the National Capitol. 1894; rpt. New York:
      Johnson Reprint, 1968.

HC98 Lawson, Elizabeth. The Gentleman from Mississippi:
      Our First Negro Senator, Hiram R. Revels. New
      York: Author, 1960.

HC99 Levy, Eugene. James Weldon Johnson: Black Leader,
      Black Voice. Chicago: Univ. of Chicago Press,
      1973.

HC100 Lewis, Claude. Adam Clayton Powell. Greenwich,
       Conn.: Fawcett, 1963.

HC101 Lewis, David L. King: A Critical Biography. New
       York: Praeger, 1970.

HC102 Lokos, Lionel. House Divided: The Life and Legacy
of Martin Luther King. New Rochelle, N.Y.: Ar-
lington, 1968.

HC103 Lovett, Robert Morss. "Du Bois." Phylon, 2 (3rd
Qrtr 1941), 214-217.

HC104 Lynch, Hollis R. Edward Wilmot Blyden: Pan-Negro
Patriot, 1832-1912. London: Oxford Univ. Press,
1967.

HC105 _____. "Introduction to the Atheneum Edition."
In Garvey, A78a:n. pag.

HC106a Lynch, John R. The Facts of Reconstruction. 1913;
rpt. New York: Arno, 1968.

HC106b _____. The Facts of Reconstruction [1913]. Ed.
William C. Harris. Indianapolis: Bobbs-Merrill,
1970.

HC107 Lynch, John Roy. Reminiscences of an Active Life:
The Autobiography of John Roy Lynch. Ed. John
Hope Franklin. Chicago: Univ. of Chicago Press,
1970.

HC108 McGill, Ralph. "W. E. B. Du Bois." Atlantic, Nov.
1965, pp. 78-81.

HC109 McGraw, James R. "Meet the Turkey General"
[Dick Gregory]. In Gregory, A85:15-34.

HC110 Malcolm X, with the assistance of Alex Haley. The
Autobiography of Malcolm X. New York: Grove,
1965.

HC111 Mann, Kenneth Eugene. "John Roy Lynch: U.S. Congressman from Mississippi." NHB, 37 (April-May
1974), 238-241.

HC112 Marrant, John. "A Narrative of the Lord's Wonder-
ful Dealings with John Marrant, a Black" [1802]. In
Porter, A141:427-447. [Later edn., "A Narrative
of the Life of John Marrant of New York" (London:
Farncombe, n.d.), available on microfilm, New
York Public Library, Film 1845.]

HC113 Mathews, Basil. Booker T. Washington, Educator
       and Interracial Interpreter. Cambridge: Harvard
       Univ. Press, 1948.

HC114 Mathews, Marcia M. Richard Allen. Baltimore:
       Helicon, 1963. [Partly fictional.]

HC115 Meltzer, Milton. Langston Hughes, a Biography.
       New York: Crowell, 1968.

HC116 Menard, Edith. "John Willis Menard." NHB, 28
       (Dec. 1964), 53-54.

HC117 _____. "John Willis Menard." NHB, 31 (Nov.
       1968), 10-11.

HC118 Miller, Floyd. "The Father of Black Nationalism:
       Another Contender" [Lewis Woodson]. Civil War His-
       tory, 17 (Dec. 1971), 310-319.

HC119 Miller, William Robert. Martin Luther King, Jr.:
       His Life, Martyrdom and Meaning for the World.
       New York: Weybright, 1968.

HC120 Moore, Alonzo D. "Memoir of the Author" [William
       Wells Brown]. In Brown, HC445:9-35.

HC121 Morse, W. H. "Lemuel Haynes." JNH, 4 (Jan.
       1919), 22-32.

HC122 Moton, Robert Russa. Finding a Way Out: An Auto-
       biography. Garden City, N. Y.: Doubleday, 1921.

HC123 Nadelson, Regina. Who Is Angela Davis? The Biog-
       raphy of a Revolutionary. New York: Wyden, 1972.

HC124 Neary, John. Julian Bond: Black Rebel. New York:
       Morrow, 1971.

HC125 Newton, Huey P., with the assistance of J. Herman
       Blake. Revolutionary Suicide. New York: Har-
       court, 1973.

HC126 Ofari, Earl. "Let Your Motto Be Resistance": The
       Life and Thought of Henry Highland Garnet. Boston:
       Beacon, 1972.

HC127 Ottley, Roi. The Lonely Warrior: The Life and
       Times of Robert S. Abbott. Chicago: Regnery,
       1955.

HC128 Page, Wilber A. "Notes on George W. Williams."
       NHB, 30 (Oct. 1967), 12.

HC129 Parker, J. A. Angela Davis: The Making of a Revo-
       lutionary. New Rochelle, N. Y.: Arlington, 1973.

HC130 Patterson, William L. The Man Who Cried Genocide:
       An Autobiography. New York: International, 1971.

HC131 Pauli, Hertha. Her Name Was Sojourner Truth. New
       York: Appleton, 1962.

HC132 Payne, Daniel Alexander. Recollections of Seventy
       Years. 1888; rpt. New York: Arno, 1968.

HC133 Peare, Catherine Owens. Mary McLeod Bethune.
       New York: Vanguard, 1951.

HC134 Pennington, James W. C. The Fugitive Blacksmith;
       or, Events in the History of James W. C. Penning-
       ton [1849]. London, 1849. Excerpt in Robinson,
       A149:123-134.

HC135 Pickens, William. Bursting Bonds. Boston: Jordan,
       1923.

HC136 "A Political Biography" [of Angela Davis]. In Davis,
       A50:171-176.

HC137 Porter, Dorothy B. "David M. Ruggles, an Apostle
       of Human Rights." JNH, 28 (Jan. 1943), 23-50.

HC138 _____. "Sarah Parker Remond, Abolitionist and
       Physician." JNH, 20 (July 1935), 287-293.

HC139 Powell, Adam Clayton, Jr. Adam by Adam: The
       Autobiography of Adam Clayton Powell, Jr. New
       York: Dial, 1971.

HC140 Powell, A. Clayton, Sr. Against the Tide: An Auto-
       biography. New York: Richard R. Smith, 1938.

HC141 Preston, Edward. Martin Luther King: Fighter for

Freedom. Garden City, N.Y.: Doubleday, 1968.

HC142 Puttkamer, Charles W., and Ruth Worthy. "William
Monroe Trotter, 1872-1934." JNH, 43 (Oct. 1958),
298-316.

HC143 Quarles, Benjamin. Frederick Douglass. Washington: Associated, 1948.

HC144 _____. "Frederick Douglass: Bridge Builder in Human Relations." NHB, 29 (Feb. 1966), 99-100, 112.

HC145 Rankin, J. E. "Introductory Sketch" [of John Mercer
Langston]. In Langston, A109:9-38.

HC146 Ransom, Reverdy C. The Pilgrimage of Harriet Ransom's Son. Nashville: Sunday School Union, n.d.

HC147 Ray, F. T. Sketch of the Life of Rev. Charles B.
Ray. New York: J. J. Little, 1887.

HC148 Reddick, Lawrence D. Crusader Without Violence:
A Biography of Martin Luther King, Jr. New York:
Harper, 1959.

HC149 Reid, C. H. "Marcus Garvey: A Social Phenomenon."
Thesis, Northwestern, 1928.

HC150 Robeson, Paul. Here I Stand. New York: Othello,
1958.

HC151 Rollin, Frank A. Life and Public Services of Martin
R. Delany. Boston: Lee and Shepard, 1868.

HC152 Rudwick, Elliott M. W. E. B. Du Bois: A Study in
Minority Group Leadership. Philadelphia: Univ. of
Pennsylvania Press, 1960.

HC153 Rustin, Bayard. "A. Philip Randolph: Dean of Civil
Rights." Crisis, 76 (April 1969), 170-173.

HC154 St. Clair, Sadie Daniel. "The Public Career of
Blanche K. Bruce." Diss., New York Univ., 1947.

HC155 Savage, W. Sherman. "The Influence of John Chavis
and Lunsford Lane on the History of North Carolina."
JNH, 25 (Jan. 1940), 14-24.

HC156 Schomburg, Arthur A.   "Two Negro Missionaries to
      the American Indians, John Marrant and John Stew-
      art."   JNH, 21 (Oct. 1936), 394-405.

HC157 Schuyler, George S.   Black and Conservative: The
      Autobiography of George S. Schuyler.   New Ro-
      chelle, N.Y.: Arlington, 1966.

HC158 Schweninger, Loren.   "John H. Rapier, Sr.: A Slave
      and Freedman in the Ante-Bellum South."   Civil
      War History, 20 (March 1974), 23-34.

HC159 Scott, Emmett J., and Lyman Beecher Stowe.
      Booker T. Washington: Builder of a Civilization.
      Garden City, N.Y.: Doubleday, 1916.

HC160 Sharma, Mohan Lal.   "Martin Luther King: Modern
      America's Greatest Theologian of Social Action."
      JNH, 53 (July 1968), 257-263.

HC161 Shaw, Peter.   "The Uses of Autobiography."   Ameri-
      can Scholar, 38 (Winter 1968-69), 136, 138, 140,
      142, 144. [Discusses Du Bois.]

HC162 Sherwood, Henry Noble.   "Paul Cuffe."   JNH, 8
      (April 1923), 153-229.

HC163a Simmons, William J.   Men of Mark: Eminent, Pro-
      gressive and Rising.   1887; rpt. New York: Arno,
      1968.

HC163b _____.   Men of Mark: Progressive and Rising
      [1887].   Chicago: Johnson, 1970.

HC164 Smith, Robert P.   "William Cooper Nell: Crusading
      Black Abolitionist."   JNH, 55 (July 1970), 182-199.

HC165 Spencer, Samuel R., Jr.   Booker T. Washington and
      the Negro's Place in American Life.   Boston: Little,
      1955.

HC166 Steiner, Stan.   "The Gentle Man: The Private Life
      and Death of Malcolm X."   Humanist, 25 (May-June
      1965), 131-132.

HC167 Sterling, Dorothy.   The Making of an Afro-American:
      Martin Robinson Delany, 1812-1885.   New York:

Doubleday, 1971.

HC168 Sterne, Emma Gelders. Mary McLeod Bethune. New York: Knopf, 1957.

HC169 Swados, Harvey. "Old Con, Black Panther, Brilliant Writer and Quintessential American" [Cleaver]. New York Times Magazine, 7 Sept. 1969, pp. 38-39, 139-154.

HC170 Swain, Lawrence. "Eldridge Cleaver." North American Review, NS 5 (July-Aug. 1968), 18-21.

HC171 Sweat, Edward F. "Francis L. Cardoza--Profile of Integrity in Reconstruction Politics." JNH, 46 (Oct. 1961), 217-232.

HC172 Tanser, H. A. "Josiah Henson, The Moses of His People." JNE, 12 (Fall 1943), 630-632.

HC173 Terrell, Mary Church. A Colored Woman in a White World. Washington: Ransdell, 1940.

HC174 Thompson, James W. An Authentic History of the Douglass Movement: Biographical Facts and Incidents in the Life of Frederick Douglass. Rochester: Rochester Herald, 1903.

HC175 Thornbrough, Emma Lou. T. Thomas Fortune: Militant Journalist. Chicago: Univ. of Chicago Press, 1972.

HC176 Torrence, Ridgely. The Story of John Hope. 1948; rpt. New York: Arno, 1969.

HC177a Truth, Sojourner. Narrative of Sojourner Truth. 1878; rpt. New York: Arno, 1968.

HC177b _____. Narrative of Sojourner Truth [1875]. Chicago: Johnson, 1970.

HC178 Turner, Henry M. "Introduction, Accompanied by a Sketch of the Life of Rev. W. J. Simmons." In Simmons, HC163a:39-63, HC163b:5-19.

HC179 Ullman, Victor. Martin R. Delany: The Beginnings of Black Nationalism. Boston: Beacon, 1971.

HC180 Uya, Okon E. From Slavery to Public Service: Robert Smalls, 1839-1915. New York: Oxford Univ.
Press, 1971.

HC181 Wahle, Kathleen O'Mara. "Alexander Crummell:
Black Evangelist and Pan-Negro Nationalist." Phylon, 29 (4th Qrtr 1968), 388-395.

HC182 Walls, William Jacob. Joseph Charles Price: Educator and Race Leader. Boston: Christopher, 1943.

HC183 Walters, Alexander. My Life and Work. New York:
Revell, 1917.

HC184a Ward, Samuel Ringgold. Autobiography of a Fugitive
Negro: His Anti-Slavery Labours in the United
States, Canada, & England. 1855; rpt. New York:
Arno, 1968.

HC184b _____. Autobiography of a Fugitive Negro: His
Anti-Slavery Labors in the United States, Canada, &
England [1855]. Chicago: Johnson, 1970.

HC185 Warner, Robert A. "Amos Gerry Beman--1812-1874,
A Memoir on a Forgotten Leader." JNH, 22 (April
1937), 200-221.

HC186 Warren, Robert Penn. "Malcolm X: Mission and
Meaning." Yale Review, 56 (Winter 1967), 161-171.

HC187 Washington, Booker T. Frederick Douglass. 1907;
rpt. New York: Haskell, 1968.

HC188 _____. My Larger Education, Being Chapters
from My Experience. 1911; rpt. Miami: Mnemosyne, 1969.

HC189 _____. The Story of My Life and Work [1900].
In Washington, A166:3-206.

HC190 _____. Working With the Hands, Being a Sequel
to "Up from Slavery" Covering the Author's Experiences in Industrial Training at Tuskegee. 1904; rpt.
New York: Negro Universities Press, 1969.

HC191 _____. Up from Slavery, An Autobiography [1901].
In Washington, A166:209-385.

HC192 Webb, Constance. Richard Wright, A Biography.
New York: Putnam, 1968.

HC193 Weisenburger, Francis P. "William Sanders Scarborough: Early Life and Years at Wilberforce."
Ohio History, 71 (Oct. 1962), 203-226.

HC194 _____. "William Sanders Scarborough: Scholarship, the Negro, Religion, and Politics." Ohio History, 72 (Jan. 1963), 25-50.

HC195 Wells, Ida B. Crusade for Justice: The Autobiography of Ida B. Wells. Ed. Alfreda M. Duster. Chicago: Univ. of Chicago Press, 1970.

HC196 Wesley, Charles H. Richard Allen: Apostle of Freedom. Washington: Associated Publishers, 1935,
1969.

HC197 Wheeler, Gerald E. "Hiram Rhoades Revels: Negro
Educator and Statesman." Thesis, Univ. of California, Berkeley, 1949.

HC198 Whitchurch, S. "The Negro Convert, A Poem; Being
the Substance of the Experience of Mr. John Marrant, a Negro." Bath: S. Hazard, n.d. [Available
on microfilm, New York Public Library, Film
1845.]

HC199 White, Walter. A Man Called White: The Autobiography of Walter White. 1948; rpt. Bloomington:
Indiana Univ. Press, 1970.

HC200 Williams, Roger M. The Bonds: An American Family. New York: Atheneum, 1971.

HC201 Work, M. N. "The Life of Charles B. Ray." JNH,
4 (Oct. 1919), 361-371.

HC202 _____, comp. "Materials from the Scrapbook of
W. A. Hayne Collected in 1874." JNH, 7 (July
1922), 311-340.

HC203 Worthy, Ruth. "A Negro in Our History: William
Monroe Trotter, 1872-1934." Thesis, Columbia,
1952.

HC204 Wright, Richard. Black Boy: A Record of Childhood
and Youth. New York: Harper, 1945.

HC205 Wyman, Lillie B. Chace. "Sojourner Truth." New
England Magazine, 24 (March 1901), 59-66.

HC206 Yates, Elizabeth. Howard Thurman: Portrait of a
Practical Dreamer. New York: John Day, 1964.

    SEE ALSO: O'Quinlivan and Speller, B21

            BIOGRAPHY--CRITICAL ESSAYS

HC207 Allen, Archie E. "John Lewis: Keeper of the
Dream." New South, 26 (Spring 1971), 15-25.

HC208 Arnold, Martin. "There Is No Rest for Roy Wilkins."
New York Times Magazine, 28 Sept. 1969, pp. 40-
41, 45, 48, 53, 55, 58, 60, 65, 68, 70. Rpt. in
Meier and Rudwick, A124:315-328.

HC209 Blodgett, Geoffrey. "John Mercer Langston and the
Case of Edmonia Lewis: Oberlin, 1862." JNH, 53
(July 1968), 201-218.

HC210 Breitman, George. The Last Year of Malcolm X:
The Evolution of a Revolutionary. New York: Merit, 1967.

HC211 Brisbane, Robert H. "His Excellency: The Provin-
cial President of Africa." Phylon, 10 (3rd Qrtr
1949), 257-264.

HC212 Brooks, Thomas R. "A Strategist Without a Movement" [Rustin]. New York Times Magazine, 16 Feb.
1969, pp. 24-25, 104-108, 111-112. Rpt. in Meier
and Rudwick, A124:329-343.

HC213 Calista, Donald J. "Booker T. Washington: Another
Look." JNH, 49 (Oct. 1964), 240-255.

HC214 Cheek, William F. "A Negro Runs for Congress:
John Mercer Langston and the Virginia Campaign of
1888." JNH, 52 (Jan. 1967), 14-34.

HC215 Coleman, Edward M. "William Wells Brown as an

Historian." JNH, 31 (Jan. 1946), 47-59.

HC216 Collier, Eugenia W. "James Weldon Johnson: Mirror of Change." Phylon, 21 (4th Qrtr 1966), 351-359.

HC217 Collyer, C. "Edward Wilmot Blyden--A Correspondent of William Ewart Gladstone." JNH, 35 (Jan. 1950), 75-78.

HC218 Contee, Clarence G. "The Emergence of Du Bois as an African Nationalist." JNH, 54 (Jan. 1969), 48-63.

HC219 Cook, Mercer. "Booker T. Washington and the French." JNH, 40 (Oct. 1955), 318-340.

HC220 De Marco, Joseph P. "The Concept of Race in the Social Thought of W. E. B. Du Bois." Philosophical Forum, NS 3 (Winter 1972), 227-242.

HC221 Diamond, Stanley. "Malcolm X: The Apostate Muslim." Dissent, 12 (Spring 1965), 193-197. Rpt. in The Radical Imagination. Ed. Michael Harrington. New York: New American Library, 1967. Pages 219-224.

HC222 Drake, Donald E., II. "Militancy in Fortune's New York Age." JNH, 55 (Oct. 1970), 307-322.

HC223 Du Bois, W. E. B. "Moton of Hampton and Tuskegee." Phylon, 1 (4th Qrtr 1940), 344-351.

HC224 Eisenberg, Bernard. "Kelly Miller: The Negro Leader as a Marginal Man." JNH, 45 (July 1960), 182-197.

HC225 Essien-Udom, E. U. "An Introduction to the Second Edition." In Garvey, A78b:vii-xxvii.

HC226 Farrison, William E. "William Wells Brown in Buffalo." JNH, 39 (Oct. 1954), 298-314.

HC227 _____. "William Wells Brown, Social Reformer." JNE, 18 (Winter 1949), 29-39.

HC228 Fishman, George. "Paul Robeson's Student Days and

the Fight Against Racism at Rutgers." Freedomways, 9 (Summer 1969), 221-229.

HC229 Flynn, John P. "Booker T. Washington: Uncle Tom
or Wooden Horse." JNH, 54 (July, 1969), 262-274.

[Fulkerson, Raymond Gerald. "Frederick Douglass
and the Anti-Slavery Crusade: His Career and
Speeches, 1817-1861." See A76.]

HC230 Gilbert, Albert C. "Architect of Men's Future--W.
E. B. Du Bois." Freedomways, 2 (Winter 1962),
33-38.

HC231 Good, Paul. " 'No Man Can Fill Dr. King's Shoes'--
but Abernathy Tries." New York Times Magazine,
26 May 1968, pp. 28-29, 91-97. Rpt. in Meier and
Rudwick, A124:284-301.

HC232 _____. "Odyssey of a Man--and a Movement"
[John Lewis]. New York Times Magazine, 25 June
1967, pp. 5, 44-48. Rpt. in Meier and Rudwick,
A124:252-266.

HC233 Guzman, Jessie P. "W. E. B. Du Bois--The Historian." JNE, 30 (Fall 1961), 377-385.

HC234 Haley, Alex. "Mr. Muhammad Speaks." Reader's
Digest, 76 (March 1960), 100-104.

HC235 Harding, Vincent. "W. E. B. Du Bois and the Black
Messianic Vision." Freedomways, 9 (Winter 1969),
44-58. Rpt. in Clarke, A37:52-68.

HC236 Harper, Frederick D. "The Influence of Malcolm X
on Black Militancy." Journal of Black Studies, 1
(June 1971), 387-402.

HC237 Heermance, J. Noel. William Wells Brown and Clo-
telle: A Portrait of the Artist in the First Negro
Novel. [Hamden, Conn.]: Archon Books, Shoe
String Press, 1969.

HC238 Himelhoch, Myra. "Frederick Douglass and Haiti's
Mole St. Nicholas." JNH, 56 (July 1971), 161-180.

HC239 Hudson, Theodore R. From LeRoi Jones to Amiri

Baraka: The Literary Works. Durham: Duke Univ.
Press, 1973.

HC240 James, Felix. "The Civic and Political Activities of
George A. Myers." JNH, 58 (April 1973), 166-178.

HC241 Jones, Wilbur D. "Blyden, Gladstone and the War."
JNH, 49 (Jan. 1964), 56-61.

HC242 Kahn, Tom, and Bayard Rustin. "The Ambiguous
Legacy of Malcolm X." Dissent, 12 (Spring 1965),
188-192.

HC243 Keating, Edward M. Free Huey! Berkeley: Ramparts, 1971.

HC244 Klingberg, Frank J. "Carter Godwin Woodson, Historian and His Contribution to American Historiography." JNH, 41 (Jan. 1956), 66-68.

HC245 Klingman, Peter D. "Josiah T. Walls and the Black
Tactics of Race in Post Civil War Florida." NHB,
37 (April-May 1974), 242-247.

HC246 Landon, Fred. "Henry Bibb, a Colonizer." JNH,
5 (Oct. 1920), 437-447.

HC247 Leary, Mary Ellen. "The Uproar Over Cleaver."
New Republic, 30 Nov. 1968, pp. 21-24.

HC248 Link, Eugene P. "The Civil Rights Activities of
Three Great Negro Physicians (1840-1940)." JNH,
52 (July 1967), 169-184. [On John S. Rock, Dan H.
Williams, and Louis Tompkins Wright.]

HC249 Lomax, Louis. To Kill a Black Man. Los Angeles:
Holoway, 1968.

HC250 McClendon, William H. "The Black Perspective of
Frederick Douglass." Black Scholar, 3 (March-
April 1972), 7-16.

HC251 Major, Reginald. Justice in the Round: The Trial of
Angela Davis. New York: Third Press, 1973.

HC252 Meier, August. "Booker T. Washington and the Negro Press: With Special Reference to the Colored

<u>American Magazine</u>." <u>JNH</u>, 38 (Jan. 1953), 67-90.

HC253 _____. "Frederick Douglass' Vision for America:
A Case Study in Nineteenth-Century Negro Protest."
In Hyman and Levy, A98:127-148.

HC254 _____. "On the Role of Martin Luther King."
<u>New Politics</u>, 4 (Winter 1965), 52-59. Rpt. in
Meier and Rudwick, A126:353-361.

HC255 _____. "The Racial and Educational Philosophy of
Kelly Miller, 1895-1915." <u>JNE</u>, 29 (Spring 1960),
121-127.

HC256 _____. "Toward a Reinterpretation of Booker T.
Washington." <u>Journal of Southern History</u>, 23 (May
1957), 220-227. Rpt. in Meier and Rudwick, A126:
125-130.

HC257 Partington, Paul G. "The Moon Illustrated Weekly--
The Precursor of the <u>Crisis</u>." <u>JNH</u>, 48 (July 1963),
206-216.

HC258 Paschal, Andrew G. "The Spirit of W. E. B. Du
Bois." <u>Black Scholar</u>, 2 (Oct. 1970), 17-28.

HC259 Quarles, Benjamin. "Douglass' Mind in the Making."
<u>Phylon</u>, 6 (1st Qrtr 1945), 5-12. Rpt. in Quarles,
HC143:1-14.

HC260 _____. "Frederick Douglass and the Woman's
Rights Movement." <u>JNH</u>, 25 (Jan. 1940), 35-44.

HC261 Rogers, Ben F. "William E. B. Du Bois, Marcus
Garvey, and Pan-Africa." <u>JNH</u>, 40 (April 1955),
154-165.

HC262 Rugaber, Walter. " 'We Can't Cuss White People Any
More. It's in Our Hands Now.' " <u>New York Times
Magazine</u>, 4 Aug. 1968, pp. 12-14, 16, 20, 23-24,
26. Rpt. in Meier and Rudwick, A124:302-314.
[On Charles Evers.]

HC263 Shepperson, George. "Frederick Douglass and Scot-
land." <u>JNH</u>, 38 (July 1953), 307-321.

HC264 Sundiata, Tiki. "A Portrait of Marcus Garvey."

Black Scholar, 2 (Sept. 1970), 7-19.

HC265 Thornbrough, Emma L. "Booker T. Washington as
Seen by His White Contemporaries." JNH, 53 (April
1968), 161-182.

HC266 _____. "More Light on Booker T. Washington and
the New York Age." JNH, 43 (Jan. 1958), 34-49.

HC267 Troy, Robert. "W. E. B. Du Bois in Retrospect."
New South, 25 (Fall 1970), 27-35.

HC268 Tucker, David M. "Miss Ida B. Wells and Memphis
Lynching." Phylon, 32 (2d Qrtr 1971), 112-122.

HC269 Walker, S. Jay. "Frederick Douglass and Woman
Suffrage." Black Scholar, 4 (March-April 1973),
24-31.

HC270 Walton, Hanes, Jr. "The Political Leadership of
Martin Luther King, Jr." Qrtrly Rev. of Higher
Education Among Negroes, 36 (July 1968), 163-171.

HC271 _____. The Political Philosophy of Martin Luther
King, Jr. Westport, Conn.: Greenwood, 1971.

HC272 Wesley, Charles H. "Carter G. Woodson--as a
Scholar." JNH, 36 (Jan. 1951), 12-24.

HC273 _____. "W. E. B. Du Bois--The Historian." JNH,
50 (July 1965), 147-162.

HC274 Yglesias, José. "Dr. King's March on Washington,
Part II." New York Times Magazine, 31 March
1968, pp. 30-31, 57-58, 60, 62, 64, 67-68, 70.
Rpt. in Meier and Rudwick, A124:267-283.

THE BLACK IMAGE IN THE WHITE MIND

HC275 Berwanger, Eugene H. The Frontier Against Slavery:
Western Anti-Negro Prejudice and the Slavery Exten-
sion Controversy. Urbana: Univ. of Illinois Press,
1967.

HC276 Bruce, Philip A. The Plantation Negro as a Freeman: Observations on His Character, Condition,

and Prospects in Virginia. 1889; rpt. Williamstown, Mass.: Corner House, 1970.

HC277 Campbell, Angus. White Attitudes Toward Black
People. Ann Arbor: Institute for Social Research,
1971.

HC278 Cantril, Hadley. "The Lynching Mob." The Psychology of Social Movements. 1941; rpt. New York:
Wiley, 1963. Pages 78-122.

HC279 Cripps, Thomas R. "The Death of Rastus: Negroes
in American Films Since 1945." Phylon, 28 (3rd
Qrtr 1967), 267-275.

HC280 Davis, David Brion. The Problem of Slavery in Western Culture. Ithaca: Cornell Univ. Press, 1966.

HC281 Degler, Carl N. "The Negro in America--Where
Myrdal Went Wrong." New York Times Magazine,
7 Dec. 1969, pp. 64-65, 152, 154-157, 159-160.

HC282 _____. "Slavery and the Genesis of American Race
Prejudice." Comparative Studies in History and Society, 2 (Oct. 1959), 49-66. Rpt. in Meier and Rudwick, A125:92-108.

HC283 Eggleston, Edward. The Ultimate Solution of the
American Negro Problem. 1913; rpt. New York:
AMS, 1973.

HC284 Elkins, Stanley M. Slavery: A Problem in American
Institutional and Intellectual Life. 2d edn. Chicago:
Univ. of Chicago Press, 1968.

HC285 Fredrickson, George M. The Black Image in the
White Mind: The Debate on Afro-American Character and Destiny, 1817-1914. New York: Harper,
1971.

HC286 Grambs, Jean Dreeden, and John C. Carr, eds.
Black Image: Education Copes with Color. Dubuque, Iowa: Brown, 1972.

HC287 Hesseltine, W. B. "Some New Aspects of the Pro-
Slavery Argument." JNH, 21 (Jan. 1936), 1-14.

HC288 Hoffman, Frederick L. Race Traits and Tendencies
of the American Negro. 1896; rpt. New York:
AMS, 1973. [Cf. Miller, SE1636.]

HC289 Jenkins, William Sumner. Pro-Slavery Thought in the
Old South. 1935; rpt. Gloucester, Mass.: Peter
Smith, 1960.

HC290 Jordan, Winthrop D. White over Black: American
Attitudes Toward the Negro, 1550-1812. Chapel
Hill: Univ. of North Carolina Press, 1968.

HC291 Lamplugh, George R. "The Image of the Negro in
Popular Magazine Fiction, 1875-1900." JNH, 57
(April 1972), 169-176.

HC292 Myrdal, Gunnar. "Racial Beliefs." In Myrdal,
HC463:83-112.

HC293 Newby, I. A. Challenge to the Court: Social Scien-
tists and the Defense of Segregation, 1954-1966.
Rev. edn. Baton Rouge: Louisiana State Univ.
Press, 1969.

HC294 _____. "Historians and Negroes." JNH, 54 (Jan.
1969), 32-47.

HC295 _____. Jim Crow's Defense: Anti-Negro Thought
in America, 1900-1930. Baton Rouge: Louisiana
State Univ. Press, 1965.

HC296 _____, ed. The Development of Segregationist
Thought. Homewood, Ill.: Dorsey, 1968.

[Ogawa, Dennis. "Small Group Communication Stereo-
types of Black Americans." See HC323.]

HC297 Pease, Jane H., and William H. Pease. "Ends,
Means, and Attitudes: Black-White Conflict in the
Antislavery Movement." Civil War History, 18
(June 1972), 117-128.

HC298 Pease, William H., and Jane H. Pease. "Antislavery
Ambivalence: Immediatism, Expediency, Race."
American Quarterly, 17 (Winter 1965), 682-695.
Rpt. in Meier and Rudwick, A125:302-314.

HC299 Phillips, Ulrich Bonnell. American Negro Slavery:
A Survey of the Supply, Employment and Control of
Negro Labor as Determined by the Plantation Re-
gime. 1918; rpt., with a foreword, "Ulrich Bonnell
Phillips & His Critics," by Eugene D. Genovese,
Baton Rouge: Louisiana State Univ. Press, 1966.

HC300 Ratner, Lorman. "Racism Persists." In Ratner,
HC535:3-27.

HC301 Reddick, Lawrence D. "Racial Attitudes in American History Textbooks of the South." JNH, 19
(July 1934), 225-265.

HC302 Schwartz, Barry N., and Robert Disch, eds. White
Racism: Its History, Pathology and Practice. New
York: Dell, 1970.

HC303 Stampp, Kenneth M. The Peculiar Institution: Slavery in the Ante-Bellum South. New York: Knopf,
1956.

HC304 Stanton, William. The Leopard's Spots: Scientific
Attitudes Toward Race in America, 1815-59. Chicago: Univ. of Chicago Press, 1960.

HC305 Szasz, Thomas S. "Blackness and Madness: Images
of Evil and Tactics of Exclusion." In Szwed, A161:
67-77.

HC306 Thorpe, Earl E. Eros and Freedom in Southern Life
and Thought. Durham, N.C.: Seeman Printery,
1967.

HC307 Voegeli, V. Jacque. Free but Not Equal: The Midwest and the Negro During the Civil War. Chicago:
Univ. of Chicago Press, 1967.

[Wander, Philip C. "The John Birch and Martin
Luther King Symbols in the Radical Right." See
HC1157.]

[_____. "Salvation Through Separation: The Image
of the Negro in the American Colonization Society."
See HC1158.]

[_____. "The Savage Child: The Image of the

Negro in the Pro-Slavery Movement." See HC1159.]

HC308 Wesley, Charles H. "The Concept of Negro Inferiority in American Thought." JNH, 25 (Oct. 1940), 540-560.

HC309 Wish, Harvey. George Fitzhugh: Propagandist of the Old South. 1943; rpt. Gloucester, Mass.: Peter Smith, 1962.

[White, Eugene E. "Anti-Racial Agitation as a Campaign Device: James K. Vardaman in the Mississippi Gubernatorial Campaign of 1903." See HC1162.]

[Williams, Donald E. "Protest Under the Cross: The Ku Klux Klan Presents Its Case to the Public, 1960." See HC1163.]

HC310 Wood, Forrest G. Black Scare: The Racist Response to Emancipation and Reconstruction. Berkeley: Univ. of California Press, 1968.

HC311 Woodward, C. Vann. "A Southern Brief for Racial Equality," HC482:184-211. Rpt. from Lewis H. Blair. A Southern Prophecy: The Prosperity of the South Dependent Upon the Elevation of the Negro [1889]. Ed. C. Vann Woodward. Boston: Little, 1964. Pages xi-xlvi.

HC312 _____. "A Southern War Against Capitalism," HC482:107-139. Rpt. from George Fitzhugh. Cannibals All! or Slaves Without Masters [1857]. Ed. C. Vann Woodward. Cambridge: Belknap Press of Harvard Univ. Press, 1960. Pages vii-xxxix.

COMMUNICATION

Communication, Interracial

HC313 Browne, Robert S. "Dialogue Between the Races--A Top Priority." TS, 16 (Sept. 1968), 5-8.

HC314 Buck, Joyce F. "The Effects of Negro and White Dialectal Variations upon Attitudes of College Students." SM, 35 (June 1968), 181-186.

HC315 Daniel, Jack L. "The Facilitation of White-Black
     Communication." Journal of Communication, 20
     (June 1970), 134-141.

HC316 Delia, Jesse G. "Dialects and the Effects of Stereo-
     types on Interpersonal Attraction and Cognitive Proc-
     esses in Impression Formation." QJS, 58 (Oct.
     1972), 285-297.

HC317 Doyle, Bertram Wilbur. The Etiquette of Race Rela-
     tions in the South: A Study in Social Control. 1937;
     rpt. Port Washington, N.Y.: Kennikat, 1968.

HC318 Du Bois, W. E. B. "The Contact of the Races."
     The Philadelphia Negro: A Social Study. 1899; rpt.
     New York: Blom, 1967. Pages 322-367.

HC319 Gregg, Richard B., and A. Jackson McCormack.
     " 'Whitey' Goes to the Ghetto: A Personal Chron-
     icle of a Communication Experience with Black
     Youths." TS, 16 (Sept. 1968), 25-30.

HC320 Hurt, H. Thomas, and Carl H. Weaver. "Negro Dia-
     lect, Ethnocentricism, and the Distortion of Infor-
     mation in the Communicative Process." CSSJ, 23
     (Summer 1972), 118-125.

HC321 Lanigan, Richard L. "Urban Crisis: Polarization
     and Communication." CSSJ, 21 (Summer 1970), 108-
     116.

     [Larson, Charles U. "The Trust Establishing Func-
     tion of the Rhetoric of Black Power." See HC1101.]

HC322 Newsom, Lionel, and William I. Gorden. "An Ex-
     change of Taped Discussions Between Students of Ne-
     gro and White Colleges." ST, 11 (Nov. 1962), 317-
     321.

HC323 Ogawa, Dennis. "Small Group Communication Stereo-
     types of Black Americans." Journal of Black Stud-
     ies, 1 (March 1971), 273-281.

HC324 Ratliffe, Sharon A., and Lyman K. Steil. "Attitudi-
     nal Differences Between Black and White College
     Students." ST, 19 (Sept. 1970), 190-198.

HC325 Rich, Andrea L. Interracial Communication. New
      York: Harper, 1974.

HC326 _____. "Some Problems in Interracial Communi-
      cation: An Interracial Group Case Study." CSSJ,
      22 (Winter 1971), 228-235.

HC327 Smith, Arthur L. Transracial Communication.
      Englewood Cliffs, N. J.: Prentice-Hall, 1973.

HC328 Williams, Ronald. "Black Communication Research:
      The Struggle To Know, The Struggle To Survive."
      In Daniel, A49:160-168.

HC329 Zinn, Howard. "Communications" [1962]. In Bracey,
      A21:692-694.

Language and Speech

HC330 Abrahams, Roger D. "Rapping and Capping: Black
      Talk as Art." In Szwed, A161:132-142.

HC331 Baratz, Joan C. "Should Black Children Learn White
      Dialect?" ASHA, 12 (Sept. 1970), 415-417. Rpt. in
      Smith, A155:3-10.

HC332 Bosmajian, Haig A. "The Language of White Rac-
      ism." College English, 31 (Dec. 1969), 263-272.
      Rpt. in Readings in Speech. 2d edn. Ed. Haig A.
      Bosmajian. New York: Harper, 1971. Pages 202-
      215. [Cf. William Kinsley, "Black and White
      Again," College English, 31 (May 1970), 862-863,
      and David Weber, "A Note on 'The Language of White
      Racism,' " ibid., pp. 863-865.]

HC333 Conrad, Earl. "The Philology of Negro Dialect."
      JNE, 13 (Spring 1944), 150-154.

HC334 Davis, Ossie. "The English Language Is My Enemy!"
      NHB, 30 (April 1967), 18. Rpt. in Smith, A155:49-
      57.

HC335 Dillard, J. L. Black English: Its History and Usage
      in the United States. New York: Random, 1972.

HC336 _____. "Non-Standard Negro Dialects:

Convergence or Divergence?" Florida FL Reporter,
6 (Fall 1968), 9-12. Rpt. in Whitten and Szwed,
A174:119-126.

HC337 Erickson, Frederick David. " 'F'get You Honky!': A
New Look at Black Dialect and the School." Elementary English, April 1969, pp. 495-499, 517. Rpt.
in Smith, A155:18-27.

HC338 Farrison, W. Edward. "Dialectology versus Negro
Dialect." CLA Journal, 13 (Sept. 1969), 21-26.

HC339 Green, Gordon C. "Negro Dialect, the Last Barrier
to Integration." JNE, 32 (Winter 1963), 81-83. Rpt.
in Smith, A155:12-17.

HC340 Haskins, Jim, and Hugh F. Butts. The Psychology of
Black Language. New York: Barnes and Noble,
1973.

HC341 Herskovits, Melville J. "The Contemporary Scene:
Language and the Arts." The Myth of the Negro
Past. 1941; rpt. Gloucester, Mass.: Peter Smith
1970. Pages 275-291.

HC342 Holt, Grace S. "The Ethno-linguistic Approach to
Speech-Language Learning." ST, 19 (March 1970),
98-100. Rpt. in Smith, A155:43-48.

[Hurt, H. Thomas, and Carl H. Weaver. "Negro
Dialect, Ethnocentricism, and the Distortion of Infor-
mation in the Communicative Process." See
HC320.]

HC343 Jones, Kirkland C. "The Language of the Black 'In-
Crowd': Some Observations on Intra-Group Communication." CLA Journal, 15 (Sept. 1971), 80-89.

[Jones, LeRoi. "Expressive Language." See SE1403.]

HC344 Kochman, Thomas. " 'Rapping' in the Black Ghetto."
Trans-action, 6 (Feb. 1969), 242-258.

HC345 _____. "Toward an Ethnography of Black American Speech Behavior." In Kochman, A108:241-264;
Smith, A155:58-86; and Whitten and Szwed, A174:
145-162.

HC346 Labov, William. <u>Language in the Inner City: Studies</u>
<u>in the Black English Vernacular.</u> Philadelphia:
Univ. of Pennsylvania Press, 1972.

HC347 _____. "The Logic of Nonstandard English." In
Williams, HC361:153-189.

HC348 McDavid, Raven I., Jr., and Virginia Glenn McDavid.
"The Relationship of the Speech of American Negroes
to the Speech of Whites." <u>American Speech,</u> 26
(Feb. 1951), 3-17.

HC349 Mitchell, Henry M. "Black English," HC1195:148-
161. Rpt. in Smith, A155:87-97.

HC350 Morse, J. Mitchell. "The Shuffling Speech of Slavery:
Black English." <u>College English</u>, 34 (March 1973),
834-839. [See "An Exchange of Letters," <u>ibid</u>., pp.
839-843.]

HC351 Pipes, William Harrison. "Mend Your Speech Pro-
fessor, Lest You Mar Your Students." <u>JNE</u>, 14
(Fall 1945), 635-642.

HC352 Podair, Simon. "Language and Prejudice Toward Negroes." <u>Phylon</u>, 17 (4th Qrtr 1956), 390-394.

[Preston, Dennis R. "Social Dialects and College
English." See HC421.]

HC353 Read, Allen Walker. "The Speech of Negroes in Colonial America." <u>JNH</u>, 24 (July 1939), 247-258.

HC354 Smith, Arthur L. "Black Language Styles" and "Functions of Black Language." In Smith, HC327:36-41,
41-43.

[Smith, Holly, comp. "A Selected Annotated Bibliography on Regional and Social Dialects." See B26.]

HC355 Spears, M. K. "You Makin' Sense." <u>New York Re-</u>
<u>view of Books</u>, 16 Nov. 1972, pp. 32-35. [Rev. of
Dillard, HC335.]

HC356 Stembridge, Jane. "Notes About a Class Held by
Stokely Carmichael." In Carmichael, A31:3-8; and
Jacobs and Landau, A99:131-137.

HC357 Stewart, William A. "Toward a History of American Negro Dialect." In Williams, HC361:351-379.

HC358 _____. "Understanding Black Language." In Szwed, A161:121-131.

HC359 Taylor, Orlando L. "Black Language: The Research Dimension." In Daniel, A49:145-159.

HC360 _____. "Some Sociolinguistic Concepts of Black Language." TS, 19 (Spring 1971), 19-26.

HC361 Williams, Frederick, ed. Language and Poverty: Perspectives on a Theme. Chicago: Markham, 1970.

   [_____, and Edward E. Rundell. "Teaching Teachers to Comprehend Negro Nonstandard English." See HC370.]

   [_____, and G. Wayne Shamo. "Regional Variations in Teacher Attitudes Toward Children's Language." See HC371.]

HC362 _____, Jack L. Whitehead, and Leslie M. Miller. "Ethnic Stereotyping and Judgments of Children's Speech." SM, 38 (Aug. 1971), 166-170.

   [Williams, Ronald. "Race and the Word." See HC432.]

HC363 Williamson, Juanita V. "Selected Features of Speech: Black and White." CLA Journal, 13 (June 1970), 420-433.

HC364 Wolfram, Walt. "Sociolinguistic Premises and the Nature of Nonstandard Dialects." ST, 19 (Sept. 1970), 177-184. Rpt. in Smith, A155:28-39.

HC365 Wood, Barbara Sundene, and Julia Curry. "Everyday Talk and School Talk of the City Black Child." ST, 8 (Nov. 1969), 282-296.

Communication in the Classroom

HC366 Cooper, June M. "Training of Teachers of Speech

for the Economically Disadvantaged Black American
Student." WS, 34 (Spring 1970), 139-143.

HC367 Daniel, Jack L. "Black Folk and Speech Education."
ST, 19 (March 1970), 123-129.

[Green, Gordon C. "Negro Dialect, the Last Barrier
to Integration." See HC339.]

HC368 Gregg, Richard, A. Jackson McCormack, and Doug-
las Pedersen. "A Description of the Interaction
Between Black Youth and White Teachers in a Ghetto
Speech Class." ST, 19 (Jan. 1970), 1-8.

[Holt, Grace S. "The Ethno-linguistic Approach to
Speech-Language Learning." See HC342.]

HC369 Rich, Andrea L., and Arthur L. Smith. "An Ap-
proach to Teaching Interracial Communication."
ST, 19 (March 1970), 138-144. Rpt. in Rich,
HC325:197-207.

HC370 Williams, Frederick, and Edward E. Rundell.
"Teaching Teachers to Comprehend Negro Nonstandard English." ST, 20 (Sept. 1971), 174-177.

HC371 Williams, Frederick, and G. Wayne Shamo. "Regional Variations in Teacher Attitudes Toward Children's Language." CSSJ, 33 (Summer 1972), 73-77.

[Williams, Frederick, Jack L. Whitehead, and Leslie M. Miller. "Ethnic Stereotyping and Judgments
of Children's Speech." See HC362.]

Communication, Nonverbal

HC372 Cooke, Benjamin G. "Nonverbal Communication
Among Afro-Americans: An Initial Classification."
In Kochman, A108:32-64.

HC373 Dubner, Frances S. "Nonverbal Aspects of Black
English." SSCJ, 37 (Summer 1972), 361-374.

HC374 Gergen, Kenneth J. "The Significance of Skin Color
in Human Relations." Color and Race. Ed. John
Hope Franklin. Boston: Houghton, 1968. Pp. 112-
128.

HC375 Johnson, Kenneth R. "Black Kinesics--Some Non-
Verbal Communication Patterns in the Black Culture."
Florida FL Reporter, 9 (Spring/Fall 1971), 17-20,
57. Rpt. in Messages: A Reader in Human Com-
munication. Ed. Jean M. Civikly. New York:
Random, 1974. Pages 103-113.

HC376 Jones, Stanley E., and John R. Aiello. "Proxemic
Behavior of Black and White First-, Third-, and
Fifth-Grade Children." Journal of Personality and
Social Psychology, 25 (Jan. 1973), 21-27.

HC377 Record, Wilson. "Sociological Theory, Intra-Racial
Color Differentiation and the Garvey Movement."
JNE, 25 (Fall 1956), 392-401.

HC378 Rich, Andrea L. "Interracial Implications of Nonverbal Communication." In Rich, HC325:161-196.

HC379 Wilkinson, Doris Y. "Status Differences and the
Black Hate Stare: 'A Conversation of Gestures.' "
Phylon, 30 (2d Qrtr 1969), 191-196.

HC380 Williams, Annette Powell. "Dynamics of a Black
Audience." In Kochman, A108:101-106.

EDUCATION

HC381 Bond, Horace Mann. The Education of the Negro in
the American Social Order. 1934; rpt., with a new
preface and an additional chapter by the author, New
York: Octagon, 1966.

HC382 _____. Negro Education in Alabama: A Study in
Cotton and Steel. 1939; rpt. New York: Octagon,
1969.

HC383 Brisbane, Robert H. "Militancy on the Black Campus." In Brisbane, HC442:101-111.

HC384 Brown, William Wells. "Chapter XXIV." In Brown,
HC444:213-219.

HC385 Bullock, Henry Allen. A History of Negro Education
in the South, from 1619 to the Present. Cambridge:
Harvard Univ. Press, 1967.

HC386 Butcher, Philip. "George W. Cable and Negro Education." JNH, 34 (April 1949), 119-134.

HC387 Caliver, Ambrose. "Certain Significant Developments in the Education of Negroes During the Past Generation." JNH, 35 (April 1950), 111-134.

HC388 Daniel, Jack L. "Black Academic Activism." Black Scholar, 4 (Jan. 1973), 44-52.

HC389 _____. "Teaching and Research in Black Communication." In Daniel, A49:171-179.

HC390 _____. "Towards Meaningful Black Studies." Crisis, 79 (Oct. 1972), 259-260.

HC391 _____, Imogene Hines, Gerlene Ross, and Gloria Walker. "Teaching Afro-American Communication." In Daniel, A49:42-53.

HC392 Draper, Theodore. "Black Studies." In Draper, HC1256:148-167.

HC393 Du Bois, W. E. B., ed. The College-Bred Negro. 1900; rpt. New York: Octagon, 1968.

HC394 _____. "Education and Illiteracy." The Philadelphia Negro: A Social Study. 1899; rpt. New York: Blom, 1967. Pages 83-96.

      [_____. The Education of Black People: Ten Critiques, 1906-1960. See A60.]

HC395 _____. "Founding the Public School." In Du Bois, HC649:637-669.

HC396 _____. The Negro Common School. 1901; rpt. New York: Octagon, 1968.

HC397 _____, and Augustus Granville Dill, eds. The College-Bred Negro American. 1910; rpt. New York: Russell, 1969.

HC398 _____. The Common School and the Negro American. 1911; rpt. New York: Russell, 1969.

HC399 "Education." In the Report of the National Advisory

Commission on Civil Disorders, HC943:424-456.

HC400 Edwards, Michael L. "A Resource Unit on Black
Rhetoric." ST, 22 (Sept. 1973), 183-188.

HC401 _____, and Jon A. Blubaugh. " 'The Black Experience' in Speech Communication Courses: A Survey." ST, 22 (Sept. 1973), 175-182.

HC402 Foster, E. C. "Carter G. Woodson's 'The Mis-Education of the Negro' Revisited: Black Colleges,
Black Studies." Freedomways, 13 (1st Qrtr 1973),
28-38.

HC403 Franklin, John Hope. "Trends in Education." In
Franklin, HC453:546-559.

HC404 Frazier, E. Franklin. "Elementary and Secondary
Schools" and "Institutions of Higher Education."
In Frazier, HC454:417-449, 450-491.

[From Servitude to Service: Being the Old South Lectures on the History and Work of Southern Institutions for the Education of the Negro. See A75.]

HC405 Funke, Loretta. "The Negro in Education." JNH,
5 (Jan. 1920), 1-21.

HC406 Gayle, Addison, Jr. "Racism and the American
University." In Gayle, A80:99-112.

HC407 Harding, Vincent. "Black Students and the 'Impos-
sible' Revolution." Ebony, Aug. 1969, pp. 141-146,
148, and Sept. 1969, pp. 97-98, 100, 102, 104.
Rpt. in The Black Revolution, A12:175-206.

HC408 Hawkins, Robert B. "A Speech Program in an Ex-
perimental College for the Disadvantaged." ST,
18 (March 1969), 115-119.

HC409 Holmes, Dwight Oliver Wendell. The Evolution of
the Negro College. 1934; rpt. New York: AMS,
1970.

HC410 Hurst, Charles G., Jr. Passport to Freedom: Education, Humanism, & Malcolm X. Hamden, Conn.:
Linnet Books, Shoe String Press, 1972.

HC411 Kilson, Martin. "Reflections on Structure and Content in Black Studies." Journal of Black Studies, 3 (March 1973), 297-314.

HC412 Litwack, Leon F. "Education: Separate and Unequal." In Litwack, HC461:113-152.

HC413 Logan, Rayford W. Howard University: The First Hundred Years, 1867-1967. New York: New York Univ. Press, 1969.

HC414 Lokos, Lionel. "The Black Rebellion on Campus," "The Black University," etc. In Lokos, HC934:147-159, 160-169, and passim.

HC415 Moss, James A. "In Defense of Black Studies." In Moss, A130:110-131.

HC416 Murray, Albert. "Black Studies and the Aims of Education." Part I: The Omni-Americans, New Perspectives on Black Experience and American Culture. New York: Outerbridge, 1970. Pages 203-217.

HC417 Myrdal, Gunnar. "The Negro School." In Myrdal, HC463:879-907.

HC418 Nash, Rosa Lee. "Toward a Philosophy of Speech Communication Education for the Black Child." ST, 19 (March 1970), 88-97.

HC419 Parker, John W. "Current Debate Practices in Thirty Negro Colleges." JNE, 9 (Jan. 1940), 32-38.

HC420 Porter, Dorothy B. "The Organized Educational Activities of Negro Literary Societies, 1828-1846." JNE, 5 (Oct. 1936), 555-576. Rpt. in Meier and Rudwick, A125:276-288, abr.

HC421 Preston, Dennis R. "Social Dialects and College English." ST, 20 (Nov. 1971), 237-246.

HC422 "Racism and the University." In Wallerstein and Starr, A163:293-397.

HC423 Ralston, Richard D. "The Role of the Black University in the Black Revolution." Journal of Black Studies, 3 (March 1973), 267-286.

HC424 Robinson, Armstead L., Craig C. Foster, and Don-
      ald H. Ogilvie, eds. Black Studies in the Univer-
      sity: A Symposium. New Haven: Yale Univ. Press,
      1969.

HC425 Rosser, James E., and E. Thomas Copeland. "Re-
      flections: Black Studies--Black Education?" Jour-
      nal of Black Studies, 3 (March 1973), 287-295.

HC426 Ruchkin, Judith Polgar. "The Abolition of 'Colored
      Schools' in Rochester, New York: 1832-1856."
      New York History, 51 (1970), 377-393.

HC427 Silberman, Charles E. "The Negro and the School."
      In Silberman, HC905:249-307.

HC428 Taylor, Orlando L. "New Directions for American
      Education: A Black Perspective." ST, 19 (March
      1970), 111-116.

HC429 Thorpe, Earl E. "Elements of Negro Thought on
      Education and Segregation." In Thorpe, HC475:282-
      309.

HC430 Turner, James. "Black Students: A Changing Per-
      spective." Ebony, Aug. 1969, pp. 135-140. In
      The Black Revolution, A12:161-173.

HC431 Washington, Booker T. "The Negro Teacher and the
      Negro School." In Washington, HC478:II, 114-147.

HC432 Williams, Ronald. "Race and the Word." TS, 19
      (Spring 1971), 27-33.

HC433 Wish, Harvey. "Negro Education and the Progres-
      sive Movement." JNH, 49 (July 1964), 184-200.

HC434 Woodson, C. G. The Education of the Negro Prior
      to 1861. 2d edn. 1919; rpt. New York: Arno,
      1968.

HC435 _____. The Mis-Education of the Negro. 1933;
      rpt. New York: AMS, 1972. [See Foster, HC
      402.]

HISTORY

History, General

HC436 Bennett, Lerone, Jr. Before the Mayflower: A History of Black America. 4th edn. Chicago: Johnson, 1969.

HC437 _____. Confrontation: Black and White. Chicago: Johnson, 1965.

HC438 Bergman, Peter M. The Chronological History of the Negro in America. New York: Harper, 1969.

HC439 Bontemps, Arna, and Jack Conroy. They Seek a City. Garden City, N.Y.: Doubleday, 1945. [Cf. HC440.]

HC440 _____. Anyplace But Here. New York: Hill, 1966. [Rev. and expanded edn. of HC439.]

HC441 Brawley, Benjamin. A Social History of the American Negro. 1921; rpt. New York: AMS, 1971.

HC442 Brisbane, Robert H. The Black Vanguard: Origins of the Negro Social Revolution, 1900-1960. Valley Forge: Judson, 1970.

HC443 Brown, William Wells. The Black Man, His Antecedents, His Genius, and His Achievements. 2d edn. 1863; rpt. New York: Johnson Reprint, 1968. [See Douglass, SE666.]

HC444 _____. My Southern Home: or, The South and Its People. 1880; rpt. New York: Negro Universities Press, 1969.

HC445 _____. The Rising Son; or, The Antecedents and Advancement of the Colored Race. 1874; rpt. New York: Negro Universities Press, 1970.

HC446 Buni, Andrew. The Negro in Virginia Politics, 1902-1965. Charlottesville: Univ. Press of Virginia, 1967.

HC447 Cromwell, John W. The Negro in American History:
Men and Women Eminent in the Evolution of the
American of African Descent. 1914; rpt. New York:
Johnson Reprint, 1968.

HC448 Cruse, Harold. The Crisis of the Negro Intellectual.
New York: Morrow, 1967.

HC449 Daniels, John. In Freedom's Birthplace: A Study of
the Boston Negroes. 1914; rpt. New York: Johnson Reprint, 1968.

HC450 Du Bois, W. E. B. The Gift of Black Folk: The Negroes in the Making of America. 1924; rpt. New
York: Johnson Reprint, 1968.

HC451 Ferris, William H. The African Abroad, or, His
Evolution in Western Civilization. 2 vols. 1913;
rpt. New York: Johnson Reprint, 1968.

HC452 Foster, William Z. The Negro People in American
History. New York: International, 1954.

HC453 Franklin, John Hope. From Slavery to Freedom: A
History of Negro Americans. 3rd edn. New York:
Knopf, 1967.

HC454 Frazier, E. Franklin. The Negro in the United
States. Rev. edn. New York: Macmillan, 1957.

HC455 Gordon, Asa H. The Georgia Negro: A History.
1937; rpt. Spartanburg, S.C.: Reprint, 1972.

HC456 _____. Sketches of Negro Life and History in
South Carolina. 2d edn. Columbia: Univ. of South
Carolina Press, 1971.

HC457 Green, Constance McLaughlin. The Secret City: A
History of Race Relations in the Nation's Capital.
Princeton: Princeton Univ. Press, 1967.

HC458 Hoover, Dwight W., ed. Understanding Negro History. Chicago: Quadrangle, 1968.

HC459 Hughes, Langston. Fight for Freedom: The Story of
the NAACP. New York: Norton, 1962.

HC460 Irvine, Keith. The Rise of the Colored Races. New
       York: Norton, 1970.

HC461 Litwack, Leon F. North of Slavery: The Negro in
       the Free States, 1790-1860. Chicago: Univ. of Chi-
       cago Press, 1961.

HC462 Meier, August, and Elliott Rudwick. From Plantation
       to Ghetto. Rev. edn. New York: Hill, 1970.

HC463 Myrdal, Gunnar, with the assistance of Richard Stern-
       er and Arnold Rose. An American Dilemma: The
       Negro Problem and Modern Democracy. Twentieth
       Anniversary Edition. New York: Harper, 1962.

HC464 Newby, I. A. Black Carolinians: A History of Blacks
       in South Carolina from 1815 to 1968. Columbia:
       Univ. of South Carolina Press, 1973.

HC465 Nichols, J. L., and William H. Crogman. Progress
       of a Race, or the Remarkable Advancement of the
       American Negro. 1920; rpt. New York: Arno,
       1969.

HC466 Nowlin, William F. The Negro in American National
       Politics. 1931; rpt. New York: AMS, 1971.

HC467 Ottley, Roi. 'New World A-Coming': Inside Black
       America. Boston: Houghton, 1943.

HC468 _____, and William J. Weatherby, eds. The Ne-
       gro in New York: An Informal Social History. New
       York: New York Public Library, 1967.

HC469 Peeks, Edward. The Long Struggle for Black Power.
       New York: Scribner's, 1971.

HC470 Powell, Adam Clayton, Jr. Marching Blacks. Rev.
       edn. New York: Dial, 1973. [1st edn., 1945, sub-
       titled "An Interpretive History of the Rise of the
       Black Common Man."]

HC471 Reddick, L. D. "A New Interpretation for Negro His-
       tory." JNH, 22 (Jan. 1937), 17-28.

HC472 Redding, Saunders. They Came in Chains: Ameri-
       cans from Africa. Rev. edn. New York:

Lippincott, 1973.

HC473 Roman, C. V. American Civilization and the Negro:
The Afro-American in Relation to National Progress.
1916; rpt. Northbrook, Ill.: Metro, 1972.

HC474 Stone, Chuck. Black Political Power in America.
Rev. edn. New York: Dell, 1970.

HC475 Thorpe, Earl E. The Mind of the Negro: An Intellectual History of Afro-Americans. 1961; rpt. Westport, Conn.: Negro Universities Press, 1970.

HC476 Toppin, Edgar A. "A Half-Century of Struggle for
Equal Rights, 1916-1965." NHB, 28 (Summer 1965),
176-177, 188-189.

HC477 Washington, Booker T. A New Negro for a New Century: An Accurate and Up-to-Date Record of the Up-
ward Struggles of the Negro Race. 1900; rpt. Miami: Mnemosyne, 1969.

HC478 _____. The Story of the Negro: The Rise of the
Race from Slavery. 2 vols. 1909; rpt. Gloucester:
Mass.: Peter Smith, 1969.

HC479 Waskow, Arthur I. From Race Riot to Sit-In, 1919
and the 1960s. Garden City, N.Y.: Doubleday,
1966.

HC480 Wesley, Charles H. Neglected History: Essays in
Negro History by a College President. [1965];
rpt. Washington: Monumental Printing Co., 1969.

HC481 Woodson, Carter G., and Charles Wesley. The Negro in Our History. 11th edn. Washington: Associated Publishers, 1966.

HC482 Woodward, C. Vann. American Counterpoint: Slavery
and Racism in the North-South Dialogue. Boston:
Little, 1971.

HC483 Wright, Richard. 12 Million Black Voices: A Folk
History of the Negro in the United States. 1941;
rpt. New York: Arno, 1969.

Antislavery Movement, 1619-1829

HC484 Adams, Alice Dana. The Neglected Period of Anti-
       Slavery in America (1808-1831). 1908; rpt. Glou-
       cester, Mass.: Peter Smith, 1964.

HC485 Aptheker, Herbert. "The Quakers and Negro Slavery."
       JNH, 25 (July 1940), 331-362.

HC486 Boyd, William M. "Southerners in the Anti-Slavery
       Movement, 1800-1830." Phylon, 9 (2d Qrtr 1948),
       153-163.

HC487 Davis, David Brion. "Part III." In Davis, HC280:
       291-482.

HC488 Drake, Thomas E. Quakers and Slavery in America.
       1950; rpt. Gloucester, Mass.: Peter Smith, 1965.

HC489 Du Bois, W. E. B. The Suppression of the African
       Slave-Trade to the United States of America, 1638-
       1870. 1898; rpt., with Du Bois' "Apologia" [1954],
       pp. 327-329, New York: Russell, 1965.

HC490 Dumond, Dwight Lowell. Antislavery: The Crusade
       for Freedom in America. Ann Arbor: Univ. of
       Michigan Press, 1961. Pages 3-157.

HC491 Franklin, John Hope. "That All Men May Be Free."
       In Franklin, HC453:126-144.

HC492 Locke, Mary Stoughton. Anti-Slavery in America
       from the Introduction of African Slaves to the Pro-
       hibition of the Slave Trade (1619-1808). 1901; rpt.
       Gloucester, Mass.: Peter Smith, 1965.

HC493 Lynd, Staughton. "The Abolitionist Critique of the
       United States Constitution." In Duberman, A57:209-
       239. Rpt. in Lynd. Class Conflict, Slavery, and
       the United States Constitution. Indianapolis:
       Bobbs-Merrill, 1967. Pages 153-183.

HC494 Staudenraus, P. J. The African Colonization Move-
       ment, 1816-1865. New York: Columbia Univ.
       Press, 1961.

HC495 Sypher, Wylie. "Hutcheson and the 'Classical' Theory of Slavery." JNH, 24 (July 1939), 263-280.

HC496 Zilversmit, Arthur. The First Emancipation: The
Abolition of Slavery in the North. Chicago: Univ.
of Chicago Press, 1967.

Antislavery Movement, 1829-1865

HC497 Abzug, Robert H. "The Influence of Garrisonian
Abolitionists' Fears of Slave Violence on the Anti-
slavery Argument." JNH, 55 (Jan. 1970), 15-28.

HC498 Aptheker, Herbert. "Militant Abolitionism." JNH,
26 (Oct. 1941), 438-484.

HC499 _____. Nat Turner's Slave Rebellion. New York:
Humanities Press, 1966.

HC500 Barnes, Gilbert Hobbs. The Antislavery Impulse,
1830-1844. 1933; rpt., with a new introduction by
William G. McLoughlin, New York: Harcourt, 1964.

HC501 Bartlett, Irving H. "The Persistence of Wendell Phillips." In Duberman, A57:102-122.

HC502 Braden, Waldo W., ed. Oratory in the Old South,
1828-1860. Baton Rouge: Louisiana State Univ.
Press, 1970.

HC503 Brawley, Benjamin. "The Negro a National Issue."
In Brawley, HC441:213-237.

HC504 Brooks, Elaine. "Massachusetts Anti-Slavery Society."
JNH, 30 (July 1945), 311-330.

HC505 Brown, William Wells. "The Abolitionists." In
Brown, HC445:393-412.

HC506 Cheatham, Thomas R. "The Rhetorical Structure of
the Abolitionist Movement Within the Baptist Church:
1833-1845." Diss., Purdue, 1969.

HC507 Craven, Avery. The Coming of the Civil War. 2d
edn. Chicago: Univ. of Chicago Press, 1957.

HC508 Davis, David Brion. "The Emergence of Immediatism
in British and American Antislavery Thought." Mississippi Valley Historical Review, 49 (Sept. 1962),
209-230.

        [_____. The Slave Power Conspiracy and the Para-
        noid Style. See HC1061.]

HC509 Dillon, Merton L. "The Abolitionists as a Dissenting
Minority." In Young, A182:85-108.

HC510 Donald, David. Charles Sumner and the Coming of
the Civil War. New York: Knopf, 1961.

HC511 Duberman, Martin B. "The Abolitionists and Pyschol-
ogy." JNH, 47 (July 1962), 183-191.

HC512 _____. "The Northern Response to Slavery." In
Duberman, A57:395-413.

HC513 Dumond, Dwight Lowell. Antislavery: The Crusade
for Freedom in America. Ann Arbor: Univ. of
Michigan Press, 1961. Pages 158-372.

HC514 _____. Antislavery Origins of the Civil War in the
United States. Ann Arbor: Univ. of Michigan Press,
1939.

HC515 Elkins, Stanley M. "The Abolitionist as Transcendent-
alist." In Elkins, HC284:175-193.

HC516 Filler, Louis. The Crusade Against Slavery, 1830-
1860. New York: Harper, 1960.

HC517 Fladeland, Betty. James Gillespie Birney: Slaveholder to Abolitionist. Ithaca: Cornell Univ. Press,
1955.

HC518 _____. "Who Were the Abolitionists?" JNH, 49
(April 1964), 99-115.

HC519 Franklin, John Hope. "Slavery and Intersectional
Strife." In Franklin, HC453:242-270.

HC520 Gara, Larry. "Slavery and the Slave Power: A Cru-
cial Distinction." Civil War History, 15 (March
1969), 5-18.

HC521 Grimké, Archibald H. William Lloyd Garrison, The
       Abolitionist. 1891; rpt. New York: Negro Univer-
       sities Press, 1969.

       [Guthrie, Warren. "The Oberlin-Wellington Rescue
       Case, 1859." See HC1077.]

       [Hammerback, John C. "George W. Julian's Anti-
       slavery Crusade." See HC1079.]

       [_____. "The Rhetoric of a Righteous Reform:
       George Washington Julian's 1852 Campaign Against
       Slavery." See HC1080.]

HC522 Kraditor, Aileen S. Means and Ends in American
       Abolitionism: Garrison and His Critics on Strategy
       and Tactics, 1834-1850. New York: Pantheon,
       1969.

HC523 Lerner, Gerda. "The Grimké Sisters and the Struggle
       Against Race Prejudice." JNH, 48 (Oct. 1963), 277-
       291.

HC524 Lofton, Williston H. "Abolition and Labor." JNH,
       33 (July 1948), 249-283.

HC525 Ludlum, Robert P. "The Antislavery 'Gag Rule':
       History and Argument." JNH, 26 (April 1941), 203-
       243.

HC526 McPherson, James M. "The Fight Against the Gag
       Rule: Joshua Levitt and Antislavery Insurgency in
       the Whig Party, 1839-1842." JNH, 48 (July 1963),
       177-195.

HC527 Martyn, Carlos. Wendell Phillips: The Agitator.
       1890; rpt. New York: Negro Universities Press,
       1969.

HC528 Merrill, Walter M. Against Wind and Tide: A Biog-
       raphy of William Lloyd Garrison. Cambridge: Har-
       vard Univ. Press, 1963.

       [Mohrmann, G. P. "Consistency Theory: The Im-
       pending Crisis of the South." See HC1106.]

HC529 Nuermberger, Ruth Ketring. The Free Produce

Movement: A Quaker Protest Against Slavery.
1942; rpt. New York: AMS, 1970.

HC530 Nye, Russel B. William Lloyd Garrison and the Hu-
manitarian Reformers. Boston: Little, 1955.

[Oliver, Robert T. "The Antislavery Crusade, 1831-
1865." See HC1112.]

HC531 Owsley, Frank L. "The Fundamental Cause of the
the Civil War: Egocentric Sectionalism." Journal
of Southern History, 7 (Feb. 1941), 3-18.

HC532 Pease, Jane H., and William H. Pease. Bound with
Them in Chains: A Biographical History of the
Antislavery Movement. Westport, Conn.: Green-
wood, 1972.

[Pease, William H., and Jane H. Pease. "Anti-
slavery Ambivalence: Immediatism, Expediency,
Race." See HC298.]

HC533 Perry, Lewis. Radical Abolitionism: Anarchy and
the Government of God in Antislavery Thought. Ithaca: Cornell Univ. Press, 1973.

HC534 Quarles, Benjamin. "The Breach Between Douglass
and Garrison." JNH, 23 (April 1938), 144-154.

HC535 Ratner, Lorman. Powder Keg: Northern Opposition
to the Antislavery Movement, 1831-1840. New
York: Basic, 1968.

HC536 Rice, Madeleine Hooke. American Catholic Opinion
in the Slavery Controversy. 1944; rpt. Gloucester,
Mass.: Peter Smith, 1964.

HC537 Richards, Leonard L. "Gentlemen of Property and
Standing": Anti-Abolition Mobs in Jacksonian America. New York: Oxford Univ. Press, 1970.

HC538 Savage, W. Sherman. The Controversy over the Distribution of Abolition Literature 1830-1860. 1938;
rpt. New York: Negro Universities Press, 1968.

HC539 Sears, Lorenzo. Wendell Phillips: Orator and Agitator. 1909; rpt. New York: Blom, 1967.

HC540 Shanks, Caroline L.   "The Biblical Anti-Slavery Argument of the Decade 1830-1840."   JNH, 16 (April
1931), 132-157.

HC541 Sherwin, Oscar.   Prophet of Liberty: The Life and
Times of Wendell Phillips.   New York: Bookman,
1958.

HC542 Shockley, Ann Allen.   "American Anti-Slavery Literature: An Overview--1693-1859."   NHB, 37 (April-
May 1974), 232-235.

HC543 Smallwood, Osborn T.   "The Historical Significance
of Whittier's Anti-Slavery Poems as Reflected by
Their Political and Social Background."   JNH, 35
(April 1950), 150-173.

HC544 Smiley, David L.   "Cassius M. Clay and John G. Fee:
A Study in Southern Anti-Slavery Thought."   JNH, 42
(July 1957), 201-213.

HC545 Stampp, Kenneth M.   "An Analysis of T. R. Dew's
Review of the Debates in the Virginia Legislature."
JNH, 27 (Oct. 1942), 380-387.

HC546 _____.   "The Fate of the Southern Antislavery
Movement."   JNH, 28 (Jan. 1943), 10-22.

HC547 Stewart, James B.   "The Aims and Impact of Garrisonian Abolitionism, 1840-1860."   Civil War History,
15 (Sept. 1969), 197-209.

HC548 Stowe, Harriet Beecher.   A Key to Uncle Tom's Cab-
in.   1853; rpt. Port Washington, N.Y.: Kennikat,
1968.

HC549 Thomas, Benjamin.   Theodore Weld, Crusader for
Freedom.   New Brunswick, N.J.: Rutgers Univ.
Press, 1950.

HC550 Thomas, John L.   The Liberator: William Lloyd Garrison, A Biography.   Boston: Little, 1963.

HC551 Turner, Lorenzo D.   Anti-Slavery Sentiment in American Literature Prior to 1865.   1929; rpt.   Port
Washington, N.Y.: Kennikat, 1966.   [First publ.,
without bibliography and index, in JNH, 14 (Oct.

1929), 371-522.]

[Weaver, Richard L., II. "The Negro Issue: Agitation in the Michigan Lyceum." See HC1160.]

HC552 Weld, Theodore Dwight, comp. American Slavery As It Is: Testimony of a Thousand Witnesses. 1839; rpt. New York: Arno, 1968.

HC553 Woodward, C. Vann. "The Northern Crusade Against Slavery." New York Review of Books, 27 Feb. 1969, pp. 5-6, 8, 10-11. Rpt. in Woodward, HC482:140-162, rev. and enlarged.

HC554 Wyatt-Brown, Bertram. "The Abolitionists' Postal Campaign of 1835." JNH, 50 (Oct. 1965), 227-238.

HC555 _____. Lewis Tappan and the Evangelical War Against Slavery. Cleveland: Press of Case Western Reserve Univ., 1969.

HC556 _____. "William Lloyd Garrison and Antislavery Unity." Civil War History, 13 (March 1967), 5-24.

HC557 Zorn, Roman J. "The New England Anti-Slavery Society: Pioneer Abolition Organization." JNH, 42 (July 1957), 157-176.

Black Abolitionists

HC558 Aptheker, Herbert. "One Continual Cry": David Walker's Appeal to the Colored Citizens of the World (1829-1830), Its Setting and Its Meaning. New York: Humanities Press, 1965.

HC559 Bell, Howard H. "The American Moral Reform Society, 1836-1841." JNE, 27 (Winter 1958), 34-40.

HC560 _____. "Expressions of Negro Militancy in the North, 1840-1860." JNH, 45 (Jan. 1960), 11-20.

HC561 _____. "Free Negroes of the North 1830-1835: A Study in National Cooperation." JNE, 26 (Fall 1957), 447-455.

HC562 _____. "National Negro Conventions of the Middle

1840's: Moral Suasion vs. Political Action."   JNH,
42 (Oct. 1957), 247-260.   Rpt. in Meier and Rudwick, A125:315-326.

HC563 _____.   "Negro Nationalism: A Factor in Emigration Projects, 1858-1861."   JNH, 47 (Jan. 1962),
42-53.

HC564 _____.   A Survey of the Negro Convention Movement, 1830-1861.   1953; rpt.   New York: Arno,
1969.

HC565 Bennett, Lerone, Jr.   "The First Freedom Movement."   In Bennett, HC437:46-77.

HC566 _____.   "Slave Revolts and Insurrections" and "The
Generation of Crisis."   In Bennett, HC436:97-126,
127-159.

HC567 Borome, Joseph A.   "Robert Purvis and His Early
Challenge to American Racism."   NHB, 30 (May
1967),   8-10.

HC568 Brawley, Benjamin.   "The Negro Reply, I: Revolt"
and "The Negro Reply, II: Organization and Agitation."   In Brawley, HC441:132-154, 155-171.

HC569 Cromwell, John W.   "The Early Negro Convention
Movement."   American Negro Academy, Occasional
Papers No. 9.   Washington: The Academy, 1904.
Rpt. rev. as "The Early Convention Movement" in
Cromwell, HC447:27-46.

HC570 Dick, Robert C.   "Rhetoric of the Negro Ante-Bellum
Protest Movement."   Diss., Stanford, 1969.

     + [_____.   "Negro Oratory in the Anti-Slavery Socie-
ties: 1830-1860."   See HC1063.]

     + [_____.   "Rhetoric of Ante-Bellum Black Separa-
tism."   See HC1064.]

HC571 Dumond, Dwight Lowell.   "Insurrections" and "Free
Negroes."   In Dumond, HC490:109-118, 119-125.

HC572 _____.   "Fugitive Slaves and the People," "Fugitive Slaves and the Law," and "Negro Leaders."

In Dumond, HC513:305-314, 315-325, 326-334.

HC573 Foner, Philip S. "The First Publicly-Elected Black
Official in the United States Reports His Election."
NHB, 37 (April-May 1974), 237. [On John Mercer
Langston, 1855.]

HC574 Foster, William Z. "The Early Negro Liberation
Movement" and "Slave Revolts and Fugitive Slaves."
In Foster, HC452:93-104, 164-175.

HC575 Franklin, John Hope. "Black Abolitionists" and "The
Underground Railroad." In Franklin, HC453:249-
253, 253-260.

HC576 Gara, Larry. The Liberty Line: The Legend of the
Underground Railroad. Lexington: Univ. of Kentucky Press, 1961.

HC577 _____. "The Professional Fugitive in the Abolition Movement." Wisconsin Magazine of History,
48 (Spring 1965), 196-204.

HC578 _____. "Propaganda Uses of the Underground
Railroad." Mid-America, 23 (July 1952), 155-171.

HC579 _____. "The Underground Railroad: A Re-evalu-
ation." Ohio Historical Quarterly, 69 (July 1960),
217-230.

HC580 _____. "William Still and the Underground Railroad." Pennsylvania History, 28 (Jan. 1961), 33-
44. Rpt. in Meier and Rudwick, A125:327-335.

HC581 Gliozzo, Charles A. "John Jones and the Black Convention Movement, 1848-1856." Journal of Black
Studies, 3 (Dec. 1972), 227-236.

HC582 Gross, Bella. "The First National Negro Convention." JNH, 31 (Oct. 1946), 435-443.

HC583 _____. "Freedom's Journal and the Rights of
All." JNH, 17 (July 1932), 241-286.

HC584 Kennicott, Patrick C. "Black Persuaders in the Anti-
slavery Movement." SM, 37 (March 1970), 15-24.
Rpt. in Journal of Black Studies, 1 (Sept. 1970),
5-20, rev.

HC585 Litwack, Leon F. "Abolitionism: White and Black"
and "The Crisis of the 1850's." In Litwack, HC461:
214-246, 247-279.

HC586 _____. "The Emancipation of the Negro Aboliton-
ist." In Duberman, A57:137-155.

HC587 Loggins, Vernon. "Writings of the Leading Negro
Antislavery Agents, 1840-1865." In Loggins, HC
992:127-175.

HC588 Meier, August. "The Emergence of Negro Nationalism." Midwest Journal, 4 (Winter 1951-1952), 98-
104.

HC589 _____, and Elliott Rudwick. "Negroes in the Ante-
Bellum Cities: Manumission, Alienation, and Protest." In Meier and Rudwick, HC462:104-136.

HC590 Pease, Jane H., and William H. Pease. "Black
Power--The Debate in 1840." Phylon, 29 (1st Qrtr
1968), 19-26.

HC591 _____. "Negro Conventions and the Problem of
Black Leadership." Journal of Black Studies, 2
(Sept. 1971), 29-44.

HC592 Quarles, Benjamin. "Abolition's Different Drummer:
Frederick Douglass." In Duberman, A57:123-134.

HC593 _____. Black Abolitionists. New York: Oxford
Univ. Press, 1969.

HC594 _____. "Freedom's Black Vanguard." Key Issues
in the Afro-American Experience. Ed. Nathan I.
Huggins, Martin Kilson, and Daniel M. Fox. New
York: Houghton, 1971. I, 174-190.

HC595 _____. "Ministers Without Portfolio." JNH, 39
(Jan. 1954), 27-42.

HC596 Siebert, Wilbur H. The Underground Railroad from
Slavery to Freedom. 1898; rpt. Gloucester, Mass.:
Peter Smith, 1968.

HC597 Sorin, Gerald. "The Black Abolitionists." Abolitionism: A New Perspective. New York: Praeger,
1972. Pages 99-119.

HC598a Still, William. The Underground Rail Road. 1872;
       rpt. New York: Arno, 1968.

HC598b _____. The Underground Railroad [1872]. Chi-
       cago: Johnson, 1970.

HC599 Thorpe, Earl E. "Elements of the Thought of Free
      Negroes During the 1850s." In Thorpe, HC475:165-
      180.

HC600 Washington, Booker T. "The Negro Abolitionists."
      In Washington, HC478:I, 279-309.

HC601 Wesley, Charles H. "The Negro in the Organization
      of Abolition." Phylon, 2 (3rd Qrtr 1941), 223-235.
      Rpt. in Wesley, HC480:77-85.

HC602 _____. "The Negroes of New York in the Emanci-
      pation Movement." JNH, 24 (Jan. 1939), 65-103.

HC603 _____. "The Participation of Negroes in Anti-
      Slavery Political Parties." JNH 29 (Jan. 1944),
      32-74. Rpt. in Wesley, HC480:56-77.

Civil War

HC604 Bennett, Lerone, Jr. "Black, Blue, and Gray: The
      Negro in the Civil War." In Bennett, HC436:160-
      182.

HC605 Brawley, Benjamin. "The Civil War and Emancipa-
      tion." In Brawley, HC441:252-261.

HC606 Foster, William Z. "The Negro People in the Civil
      War." In Foster, HC452:271-283.

HC607 Franklin, John Hope. "Civil War." In Franklin,
      HC453:271-296.

HC608 Frazier, E. Franklin. "The Civil War and Emanci-
      pation." In Frazier, HC454:103-122.

HC609 McPherson, James M. "Abolitionist and Negro Op-
      position to Colonization During the Civil War."
      Phylon, 26 (4th Qrtr 1965), 391-399.

HC610 _____. Marching Toward Freedom: The Negro
in the Civil War, 1861-1865. New York: Knopf,
1967.

HC611 _____. The Negro's Civil War: How American
Negroes Felt and Acted During the War for the Union.
New York: Pantheon, 1965.

[_____. The Struggle for Equality: Abolitionists
and the Negro in the Civil War and Reconstruction.
See HC693.]

HC612 Meier, August, and Elliott Rudwick. "A Dream Betrayed: Negroes During the Civil War and Reconstruction." In Meier and Rudwick, HC462:137-147.

HC613 Quarles, Benjamin. The Negro in the Civil War.
Boston: Little, 1953.

HC614 Silver, James W. Confederate Morale and Church
Propaganda. 1957; Gloucester, Mass.: Peter
Smith, 1964.

HC615 Thorpe, Earl E. "The Negro and American Wars."
In Thorpe, HC475:187-201.

HC616 Wesley, Charles H. "The Civil War and the Negro-
American." JNH, 47 (April 1962), 77-96.

HC617 _____. Negro Americans in the Civil War. New
York: Publishers Co., 1967.

HC618 Woodson, Carter G. "The Civil War and the Church."
In Woodson, HC1188:164-179.

Reconstruction

HC619 Abbott, Martin. The Freedmen's Bureau in South
Carolina, 1865-1872. Chapel Hill: Univ. of North
Carolina Press, 1967.

HC620 _____. "Freedom's Cry: Negroes and Their Meet-
ings in South Carolina, 1865-1869." Phylon, 20
(3rd Qrtr 1959), 263-272.

HC621 Alexander, Thomas B. Political Reconstruction in

Tennessee. 1950; rpt. New York: Russell, 1968.

HC622 _____. Thomas A. R. Nelson of East Tennessee.
Nashville: Tennessee Historical Commission, 1956.

HC623 Allen, James S. Reconstruction: The Battle for
Democracy, 1865-1876. New York: International,
1937.

HC624 Aptheker, Herbert. "South Carolina Negro Conventions, 1865." JNH, 31 (Jan. 1946), 91-97.

HC625 Barksdale, Ethelbert. "Reconstruction in Mississippi."
In Herbert, A91:321-348.

HC626 Belz, Herman. Reconstructing the Union: Theory
and Policy during the Civil War. Ithaca: Cornell
Univ. Press, 1969.

HC627 Bennett, Lerone, Jr. "Black Power in Dixie." In
Bennett, HC436:183-219.

HC628 _____. Black Power, U.S.A.: The Human Side
of Reconstruction, 1867-1877. Chicago: Johnson,
1967.

HC629 _____. "The Revolution that Failed." In Bennett,
HC437:78-86.

HC630 Bentley, George R. A History of the Freedmen's
Bureau. 1955; rpt. New York: Octagon, 1970.

HC631 Blackburn, George M. "Radical Republican Motiva-
tion: A Case History." JNH, 54 (April 1969), 109-
126.

HC632 Bond, Horace Mann. "Social and Economic Forces
in Alabama Reconstruction." JNH, 23 (July 1938),
290-348.

HC633 _____. "Social Classes and the Beginning of Reconstruction," "The Origin of Tax-Supported Schools
for Negroes," and "Profit and Loss at the End of
Legal Reconstruction." In Bond, HC381:14-36, 37-
57, 58-83.

HC634 Brawley, Benjamin. "The Era of Enfranchisement."

In Brawley, HC441:262-286.

HC635 Brock, W. R. An American Crisis: Congress and
Reconstruction, 1865-1867. London: Macmillan,
1963.

HC636 Brown, William Garrott. "The Ku Klux Movement."
Atlantic, May 1901, pp. 634-644. Rpt. in Current,
A47:95-115.

HC637 Brown, William Wells. "The New Era." In Brown,
HC445:413-417.

HC638 Carpenter, John A. "Atrocities in the Reconstruction Period." JNH, 47 (Oct. 1962), 234-247.

HC639 Chamberlain, Daniel H. "Reconstruction in South
Carolina." Atlantic, April 1901, pp. 473-484. Rpt.
in Current, A47:73-94.

HC640 Clayton, Powell. The Aftermath of the Civil War, in
Arkansas. 1915; rpt. New York: Negro Universities Press, 1969.

HC641 Conway, Alan. The Reconstruction of Georgia. Minneapolis: Univ. of Minnesota Press, 1966.

HC642 Coulter, E. Merton. The Civil War and Readjust-
ment in Kentucky. 1926; rpt. Gloucester, Mass.:
Peter Smith, 1966.

HC643 _____. The South During Reconstruction, 1865-
1877. Baton Rouge: Louisiana State Univ. Press,
1947. [See Franklin, HC667.]

HC644 _____. William G. Brownlow: Fighting Parson of
the Southern Highlands. 1937; rpt. Knoxville: Univ.
of Tennessee Press, 1971.

HC645 Cox, LaWanda, and John H. Cox. Politics, Principle,
and Prejudice, 1865-1866: Dilemma of Reconstruction America. New York: Free Press, 1963.

HC646 Crouch, Barry A., and L. J. Schultz. "Crisis in
Color: Racial Separation in Texas During Reconstruction." Civil War History, 16 (March 1969),
37-49.

HC647 Davis, William Watson. The Civil War and Reconstruction in Florida. 1913; rpt. Gainesville: Univ.
of Florida Press, 1964.

HC648 Dennett, John Richard. The South as It Is: 1865-
1866. Ed. Henry M. Christman. New York: Viking, 1965.

HC649 Du Bois, W. E. B. Black Reconstruction in America:
An Essay Toward a History of the Part Which Black
Folk Played in the Attempt to Reconstruct Democ-
racy in America, 1860-1880. 1935; rpt. New York:
Russell, 1962.

HC650 _____. "The Freedmen's Bureau." Atlantic,
March 1901, pp. 354-365. Rpt. in Current, A47:
52-72, and rev. as "Of the Dawn of Freedom" in
Du Bois, A65:13-40.

HC651 _____. "Reconstruction, Seventy-Five Years After." Phylon, 4 (3rd Qrtr 1943), 205-212. Rpt. in
Du Bois, A66:79-88.

HC652 _____. "Reconstruction and Its Benefits." American Historical Review, 15 (July 1910), 781-799.
Rpt. in Drimmer, A56:273-292.

HC653 Dunning, William Archibald. Essays on the Civil
War and Reconstruction. Rev. edn. 1904; rpt.
Gloucester, Mass.: Peter Smith, 1969.

HC654 _____. Reconstruction, Political & Economic,
1865-1877. New York: Harper, 1907.

HC655 _____. "The Undoing of Reconstruction." Atlantic, Oct. 1901, pp. 437-449. Rpt. in Current, A47:
134-156, and in Dunning, HC653:353-385.

HC656 Durden, Robert F. "The Prostrate State Revisited:
James S. Pike and South Carolina Reconstruction."
JNH, 39 (April 1954), 87-110.

HC657 Eckenrode, Hamilton James. The Political History
of Virginia during the Reconstruction. 1904; rpt.
Gloucester, Mass.: Peter Smith, 1966.

HC658 Fehrenbacher, Don E. "Disunion and Reunion."

The Reconstruction of American History.   Ed. John
Higham. New York: Harper, 1962. Pages 98-
118.

HC659 Fertig, James Walter. The Secession and Reconstruction of Tennessee. 1898; rpt. New York:
AMS, 1972.

HC660 Ficklen, John Rose. History of Reconstruction in
Louisiana (Through 1868). 1910; rpt. Gloucester,
Mass.: Peter Smith, 1966.

HC661 Fischer, Roger A. "A Pioneer Protest: The New
Orleans Street-Car Controversy of 1867." JNH,
53 (July 1968), 219-233.

HC662 Fishback, William M. "Reconstruction in Arkansas."
In Herbert, A91:294-320.

HC663 Fleming, Walter L. Civil War and Reconstruction
in Alabama. 1905; rpt. Gloucester, Mass.: Peter
Smith, 1949.

HC664 _____. The Freedmen's Savings Bank: A Chapter
in the Economic History of the Negro Race. 1927;
rpt. Westport, Conn.: Negro Universities Press,
1970.

HC665 _____, ed. Documentary History of Reconstruction: Political, Military, Social, Religious, Educational & Industrial, 1865 to the Present Time. 2
vols. 1906, 1907; rpt. Gloucester, Mass.: Peter
Smith, 1960.

HC666 Franklin, John Hope. "The Effort To Attain Peace."
In Franklin, HC453:297-323.

HC667 _____. "Whither Reconstruction Historiography?"
JNE, 17 (Fall 1948), 446-461. [Rev. of Coulter,
HC643.]

HC668 Frazier, E. Franklin. "Reconstruction: Period of
Acute Race Conflict." In Frazier, HC454:123-146.

HC669 Fredrickson, George M. "Race and Reconstruction."
In Fredrickson, HC285:165-197.

HC670 Garner, James Wilford. Reconstruction in Missis-
       sippi. 1901; rpt. Gloucester, Mass.: Peter Smith,
       1964.

HC671 Gray, Daniel Savage. "Bibliographical Essay: Black
       Views on Reconstruction." JNH, 58 (Jan. 1973),
       73-85.

HC672 Hamilton, J. G. de Roulhac. Reconstruction in North
       Carolina. 1914; rpt. Gloucester, Mass.: Peter
       Smith, 1964.

HC673 Hemphill, John J. "Reconstruction in South Carolina."
       In Herbert, A91:85-111.

HC674 Henry, Robert Selph. The Story of Reconstruction.
       1938; rpt. Gloucester, Mass.: Peter Smith, 1963.

HC675 Herbert, Hilary A. "The Conditions of the Recon-
       struction Problem." Atlantic, Feb. 1901, pp. 145-
       157. Rpt. in Current, A47:29-51.

HC676 _____. "Reconstruction at Washington." In Her-
       bert, A91:1-28.

HC677 _____. "Reconstruction in Alabama." In Herbert,
       A91:29-69.

HC678 _____. "Sunrise." In Herbert, A91:430-442.

HC679 Hesseltine, William B. Lincoln's Plan of Reconstruc-
       tion. 1960; rpt. Gloucester, Mass.: Peter Smith,
       1963.

HC680 Horn, Stanley F. Invisible Empire: The Story of the
       Ku Klux Klan 1866-1871. 1939; rpt. New York:
       Haskell, 1968.

HC680a Jones, Ira P. "Reconstruction in Tennessee." In
       Herbert, A91:169-215.

HC681 Kendrick, Benj. B. The Journal of the Joint Com-
       mittee of Fifteen on Reconstruction: 39th Congress,
       1865-1867. 1914; rpt. New York: Negro Univer-
       sities Press, 1969.

HC682 Krug, Mark M. "On Rewriting of the Story of

Reconstruction in the U.S. History Textbooks."
JNH, 46 (April 1961), 133-153.

HC683 Leigh, Frances B[utler]. Ten Years on a Georgia
Plantation Since the War. 1883; rpt. New York:
Negro Universities Press, 1969.

HC684 Long, O. S., and William L. Wilson. "Reconstruction in West Virginia." In Herbert, A91:258-284.

HC684a Lonn, Ella. Reconstruction in Louisiana After 1868.
1918; rpt. Gloucester, Mass.: Peter Smith, 1967.

HC685 Low, W. A. "The Freedmen's Bureau and Civil
Rights in Maryland." JNH, 37 (July 1952), 221-
247.

HC686 _____. "The Freedmen's Bureau and Education
in Maryland." Maryland Historical Magazine, 47
(March 1952), 29-39.

HC687 Lynch, John R. "More About the Historical Errors
of James F. Rhodes." JNH, 3 (April 1918), 139-
157.

HC688 _____. "Some Historical Errors of James Ford
Rhodes." JNH, 2 (Oct. 1917), 345-368.

HC689 _____. "The Tragic Era" [letter]. JNH, 16
(Jan. 1931), 103-120.

HC690 Lynd, Staughton. "Rethinking Slavery and Reconstruction." JNH, 50 (July 1965), 198-209.

HC691 McCall, S. W. "Washington During Reconstruction."
Atlantic, June 1901, pp. 817-826. Rpt. in Current,
A47:116-133.

HC692 McPherson, Edward. The Political History of the
United States of America During the Period of Re-
construction. 2d edn. 1875; rpt. New York:
Negro Universities Press, 1969.

HC693 McPherson, James M. The Struggle for Equality:
Abolitionists and the Negro in the Civil War and
Reconstruction. Princeton: Princeton Univ. Press,
1964.

HC694 Meier, August. "Negroes in the First and Second
       Reconstructions of the South." Civil War History,
       13 (June 1967), 114-130.

HC695 _____, and Elliott Rudwick. "A Dream Betrayed:
       Negroes During the Civil War and Reconstruction."
       In Meier and Rudwick, HC462:147-176.

HC696 Morton, Richard L. The Negro in Virginia Politics,
       1865-1902. 1919; rpt. Spartanburg, S.C.: Re-
       print, 1973.

HC697 Murphy, L. E. "The Civil Rights Law of 1875."
       JNH, 12 (April 1927), 110-127. [See John R.
       Lynch, letter, JNH, 12 (Oct. 1927), 667-669.]

HC698 Nathans, Elizabeth Studley. Losing the Peace:
       Georgia Republicans and Reconstruction, 1865-1871.
       Baton Rouge: Louisiana State Univ. Press, 1968.

HC699 Neal, John Randolph. Disunion and Restoration in
       Tennessee. 1899; rpt. Freeport, N.Y.: Books
       for Libraries, 1971.

HC700 Page, Thomas Nelson. "The Southern People During
       Reconstruction." Atlantic, Sept. 1901, pp. 289-304.

HC701 Pasco, Samuel. "Reconstruction in Florida." In
       Herbert, A91:140-168.

HC702 Patton, James Welch. Unionism and Reconstruction
       in Tennessee, 1860-1869. 1934; rpt. Gloucester,
       Mass.: Peter Smith, 1966.

HC703 Pease, William H. "Three Years Among the Freed-
       men: William C. Gannett and the Port Royal Ex-
       periment." JNH, 42 (April 1957), 98-117.

HC704 Perry, Bliss. "Reconstruction and Disfranchisement."
       Atlantic, Oct. 1901, pp. 433-437. Rpt. as "Con-
       cluding Commentary" in Current, A47:157-165.

HC705 Phelps, Albert. "New Orleans and Reconstruction."
       Atlantic, July 1901, pp. 121-131.

HC706 Ramsdell, Charles William. Reconstruction in Texas.
       1910; rpt. Gloucester, Mass.: Peter Smith, 1964.

HC707 Report of the Joint Committee on Reconstruction, at the
      First Session Thirty-Ninth Congress. 1866; rpt.
      Westport, Conn.: Negro Universities Press, 1969.

HC708 Reynolds, John S. Reconstruction in South Carolina,
      1865-1877. 1905; rpt. New York: Negro Univer-
      sities Press, 1969.

HC709 Rice, Lawrence D. The Negro in Texas, 1874-1900.
      Baton Rouge: Louisiana State Univ. Press, 1971.

HC710 Richardson, Joe M. The Negro in the Reconstruction
      of Florida, 1865-1877. Florida State Univ. Studies,
      No. 46. Tallahassee: Florida State Univ., 1965.

HC711 Riddleberger, Patrick W. "The Radicals' Abandon-
      ment of the Negro During Reconstruction." JNH,
      45 (April 1960), 88-102.

HC712 Sage, B. J. "Reconstruction in Louisiana." In Her-
      bert, A91:383-429.

HC713 Schurz, Carl. Report on the Condition of the South.
      1865; rpt. New York: Arno, 1969. Also in
      Speeches, Correspondence and Political Papers of
      Carl Schurz. Ed. Frederic Bancroft. New York:
      Putnam's, 1913. I, 279-374.

HC714 Scott, Eben Greenough. Reconstruction During the
      Civil War in the United States of America. 1895;
      rpt. New York: Negro Universities Press, 1969.

HC715 Shapiro, Herbert. "Afro-American Responses to
      Race Violence During Reconstruction." Science &
      Society, 36 (Summer 1972), 158-170.

HC716 Simkins, Francis Butler, and Robert Hilliard Woody.
      South Carolina During Reconstruction. 1932; rpt.
      Gloucester, Mass.: Peter Smith, 1966.

HC717 Stampp, Kenneth M. The Era of Reconstruction,
      1865-1877. New York: Knopf, 1965.

HC718 Stewart, Charles. "Reconstruction in Texas." In
      Herbert, A91:349-382.

HC719 Stiles, Robert. "Reconstruction in Virginia." In

Herbert, A91:216-257.

HC720 Taylor, A. A. "Historians of the Reconstruction."
JNH, 23 (Jan. 1938), 16-34.

HC721 _____. The Negro in South Carolina During the
Reconstruction. Washington: Association for the
Study of Negro Life and History, 1924. Rpt. from
JNH, 9 (July 1924), 241-364, and (Oct. 1924), 381-
569.

HC722 _____. The Negro in Tennessee, 1865-1880.
1941; rpt. Spartanburg, S.C.: Reprint, 1974.

HC723 _____. The Negro in the Reconstruction of Virginia. 1926; rpt. New York: Russell, 1969. Rpt.
from JNH, 11 (April 1926), 243-415, and (July
1926), 425-537.

HC724 Thompson, C. Mildred. Reconstruction in Georgia:
Economic, Social, Political, 1865-1872. 1915; rpt.
Gloucester, Mass.: Peter Smith, 1964.

HC725 Thorpe, Earl E. "Shadow of the Plantation." In
Thorpe, HC475:237-265.

HC726 Tourgee, Albion W. The Invisible Empire: A Con-
cise Review of the Epoch. 1883; rpt. Ridgewood,
N.J.: Gregg, 1968.

HC727 Trefousse, Hans L. The Radical Republicans: Lincoln's Vanguard for Racial Justice. New York:
Knopf, 1969.

HC728 Turner, Henry G. "Reconstruction in Georgia." In
Herbert, A91:112-139.

HC729 Vance, Zebulon B. "Reconstruction in North Carolina." In Herbert, A91:70-84.

HC730 Vest, George G. "Reconstruction in Missouri." In
Herbert, A91:285-293.

HC731 Wallace, John. Carpetbag Rule in Florida: The Inside Workings of the Reconstruction of Civil Government after the Close of the Civil War. 1888; rpt.
Gainesville: Univ. of Florida Press, 1964.

HC732 Warmoth, Henry Clay. War, Politics, and Reconstruction: Stormy Days in Louisiana. 1930; rpt.
New York: Negro Universities Press, 1970.

HC733 Wharton, Vernon Lane. The Negro in Mississippi,
1865-1890. 1947; rpt. New York: Harper, 1965.

HC734 _____. "The Race Issue in the Overthrow of Reconstruction in Mississippi." Phylon, 2 (4th Qrtr
1941), 362-370. Rpt. in Meier and Rudwick, A125:
369-377.

HC735 White, Howard A. The Freedmen's Bureau in Louisiana. Baton Rouge: Louisiana State Univ. Press,
1970.

HC736 Williamson, Joel. After Slavery: The Negro in South
Carolina During Reconstruction, 1861-1877. Chapel
Hill: Univ. of North Carolina Press, 1965.

HC737 Wilson, Theodore Brantner. The Black Codes of the
South. University, Ala.: Univ. of Alabama Press,
1965.

HC738 Wilson, Woodrow. "The Reconstruction of the Southern States." Atlantic, Jan. 1901, pp. 1-15. Rpt.
in Current, A47:3-28.

HC739 Wood, Forrest G. "On Revising Reconstruction History: Negro Suffrage, White Disfranchisement, and
Common Sense." JNH, 51 (April 1966), 98-113.

HC740 Woodward, C. Vann. "The Political Legacy of the
First Reconstruction." JNE, 26 (Summer 1957),
231-240. Rpt. in The Burden of Southern History.
Rev. edn. Baton Rouge: Louisiana State Univ.
Press, 1968. Pages 89-107.

HC741 _____. Reunion and Reaction: The Compromise
of 1877 and the End of Reconstruction. Boston:
Little, 1951.

HC742 _____. "Seeds of Failure in Radical Race Policy."
In Woodward, HC482:163-183. Rpt. from Proceed-
ings of the American Philosophical Society, 110
(Feb. 1966), 1-9.

Black Politicians

HC743 Andrews, Norman P. "The Negro in Politics." JNH,
5 (Oct. 1920), 420-436.

HC744 Bacote, C. A. "The Negro in Atlanta Politics."
Phylon, 16 (4th Qrtr 1955), 333-350.

HC745 Bennett, Lerone, Jr. "Black Power in Dixie." In
Bennett, HC436:200-213.

HC746 Bernstein, Leonard. "The Participation of Negro
Delegates in the Constitutional Convention of 1868 in
North Carolina." JNH, 34 (Oct. 1949), 391-409.

[Bradley, Bert. "Negro Speakers in Congress: 1869-
1875." See HC1046.]

HC747 Brawley, Benjamin. "The Negro in Congress." In
Brawley, HC12:120-126.

HC748 Brewer, J. Mason. Negro Legislators of Texas and
Their Descendants: A History of the Negro in Texas
Politics from Reconstruction to Disfranchisement.
Dallas: Mathis, 1935.

HC749 Bryant, Lawrence C. Negro Lawmakers in the South
Carolina Legislature, 1869-1902. Orangeburg,
S.C.: School of Graduate Studies, South Carolina
State College, 1968.

HC750 _____. Negro Senators and Representatives in the
South Carolina Legislature, 1868-1902. Orangeburg,
S.C.: School of Graduate Studies, South Carolina
State College, 1968.

HC751 Cartwright, Joseph H. "Black Legislators in Tennes-
see in the 1800's: A Case Study in Black Political
Leadership." Tennessee Historical Quarterly, 32
(Fall 1973), 265-284.

[Christopher, Maurine. America's Black Congressmen. See HC24.]

HC752 Clayton, Edward T. The Negro Politician: His Success and Failure. Chicago: Johnson, 1964.

HC753 Coulter, E. Merton. Negro Legislators in Georgia
During the Reconstruction Period. Athens: Georgia
Historical Quarterly, 1968.

HC754 Elmore, Joseph Elliot. "North Carolina Negro Congressmen, 1875-1901." Thesis, Univ. of North
Carolina, 1964.

HC755 Franklin, John Hope. "Political Currents." In
Franklin, HC453:315-323.

HC756 Gosnell, Harold F. Negro Politicians: The Rise of
Negro Politics in Chicago. 1935; rpt. with an in-
troduction by James Q. Wilson, Chicago: Univ. of
Chicago Press, 1966.

HC757 Johnston, James Hugo. "The Participation of Negroes
in the Government of Virginia from 1877 to 1888."
JNH, 14 (July 1929), 251-271.

HC758 Katz, William. "George Henry White: A Militant Negro Congressman in the Age of Booker T. Washington." NHB, 29 (March 1966), 125-126, 134,
138-139.

HC759 Meier, August, and Elliott Rudwick. "A Dream Betrayed: Negroes During the Civil War and Reconstruction." In Meier and Rudwick, HC462:167-171.

HC760 "Negroes in Congress, 1868-1895." NHB, 31 (Nov.
1968), 12-13.

HC761 Robinson, George F., Jr. "The Negro in Politics in
Chicago." JNH, 17 (April 1932), 180-229.

HC762 Smith, Samuel Denny. The Negro in Congress, 1870-
1901. Chapel Hill: Univ. of North Carolina Press,
1940.

HC763 Taylor, Alrutheus A. "Negro Congressmen a Generation After." JNH, 7 (April 1922), 127-171.

HC764 "Three Negro Senators of the United States: Hiram
R. Revels, Blanche K. Bruce and Edward W.
Brooke." NHB, 30 (Jan. 1967), 4-5, 12.

HC765 Van Deusen, John G. "The Negro in Politics."

JNH, 21 (July 1936), 256-274.

HC766 Walton, Hanes, Jr. The Negro in Third Party Politics. Philadelphia: Dorrance, 1969.

HC767 _____. Black Political Parties: An Historical and
Political Analysis. New York: Free Press, 1972.

HC768 _____, and Ronald Clark. "Black Presidential
Candidates Past and Present." New South, 27
(Spring 1972), 14-22.

HC769 Walton, Norman W. "James T. Rapier: Congressman from Alabama." NHB, 30 (Nov. 1967), 6-10.

HC770 Wharton, Vernon Lane. "The Negro and Politics,
1870-1875." In Wharton, HC733:157-180.

HC771 Wilson, James Q. Negro Politics: The Search for
Leadership. New York: Free Press, 1960.

HC772 _____. "Two Negro Politicians: An Interpretation." Midwest Journal of Politics, 4 (Nov. 1960),
346-369. Rpt. in Meier and Rudwick, A126:376-
393.

HC773 Woodson, Carter G. "The Call of Politics." In
Woodson, HC1188:198-223.

HC774 Work, Monroe N., comp. "Some Negro Members of
Reconstruction Conventions and Legislatures of Congress." JNH, 5 (Jan. 1920), 63-119.

Post-Reconstruction, 1877-1895

HC775 Abramovitz, Jack. "The Negro in the Populist Movement." JNH, 38 (July 1953), 257-289.

HC776 Barrows, Isabel C., ed. First Mohonk Conference
on the Negro Question. 1890-1891; rpt. New York:
Negro Universities Press, 1969.

HC777 Bennett, Lerone, Jr. "The Birth of Jim Crow."
In Bennett, HC436:220-226.

HC778 _____. "The Revolution that Failed." In Bennett,

HC437:86-109.

HC779 Bond, Horace Mann. "The Middle Period: The Social Structure Solidified." In Bond, HC381:84-115.

HC780 Brawley, Benjamin. "The Negro in the New South."
In Brawley, HC441:287-296.

HC781 Crowe, Charles. "Tom Watson, Populists, and
Blacks Reconsidered." JNH, 55 (April 1970), 99-
116.

HC782 Fishel, Leslie H., Jr. "Repercussions of Reconstruction: The Northern Negro, 1870-1883." Civil
War History, 14 (Dec. 1968), 325-345.

HC783a Fortune, T. Thomas. Black and White: Land,
Labor, and Politics in the South. 1884; rpt. New
York: Arno, 1968.

HC783b _____. Black and White: Land, Labor, and
Politics in the South [1884]. Chicago: Johnson,
1970.

HC784 Franklin, John Hope. "Losing the Peace." In
Franklin, HC453:324-343.

HC785 Frazier, E. Franklin. "New Forms of Accommodation." In Frazier, HC454:147-168.

HC786 Fredrickson, George M. "The New South and the
New Paternalism, 1877-1890." In Fredrickson,
HC285:198-227.

HC787 Garvin, Roy. "Benjamin, or 'Pap,' Singleton, and
His Followers." JNH, 33 (Jan. 1948), 7-23.

HC788 Logan, Frenise A. The Negro in North Carolina,
1876-1894. Chapel Hill: Univ. of North Carolina
Press, 1964.

HC789 Logan, Rayford W. The Betrayal of the Negro, from
Rutherford B. Hayes to Woodrow Wilson. New enl.
edn. New York: Collier, 1965.

HC790 Meier, August, and Elliott Rudwick. "A Strange
Chapter in the Career of 'Jim Crow.' " In Meier

and Rudwick, A126:14-19.

HC791 _____. " 'Up from Slavery': The Age of Accommodation." In Meier and Rudwick, HC462:177-193.

HC792 Schwendemann, Glen. "St. Louis and the 'Exodusters'
of 1879." JNH, 46 (Jan. 1961), 32-46.

HC793 Shapiro, Herbert. "The Populists and the Negro: A
Reconsideration." In Meier and Rudwick, A126:27-36.

HC794 Thorpe, Earl E. "Shadow of the Plantation." In
Thorpe, HC475:265-281.

HC795 Tindall, George B. "The Question of Race in the South
Carolina Constitutional Convention of 1895." JNH, 37
(July 1952), 277-303. Rpt. in Meier and Rudwick,
A126:37-55.

HC796 _____. South Carolina Negroes, 1877-1900. Columbia: Univ. of South Carolina Press, 1952.

HC797 Van Deusen, John G. "The Exodus of 1879." JNH,
21 (April 1936), 111-129.

HC798 Weaver, Valeria W. "The Failure of Civil Rights
1875-1883 and Its Repercussions." JNH, 54 (Oct.
1969), 368-382.

HC799 Woodward, C. Vann. "The Birth of Jim Crow."
American Heritage, 15 (April 1964), 52-55, 100-103.
Rpt. as "The National Decision Against Equality" in
Woodward, HC482:212-233, rev.

HC800 _____. "The Strange Career of a Historical Controversy." In Woodward, HC482:234-260.

HC801 _____. The Strange Career of Jim Crow. 3rd
rev. edn. New York: Oxford Univ. Press, 1974.

Afro-Americans and the Labor Movement

HC802 Bloch, Herman D. "Labor and the Negro 1866-1910."
JNH, 50 (July 1965), 163-184.

HC803 Du Bois, W. E. B. Black Reconstruction in America.

In Du Bois, HC649:353-367 and passim.

HC804 Foner, Philip S. "The IWW and the Black Worker."
JNH, 55 (Jan. 1970), 45-64.

HC805 Foster, William Z. "The National Labor Union" and
"Knights of Labor and American Federation of Labor." In Foster, HC452:345-354, 365-375.

HC806 Howe, Irving, and B. J. Widick. "The U.A.W.
Fights Race Prejudice." Commentary, 8 (Sept.
1949), 261-268. Rpt. in Meier and Rudwick, A126:
235-244.

HC807 Mandel, Bernard. "Samuel Gompers and the Negro
Workers, 1886-1914." JNH, 40 (Jan. 1955), 34-60.
Rpt. in Meier and Rudwick, A126:75-93.

HC808 Meier, August, and Elliott Rudwick. "'Up from
Slavery': The Age of Accommodation." In Meier
and Rudwick, HC462:189-191.

HC809 Northrup, Herbert R. "Organized Labor and Negro
Workers." Journal of Political Economy, 51 (June
1943), 206-221. Rpt. in Sternsher, A158:127-149.

HC810 Spero, Sterling D., and Abram L. Harris. The
Black Worker: The Negro and the Labor Movement.
1931; rpt. Port Washington, N.Y.: Kennikat, 1966.

HC811 Wesley, Charles. "Organized Labor and the Negro."
In Calverton, A30:339-362.

The Era of Booker T. Washington, 1895-1915

HC812 Abramovitz, Jack. "Crossroads of Negro Thought,
1890-1915." Social Education, 18 (March 1954),
117-120.

HC813 _____. "The Emergence of Booker T. Washington as a National Negro Leader." Social Education,
32 (May 1968), 445-451.

HC814 Bennett, Lerone, Jr. "The Birth of Jim Crow" and
"From Booker T. Washington to Martin Luther
King, Jr." In Bennett, HC436:226-241, 274-278.

HC815 _____. "The Lions and the Foxes." In Bennett,
       HC437:113-133.

HC816 Bernstein, Barton J. "Plessy v. Ferguson: Conserv-
       ative Sociological Jurisprudence." JNH, 48 (July
       1963), 196-205.

HC817 Brawley, Benjamin. " 'The Vale of Tears,' 1890-
       1910." In Brawley, HC441:297-340.

HC818 Crowe, Charles. "Racial Massacre in Atlanta, Sep-
       tember 22, 1906." JNH, 54 (April 1969), 150-173.

HC819 _____. "Racial Violence and Social Reform--Ori-
       gins of the Atlanta Riot of 1906." JNH, 53 (July
       1968), 234-256.

HC820 Franklin, John Hope. "Philanthropy and Self-Help"
       and "Dawn of a New Century." In Franklin, HC453:
       382-412, 433-451.

HC821 Fredrickson, George M. The Black Image in the
       White Mind. In Fredrickson, HC285:228-319.

HC822 Harlan, Louis R. "Booker T. Washington and the
       White Man's Burden." American Historical Review,
       71 (Jan. 1966), 441-467.

HC823 _____. "Booker T. Washington in Biographical
       Perspective." American Historical Review, 75 (Oct.
       1970), 1581-1599.

HC824 _____. "The Secret Life of Booker T. Washing-
       ton." Journal of Southern History, 37 (Aug. 1971),
       393-416.

HC825 Meier, August. Negro Thought in America, 1880-
       1915: Racial Ideologies in the Age of Booker T.
       Washington. Ann Arbor: Univ. of Michigan Press,
       1963.

HC826 _____. "Toward a Reinterpretation of Booker T.
       Washington." Journal of Southern History, 23 (May
       1957), 220-227.

HC827 _____, and Elliott Rudwick. " 'Up from Slavery':
       The Age of Accommodation." In Meier and

Rudwick, HC462:193-212.

HC828 Newman Richard. "Washington and Du Bois: Integration and Separation in American Negro Protest."
Boston University Journal, 18 (Spring 1970), 43-48.

HC829 Olsen, Otto H., ed. The Thin Disguise: Turning
Point in Negro History. "Plessy v. Ferguson," A
Documentary Presentation (1864-1896). New York:
Humanities Press, 1967.

HC830 Rudwick, Elliott M. "The Niagara Movement." JNH,
42 (July 1957), 177-200. Rpt. in Meier and Rudwick, A126:131-148. Rpt. as "Niagara Movement:
The Protest" in Rudwick, HC152:94-119, rev.

HC831 _____. "Race Leadership Struggle: Background
of the Boston Riot of 1903." JNE, 31 (Winter 1962),
16-24. Rev. version in Rudwick, HC152:65-76.

HC832 Thorpe, Earl E. "The Washington-Du Bois Controversy." In Thorpe, HC475:310-334.

HC833 Walden, Daniel. "The Contemporary Opposition to
the Political Ideals of Booker T. Washington." JNH,
45 (April 1960), 103-115.

HC834 Washington, Booker T. The Future of the American
Negro. 1899; rpt. New York: Haskell, 1968.

From BTW to the New Deal, 1915-1933

HC835 Aron, Birgit. "The Garvey Movement: Shadow and
Substance." Phylon, 8 (4th Qrtr 1947), 337-343.

HC836 Bennett, Lerone, Jr. "From Booker T. Washington
to Martin Luther King, Jr." In Bennett, HC436:
278-299.

HC837 _____. "The Lions and the Foxes." In Bennett,
HC437:133-160.

HC838 Brawley, Benjamin. "The Negro in the New Age."
In Brawley, HC441:341-371.

HC839 Brisbane, Robert Hughes, Jr. "Some New Light on

the Garvey Movement." JNH, 36 (Jan. 1951), 53-
62.

HC840 Contee, Clarence G. "Du Bois, the NAACP, and the
Pan-African Congress of 1919." JNH, 57 (Jan.
1972), 13-28.

HC841 Cripps, Thomas R. "The Reaction of the Negro to
the Motion Picture Birth of a Nation." Historian,
25 (May 1963), 344-362. Rpt. in Meier and Rudwick, A126:149-161.

HC842 Cruse, Harold. "Harlem Background--The Rise of
Economic Nationalism and Origins of Cultural Revolution." In Cruse, HC448:11-63.

HC843 Diggs, Irene. "The Amenia Conferences: A Neglected
Aspect of the Afro-American Struggle." Freedomways, 13 (2d Qrtr 1973), 117-134.

HC844 Donald, Henderson H. "The Negro Migration of 1916-
1918." JNH, 6 (Oct. 1921), 383-498.

HC845 Elkins, W. F. "The Influence of Marcus Garvey on
Africa: A British Report of 1922." Science & Society, 32 (Summer 1968), 321-323.

HC846 _____. "Marcus Garvey, the Negro World, and
the British West Indies: 1919-1920." Science & Society, 36 (Spring 1972), 63-77.

HC847 Fierce, Milfred C. "Economic Aspects of the Marcus
Garvey Movement." Black Scholar, 3 (March-April
1972), 50-61.

HC848 Franklin, John Hope. "In Pursuit of Democracy,"
"Democracy Escapes," and "A Harlem Renaissance."
In Franklin, HC453:452-476, 477-497, 498-513.

HC849 Frazier, E. Franklin. "The Garvey Movement."
Opportunity, 4 (Nov. 1926), 346-348. Rpt. in Meier
and Rudwick, A126:204-208.

HC850 _____. "The Garvey Movement." In Frazier,
HC454:528-531.

HC851 James, C. L. R. "Marcus Garvey." A History of

Negro Revolt. 1938; rpt. New York: Haskell, 1969. Pages 63-71.

HC852 Kellogg, Charles Flint. NAACP: A History of the National Association for the Advancement of Colored People. Vol. I, 1909-1920. Baltimore: Johns Hopkins Press, 1967.

HC853 Meier, August, and Elliott Rudwick. "Black Men in the Urban Age: The Rise of the Ghetto." In Meier and Rudwick, HC462:213-238.

HC854 Miller, Kelly. Kelly Miller's History of the World War for Human Rights. N.p., 1919.

HC855 Moses, Wilson J. "A Reappraisal of the Garvey Movement." Black Scholar, 4 (Nov.-Dec. 1972), 38-49.

HC856 Ovington, Mary White. "The National Association for the Advancement of Colored People." JNH, 9 (April 1924), 107-116.

HC857 Record, Wilson. "Negro Intellectual Leadership in the National Association for the Advancement of Colored People: 1910-1940." Phylon, 17 (4th Qrtr 1956), 375-389.

HC858 Reid, Ira De A. "Negro Movements and Messiahs, 1900-1949." Phylon, 10 (4th Qrtr 1949), 362-369.

HC859 Thorpe, Earl E. "The Negro and American Wars." In Thorpe, HC475:204-217.

HC860 Wood, L. Hollingsworth. "The Urban League Movement." JNH, 9 (April 1924), 117-126.

HC861 Zickefoose, Harold E. "The Garvey Movement." Thesis, State Univ. of Iowa, 1931.

The New Deal, 1933-1941

HC862 Allen, James S. The Negro Question in the United States. New York: International, 1936.

HC863 Bennett, Lerone, Jr. "The Lions and the Foxes."

In Bennett, HC437:160-166.

HC864 Brisbane, Robert H. "Blacks, Reds, and the Great
Depression." In Brisbane, HC442:133-159.

HC865 Bunche, Ralph J. The Political Status of the Negro
in the Age of FDR [1940]. Chicago: Univ. of Chicago Press, 1973.

HC866 Cruse, Harold. "Jews and Negroes in the Communist Party" and "The National Negro Congress." In
Cruse, HC448:147-170, 171-180.

HC867 Fishel, Leslie H., Jr. "The Negro in the New Deal
Era." Wisconsin Magazine of History, 48 (Winter
1964), 111-126. Rpt. in Sternsher, A158:7-28; and
in Fishel and Quarles, A72:447-453, abr.

HC868 Fontaine, W. T. "An Interpretation of Contemporary
Negro Thought from the Standpoint of the Sociology
of Knowledge." JNH, 25 (Jan. 1940), 6-13.

HC869 Foster, William Z. "The Economic Crisis and the
New Deal" and "The Negro and the New Trade Unionism." In Foster, HC452:479-491, 492-504.

HC870 Franklin, John Hope. "The New Deal." In Franklin,
HC453:523-545.

HC871 Hoffman, Erwin D. "The Genesis of the Modern
Movement for Equal Rights in South Carolina, 1930-
1939." JNH, 44 (Oct. 1959), 346-369. Rpt. in
Sternsher, A158:194-214.

HC872 Meier, August, and Elliott Rudwick. "Black Men in
the Urban Age: The Rise of the Ghetto." In Meier
and Rudwick, HC462:238-246.

[Sternsher, Bernard, ed. The Negro in Depression
and War: Prelude to Revolution, 1930-1945. See
A158.]

World War II, 1941-1945

HC873 Bennett, Lerone, Jr. "Gandhi in Harlem." In Bennett, HC437:169-196.

HC874 Brisbane, Robert H. "The Original March on Wash-
       ington" and "The Politics of FEPC." In Brisbane,
       HC442:161-169, 171-183.

HC875 Foster, William Z. "Fascism and World War II."
       In Foster, HC452:505-517.

HC876 Franklin, John Hope. "Fighting for the Four Free-
       doms." In Franklin, HC453:573-607.

HC877 Garfinkel, Herbert. When Negroes March: The
       March on Washington Movement in the Organization-
       al Politics for FEPC. Glencoe, Ill.: Free Press,
       1959.

HC878 Hughes, Langston. "World War II." In Hughes, HC
       459:90-109. [See also 83-86.]

HC879 Meier, August, and Elliott Rudwick. "Black Men in
       the Urban Age: The Rise of the Ghetto." In Meier
       and Rudwick, HC462:246-248.

HC880 Thorpe, Earl E. "The Negro and American Wars."
       In Thorpe, HC475:217-221.

The Cold War Era, 1945-1955

HC881 Bennett, Lerone, Jr. "Bigger in Wonderland." In
       Bennett, HC437:199-223.

HC882 Black, Algernon D. "Civil Rights and Ethical Re-
       sponsibilities." Humanist, 11 (March-April 1951),
       53-58.

HC883 Brisbane, Robert H. "The First Assault on Plessy
       v. Ferguson" and "The New Urban League." In
       Brisbane, HC442:185-202. 203-211.

HC884 Foster, William Z. "The Negro and the Cold War."
       In Foster, HC452:518-530.

HC885 Franklin, John Hope. "The Post-War Years." In
       Franklin, HC453:608-622.

HC886 Meier, August, and Elliott Rudwick. CORE: A Study
       in the Civil Rights Movement, 1942-1968. In Meier

and Rudwick, HC903:3-71.

The Civil Rights Movement, 1955-1964

HC887 Aptheker, Herbert. Soul of the Republic: The Negro
    Today. New York: Marzani, 1964.

HC888 Bennett, Lerone, Jr. "From Booker T. Washington
    to Martin Luther King, Jr." and "The Bitter Har-
    vest." In Bennett, HC436:313-324, 325-348.

HC889 _____. "Confrontation II: America Face to Face."
    In Bennett, HC437:251-304.

HC890 _____. "Mood: Project 'C.' " In Bennett, A11:
    3-23.

HC891 Brisbane, Robert H. "We Shall Overcome." In
    Brisbane, HC442:237-250.

HC892 Clark, Kenneth B. "The Civil Rights Movement:
    Momentum and Organization." Daedalus, 95 (Winter
    1966), 241-264. Rpt. in Geschwender, A81:47-64.

HC893 Franklin, John Hope. "The Negro Revolution." In
    Franklin, HC453:623-652.

HC894 Graham, Hugh Davis. Crisis in Print: Desegrega-
    tion and the Press in Tennessee. Nashville: Van-
    derbilt Univ. Press, 1967.

HC895 Harding, Vincent. "Black Radicalism: The Road
    from Montgomery." In Young, A182:321-354.

HC896 Hoffer, Eric. "The Negro Revolution." The Temper
    of Our Time. New York: Harper, 1967. Pages
    41-57.

HC897 Jacobs, Paul, and Saul Landau. "SNCC--One Man,
    One Vote." In Jacobs and Landau, A99:15-26.

HC898 King, Martin Luther, Jr. Stride toward Freedom:
    The Montgomery Story. New York: Harper, 1958.

HC899 Laue, James H. "An Example: The Civil Rights Move-
    ment." In Wm. Bruce Cameron. Modern Social

Movements: A Sociological Outline. New York:
Random, 1966. Pages 111-120.

HC900 Long, Margaret. "March on Washington." New
South, 18 (Sept. 1963), 3-19.

HC901 Mayfield, Julian. "Challenge to Negro Leadership:
The Case of Robert Williams." Commentary, 31
(April 1961), 297-305.

HC902 Meier, August, and Elliott Rudwick. "The Black Revolt." In Meier and Rudwick, HC462:251-273.

HC903 _____. CORE: A Study in the Civil Rights Movement, 1942-1968. New York: Oxford Univ. Press,
1973.

HC904 Pettigrew, Thomas F. "Actual Gains and Psychological Losses: The Negro American Protest." JNE,
32 (Fall 1963), 493-506. Rpt. in Meier and Rudwick, A126:318-332.

HC905 Silberman, Charles E. Crisis in Black and White.
New York: Random, 1964.

[Simons, Herbert W. "Patterns of Persuasion in the
Civil Rights Struggle." See HC1134.]

[Smith, Donald Hugh. "Civil Rights: A Problem in
Communication." See HC1142.]

[_____. "Martin Luther King: In the Beginning
at Montgomery." See HC1144.]

HC906 Southern Regional Council. "Direct Action in the
South." New South, 18 (Oct.-Nov. 1963), 1-32.

HC907 Tucker, Sterling. "The Death of a Movement." In
Tucker, HC1247:7-36.

HC908 Valien, Preston. "The Montgomery Bus Protest as
a Social Movement." Race Relations: Problems
and Theory. Ed. Jitsuichi Masuoka and Preston
Valien. Chapel Hill: Univ. of North Carolina Press,
1961. Pages 112-127.

HC909 Woodward, C. Vann. "The Great Civil Rights

Debate." Commentary, Oct. 1957, pp. 283-291.

HC910 _____. "What Happened to the Civil Rights Move-
ment." Harper's Magazine, Jan. 1967, pp. 29-37.
Rpt. in The Burden of Southern History. Rev. edn.
Baton Rouge: Louisiana State Univ. Press, 1968.
Pages 29-37.

HC911 Zinn, Howard. SNCC: The New Abolitionists. 2d
edn. Boston: Beacon, 1965.

Black Protest, 1964-1974

HC912 Allen, Robert L. Black Awakening in Capitalist
America: An Analytic History. Garden City, N.Y.:
Doubleday, 1969. [Also publ. as A Guide to Black
Power in America: An Historical Analysis. Lon-
don: Gollancz, 1970.]

HC913 Anthony, Earl. Picking Up the Gun: A Report on
the Black Panthers. New York: Dial, 1970. [See
Charyn, HC917.]

HC914 Bell, Inge Powell. "Emergence of Black Power."
In Bell, HC1229:187-190.

HC915 Bennett, Lerone, Jr. "The Bitter Harvest." In Bennett, HC436:348-376.

[Brooks, Robert D. "Black Power: The Dimensions
of a Slogan." See HC1050.]

[Burgess, Parke G. "The Rhetoric of Black Power:
A Moral Demand?" See HC1055.]

HC916 Carmichael, Stokely, and Charles V. Hamilton.
Black Power: The Politics of Liberation in America. New York: Random, 1967.

HC917 Charyn, Marlene. Rev. of Anthony, HC913, in Saturday Review, 28 Feb. 1970, pp. 38-40.

HC918 Clarke, Stephen, et al. The Black Man in Search of
Power: A Survey of the Black Revolution Across
the World. London: Nelson, 1968. [See pp. 75-
121.]

HC919 Cruse, Harold. "Behind the Black Power Slogan."
        Rebellion or Revolution? New York: Morrow,
        1968. Pages 193-258.

HC920 _____. "Postscript on Black Power--The Dialogue
        Between Shadow and Substance." In Cruse, HC448:
        544-565.

HC921 Danzig, David. "In Defense of 'Black Power.'"
        Commentary, 42 (Sept. 1966), 41-46.

HC922 Draper, Theodore. "The Black Panthers" and "Black
        Power." In Draper, HC1256:97-117, 118-131.

HC923 Duberman, Martin. "Black Power in America."
        Partisan Review, 35 (Winter 1968), 34-48. Rpt. in
        Meier and Rudwick, A126:394-405; and in Young,
        A182:303-317.

HC924 Fairfield, Roy P. "Mutual Challenge: The Negro and
        Humanism." Humanist, 25 (July-Aug. 1965), 149-
        153.

        [Flynt, Wayne. "The Ethics of Democratic Persua-
        sion and the Birmingham Crisis." See HC1069.]

HC925 Fry, John R. "Black Power and Christian Responsi-
        bility." Fire and Blackstone. Philadelphia: Lip-
        pincott, 1969. Pages 97-146.

HC926 Gayle, Addison, Jr. "Black Power and Existential
        Politics" and "Black Power or Black Fascism?"
        In Gayle, A80:71-79, 80-87.

HC927 Gerlach, Luther P., and Virginia H. Hine. "The So-
        cial Organization of a Movement of Revolutionary
        Change: Case Study, Black Power." In Whitten and
        Szwed, A174:385-400.

HC928 Goodheart, Eugene. "The Rhetoric of Violence."
        Nation, 6 April 1970, pp. 399-402.

        [Gregg, Richard B., A. Jackson McCormack, and
        Douglas J. Pedersen. "The Rhetoric of Black Pow-
        er: A Street-Level Interpretation." See HC1075.]

HC929 Grier, William H., and Price M. Cobbs. Black

Rage. New York: Basic, 1968.

HC930 Hamilton, Charles V. "Riots, Revolts and Relevant
       Response." In Barbour, A8:171-178.

HC931 _____. "How Black Is Black?" Ebony, Aug. 1969,
       pp. 45-48, 52. Rpt. in The Black Revolution, A12:
       23-29.

       [Hess, Richard, and Paul Harper. "A Kind of Alice
       in Wonderland: The Riot Report--an Analysis of Its
       Effects." See HC1086.]

       [King, Martin Luther, Jr. Where Do We Go from
       Here: Chaos or Community? See SE1464.]

       [Klumpp, James F. "Nonviolence and Black Power:
       Civil Rights as a Mass Movement." See HC1099.]

HC932 Ladner, Joyce. "What 'Black Power' Means to Ne-
       groes in Mississippi." Trans-Action, 5 (Nov. 1967),
       7-15. Rpt. in Rose, A151:249-265.

       [Larson, Charles U. "The Trust Establishing Func-
       tion of the Rhetoric of Black Power." See HC1101.]

HC933 Lasch, Christopher. "The Trouble with Black Pow-
       er." New York Review of Books, 29 Feb. 1968,
       pp. 4-13. Rpt. in Katope and Zolbrod, A105:412-
       430; and in Rose, A151:267-291.

HC934 Lokos, Lionel. The New Racism: Reverse Discrimi-
       nation in America. New Rochelle, N.Y.: Arling-
       ton, 1971.

       [McPherson, Dorothy. "Black Power in Print." See
       B16.]

HC935 Major, Reginald. A Panther Is a Black Cat. New
       York: Morrow, 1971.

HC936 Margolis, Joseph, and Clorinda Margolis. "Black
       and White on Black and White." Humanist, 29
       (July-Aug. 1969), n. pag. Rpt. in Moss, A130:3-12.

HC937 Marine, Gene. The Black Panthers. New York:
       New American Library, 1969.

HC938 Meier, August, and Elliott Rudwick. "The Black Revolt." In Meier and Rudwick, HC462:273-298.

HC939 _____. "CORE in Decline: The Road Toward Black Power, 1964-1966" and "Epilogue." In Meier and Rudwick, HC903:329-408, 409-431.

HC940 Morsell, John A. "Black Progress or Illiberal Rhetoric?" Crisis, June-July 1973, pp. 200-203. [See Wattenberg and Scammon, HC954.]

HC941 "The Panthers and the Law." Newsweek, 23 Feb. 1970, pp. 26-30.

HC942 Patterson, Eugene. "Rap, Stokely and Booker T., a Document." JNH, 52 (Oct. 1967), 325-326.

HC943 Report of the National Advisory Commission on Civil Disorders. New York: Dutton, 1968. [See Hess and Harper, HC1086.]

HC944 Roberts, Gene. "The Story of Snick: From 'Freedom High' to Black Power." New York Times Magazine, 25 Sept. 1966, pp. 27-29, 119-120, 122, 124, 126, 128. Rpt. in Meier and Rudwick, A124:139-153.

HC945 Schanche, Don A. The Panther Paradox: A Liberal's Dilemma. New York: McKay, 1970.

[Scott, Robert L. "Black Power Bends Martin Luther King." See HC1126.]

[_____. "Justifying Violence: The Rhetoric of Militant Black Power." See HC1127.]

[_____. "Rhetoric, Black Power, and Baldwin's 'Another Country.'" See HC1128.]

[_____, and Wayne Brockriede. "Hubert Humphrey Faces the 'Black Power' Issue." See HC1129.]

[_____. "The Rhetoric of Black Power: Order and Disorder in the Future." See HC1130.]

[Scott, Robert L., and Donald K. Smith. "The Rhetoric of Confrontation." See HC1131.]

HC946 Seale, Bobby. Seize the Time: The Story of the
       Black Panther Party and Huey P. Newton. New
       York: Random, 1970.

HC947 Sheehy, Gail. Panthermania: The Clash of Black
       Against Black in One American City. New York:
       Harper, 1971.

HC948 Sleeper, C. Freeman. Black Power and Christian
       Responsibility: Some Biblical Foundations for Social
       Ethics. Nashville: Abingdon, 1969.

       [Smith, Arthur L. Rhetoric of Black Revolution.
       See HC1246.]

       [Smith, D. H. "Rhetoric of Riots." See HC1145.]

       [Spike, Robert W. "The Riots as Communication."
       See HC1148.]

HC949 Stearn, Gerald Emanuel. "Rapping with the Panthers
       in White Suburbia." New York Times Magazine,
       8 March 1970, pp. 28-29, 110-115.

HC950 Steel, Ronald. "Letter from Oakland: The Panthers."
       New York Review of Books, 11 Sept. 1969, pp. 14-
       23.

HC951 Stern, Sol. "The Call of the Black Panthers." New
       York Times Magazine, 6 Aug. 1967, pp. 10-11, 62,
       64, 67-68. Rpt. in Meier and Rudwick, A124:230-
       242.

HC952 Stone, Chuck. "The National Conference on Black
       Power." In Barbour, A8:189-198.

       [Tucker, Sterling. For Blacks Only: Black Strate-
       gies for Change in America. See HC1247.]

       [Van Graber, Marilyn. "Functional Criticism: A
       Rhetoric of Black Power." See HC1154.]

HC953 Vincent, Theodore G. Black Power and the Garvey
       Movement. Berkeley: Ramparts, 1971.

HC954 Wattenberg, Ben J., and Richard M. Scammon.
       "Black Progress and Liberal Rhetoric." Commentary,

55 (April 1973), 35-44. [See Morsell, HC940.]

HC955 Wills, Garry. The Second Civil War: Arming for
      Armageddon. New York: New American Library,
      1968.

HC956 Wright, Nathan, Jr. "The Crisis Which Bred Black
      Power." In Barbour, A8:103-118; and in Rose,
      A151:183-195.

HC957 Zinn, Howard. "American Liberalism, Source of Ne-
      gro Radicalism." Boston Univ. Journal, 16 (Winter
      1968). Rpt. in Moss, A130:132-141.

HC958 Zolberg, Aristide, and Vera Zolberg. "The Ameri-
      canization of Frantz Fanon." Public Interest, 9
      (Fall 1967), 49-63. Rpt. in Rose, A151:197-211.

                        LITERATURE

Literature, Art, and Music

HC959 Abramson, Doris. "Negro Playwrights in America."
      Columbia Forum, 12 (Spring 1969), 11-17.

HC960 Bailey, Peter. "The Black Theater." Ebony, Aug.
      1969, pp. 126-128, 130-132, 134. Rpt. in The
      Black Revolution, A12:149-159.

HC961 Baker, David N. "The Rhetorical Dimensions of
      Black Music: Past and Present." In Daniel, A49:
      3-27.

HC962 Berek, Peter. "Using Black Magic with the Word on
      the World." Saturday Review, 30 Nov. 1968, pp.
      35-37. [Rev. of Jones and Neal, A103.]

HC963 Bigsby, C. W. E. Confrontation and Commitment: A
      Study of Contemporary American Drama 1959-66.
      [Columbia]: Univ. of Missouri Press, 1967.

HC964 Bone, Robert. The Negro Novel in America. Rev.
      edn. New Haven: Yale Univ. Press, 1965.

HC965 Brawley, Benjamin. "Drama and Stage, 1916-1936."

In Brawley, HC13:269-296.

HC966 _____. The Negro in Literature and Art in the
United States. 1929; rpt. New York: AMS, 1971.
[Rev. and enl. edn., Brawley, HC13.]

HC967 _____. "The Promise of Negro Literature."
JNH, 19 (Jan. 1934), 53-59.

HC968 _____. "Three Negro Poets: Horton, Mrs. Harper and Whitman." JNH, 2 (Oct. 1917), 384-392.

HC969 Bronz, Stephen H. Roots of Negro Racial Conscious-
ness: The 1920's, Three Harlem Renaissance Authors. New York: Libra, 1964.

HC970 Brown, Sterling. "Negro Folk Expression: Spirituals,
Seculars, Ballads and Work Songs." Phylon, 14
(1st Qrtr 1953), 45-61. Rpt. in Meier and Rudwick,
A126:209-226.

HC971 Chamberlain, John. "The Negro as Writer." Bookman, 70 (Feb. 1930), 603-611.

HC972 Clay, Eugene. "The Negro in Recent American Literature." American Writers' Congress. Ed. Henry
Hart. New York: International, 1935. Pages 145-
153.

HC973 Courlander, Harold. Negro Folk Music, U.S.A. New
York: Columbia Univ. Press, 1963.

HC974 Cruse, Harold. "The Harlem Black Arts Theater--
New Dialogue with the Lost Black Generation," "Intellectuals and the Theater of the 1960's--As Medi-
um and Dialogue," and "Negro Writers' Conferences
--The Dialogue Distorted." In Cruse, HC448:533-
543, 520-532, 498-519.

HC975 Fisher, Miles Mark. Negro Slave Songs in the United
States. 1953; rpt. New York: Russell, 1968.

HC976 Frazier, E. Franklin. "Negro Press and Literature." In Frazier, HC454:492-519.

HC977 Garrett, Romeo B. "African Survivals in American
Culture." JNH, 51 (Oct. 1966), 239-245. Rpt. in

Smith, A155:356-362.

HC978 Gayle, Addison, Jr. "Cultural Nationalism: The Black Novelist in America." In Gayle, A80:198-209.

HC979 _____. "The Literature of Protest." NHB, 29 (Dec. 1965), 61-62.

HC980 Gibson, Donald B. "Wright's Invisible Native Son." American Quarterly, 21 (Winter 1969), 728-738.

HC981 Gloster, Hugh M. Negro Voices in American Fiction. 1948; rpt. New York: Russell, 1965.

HC982 _____. "Richard Wright: Interpreter of Racial and Economic Maladjustments." Opportunity, 19 (Dec. 1941), 361-365, 383.

HC983 Gordon, Eugene. "Social and Political Problems of the Negro Writer." American Writers' Congress. Ed. Henry Hart. New York: International, 1935. Pages 141-145.

HC984 Hughes, Carl Milton. The Negro Novelist: A Discussion of the Writings of American Negro Novelists, 1940-1950. New York: Citadel, 1953.

HC985 Hyman, Stanley Edgar. "American Negro Literature and the Folk Tradition." The Promised End: Essays and Reviews, 1942-1962. Cleveland: World, 1963. Pages 295-315. [Enl. version of "The Folk Tradition." Partisan Review, 25 (Spring 1958), 197-211.]

HC986 Jahn, Janheinz. Neo-African Literature: A History of Black Writing. Tr. Oliver Coburn and Ursula Lehrburger. New York: Grove, 1969.

HC987 Johnson, James W., and John Rosamond Johnson, eds. The Books of American Negro Spirituals. New York: Viking, 1940.

[Jones, LeRoi. "The Myth of a 'Negro Literature.'" See SE1401.]

HC988 _____. "The Revolutionary Theatre." In Jones, A102:210-215; and in Katope and Zolbrod, A105: 408-411.

HC989 Krehbiel, Henry Edward. Afro-American Folksongs:
       A Study in Racial and National Music. 1914; rpt.
       New York: Ungar, 1962.

HC990 Lewin, Olive. "Folk Music Research in Jamaica."
       In Daniel, A49:121-135.

HC991 Llorens, David. "Ameer (Leroi Jones) Baraka."
       Ebony, Aug. 1969, pp. 75-78, 80-83. Rpt. in The
       Black Revolution, A12:65-78.

HC992 Loggins, Vernon. The Negro Author: His Develop-
       ment in America to 1900. 1931; rpt. Port Wash-
       ington, N.Y.: Kennikat, 1964.

HC993 MacLeod, Norman. "The Poetry and Argument of
       Langston Hughes." Crisis, 45 (Nov. 1938), 358-
       359.

HC994 Martin, Kathryn. "The Relationship of Theatre of
       Revolution and Theology of Revolution to the Black
       Experience." TS, 19 (Spring 1971), 35-41.

HC995 Murray, Albert. "James Baldwin, Protest Fiction,
       and the Blues Tradition." Part I: The Omni-Amer-
       icans, New Perspectives on Black Experience and
       American Culture. New York: Outerbridge, 1970.
       Pages 142-168.

HC996 Neal, Larry. "And Shine Swam On." In Jones and
       Neal, A103:638-656.

HC997 _____. "Black Art and Black Liberation."
       Ebony, Aug. 1969, pp. 54-58, 62. Rpt. in The
       Black Revolution, A12:31-53.

HC998 "The Negro in Literature: The Current Scene."
       Phylon, 11 (4th Qrtr 1950), 297-394.

       [Ralph, George, comp. The American Theater, The
       Negro, and the Freedom Movement: A Bibliogra-
       phy. See B24.]

HC999 Riach, W. A. D. " 'Telling It Like It Is': An Exam-
       ination of Black Theatre as Rhetoric." QJS, 56
       (April 1970), 179-186.

HC1000 Robinson, William H. "Orator Poets." In Robinson, A148:3-94.

HC1001 Roth, Philip. "Channel X: Two Plays on the Race
Conflict." New York Review of Books, 28 May 1964,
pp. 10-13.

HC1002 Rourke, Constance. "Traditions for a Negro Literature." The Roots of American Culture. New York:
Harcourt, 1942. Pages 262-274.

HC1003 Scarborough, Dorothy. On the Trail of Negro Folk-
Songs. 1925; rpt. Hatboro, Pa.: Folklore Associates, 1963.

HC1004 Sherman, Alfonso. "Little Known Black Heroes in
Ante-Bellum Drama." ST, 19 (March 1970), 130-
137.

HC1005 Sidran, Ben. Black Talk. New York: Holt, 1971.

HC1006 Spellman, A. B. "Not Just Whistling Dixie." In
Jones and Neal, A103:159-168.

HC1007 Thorpe, Earl E. "The Mind of the Negro Writer
and Artist." In Thorpe, HC475:451-495.

HC1008 Turner, Darwin, "Paul Laurence Dunbar: The Rejected Symbol." JNH, 52 (Jan. 1967), 1-13.

HC1009 White, Newman I. American Negro Folk-Songs.
1928; rpt. with a foreword by Bruce Jackson, Hatboro, Pa.: Folklore Associates, 1965.

HC1010 Work, John W. American Negro Songs and Spirituals. 1940; rpt. New York: Bonanza, n.d.

HC1011 Wright, Richard. "The Literature of the Negro in
the United States." In Wright, A181:69-105.

Literature--Slave Narratives

HC1012 Brawley, Benjamin. "Slave Narratives." In Brawley, HC13:63-67.

HC1013 Heermance, J. Noel. "Slave Narratives as a Genre:

Frederick Douglass as Prototype," "Slave Narratives Continued: Unique Personalities and Purposes,"
and "Narrative of William W. Brown, a Fugitive
Slave." In Heermance, HC237:76-90, 91-118, 119-
132.

HC1014 Jahn, Janheinz. "The Accounts of Escaped Slaves
(United States)." In Jahn, HC986:125-128.

[Loggins, Vernon. The Negro Author. In Loggins,
HC992:212-232.]

HC1015 Nichols, Charles H. Many Thousand Gone: The Ex-
Slaves' Account of Their Bondage and Freedom.
Leiden: E. J. Brill, 1963.

HC1016 Osofsky, Gilbert. "Puttin' On Ole Massa: The Significance of Slave Narratives." In Osofsky, HC1017:
9-44.

HC1017   , ed. Puttin' On Ole Massa: The Slave
Narratives of Henry Bibb, William Wells Brown, and
Solomon Northup. New York: Harper, 1969.

HC1018 Rawick, George P., ed. The American Slave: A
Composite Autobiography. 8 vols. Westport, Conn.:
Negro Universities Press, 1971-.

HC1019 Yetman, Norman R. "The Background of the Slave
Narrative Collection." American Quarterly, 19 (Fall
1967), 534-553.

[For representative slave narratives, see:
    Solomon Bayley, SE78
    Henry Bibb, SE94
    William Wells Brown, SE218
    Frederick Douglass, HC40
    Briton Hammon, SE1187
    Josiah Henson, SE1230
    Solomon Northup, SE1778
    James W. C. Pennington, HC134
    Moses Roper, SE1988
    Venture Smith, SE2110
    Samuel Ringgold Ward, HC184a or HC184b.]

PUBLIC ADDRESS

Public Address--Overview

HC1020 Andrews, James R. A Choice of Worlds: The Practice and Criticism of Public Discourse. New York:
Harper, 1973.

HC1021 Bennett, Winfield DeWitt. "A Survey of American
Negro Oratory (1619-1900)." Thesis, George Washington Univ., 1935.

HC1022 Black, Edwin. Rhetorical Criticism: A Study in
Method. New York: Macmillan, 1965.

HC1023 Boulware, Marcus H. The Oratory of Negro Leaders: 1900-1968. Westport, Conn.: Negro Universities Press, 1969.

HC1024 Griffin, Leland M. "The Rhetoric of Historical
Movements." QJS, 38 (April 1952), 184-188.

HC1025 Heermance, J. Noel. "Negro Abolitionism: Its
Physical and Literary Expression" and "Negro Oratory Prior to Brown." In Heermance, HC237:24-30,
31-45.

HC1026 Hillbruner, Anthony. Critical Dimensions: The Art
of Public Address Criticism. New York: Random,
1966.

HC1027 Kennicott, Patrick C. "Negro Antislavery Speakers
in America." Diss., Florida State Univ., 1967.

HC1028 Mohrmann, G. P., Charles J. Stewart, and Donovan
J. Ochs, eds. Explorations in Rhetorical Criticism.
University Park, Pa.: Pennsylvania State Univ.
Press, 1973.

HC1029 Moseberry, Lowell Tillry. "An Historical Study of
Negro Oratory in the United States to 1915." Diss.,
Univ. of Southern California, 1955.

HC1030 Nilsen, Thomas R., ed. Essays on Rhetorical Criticism. New York: Random, 1968.

HC1031 Scott, Robert L. , and Bernard L. Brock, eds.
Methods of Rhetorical Criticism: A Twentieth-Century Perspective. New York: Harper, 1972.

HC1032 Smith, Arthur L. "Theoretical and Research Issues
in Black Communication. " In Daniel, A49:136-144.

HC1033 Thonssen, Lester, A. Craig Baird, and Waldo W.
Braden. Speech Criticism. 2d edn. New York:
Ronald, 1970.

HC1034 Wichelns, Herbert A. "The Literary Criticism of
Oratory" [1925]. In Scott and Brock, HC1031:27-60.

Public Address--Critical Essays

HC1035 Anatol, Karl W. , and John R. Bittner. "Kennedy
on King: The Rhetoric of Control. " TS, 16 (Sept.
1968), 31-34.

HC1036 Asinof, Eliot. "Dick Gregory Is Not So Funny Now."
New York Times Magazine, 17 March 1968, pp. 37-
45. Rpt. in Auer, A5:409-413.

HC1037 Banninga, Jerald L. "John Quincy Adams on the
Right of a Slave To Petition Congress." SSCJ, 38
(Winter 1972), 151-163.

HC1038 Berquist, Goodwin, and James Greenwood. "Protest Against Racism: 'The Birth of a Nation' in
Ohio." Rhetoric of the People. Ed. Harold Barrett. Amsterdam: Rodopi, 1974. Pages 221-239.

HC1039 Black, Edwin. "The 'Vision' of Martin Luther
King." Literature as Revolt and Revolt as Literature: Three Studies in the Rhetoric of Non-Oratori-
cal Forms. The Proceedings of the Fourth Annual
University of Minnesota Spring Symposium in Speech-
Communication. May 3, 1969. Minneapolis: n.p.,
n.d. Pages 7-16.

HC1040 Borden, Karen Wells. "Black Rhetoric in the 1960s:
Sociohistorical Perspectives." Journal of Black
Studies, 3 (June 1973), 423-431.

HC1041 Boskin, Joseph. "Humor in the Civil Rights

Movement." Boston University Journal, 18 (Spring 1970), 2-7.

HC1042 Bosmajian, Haig A. "The Letter from Birmingham Jail." Midwest Quarterly, 8 (Winter 1967), 127-143. Rpt. in Smith, A155:195-209. [See King, SE 1438.]

HC1043 Boulware, Marcus H. " 'The Crusader': Robert Williams." NHB, 29 (Jan. 1966), 81-82.

HC1044 _____. "Minister Malcolm, Orator Profundo." NHB, 30 (Nov. 1967), 12-14.

HC1045 _____. "Roscoe Conkling Simmons: The Golden Voiced Politico." NHB, 29 (March 1966), 131-132.

HC1046 Bradley, Bert. "Negro Speakers in Congress: 1869-1875." SSJ, 17 (May 1953), 216-225.

HC1047 Bradley, Pearl G. "A Rhetorical Analysis of John F. Kennedy's Civil Rights Speech." CLA Journal, 9 (Dec. 1965), 171-176.

HC1048 Brockriede, Wayne, and Robert L. Scott. "Stokely Carmichael: Two Speeches on Black Power." CSSJ, 19 (Spring 1968), 3-13. Rpt. in Scott and Brockriede, A154:112-131; and in Smith, A155:176-192.

HC1049 Brodwin, Stanley. "The Veil Transcended: Form and Meaning in W. E. B. Du Bois' 'The Souls of Black Folk.' " Journal of Black Studies, 2 (March 1972), 303-321.

HC1050 Brooks, Robert D. "Black Power: The Dimensions of a Slogan." WS, 34 (Spring 1970), 108-114. Rpt. in Smith, A155:338-346.

HC1051 Brown, Lloyd W. "The Image-Makers: Black Rhetoric and White Media." In Daniel, A49:28-41.

HC1052 _____. "Ralph Ellison's Exhorters: The Role of Rhetoric in Invisible Man." CLA Journal, 13 (March 1970), 289-303.

HC1053 Brownlow, Paul C. "The Pulpit and Black America: 1865-1877." QJS, 58 (Dec. 1972), 431-440.

HC1054 Brustein, Robert. "Everybody's Protest Play." New Republic, 16 May 1964, pp. 35-37. Rpt. in Seasons of Discontent: Dramatic Opinions, 1959-1965. New York: Simon, 1965. Pages 161-165.

HC1055 Burgess, Parke G. "The Rhetoric of Black Power: A Moral Demand?" QJS, 54 (April 1968), 122-133. Rpt. in Smith, A155:248-266.

HC1056 Campbell, Finley C. "Voices of Thunder, Voices of Rage: A Symbolic Analysis of a Selection from Malcolm X's Speech, 'Message to the Grass Roots.'" ST, 19 (March 1970), 101-110. Rpt. in Smith, A155:141-156.

HC1057 Campbell, Karlyn Kohrs. "The Rhetoric of Radical Black Nationalism: A Case Study in Self-Conscious Criticism." CSSJ, 22 (Fall 1971), 151-160.

HC1058 Chaffee, Mary Law. "William E. B. Du Bois' Concept of the Racial Problem in the United States." JNH, 41 (July 1956), 241-258.

HC1059 Cummings, Melbourne S. "Problems of Researching Black Rhetoric." Journal of Black Studies, 2 (June 1972), 503-508.

HC1060 Daniel, Jack L. "The Study of Black Rhetoric." Black Lines, 1 (Fall 1970), 7-15.

HC1061 Davis, David Brion. The Slave Power Conspiracy and the Paranoid Style. Baton Rouge: Louisiana State Univ. Press, 1969.

HC1062 Delaney, Marion Agnes. "Dominant Themes in the Oratory of Booker T. Washington." Thesis, Univ. of Tennessee, 1968.

HC1063 Dick, Robert C. "Negro Oratory in the Anti-Slavery Societies: 1830-1860." WS, 28 (Winter 1964), 5-14. Rpt. in Smith, A155:111-122.

HC1064 _____. "Rhetoric of Ante-Bellum Black Separatism." NHB, 34 (Oct. 1971), 133-137.

HC1065 Epps, Archie. "The Theme of Exile in the Harvard
Speeches." In Malcolm X, A122:82-99. Rpt. in
Smith, A155:231-246.

HC1066 Ernst, Robert. "Negro Concepts of Americanism."
JNH, 39 (July 1954), 206-219.

HC1067 Ferris, Maxine Schnitzer. "The Speaking of Roy
Wilkins." CSSJ, 16 (May 1965), 91-98. Rpt. in
Auer, A5:367-376.

HC1068 Ferris, William H. "The American Negro's Contribution to Literature, Music and Oratory." In Ferris, HC451:255-278.

HC1069 Flynt, Wayne. "The Ethics of Democratic Persuasion and the Birmingham Crisis." SSJ, 35 (Fall
1969), 40-53.

HC1070 Fulkerson, Gerald. "Frederick Douglass and the
Kansas-Nebraska Act: A Case Study in Agitational
Versatility." CSSJ, 23 (Winter 1972), 261-269.

HC1071 Gayle, Addison, Jr. "The Dialectic of 'The Fire
Next Time.' " NHB, 30 (April 1967), 15-16.

HC1072 Goldman, Mark. "A Study of Message-Change and
Reaction in Senator Edward W. Brooke's Views on
the Vietnam War." TS, 17 (Sept. 1969), 60-62.

HC1073 Gottschalk, Jane. "The Rhetorical Strategy of
Booker T. Washington." Phylon, 27 (Winter 1966),
388-395.

HC1074 Gregg, Richard B. "The Ego-Function of the Rhetoric of Protest." Philosophy & Rhetoric, 4 (Spring
1971), 71-91.

HC1075 _____, A. Jackson McCormack, and Douglas J.
Pedersen. "The Rhetoric of Black Power: A Street-
Level Interpretation." QJS, 55 (April 1969), 151-
160. Rpt. in Smith, A155:267-282.

HC1076 Gronbeck, Bruce E. "The Rhetoric of Social-Institu-
tional Change: Black Action at Michigan." In Mohrmann, HC1028:96-123.

HC1077 Guthrie, Warren. "The Oberlin-Wellington Rescue
       Case, 1859." In Auer, A4:85-97.

HC1078 Hale, Frank W., Jr. "A Critical Analysis of the
       Speaking of Frederick Douglass." Thesis, Univ. of
       Nebraska, 1951.

HC1079 Hammerback, John C. "George W. Julian's Anti-
       slavery Crusade." WS, 37 (Summer 1973), 157-165.

HC1080 _____. "The Rhetoric of a Righteous Reform:
       George Washington Julian's 1852 Campaign Against
       Slavery." CSSJ, 22 (Summer 1971), 85-93.

HC1081 Hannerz, Ulf. "The Rhetoric of Soul: Identification
       in Negro Society." Race, 9 (April 1968), 453-465.
       Rpt. in Meier and Rudwick, A126:481-492; in Rose,
       A152:301-314; and in Smith, A155:306-321.

HC1082 Harris, Thomas E., and Patrick C. Kennicott.
       "Booker T. Washington: A Study of Conciliatory
       Rhetoric." SSCJ, 37 (Fall 1971), 47-59. Rpt. in
       Smith, A155:124-138.

HC1083 Hawthorne, Lucia S. "The Public Address of Black
       America." In Daniel, A49:54-66.

HC1084 Heermance, J. Noel. "William Wells Brown as Ora-
       tor." In Heermance, HC237:46-75.

HC1085 Hendrix, J. A. "Black Rhetoric: The Ideological
       Cyclorama." SSJ, 35 (Fall 1969), 92-95.

HC1086 Hess, Richard, and Paul Harper. "A Kind of Alice
       in Wonderland: The Riot Report--An Analysis of Its
       Effects." Speaker and Gavel, 7 (March 1970), 87-
       93.

HC1087 Hicks, Granville. "Gun in the Hand of a Hater."
       Saturday Review, 2 May 1964, pp. 27-28. Rpt. in
       Literary Horizons: A Quarter Century of American
       Fiction. New York: New York Univ. Press, 1970.
       Pages 98-101.

HC1088 Hitchcock, Orville A., and Ota Thomas Reynolds.
       "Ford Douglass' Fourth of July Oration, 1860." In
       Auer, A4:133-151.

HC1089 Honan, William Holmes. "John Jasper and the Sermon that Moved the Sun." SM, 23 (Nov. 1956), 255-261.

HC1090 Hurst, Charles G., Jr. "The Message and the Humanism of Malcolm X." In Hurst, HC410:177-193.

HC1091 Illo, John. "The Rhetoric of Malcolm X." Columbia Forum, 9 (Spring 1966), 5-12. Rpt. in Smith, A155:158-175.

HC1092 Jefferson, Pat. "The Magnificent Barbarian at Nashville." SSJ, 33 (Winter 1967), 77-87.

HC1093 _____. "The Schizoid Image of Stokely Carmichael." In Auer, A5:389-398.

HC1094 _____. " 'Stokely's Cool': Style." TS, 16 (Sept. 1968), 19-24.

HC1095 Kane, Peter E. "The Powell Affair." Speaker and Gavel, 4 (May 1967), 93-99. Rpt. in Weiss and Brock, A172:9-15.

HC1096 Kennicott, Patrick C., and Wayne E. Page. "H. Rap Brown: The Cambridge Incident." QJS, 57 (Oct. 1971), 325-334.

HC1097 Kerr, Harry P. "Brooke's Dilemma." Speaker and Gavel, 4 (Jan. 1967), 48-49, 53. Rpt. in Weiss and Brock, A172:7-8.

HC1098 King, Andrew A. "The Rhetorical Legacy of the Black Church." CSSJ, 22 (Fall 1971), 179-185.

HC1099 Klumpp, James F. "Nonviolence and Black Power: Civil Rights as a Mass Movement." Speaker and Gavel, 6 (March 1969), 71-76. Rpt. in Weiss and Brock, A172:61-66.

HC1100 Ladner, Cornelius. "A Critical Analysis of Four Anti-Slavery Speeches of Frederick Douglass." Thesis, Univ. of Iowa, 1947.

HC1101 Larson, Charles U. "The Trust Establishing Function of the Rhetoric of Black Power." CSSJ, 21 (Spring 1970), 52-56. Rpt. in Smith, A155:329-336.

HC1102 McEdwards, Mary G. "Agitative Rhetoric: Its Nature and Effect." WS, 32 (Winter 1968), 36-43.
Rpt. in Auer, A5:7-14.

HC1103 Mann, Kenneth Eugene. "Nineteenth Century Black Militant: Henry Highland Garnet's Address to the Slaves." SSJ, 36 (Fall 1970), 11-21.

HC1104 Meier, August, and Elliott Rudwick. "Black Violence in the Twentieth Century: A Study in Rhetoric and Retaliation." The History of Violence in America: Historical and Comparative Perspectives. Ed.
Hugh Davis Graham and Ted Robert Gurr. New York: Praeger, 1969. Pages 399-412. Rpt. in Geschwender, A81:404-413. [Cf Elliott Rudwick and August Meier. "Negro Retaliatory Violence in the Twentieth Century." New Politics, 5 (Winter 1966), 41-51. Rpt. in Meier and Rudwick, A126:407-417.]

HC1105 _____. "Radicals and Conservatives: Black Protest in Twentieth-Century America." In Rose, A151:119-147.

HC1106 Mohrmann, G. P. "Consistency Theory: The Impending Crisis of the South." In Mohrmann, HC1028: 191-206.

HC1107 Montgomery, Janey Weinhold. "A Comparative Analysis of the Rhetoric of Two Negro Women Orators: Sojourner Truth and Frances E. Watkins Harper." Fort Hays Studies, Literature Series, No. 6. Hays: Fort Hays Kansas State College, 1968.

HC1108 Moore, Carl. "A Course in the Rhetoric of Black Power." Journal of Black Studies, 2 (June 1972), 511-515.

HC1109 Morrison, Matthew C. "Marshall Keeble's Eloquence of Humor." TS, 17 (Nov. 1969), 35-38.

HC1110 Mowe, Gregory, and W. Scott Nobles. "James Baldwin's Message for White America." QJS, 58 (April 1972), 142-151.

HC1111 "Observations of Parker Pillsbury on the First Public Speech of Frederick Douglass." NHB, 30 (Feb. 1967), 6.

HC1112 Oliver, Robert T. "The Antislavery Crusade, 1831-
1865" and "Restriction, Reconstruction and Reconcil-
iation, 1865-1886." History of Public Speaking in
America. Boston: Allyn, 1965. Pages 226-269,
315-357.

HC1113 Palmer, Edward Nelson. "Father Divine Is God:
An Analysis of Propaganda Techniques." Qrtrly
Rev. of Higher Education Among Negroes, 13 (July
1945), 253-264.

HC1114 Phifer, Elizabeth Flory, and Dencil R. Taylor.
"Carmichael in Tallahassee." SSJ, 33 (Winter
1967), 88-92.

HC1115 Phifer, Gregg. "Ralph Bunche, Negro Spokesman."
American Public Address: Studies in Honor of Al-
bert Craig Baird. Ed. Loren Reid. Columbia:
Univ. of Missouri Press, 1961. Pages 293-310.

HC1116 Pickens, William. "Humor in Speech." American
Aesop: Negro and Other Humor. 1926; rpt. New
York: AMS, 1969. Pages ix-xx.

HC1117 Pollock, Art. "Stokely Carmichael's New Black
Rhetoric." SSCJ, 37 (Fall 1971), 92-94.

HC1118 Powers, Lloyd D. "Chicano Rhetoric: Some Basic
Concepts." SSCJ, 38 (Summer 1973), 340-346.

HC1119 Reynolds, Peggy. "The Ballot or the Bullet: One-
Man Dialectic." Speaker and Gavel, 7 (Jan. 1970),
37-40. Rpt. in Weiss and Brock, A172:87-90.

HC1120 Rich, Andrea L., and Arthur L. Smith. "Malcolm
X: Architect of Black Revolution." Rhetoric of
Revolution: Samuel Adams, Emma Goldman, Malcolm X. Durham, N.C.: Moore, n.d. Pages 143-
212.

HC1121 Richardson, Larry S. "Stokely Carmichael: Jazz
Artist." WS, 34 (Summer 1970), 212-218. Rpt. in
Smith, A155:347-355.

HC1122 Ritchie, Gladys. "The Sit-In: A Rhetoric of Human
Action." TS, 18 (Winter 1970), 22-25.

HC1123 Rothwell, J. Dan.   "Verbal Obscenity: Time for
Second Thoughts."   WS, 35 (Fall 1971), 231-242.

HC1124 Rudwick, Elliott M.   "Du Bois versus Garvey:
Race Propagandists at War."   JNE, 28 (Fall 1959),
421-429.

HC1125 Schechter, William.   The History of Negro Humor
in America.   New York: Fleet, 1970.

HC1126 Scott, Robert L.   "Black Power Bends Martin
Luther King."   Speaker and Gavel, 5 (March 1968),
80-86.   Rpt. in Scott and Brockriede, A154:166-
177; and in Weiss and Brock, A172:25-31.

HC1127 _____.   "Justifying Violence: The Rhetoric of
Militant Black Power."   CSSJ, 19 (Summer 1968),
96-104.   Rpt. in Scott and Brockriede, A154:132-
145.

HC1128 _____.   "Rhetoric, Black Power, and Baldwin's
'Another Country.' "   Journal of Black Studies, 1
(Sept. 1970), 21-34.

HC1129 _____, and Wayne Brockriede.   "Hubert Humph-
rey Faces the 'Black Power' Issue."   Speaker and
Gavel, 4 (Nov. 1966), 11-17.   Rpt. in Scott and
Brockriede, A154:74-83; and in Weiss and Brock,
A172:1-6.

HC1130 _____.   "The Rhetoric of Black Power: Order
and Disorder in the Future."   In Scott and Brockriede, A154:194-201.

HC1131 Scott, Robert L., and Donald K. Smith.   "The Rhetoric of Confrontation."   QJS, 55 (Feb. 1969), 1-8.
Rpt. in Katope and Zolbrod, A105:202-211.

HC1132 Sherman, Joan R.   "James Monroe Whitfield, Poet
and Emigrationist: A Voice of Protest and Despair."
JNH, 57 (April 1972), 169-176.

HC1133 Shiffrin, Steven H.   "The Rhetoric of Black Violence in the Antebellum Period: Henry Highland
Garnet."   Journal of Black Studies, 2 (Sept. 1971),
45-56.

HC1134 Simons, Herbert W. "Patterns of Persuasion in the Civil Rights Struggle." TS, 15 (Feb. 1967), 25-27. Rpt. in Auer, A5:45-49.

HC1135 Smith, Arthur L. "The Frames of Black Protest Speaking." In Smith, A155:284-291.

HC1136 _____. "Henry Highland Garnet: Black Revolutionary in Sheep's Vestments." CSSJ, 21 (Summer 1970), 93-98. Rpt. in Smith, A155:101-109.

HC1137 _____. "Markings of an African Concept of Rhetoric." TS, 19 (Spring 1971), 13-18. Rpt. in Smith, A155:363-372.

HC1138 _____. "The Rhetoric of Psychical and Physical Emigration." In Smith, A155:375-387.

HC1139 _____. "Socio-Historical Perspectives of Black Oratory." QJS, 56 (Oct. 1970), 264-269. Rpt. in Smith, A155:295-304.

HC1140 _____. "Some Characteristics of the Black Religious Audience." SM, 37 (Aug. 1970), 207-210.

HC1141 _____. "Topics of Revolutionary Rhetoric." In Smith, HC1246:43-61. Rpt. in Smith, A155:213-228.

HC1142 Smith, Donald Hugh. "Civil Rights: A Problem in Communication." Phylon, 27 (4th Qrtr 1966), 379-387.

HC1143 _____. "An Exegesis of Martin Luther King, Jr.'s Social Philosophy." Phylon, 31 (1st Qrtr 1970), 89-97.

HC1144 _____. "Martin Luther King, Jr.: In the Beginning at Montgomery." SSJ, 34 (Fall 1968), 8-17.

HC1145 _____. "Rhetoric of Riots." Contemporary Review, 213 (Oct. 1968), 178-184.

HC1146 _____. "Social Protest ... and the Oratory of Human Rights." TS, 15 (Sept. 1967), 2-8. Rpt. in Auer, A5:438-449.

HC1147 Sowande, Fela. "The Quest of an African World

View: The Utilization of African Discourse." In Daniel, A49:67-117.

HC1148 Spike, Robert W. "The Riots as Communication." Christianity and Crisis, 26 (19 Sept. 1966), 193-194.

HC1149 Steinkraus, Warren E. "Martin Luther King's Personalism and Non-Violence." Journal of the History of Ideas, 34 (Jan.-March 1973), 97-111.

HC1150 Tewell, Fred. "How Negroes Communicate in an American Community." TS, 6 (April 1958), 15-17.

HC1151 Thorpe, Earl E. "Hostility, Revenge and Protest as Elements in Negro Thought," "Some Sources of the Negro's Faith in Himself and in American Democracy," "Capitalism, Socialism and Communism in Negro Thought," and "The Philosophy of Negro History." In Thorpe, HC475:75-103, 150-164, 420-440, 441-450.

HC1152 Thurber, John H., and John L. Petelle. "The Negro Pulpit and Civil Rights." CSSJ, 19 (Winter 1968), 273-278.

HC1153 Trank, Douglas M. "The Negro and the Mormons: A Church in Conflict." WS, 35 (Fall 1971), 220-230.

HC1154 Van Graber, Marilyn. "Functional Criticism: A Rhetoric of Black Power." In Mohrmann, HC1028: 207-222.

HC1155 Wagner, Gerard A. "Sojourner Truth: God's Appointed Apostle of Reform." SSJ, 28 (Winter 1962), 123-130.

HC1156 Wallace, Karl R. "Booker T. Washington." A History and Criticism of American Public Address. Ed. William Norwood Brigance. 1943; rpt. New York: Russell, 1960. I, 407-433.

HC1157 Wander, Philip C. "The John Birch and Martin Luther King Symbols in the Radical Right." WS, 35 (Winter 1971), 4-14.

HC1158 _____. "Salvation Through Separation: The

Image of the Negro in the American Colonization Society." QJS, 57 (Feb. 1971), 57-67.

HC1159 _____. "The Savage Child: The Image of the Negro in the Pro-Slavery Movement." SSCJ, 37 (Summer 1972), 335-360.

HC1160 Weaver, Richard L., II. "The Negro Issue: Agitation in the Michigan Lyceum." CSSJ, 22 (Fall 1971), 196-201.

HC1161 Weiss, Samuel A. "The Ordeal of Malcolm X." South Atlantic Quarterly, 67 (Winter 1968), 53-63.

HC1162 White, Eugene E. "Anti-Racial Agitation as a Campaign Device: James K. Vardaman in the Mississippi Gubernatorial Campaign of 1903." SSJ, 10 (Jan. 1945), 49-56.

HC1163 Williams, Donald E. "Protest Under the Cross: The Ku Klux Klan Presents Its Case to the Public, 1960." SSJ, 27 (Fall 1961), 43-55. Rpt. in Auer, A5:415-426.

RELIGION

Churches and Preachers

HC1164 Boorstin, Daniel J. "Invisible Communities: The Negroes' Churches." The Americans: The National Experience. New York: Random, 1965. Pages 190-199.

HC1165 Caldwell, Erskine. "At the Other End of Town." Deep South: Memory and Observation. New York: Weybright, 1968. Pages 191-257.

HC1166 Cantril, Hadley, and Muzafer Sherif. "The Kingdom of Father Divine." Journal of Abnormal and Social Psychology, 33 (April 1938), 147-167. Rpt. in The Psychology of Social Movements. 1941; rpt. New York: Wiley, 1963. Pages 123-143.

HC1167 Cromwell, John W. "The Negro Church." In Cromwell, HC447:61-70.

HC1168 Du Bois, W. E. B. "Of the Faith of the Fathers."
In Du Bois, A65:189-206.

HC1169 _____, ed. The Negro Church. 1903; rpt. New
York: Octagon, 1968.

[Faduma, Orishatukeh. "The Defects of the Negro
Church." See SE877.]

HC1170 Frazier, E. Franklin. "The Negro Church." In
Frazier, HC454:334-366.

HC1171 Hamilton, Charles V. The Black Preacher in America. New York: Morrow, 1972.

HC1172 Harding, Vincent. "Religion and Resistance Among
Antebellum Negroes, 1800-1860." In Meier and
Rudwick, A125:179-197.

HC1173 Herskovits, Melville J. "The Contemporary Scene:
Africanisms in Religious Life." The Myth of the
Negro Past. 1941; rpt. Gloucester, Mass.: Peter
Smith, 1970. Pages 207-260.

HC1174 Johnston, Ruby F. The Development of Negro Religion. New York: Philosophical Library, 1954.

[King, Andrew A. "The Rhetorical Legacy of the
Black Church." See HC1098.]

HC1175 Lincoln, C. Eric. "Key Man of the South--The Ne-
gro Minister." New York Times Magazine, 12
July 1964, pp. 20, 36-37, 40. Rpt. in Lincoln,
A111:123-132.

HC1176 Litwack, Leon F. "The Church and the Negro."
In Litwack, HC461:187-213.

HC1177 Marx, Gary T. "Religion: Opiate or Inspiration
of Civil Rights Militancy Among Negroes?" American Sociological Review, 32 (Feb. 1967), 64-72.
Rpt. in Meier and Rudwick, A126:362-375.

HC1178 Mays, Benjamin Elijah, and Joseph William Nicholson. The Negro's Church. 1933; rpt. New York:
Russell, 1969.

HC1179 Myrdal, Gunnar. "The Negro Church." In Myrdal,
       HC463:858-878.

HC1180 Payne, Daniel A. History of the African Methodist
       Episcopal Church. Ed. C. S. Smith. 1891; rpt.
       New York: Johnson Reprint, 1968.

HC1181 _____. The Semi-Centenary and the Retrospec-
       tion of the African Meth[odist] Episcopal Church in
       the United States of America. 1866; rpt. Free-
       port, N.Y.: Books for Libraries, 1972.

HC1182 Phillips, C. H. The History of the Colored Method-
       ist Episcopal Church in America. 1898; rpt. New
       York: Arno, 1972.

       [Smith, Arthur L. "Some Characteristics of the
       Black Religious Audience." See HC1140.]

HC1183 Smith, Charles Spencer. A History of the African
       Methodist Episcopal Church ... 1856-1922. 1922;
       rpt. New York: Johnson Reprint, 1968.

HC1184 Taylor, Alrutheus Ambush. "Religious Efforts
       Among the Negroes." In Taylor, HC723:174-193.

HC1185 Thorpe, Earl E. "The Negro's Church and God."
       In Thorpe, HC475:104-135.

       [Thurber, John H., and John L. Petelle. "The Ne-
       gro Pulpit and Civil Rights." See HC1152.]

HC1186 Turner, Henry M. The Genius and Theory of Meth-
       odist Polity, or the Machinery of Methodism.
       1885; rpt. Northbrook, Ill.: Metro, 1972.

HC1187 Washington, Booker T. "The Negro Preacher and
       the Negro Church." In Washington, HC478:I, 251-
       278.

HC1188 Woodson, Carter G. The History of the Negro
       Church. 3rd edn. Washington: Associated Pub-
       lishers, 1972.

HC1189 Woolridge, Nancy Bullock. "The Slave Preacher--
       Portrait of a Leader." JNE, 14 (Winter 1945),
       28-37.

Old-Time Negro Preaching

HC1190 Brown, William Wells. "Chapter XX." In Brown,
        HC444:188-198.

HC1191 Holt, Grace Sims. "Stylin' Outta the Black Pulpit."
        In Kochman, A108:189-204.

        [Hyman, Stanley Edgar. "American Negro Litera-
        ture and the Folk Tradition." See HC985:310-312.]

HC1192 Johnson, Charles S. "Religion and the Church."
        Shadow of the Plantation. Chicago: Univ. of Chi-
        cago Press, 1934. Pages 150-179. Rpt. in Bracey,
        A21:580-587, excerpt.

HC1193 Johnson, James Weldon. "Preface." God's Trom-
        bones: Seven Negro Sermons in Verse. New York:
        Viking, 1927. Pages 1-11.

HC1194 McGhee, Nancy B. "The Folk Sermon: A Facet of
        the Black Literary Heritage." CLA Journal, 13
        (Sept. 1969), 51-61.

HC1195 Mitchell, Henry H. Black Preaching. Philadelphia:
        Lippincott, 1970.

HC1196 Pipes, William Harrison. "Old-Time Negro Preach-
        ing: An Interpretative Study." QJS, 31 (Feb. 1945),
        15-21.

HC1197 _____. Say Amen, Brother! Old-Time Negro
        Preaching: A Study in American Frustration. 1951;
        rpt. Westport, Conn.: Negro Universities Press,
        1970.

HC1198 Rosenberg, Bruce A. The Art of the American
        Folk Preacher. New York: Oxford Univ. Press,
        1970.

HC1199 Taylor, Alrutheus Ambush. "The Impression the
        Church Made." In Taylor, HC723:194-207.

The Black Muslims

HC1200 Baldwin, James. "Down at the Cross." In Baldwin, SE68:29-120.

HC1201 Bibb, Leon Douglas. "They Preach Black To Be
the Ideal." NHB, 28 (March 1965), 132-133.

HC1202 Bontemps, Arna, and Jack Conroy. "Beloved and
Scattered Millions." In Bontemps and Conroy,
HC439:174-183.

HC1203 Burns, W. Haywood. "Black Muslims in America:
A Reinterpretation." Race, 5 (July 1963), 26-37.

HC1204 Cameron, Wm. Bruce. "An Example: The Black
Muslims." Modern Social Movements: A Sociological Outline. New York: Random, 1966. Pages
33-36.

[Cleaver, Eldridge. "The Decline of the Black Muslims." See SE378.]

HC1205 Davis, Charles H., Jr. Black Nationalism and the
Nation of Islam. 4 pts. [Pamphlets] Los Angeles:
Operation Education, 1962. [Rev. of Essien-Udom,
HC1207.]

HC1206 Draper, Theodore. "The Nation of Islam." In
Draper, HC1256:69-85.

HC1207 Essien-Udom, E. U. Black Nationalism: A Search
for an Identity in America. Chicago: Univ. of Chicago Press, 1962. [See Davis, HC1205.]

HC1208 Hatchett, John F. "The Moslem Influence Among
American Negroes." Journal of Human Relations,
10 (Summer 1962), 375-382.

HC1209 Hentoff, Nat. "Elijah in the Wilderness." Reporter,
4 Aug. 1960, pp. 37-40.

HC1210 Howard, John R. "The Making of a Black Muslim."
Trans-Action, 4 (Dec. 1966), 15-21. Rpt. in Geschwender, A81:449-458.

HC1211 Laue, James H. "A Contemporary Revitalization
Movement in American Race Relations: The 'Black
Muslims.' " Social Forces, 42 (March 1964), 315-
324. Rpt. in Geschwender, A81:436-448.

HC1212 Lincoln, C. Eric. "The Black Muslims." Progressive, 26 (Dec. 1962), 43-44, 46-48. Rpt. in Lincoln, A111:51-61.

HC1213 _____. The Black Muslims in America. [Rev.
edn.] Boston: Beacon, 1973.

HC1214 _____. "Black Nationalism and Christian Conscience." In Lincoln, A111:90-99.

HC1215 _____. "The Black Muslims as a Protest Movement." Assuring Freedom to the Free: A Century
of Emancipation in the USA. Ed. Arnold M. Rose.
Detroit: Wayne State Univ. Press, 1964. Pages
220-240.

HC1216 _____. "Extremist Attitudes in the Black Muslim Movement." New South, 18 (Jan. 1963), 3-10.
Rpt. in Lincoln, A111:62-75.

HC1217 Lokos, Lionel. "The Black Muslims." In Lokos,
HC934:25-40.

HC1218 Lomax, Louis E. When the Word Is Given: A Report on Elijah Muhammad, Malcolm X, and the
Black Muslim World. Cleveland: World, 1963.

HC1219 Meier, August. "The Black Muslims: Racism in
Reverse?" Liberation, April 1967, pp. 9-13.

HC1220 "The Muslims' Farm." Newsweek, 8 Dec. 1969,
pp. 52, 57.

HC1221 Parenti, Michael. "The Black Muslims: From
Revolution to Institution." Social Research, 31
(Summer 1964), 175-194.

HC1222 Roach, Mildred. "Muslims and Negro Freedom."
Freedomways, 4 (Spring 1964), 260-266.

HC1223 Samuels, Gertrude. "Two Ways: Black Muslim
and N.A.A.C.P." New York Times Magazine, 12

May 1963, pp. 26-27, 86-88. Rpt. in Meier and
Rudwick, A124:37-45.

HC1224 Shack, William S. "Black Muslims: A Nativist Religious Movement Among Negro Americans." Race,
3 (Nov. 1961), 57-67.

HC1225 Sherwin, Mark. The Extremists. New York: St.
Martin's, 1963. [See pp. 190-212.]

HC1226 Silberman, Charles E. "Civil Rights and Self-Im-
provement." In Silberman, HC905:148-161.

[Williams, Daniel T., comp. "The Black Muslims
in the United States: A Selected Bibliography,
1964." See B32.]

HC1227 Worthy, William. "The Nation of Islam: Impact
and Prospects." Midstream, Spring 1962, pp. 26-
33.

STRATEGY AND TACTICS

HC1228 Bailey, Harry A., Jr. "Negro Interest Group Strategies." Urban Affairs Quarterly, 4 (Sept. 1969),
26-38. Rpt. in Geschwender, A81:126-135.

HC1229 Bell, Inge Powell. CORE and the Strategy of Nonviolence. New York: Random, 1968.

HC1230 Bennett, Lerone, Jr. "Structure: The Black Establishment" and "Tea and Sympathy: Liberals and Other White Hopes." In Bennett, A11:25-45, 75-104.

HC1231 Bunche, Ralph J. "A Critical Analysis of the Tac-
tics and Programs of Minority Groups." JNE, 4
(July 1935), 308-320. Rpt. in Broderick and Meier,
A26:161-179.

HC1232 _____. "The New Negro Alliance." In Bracey,
A22:377-386.

HC1233 _____. "The Programs of Organizations Devoted
to the Improvement of the Status of the American
Negro." JNE, 8 (July 1939), 539-550. Rpt. in
Meier and Rudwick, A126:245-256.

HC1234 Danzig, David. "The Meaning of Negro Strategy."
Commentary, 37 (Feb. 1964), 41-46.

HC1235 Killian, Lewis M., and Charles U. Smith. "Negro
Protest Leaders in a Southern Community." Social
Forces, 38 (March 1960), 253-257. Rpt. in Meier
and Rudwick, A126:334-341.

HC1236 Lincoln, C. Eric. "The Spectrum of Black Protest."
In Lincoln, HC1213:251-279.

HC1237 McLaurin, Charles. "Notes on Organizing." In
Jacobs and Landau, A99:137-140.

HC1238 Meier, August. "The Dilemmas of Negro Protest
Strategy." New South, 21 (Spring 1966), 1-18.

HC1239 _____. "Negro Protest Movements and Organizations." JNE, 32 (Fall 1963), 437-450.

     [_____, and Elliott Rudwick. "Black Violence in
     the Twentieth Century: A Study in Rhetoric and Re-
     taliation." See HC1104.]

HC1240 Oppenheimer, Martin. "Current Negro Protest Activities and the Concept of Social Movement."
Phylon, 24 (2d Qrtr 1963), 154-159.

HC1241 _____. "The Southern Student Sit-Ins: Intra-
Group Relations and Community Conflict." Phylon,
27 (Spring 1966), 20-26. Rpt. in Geschwender, A81:
144-150.

HC1242 _____, and George Lakey. A Manual for Direct
Action. Chicago: Quadrangle, 1965.

HC1243 Phillips, William M., Jr. "The Boycott: A Negro
Community in Conflict." Phylon, 22 (Spring 1961),
24-30. Rpt. in Geschwender, A81:150-155.

HC1244 Record, Wilson. "Extremist Movements Among
American Negroes." Phylon, 17 (1st Qrtr 1956),
17-23.

HC1245 _____. "Intellectuals in Social and Racial Movements." Phylon, 15 (3rd Qrtr 1954), 231-242.

     [Scott, Robert L., and Donald K. Smith. "The

Rhetoric of Confrontation." See HC1131.]

[Simons, Herbert W. "Patterns of Persuasion in the Civil Rights Struggle." See HC1134.]

HC1246 Smith, Arthur L. Rhetoric of Black Revolution. Boston: Allyn, 1969.

[Smith, D. H. "Rhetoric of Riots." See HC1145.]

[Spike, Robert W. "The Riots as Communication." See HC1148.]

HC1247 Tucker, Sterling. For Blacks Only: Black Strategies for Change in America. Grand Rapids, Mich.: Eerdmans, 1971.

HC1248 Ware, Gilbert. "Lobbying as a Means of Protest: The NAACP as an Agent of Equality." JNE, 33 (Spring 1964), 103-110.

HC1249 Wildavsky, Aaron. "The Empty-Head Blues: Black Rebellion and White Reaction." Public Interest, 11 (Spring 1968), 3-16. Rpt. in Rose, A151:293-307.

HC1250 Wilson, James Q. "The Strategy of Protest: Problems of Negro Civic Action." Journal of Conflict Resolution, 5 (Summer 1961), 291-303.

HC1251 Winston, Henry. Strategy for a Black Agenda: A Critique of New Theories of Liberation in the United States and Africa. New York: International, 1973.

HC1252 Zanden, James W. Vander. "The Non-Violent Resistance Movement Against Segregation." American Journal of Sociology, 68 (March 1963), 544-550. Rpt. in Geschwender, A81:136-143.

HC1253 Zinn, Howard. "Abolitionists, Freedom-Riders, and the Tactics of Agitation." In Duberman, A57:418-451.

THEMES: NATIONALISM AND PAN-AFRICANISM

HC1254 Bell, Howard H. "Introduction." Search for a Place: Black Separatism and Africa, 1960. Ed.

Howard H. Bell.   Ann Arbor: Univ. of Michigan
Press, 1969.   Pages 1-22.

HC1255 Bell, Inge Powell.   "Black Nationalism."   In Bell,
HC1229:46-50.

[Campbell, Karlyn Kohrs.   "The Rhetoric of Radical
Black Nationalism: A Case Study in Self-Conscious
Criticism."   See HC1057.]

[Cleaver, Eldridge.   "Rallying Round the Flag."
See SE374.]

[Dick, Robert C.   "Rhetoric of Ante-Bellum Black
Separatism."   See HC1064.]

HC1256 Draper, Theodore.   The Rediscovery of Black Nationalism.   New York: Viking, 1970.   [See Foner,
HC1259.]

HC1257 Du Bois, W. E. B.   Black Folk Then and Now: An
Essay in the History and Sociology of the Negro
Race.   1939; rpt.   New York: Octagon, 1970.

HC1258 _____.   The World and Africa: An Inquiry into
the Part Which Africa Has Played in World History.
Enl. edn.   New York: International, 1965.

[Essien-Udom, E. U.   Black Nationalism: A Search
for an Identity in America.   See HC1207.]

HC1259 Foner, Eric.   "In Search of Black History."   New
York Review of Books, 22 Oct. 1970, pp. 11-14.
[Rev. of Draper, HC1256.]

HC1260 Genovese, Eugene D.   "The Legacy of Slavery and
the Roots of Black Nationalism."   Studies on the
Left, 6 (Nov.-Dec. 1966), 3-26.   Rpt. in Rose,
A151:31-51.

HC1261 Gill, Robert Lewis, and Roberta Louise Gill.   "International Implications of Black Power as Viewed
by Their Advocates."   Qrtrly Rev. of Higher Education Among Negroes, 37 (Oct. 1969), 153-176.

HC1262 Gregor, A. James.   "Black Nationalism: A Pre-
liminary Analysis of Negro Radicalism."   Science

& Society, 27 (Fall 1963), 415-432.

HC1263 Hamilton, Charles V. "Pan-Africanism and the
Black Struggle in the U.S." Black Scholar, 2
(March 1971), 10-15.

HC1264 Holloway, Anne Forrester. "Pan-African Activism
in the 20th Century." In Moss, A130:142-155.

HC1265 Jones, LeRoi. "The Legacy of Malcolm X and the
Coming of the Black Nation." In Jones, A102:238-
250.

HC1266 Lynch, Hollis R. "Pan-Negro Nationalism in the
New World, Before 1862." Boston University Papers on Africa. Boston: Boston Univ. Press,
1966. II, 149-179. Rpt. in Meier and Rudwick,
A125:42-65.

HC1267 Redkey, Edwin S. "Bishop Turner's African
Dream." Journal of American History, 54 (Sept.
1967), 271-290.

HC1268 _____. Black Exodus: Black Nationalist and
Back-to-Africa Movements, 1890-1910. New Haven:
Yale Univ. Press, 1969.

HC1269 _____. "The Flowering of Black Nationalism:
Henry M. Turner and Marcus Garvey." Key Issues
in the Afro-American Experience. Ed. Nathan I.
Huggins, Martin Kilson, and Daniel M. Fox. New
York: Houghton, 1971. II, 107-124.

[Rogers, Ben F. "William E. B. Du Bois, Marcus
Garvey, and Pan-Africa." See HC261.]

HC1270 Shepperson, George. "Pan-Africanism and 'Pan-
Africanism': Some Historical Notes." Phylon, 23
(4th Qrtr 1962), 346-358.

HC1271 Smith, Ed. Where To, Black Man? Chicago:
Quadrangle, 1967.

HC1272 Stuckey, Sterling. "Du Bois, Woodson and the Spell
of Africa." Negro Digest, 16 (Feb. 1967), 20-24,
60-74.

[_____, ed. The Ideological Origins of Black Nationalism. See A160.]

HC1273 Tucker, Sterling. "The Dangers and Uses of Separatism." In Tucker, HC1247:92-119.

HC1274 Weisbord, Robert G. Ebony Kinship: Africa, Africans, and the Afro-American. Westport, Conn.:
Greenwood, 1973.

HC1275 Wright, Richard. Black Power: A Record of Reactions in a Land of Pathos. New York: Harper,
1954.

SECTION IV

SPEECHES AND ESSAYS (SE)

SE1   Abbott, Robert S. "A Message to Youth." 15 Aug. 1931. In Foner, A74:779.

ABBOTT, ROBERT S. See Ottley, HC127.

SE2   Abernathy, Ralph David. "They Didn't Know Who He Was." 15 Jan. 1969. In Hale, A90:331-337.

SE3   _____. "The Kerner Report, Promises and Realities." 5 March 1969. In Foner, A74:1145-1152.

SE4   _____. "Address to the Congress of African Peoples." Sept. 1970. In Jones, A101:9-11.

SE5   _____. "Some International Dimensions of the Peace Movement." 1971. Freedomways, 11 (3rd Qrtr 1971), 237-240.

ABERNATHY, RALPH. See Good, HC231.

SE6   Adams, E. J. "These Are Revolutionary Times." 19 March 1867. In Foner, A74:343-344.

SE7   "Address to a Reconstruction Meeting." 19 April 1867. JNH, 2 (Oct. 1917), 431.

SE8   "Address to the Female Literary Association of Philadelphia." May 1832. In Porter, A141:127-128.

SE9   African Blood Brotherhood. "Program of the African Blood Brotherhood." 1922. In Aptheker, A2:414-420.

SE10 Alexander, Sadie T. M. "Founders Day Address." 11 April 1963. In Williams and Williams, A175:149-156.

ALEXANDER, SADIE MOSSELL.   See Boulware,
HC1023:101-102.

SE11 Allen, George R.   "Essay, to the American Convention for Promoting the Abolition of Slavery, and Improving the Condition of the African Race."   21 Oct.
1828.   In Porter, A141:572-573.

SE12 Allen, Richard.   "To the People of Color."   1793.   In
Allen, HC2:72-74.   Rpt. in Golden and Rieke, A82:
76-77.

[_____, and Absalom Jones.   See Jones, SE1395.]

SE13 Allen, Richard.   "Address to the Public, and People
of Colour."   March 1808.   In Porter, A141:415-417.

SE14 _____.   "An Address to Those Who Keep Slaves and
Approve the Practice."   N.d.   In Allen, HC2:69-71.

SE15 _____.   "A Short Address to the Friends of Him
Who Hath No Helper."   N.d.   In Allen, HC2:75-89.

ALLEN, RICHARD.   See Allen, HC2; Allen, HC3;
Mathews, HC114; Simmons, HC163a:491-497 or HC
163b:329-334; Wesley, HC196; Woodson, HC1188:
62-68; and Langston, SE1493.

SE16 Allen, Samuel W.   "The Civil Rights Struggle."   18
Dec. 1968.   In Wright, A179:236-250.

SE17 Allen, William G.   Wheatley, Banneker and Horton;
With Selections from the Poetical Works of Wheat-
ley and Horton.   1849; rpt.   Freeport, N.Y.:
Books for Libraries, 1970.

SE18 _____.   Letter to Frederick Douglass.   30 Dec.
1851.   In Woodson, A176:288-290.

SE19 _____.   "Orators and Oratory."   22 June 1852.   In
Cromwell, A42:246-251, excerpt.

SE20 _____.   Letter to Frederick Douglass.   25 Oct.
1852.   In Woodson, A176:282-284.

SE21 _____.   "Placido."   1853.   In Griffiths, A86:256-
263.

SE22 _____. The American Prejudice against Color: An
Authentic Narration, Showing How Easily the Nation
Got into an Uproar. 1853; rpt. New York: Arno,
1969.

SE23 _____. Letter to William Lloyd Garrison. 20 June
1853. In Woodson, A176:284-287.

SE24 American Moral Reform Society. "Declaration of Sentiment." Aug. 1837. In Porter, A141:200-204.

SE25 _____. "To the American People." Aug. 1837. In
Porter, A141:204-209. [Signed by William Whipper.]

SE26 American Negro Labor Congress. "A Call to Action."
1925. In Aptheker, A2:488-493.

SE27 _____. "Program of the American Negro Labor
Congress." 1930. In Aptheker, A2:660-671.

SE28 American Society of Free Persons of Colour. "Ad-
dress to the Free People of Colour of These United
States." 20 Sept. 1830. In Porter, A141:179-181.
[Signed by Richard Allen.]

SE29 Anderson, Charles W. "The Limitless Possibilities of
the Negro Race." 5 June 1897. In Dunbar, A70:
211-218.

SE30 Anderson, Marian. "Committee IV, on the Report of
the Trusteeship Council." 5 Nov. 1958. In Hill,
A93:222-224.

SE31 Anderson, S. E. "Revolutionary Black Nationalism
and the Pan-African Idea." 1970. In Barbour,
A9:99-123.

SE32 Anderson, S. W. "The World To Come." 1890. In
Brawley, A25:175-187.

SE33 Anthony, Earl. "Pan-African Socialism." 1971.
Black Scholar, 3 (Oct. 1971), 40-45.

ANTHONY, EARL. See Anthony, HC913.

SE34 "Appeal of Forty Thousand [Pennsylvania] Citizens,
Threatened with Disfranchisement." 14 March

1838. In Aptheker, A1:176-186; in Bracey, A21:
130-143; and in Woodson, A177:96-103, excerpt.

SE35 Arnett, Benjamin W. "The Afro-American Press."
1890. In Penn, A139:456-459.

SE36 _____. "Episcopal Address." May 1896. In
Smith, HC1183:195-199, excerpt.

ARNETT, BENJAMIN W. See Simmons, HC163a:883-
891 or HC163b:625-631.

SE37 Atlanta Black Men. "Petition to the Government
Against Lynching." 5 March 1918. In Aptheker,
A2:199-201.

SE38 Bagnall, Robert W. "Negroes in New Abolition Movement." Dec. 1925. In Aptheker, A2:498-504.

SE39 Baldwin, James. "The Harlem Ghetto: Winter 1948;
The Vicious Circle of Frustration and Prejudice."
Feb. 1948. Commentary, Feb. 1948, pp. 165-170.
Rpt. as "The Harlem Ghetto" in Baldwin, A7:51-64.

SE40 _____. "Journey to Atlanta." Oct. 1948. In
Baldwin, A7:65-75.

SE41 _____. "Everybody's Protest Novel." June 1949.
Partisan Review, 16 (June 1949), 578-585. Rpt. in
Baldwin, A7:13-22.

SE42 _____. "Encounter on the Seine: Black Meets
Brown." June 1950. In Baldwin, A7:103-109.

SE43 _____. "Many Thousands Gone." Nov. 1951.
Partisan Review, 18 (Nov.-Dec. 1951), 665-680.
Rpt. in Baldwin, A7:23-42; and in Chapman, A32:
590-604.

SE44 _____. "Stranger in the Village." Oct. 1953.
Harper's Magazine, Oct. 1953, pp. 42-48. Rpt.
in Baldwin, A7:143-158.

SE45 _____. "A Question of Identity." July 1954.
Partisan Review, 21 (July-Aug. 1954), 402-410.
Rpt. in Baldwin, A7:110-122.

SE46 _____. "The Male Prison." Dec. 1954. In Baldwin, A6:155-162.

SE47 _____. "Life Straight in De Eye; Carmen Jones: Film Spectacular in Color." Jan. 1955. Commentary, Jan. 1955, pp. 74-77. Rpt. as "Carmen Jones: The Dark Is Light Enough" in Baldwin, A7:43-50.

SE48 _____. "Equal in Paris: An Autobiographical Story." March 1955. Commentary, March 1955, pp. 251-259. Rpt. in Baldwin, A7:123-142.

SE49 _____. "Me and My House...." Nov. 1955. Harper's Magazine, Nov. 1955, pp. 54-61. Rpt. as "Notes of a Native Son" in Baldwin, A7:76-102.

SE50 _____. "Faulkner and Desegregation." Fall 1956. Partisan Review, 23 (Fall 1956), 568-573. Rpt. in Baldwin, A6:117-126.

SE51 _____. "Princes and Powers." Jan. 1957. Encounter, Jan. 1957, pp. 52-60. Rpt. in Baldwin, A6:13-55.

SE52 _____. "The Hard Kind of Courage." Oct. 1958. Harper's Magazine, Oct. 1958, pp. 61-65. Rpt. as "A Fly in the Buttermilk" in Baldwin, A6:83-97.

SE53 _____. "The Discovery of What It Means To Be an American." Jan. 1959. New York Times Book Review, 25 Jan. 1959, pp. 4, 22. Rpt. in Baldwin, A6:3-12.

SE54 _____. "A Letter from the South: Nobody Knows My Name." Winter 1959. Partisan Review, 26 (Winter 1959), 72-82. Rpt. (with title and subtitle reversed) in Baldwin, A6:98-116.

SE55 _____. "The Precarious Vogue of Ingmar Bergman." April 1960. Esquire, April 1960, pp. 128-129, 132. Rpt. as "The Northern Protestant" in Baldwin, A6:163-180.

SE56 _____. "Fifth Avenue, Uptown: A Letter from Harlem." July 1960. In Baldwin, A6:56-71.

SE57 _____. "Notes for a Hypothetical Novel: An Address." 22 Oct. 1960. In Baldwin, A6:141-154.

SE58 _____. "In Search of a Majority." 1960. In Baldwin, A6:127-137.

SE59 _____. "The Dangerous Road Before Martin Luther King." Feb. 1961. Harper's Magazine, Feb. 1961, pp. 33-42.

SE60 _____. "A Negro Assays the Negro Mood." March 1961. New York Times Magazine, 12 March 1961, pp. 25, 103-104. Rpt. as "East River, Downtown: Postscript to a Letter from Harlem" in Baldwin, A6:72-82.

SE61 _____. "The Black Boy Looks at the White Boy." May 1961. Esquire, May 1961, pp. 102, 104-106. Rpt. in Baldwin, A6:216-241.

SE62 _____. "Alas, Poor Richard." 1961. In Baldwin, A6:181-215.

SE63 _____. "The Artist's Struggle for Integrity." Feb. 1963. Liberation, 8 (March 1963), 9-11. Rpt. in Goodman, A83:380-387.

SE64 _____. "Interview with Kenneth B. Clark." 24 May 1963. Freedomways, 3 (Summer 1963), 361-368. Rpt. in Clark, A34:4-14; and in John Henrik Clarke, ed. Harlem: A Community in Transition. New York: Citadel, 1964. Pages 123-130.

SE65 _____. "We Can Change the Country." 22 Sept. 1963. Liberation, 8 (Oct. 1963), 7-8. Rpt. in Goodman, A83:341-345.

SE66 _____. "The Negro Child--His Self-Image." 16 Oct. 1963. In Hale, A90:22-28.

SE67 _____. "What Price Freedom?" Nov. 1963. Freedomways, 4 (Spring 1964), 191-195.

SE68 _____. The Fire Next Time. New York: Dial, 1963.
       Contains: "My Dungeon Shook: Letter to My Nephew on the One Hundredth Anniversary of

the Emancipation," pp. 17-24. "Down at the
Cross: Letter from a Region in My Mind," pp.
29-120.

SE69 _____ . "The American Dream Is at the Expense
of the American Negro." Feb. 1965. In Foner,
A74:1013-1017.

SE70 _____ . "A Letter to Americans." Freedomways,
8 (Spring 1968), 112-116.

SE71 _____ , and Margaret Mead. A Rap on Race [con-
versation]. 26-27 Aug. 1970. Philadelphia: Lippincott, 1971.

SE72 Baldwin, James. "An Open Letter to My Sister, Ang-
ela Davis." 19 Nov. 1970. New York Review of
Books, 7 Jan. 1971, pp. 15-16. Rpt. in Davis,
A50:13-18.

SE73 _____ . No Name in the Street. New York: Dial,
1972.
Contains: "Take Me to the Water," pp. 3-81.
"To Be Baptized," pp. 85-195.

BALDWIN, JAMES. See Bennett, HC437:205-211;
Cruse, HC448:193-196, 481-491; Bigsby, HC963:126-
137; Bone, HC964:215-239; Murray, HC995; Roth,
HC1001; Brustein, HC1054; Gayle, HC1071; Hicks,
HC1087; Mowe and Nobles, HC1110; Scott, HC1128;
and Cleaver, SE373.

SE74 Baltimore Afro-American. "Worthwhile Exchange."
14 June 1969. In Fishel and Quarles, A72:589.

SE75 Banneker, Benjamin. "Letter to the Secretary of
State, with His Answer." 19 Aug. 1791 and 30 Aug.
1791. In Porter, A141:324-328; and in Woodson,
A176:xxiv-xxviii.

[Barbadoes, James G., and Robert Roberts. See Roberts, SE1970.]

SE76 Barnett, Ferdinand L. "Race Unity." May 1879.
In Foner, A74:462-466.

SE77 Barrett, B. F. "The Unreasonable Prejudices Against

People of Color in Philadelphia." 23 Sept. 1866.
In Foner, A74:337-341.

SE78 Bayley, Solomon. "A Narrative of Some Remarkable
Incidents in the Life of Solomon Bayley, Formerly
a Slave." 1825. In Porter, A141:587-613.

SE79 Beckham, Edgar F. "What We Mean by 'The Black
University.' " Oct. 1968. In Wallerstein and Starr,
A163:356-360.

SE80 Belafonte, Harry. "Martin Luther King and W. E. B.
Du Bois: A Personal Tribute." 30 Jan. 1972.
Freedomways, 12 (1st Qrtr 1972), 17-21.

SE81 Bell, J. W. "The Teaching of Negro History." 23
Nov. 1922. JNH, 8 (April 1923), 123-127.

[Bell, Philip, and Samuel Ennals. See Ennals, SE872.]

[Beman, Amos G., and Joseph Gilbert. See Gilbert,
SE1024.]

BEMAN, AMOS G. See Warner, HC185.

SE82 Bennett, Lerone, Jr. "Of Time, Space, and Revolution." Aug. 1969. In The Black Revolution, A12:
1-21.

SE83 Berrian, Henry, and Henry N. Merriman. "Resolutions on Colonization." 8 Aug. 1831. In Garrison,
A77:30-31.

SE84 Bertonneau, Arnold. "Every Man Should Stand Equal
Before the Law." 12 April 1864. In Foner, A74:
304-307.

SE85 Bethune, Mary McLeod. "The Problems of the City
Dweller." 1925. Opportunity, 3 (Feb. 1925), 54-55.

SE86 _____. "Clarifying Our Vision with the Facts." 31
Oct. 1937. JNH, 23 (Jan. 1938), 10-15.

SE87 _____. " 'I'll Never Turn Back No More!' " 1938.
Opportunity, 16 (Nov. 1938), 324-326.

SE88 _____. "The Adaptation of the History of the Negro

to the Capacity of the Child." 11 Nov. 1938. <u>JNH</u>,
24 (Jan. 1939), 9-13.

SE89 _____. "'Certain Unalienable Rights.'" 1944. In
Logan, A115:248-258.

SE90 _____. "My Secret Talks with FDR." 1949.
<u>Ebony</u>, April 1949, pp. 42-51. Rpt. in Sternsher,
A158:53-65.

SE91 _____. "The Negro in Retrospect and Prospect."
29 Oct. 1949. <u>JNH</u>, 35 (Jan. 1950), 9-19.

SE92 _____. "True Leadership Is Timeless." 1950.
<u>NHB</u>, 13 (May 1950), 173.

SE93 _____. "The Torch Is Ours." 27 Oct. 1950. <u>JNH</u>,
36 (Jan. 1951), 9-11.

BETHUNE, MARY McLEOD. See Bullock, HC19:103-
108; Holt, HC86; Peare, HC133; Sterne, HC168; and
Boulware, HC1023:107-111.

SE94 Bibb, Henry. <u>Narrative of the Life and Adventures of</u>
<u>Henry Bibb, an American Slave</u> [1849]. In Osofsky,
HC1017:51-171.

BIBB, HENRY. See Landon, HC246; Brown, HC443:
86-88; and Quarles, HC593:61-62.

SE95 Billingsley, Andrew. "The Black Presence in American Higher Education." July 1969. In Wright,
A179:126-149.

SE96 Blyden, Edward Wilmot. "Liberia as She Is; and the
Present Duty of Her Citizens." 27 July 1857. In
Blyden, A13:63-65, excerpt.

SE97 _____. "Vindication of the African Race." 1857.
In Blyden, A15:31-64.

SE98 _____. "A Eulogy Pronounced on the Reverend John
Day." 2 March 1859. In Blyden, A15:127-149;
and in Blyden, A13:67-75, excerpt.

SE99 _____. "A Chapter in the History of the African
Slave-Trade." June 1859. In Blyden, A15:151-167.

SE100 _____. "Hope for Africa." 21 July 1861. In Blyden, A15:4-29.

SE101 _____. "Inaugural Address at the Inauguration of
Liberia College." 23 Jan. 1862. In Blyden, A15:
95-123; and in Blyden, A13:219-222, excerpt.

SE102 _____. "An Address before the Maine State Colonization Society." 26 June 1862. In Blyden, A13:
11-20.

SE103 _____. "The Call of Providence to the Descend-
ants of Africa in America." 1862. In Blyden,
A15:67-91; in Brotz, A27:112-126; and in Blyden,
A13:25-33, abr.

SE104 _____. "Our Origin, Dangers and Duties." 26
July 1865. In Blyden, A13:77-79, excerpt.

SE105 _____. "Liberia as a Means, Not an End." 26
July 1867. In Blyden, A13:81-84, abr.

SE106 _____. "Mohammedanism in Western Africa."
Jan. 1871. In Blyden, A14:173-188; and in Blyden,
A13:273-279, excerpt.

SE107 _____. "Liberia--Its Status and Its Field." Sept.-
Oct. 1872. In Blyden, A13:93-98, abr.

SE108 _____. "Mohammedanism and the Negro Race."
Nov. 1875. In Blyden, A14:1-24; and in Blyden,
A13:281-294, abr.

SE109 _____. "Christianity and the Negro Race." May
1876. In Blyden, A14:25-45.

SE110 _____. "Christian Missions in West Africa." Oct.
1876. In Blyden, A14:46-70.

SE111 _____. "Islam and Race Distinctions." Nov. 1876.
In Blyden, A14:241-259.

SE112 _____. "Africa and the Africans." Aug. 1878.
In Blyden, A14:260-283.

SE113 _____. "Echoes from Africa." Dec. 1878. In
Blyden, A14:130-151; and in Blyden, A13:159-161,
excerpt.

SE114 _____. "Ethiopia Stretching Out Her Hands unto God; or, Africa's Service to the World." May 1880. In Blyden, A14:113-129; and in Blyden, A13:35-37, excerpt.

SE115 _____. "The Aims and Methods of a Liberal Education for Africans." 5 Jan. 1881. In Blyden, A14:71-93; and in Blyden, A13:231-245, abr.

SE116 _____. "Philip and the Eunuch." 1882. In Blyden, A14:152-172.

SE117 _____. "The Origin and Purpose of African Colonization." 14 Jan. 1883. In Blyden, A14:94-112; in Golden and Rieke, A82:329-345; and in Blyden, A13:39-43, excerpt.

SE118 _____. "Sierra Leone and Liberia: Their Origin, Work, and Destiny." April 1884. In Blyden, A14: 189-240.

SE119 _____. "The Life of Lord Lawrence and Its Lessons." 1887. In Blyden, A14:284-305.

SE120 _____. "The Mohammedans of Nigritia." 1887. In Blyden, A14:306-336; and in Blyden, A13:295-301, excerpt.

SE121 _____. "African Colonization." 1887. In Blyden, A14:337-373.

SE122 _____. "The African Problem and the Method of Its Solution." 19 Jan. 1890. In Brotz, A27:126-139; in Foner, A74:541-556; and in Blyden, A13:45-52, abr.

SE123 _____. The African Problem, and Other Discourses, Delivered in America in 1890. London: Whittingham, 1890.
    Contains: "The African Problem" (SE122).
"The Elements of Permanent Influence."
"Problems Before the Church."
"The Koran in Africa."

SE124 _____. "A Chapter in the History of Liberia." July 1892. In Blyden, A13:99-117, abr.

SE125 _____. "Study and Race." 19 May 1893. In

Blyden, A13:195-204.

SE126 _____. "The African Problem." Sept. 1895.
North American Review, 161 (Sept. 1895), 327-339.
Rpt. in Blyden, A13:317-321, excerpt.

SE127 _____. "The Negro in the United States." Jan.
1900. In Blyden, A13:53-57, abr.

SE128 _____. "The Liberian Scholar." 21 Feb. 1900.
In Blyden, A13:265-268, excerpt.

SE129 _____. "West Africa." Sept. 1901. In Blyden,
A13:323-326, excerpt.

SE130 _____. West Africa Before Europe and Other Addresses, Delivered in England in 1901 and 1903.
London: Phillips, 1905.

SE131 _____. "Some Problems of West Africa." 26
June 1903. In Blyden, A13:327-334, excerpt.

SE132 _____. "The Political Outlook for Africa." 15
Aug. 1903. In Dunbar, A70:263-264.

SE133 _____. "The Three Needs of Liberia." 26 Jan.
1908. In Blyden, A13:119-125, abr.

BLYDEN, EDWARD WILMOT. See Billingsley, HC10;
Holden, HC82; Lynch, HC104; Simmons, HC163a:
916-921 or HC163b:651-654; Collyer, HC217; Jones,
HC241; Cromwell, HC447:235-239; and Redkey,
HC1268:47-72.

SE134 Boggs, Grace Lee. "Toward a New System of Education." 8 Oct. 1968. In Wright, A179:186-197.

SE135 Boggs, James. "The Meaning of the Black Revolt in
the U.S.A." 1963. In Boggs, A16:9-18.

SE136 _____. "Integration and Democracy: Two Myths
That Have Failed." Fall 1964. In Boggs, A16:33-
38.

SE137 _____. "Culture and Black Power." Jan. 1967.
In Boggs, A16:63-69.

SE138 _____. "Black Power: A Scientific Concept Whose Time Has Come." April 1967. In Boggs, A16:51-62; and in Jones and Neal, A103:105-118.

SE139 _____. "The Basic Issues and the State of the Nation." Nov. 1967. In Boggs, A16:70-78; and in Bracey, A22:523-531.

SE140 _____. "The Future Belongs to the Dispossessed." 1968. In Boggs, A16:81-91.

SE141 _____. "The Labor Movement: Revolutionary or--." 1968. In Boggs, A16:91-100.

SE142 _____. "Civil Rights Legislation." 1968. In Boggs, A16:100-104.

SE143 _____. "King, Malcolm, and the Future of the Black Revolution." 1968. In Boggs, A16:104-121.

SE144 _____. "Democracy: Capitalism's Last Battle-Cry." 1968. In Boggs, A16:122-132.

SE145 _____. "The Myth and Irrationality of Black Capitalism." April 1969. In Boggs, A16:133-145.

SE146 _____, and Grace Lee Boggs. "Uprooting Racism and Racists in the United States." Oct. 1969. In Boggs, A16:146-160.

SE147 Boggs, James. "The American Revolution: Putting Politics in Command." 1970. In Boggs, A16:161-190.

SE148 _____. "The Revolutionary Struggle for Black Power." 1970. In Barbour, A9:33-48.

SE149 _____. "Blacks in the Cities: Agenda for the 70s." 1972. Black Scholar, 4 (Nov.-Dec. 1972), 50-61.

SE150 Bond, Horace Mann. "Intelligence Tests and Propaganda." June 1924. In Aptheker, A2:453-459.

SE151 _____. "A Negro Looks at His South." June 1931. Harper's Magazine, June 1933, pp. 98-108. Rpt. in Brown, A28:1028-1042.

SE152 _____. "What the San Francisco Conference Means to the Negro." 18 April 1945. JNE, 14 (Fall 1945), 627-630.

SE153 _____. "Education for Political and Social Responsibility: Its Natural History in the American College." 29 Nov. 1946. JNE, 16 (Spring 1947), 165-171.

SE154 _____. "The Present Status of Racial Integration in the United States, with Especial Reference to Education." 16 April 1952. JNE, 21 (Summer 1952), 241-250.

SE155 _____. "Reflections, Comparative, on West African Nationalist Movements." 20 Sept. 1956. Presence Africaine, Nos. 8-10 (June-Nov. 1956), 132-142.

SE156 _____. "The Search for Talent." The Inglis Lecture, Cambridge Graduate School of Education, 1957. Cambridge: Harvard Univ. Press, 1959.

SE157 _____. "Howe and Isaacs in the Bush: The Ram in the Thicket." 1961. Atlanta: Atlanta Univ. School of Education, 1961? Rpt. in Hill and Kilson, A92a:278-288 or A92b:321-333.

SE158 _____. "New England Mission for Black Freedom." July 1963. New South, 18 (July-Aug. 1963), 3-8.

BOND, HORACE MANN. See Williams, HC200:77-178.

SE159 Bond, Julian. "The Southern Youth Movement." 1962. Freedomways, 2 (Summer 1962), 308-310.

SE160 _____. "Nonviolence: An Interpretation." 1963. Freedomways, 3 (Spring 1963), 159-162.

SE161 _____. "Black Candidates: Southern Campaign Experiences." 1968. Atlanta: Voter Education Project, Southern Regional Council, n.d.

SE162 _____. "A New Movement and a New Method." May 1969. In Foner, A74:1162-1166. Rpt. as "Young, Black, and Urban" in Bond, A17:65-72 [abr. and much rev. for 1971 delivery]. [Cf. Bond, "A

New Vision, A Better Tomorrow." <u>Humanist</u>, 29
(Jan.-Feb. 1969), 11-12. Rpt. in Moss, A130:50-
54.]

SE163 _____. "The Failure of the White Minority." 10
Oct. 1969. In Wallerstein and Starr, A163:311-317;
and as "Revolution on Campus" in Bond, A17:31-37,
rev.

SE164 _____. "The People Next Door." 1969. In Bond,
A17:17-24.

SE165 _____. "Killers of the Dream." 1969. In Bond,
A17:38-43.

SE166 _____. "Uniting the Races." Jan. 1970. <u>Play-
boy</u>, Jan. 1970, pp. 128, 154. Rpt. in Littleton
and Burger, A112:362-366.

SE167 _____. "Other Voices, Other Strategies." April
1970. <u>Time</u>, 6 April 1970, pp. 23-24, 27. Rpt.
in Littleton and Burger, A112:432-436.

SE168 _____. "Black Hands, Black Sweat." 1970. In
Bond, A17:44-51.

SE169 _____. "America's Domestic Colony." 1970. In
Bond, A17:52-64.

SE170 _____. "Lincoln Revisited." 1970. In Bond,
A17:129-137.

SE171 _____. "Address to the Congress of African
Peoples." Sept. 1970. In Jones, A101:88-91

SE172 _____. "The Roots of Racism and War." 1970.
<u>Black Scholar</u>, 2 (Nov. 1970), 20-23.

SE173 _____. "The Establishment." 1971. In Bond,
A17:115-120.

SE174 _____. "A Black Southern Strategy." 1972. In
Wright, A180:137-143.

SE175 _____. "A Prophet Not Without Honor." 1972.
In Bond, A17:11-15.

SE176 _____. "A Little Political History." 1972. In

Bond, A17:25-30.

SE177 _____. "City Too Busy To Hate." 1972. In
       Bond, A17:73-86.

SE178 _____. "The Panthers and Bobby Seale, Angela
       Davis, and George Jackson." 1972. In Bond, A17:
       87-103.

SE179 _____. "Federal Bureau of Intimidation." 1972.
       In Bond, A17:104-114.

SE180 _____. "The Kent State Massacre." 1972. In
       Bond, A17:121-128.

SE181 _____. "Black Faces in High Places." 1972. In
       Bond, A17:138-146.

SE182 _____. "The Need for NAPPI." 1972. In Bond,
       A17:147-153.

SE183 _____. "America's Revolution." 1972. In Bond,
       A17:154-163.

    BOND, JULIAN. See Neary, HC124; and Williams,
    HC200:181-282.

SE184 Bonner, Marita O. "On Being Young--A Woman--
       and Colored." Dec. 1925. In Aptheker, A2:505-
       509.

SE185 Bontemps, Arna. "The Negro's Contribution Recon-
       sidered." 19 Feb. 1957. In Hill, A93:185-192.

SE186 Borders, William Holmes. "Some Negro Contribu-
       tions to American Civilization." 10 Jan. 1943. In
       Hill, A93:79-83.

SE187 Bouey, H. N. "The Fall of Man." 1890. In Braw-
       ley, A25:50-55.

    BOUEY, HARRISON N. See Simmons, HC163a:951-
    953 or HC163b:675-676.

SE188 Bowen, J. W. E. "The Comparative Status of the Ne-
       gro at the Close of the War and of To-day." 13
       Dec. 1895. In Bowen, A20:163-173.

SE189 _____. "What Achievements Did the American
Negro Make in the Nineteenth Century?" 1902. In
Culp, A46:29-34.

SE190 Bowler, William, and Lentey Craw. "Resolution of
the Free People of Color of Richmond." 24 Jan.
1817. In Garrison, A77:62-63.

SE191 Braithwaite, William Stanley. "Democracy and Art."
Aug. 1915. In Aptheker, A2:107-108.

SE192 Brawley, Benjamin. "Politics and Womanliness."
Aug. 1915. In Aptheker, A2:96-97.

SE193 Brawley, E. M. "Contending for the Faith." 1890.
In Brawley, A25:11-27.

SE194 _____. "Baptists and Sunday-School Work." 1890.
In Brawley, A25:221-232.

SE195 _____. "Baptists and General Education." 1890.
In Brawley, A25:237-250.

SE196 _____. "The Duty of Colored Baptists in View of
the Past, the Present, and the Future." 1890. In
Brawley, A25:287-300.

SE197 _____. "Is the Young Negro an Improvement,
Morally, on His Father?" 1902. In Culp, A46:
254-257.

BRAWLEY, E. M. See Simmons, HC163a:908-912 or
HC163b:645-647.

SE198 Braxton, P. H. A. "Baptists and Foreign Missions."
1890. In Brawley, A25:256-270.

BRAXTON, P. H. A. See Simmons, HC163a:1046-1051
or HC163b:753-756.

SE199 Brooke, Edward W. "Crisis in the Two-Party System." 5 Jan. 1966. In Smith and Robb, A156:144-
159.

SE200 _____. "The Problem of Civil Rights." 1966. In
Brooke, SE201:148-159. Rpt. in Littleton and Burger, A112:247-249, excerpt.

SE201 _____. The Challenge of Change: Crisis in Our
        Two-Party System. Boston: Little, 1966.

SE202 _____. "Address to the 1967 National Convention
        of the NAACP." 11 July 1967. In Williams and
        Williams, A175:113-122; and in Foner, A74:1059-
        1065, abr.

SE203 _____. "After a Long Hot Summer." Sept. 1967.
        Look, 5 Sept. 1967, pp. 26-27. Rpt. in Littleton
        and Burger, A112:314-319.

        BROOKE, EDWARD W. See Christopher, HC24:228-
        236; Cutler, HC33; "Three Negro Senators...,"
        HC764; Goldman, HC1072; and Kerr, HC1097.

SE204 Brooks, Walter H. "The Doctrine of God: His Ex-
        istence and Attributes." 1890. In Brawley, A25:
        39-49.

SE205 _____. "The Negro as a Christian." 1902. In
        Culp, A46:315-317.

SE206 Brown, Charlotte Hawkins. "Bennett College." 10
        Oct. 1943. In Hill, A93:84-88.

SE207 _____. "The Place of the Nursing Profession in
        American Life." 6 March 1949. In Hill, A93:89-
        91.

        BROWN, CHARLOTTE HAWKINS. See Boulware,
        HC1023:105-107.

SE208 Brown, D. P. "The State of the Country from a
        Black Man's Point of View." Aug. 1899. In Foner,
        A74:617-624.

SE209 Brown, Edward Everett. "Importance of Race Pride."
        5 March 1888. In Foner, A74:515-517.

SE210 Brown, H. Rap. "Colonialism and Revolution." Sum-
        mer 1967. In Brown, SE212:134-145. Rpt. in
        Smith and Robb, A156:304-312.

SE211 _____. "The Third World and the Ghetto." Oct.
        1967. In Foner, A74:1089-1091.

SE212 _____. Die Nigger Die! New York: Dial, 1969.

BROWN, H. RAP. See Kennicott and Page, HC1096.

SE213 Brown, Jere A. "The Afro-American Press." 1890.
In Penn, A139:467-471.

SE214 Brown, Morris. "Opening Sermon Preached Before
the Baltimore Annual Conference of the A.M.E.
Church." 1844. In Payne, HC1180:263-265.

SE215 Brown, Raymond. "Justice." Sept. 1970. In Jones,
A101:391-392.

SE216 Brown, Sterling A. "Count Us In." 1944. In Logan,
A115:308-344.

SE217 Brown, Tony. "Communications: Coordinator's Statement." Sept. 1970. In Jones, A101:451-454.

SE218 Brown, William Wells. Narrative of William Wells
Brown, a Fugitive Slave [1847]. In Osofsky,
HC1017:173-223.

SE219 _____. "Slavery As It Is, and Its Influence upon
the American People." 14 Nov. 1847. In Foner,
A74:90-93, excerpt.

SE220 _____. "Visit of a Fugitive Slave to the Grave of
Wilberforce." 1854. In Griffiths, A87:70-76. Rpt.
in Brawley, A24:170-174.

SE221 _____. The American Fugitive in Europe: Sketches
of Places and People Abroad ... with a Memoir of
the Author. 1855; rpt. New York: Negro Universities Press, 1969.

SE222 _____. "Address to the Annual Meeting of the
American Anti-Slavery Society." 6 May 1862. In
Aptheker, A1:470-471, excerpt.

BROWN, WILLIAM WELLS. See Brawley, HC13:59-
63; Brown, HC17; Farrison, HC50; Moore, HC120;
Simmons, HC163a:447-450 or HC163b:296-297; Cole-
man, HC215; Farrison, HC226; Farrison, HC227;
Heermance, HC237; Quarles, HC593:62-63; Loggins,
HC992:156-173; and Douglass, SE666.

SE223 Browne, Robert S. "A Case for Separation." 30
      June 1968. In Foner, A74:1121-1131. Rpt. as
      "The Case for Two Americas--One Black, One
      White." New York Times Magazine, 11 Aug. 1968,
      pp. 10, 13, 50, 51, 56, 60, 61. NYT text rpt. in
      Golden and Rieke, A82:443-450.

SE224 _____. "Financing the Black University." Nov.
      1968. In Wright, A179:85-93.

SE225 _____. "Toward Making 'Black Power' Real
      Power." 1969. In Lecky and Wright, A110:65-77.

SE226 Bruce, B. K. "In Behalf of P. B. S. Pinchback." 3
      March 1876. In Woodson, A177:267-270.

SE227 _____. "On Election Practices in Mississippi."
      31 March 1876. In Woodson, A177:270-272.

SE228 _____. "A Call for a Change in Our Indian
      Policy." 7 April 1880. In Foner, A177:472-477.

      BRUCE, BLANCHE K. See Brawley, HC12:127-132;
      Christopher, HC24:15-24; Houston, HC88; St. Clair,
      HC154; Simmons, HC163a:699-703 or HC163b:483-
      487; Cromwell, HC447:164-170; "Three Negro Sena-
      tors...," HC764; and Loggins, HC992:292-293.

SE229 Bruce, John E. "Reasons Why the Colored Ameri-
      can Should Go To Africa." Oct. 1877. In Foner,
      A74:459-461.

SE230 _____. "Reflections on the Decision in the Civil
      Rights Cases." Nov. 1883. In Bruce, A29:19-22.

SE231 _____. "Is This Our Country?" Nov. 1883. In
      Bruce, A29:23-26.

SE232 _____. "The Application of Force." 5 Oct. 1889.
      In Bruce, A29:29-32. Rpt. in Barbour, A8:51-52,
      excerpt, and in Foner, A74:537-538, excerpt.

SE233 _____. " 'The Blot on the Escutcheon.' " 1890.
      In Bruce, A29:34-43.

SE234 _____. "To the Parents." c. 1900. In Bruce,
      A29:63-67.

SE235 _____. "Some Serious Phases of the Problem of Race." 30 Dec. 1909. In Bruce, A29:92-96, excerpt.

SE236 _____. "The Sons of Africa." c. 1913. In Bruce, A29:102-103.

SE237 _____. "Present Tendencies." 20 June 1915. In Bruce, A29:109-114.

SE238 _____. "An Intellectual Battle." 25 Nov. 1915. In Bruce, A29:121-124.

   [_____. 24 Aug. 1916. Same as SE235.]

SE239 _____ ["Bruce Grit"]. The Awakening of Hezekiah Jones ... A Story Dealing with Some of the Problems Affecting the Political Rewards Due the Negro. Hopkinsville, Ky.: Phil H. Brown, 1916.

SE240 _____. "Practical Race Pride." 20 March 1917. In Bruce, A29:134-136.

SE241 _____. "The Oneness of the Darker Races." c. 1918. In Bruce, A29:136-141.

SE242 _____. "The Destiny of the Darker Races." 1918. In Bruce, A29:142-145.

SE243 _____. "Mr. Marcus Garvey." 1918. In Bruce, A29:146.

SE244 _____. "A Phillip [sic] Randolph." Dec. 1919. In Bruce, A29:156.

SE245 _____. "The Meaning of White Democracy." 1919. In Bruce, A29:157-158.

SE246 _____. "Letter to Marcus Garvey." 17 Aug. 1920. In Bruce, A29:159.

SE247 _____. "Replies to the Claim the Goals of Black and White Are Identical." c. 1921. In Golden and Rieke, A82:386-387.

SE248 _____. "Marcus Garvey and the U.N.I.A." 1922. In Bruce, A29:167-170.

SE249 _____. "The Problems that Face the Negro in
America." 28 May 1922. In Bruce, A29:171-175.

BRUCE, JOHN EDWARD. See Penn, A139:344-347.

SE250 Bruce, Roscoe Conkling. "Tuskegee Institute." 1905.
In From Servitude to Service, A75:83-113.

SE251 _____. "Freedom Through Education." 30 May
1905. In Woodson, A177:585-595.

[Bryan, R., and J. B. Vashon. See Vashon, SE2210.]

SE252 Bryant, M. Edward. "How Shall We Get Our Rights?"
4 Dec. 1887. In Foner, A74:510-514.

SE253 Bulkley, William L. "Race Prejudice as Viewed from
an Economic Standpoint." 31 May 1909. In Proceedings of the National Negro Conference, A145:89-
97. Rpt. in Foner, A74:680-686.

SE254 Bunche, Ralph J. A World View of Race. 1936; rpt.
Port Washington, N.Y.: Kennikat, 1968.
Contains: "What Is Race?" pp. 4-23.
"The Device of Race in World Economic and Po-
litical Conflict," pp. 25-36.
"Race and Imperialism," pp. 38-65.
"Race in the United States," pp. 67-96.

SE255 _____. "The Disfranchisement of the Negro." 27
Dec. 1940. In Brown, A28:925-936.

SE256 _____. "The Barriers of Race Can Be Surmounted;
Color Has Nothing To Do with Worth." 30 May
1949. Vital Speeches, 15 (1 July 1949), 572-574.

SE257 _____. "The Challenge of Human Relations." 11
Feb. 1950. In Representative American Speeches,
1949-1950. Ed. A. Craig Baird. New York: Wilson, 1950. Pages 142-153.

SE258 _____. "Democracy: A World Issue." 6 June
1950. JNE, 19 (Fall 1950), 431-438.

SE259 _____. "Prospects for Peace: U.N. Building
Firm Foundations." 28 April 1951. Vital Speeches,
17 (1 June 1951), 489-492.

SE260 _____. "Freedom Is a Blessing." 4 June 1951.
Vital Speeches, 17 (15 Aug. 1951), 663-666.

SE261 _____. "Equality Without Qualifications." 1 July
1951. Phylon, 12 (3rd Qrtr 1951), 209-218.

SE262 _____. "Toward Peace and Freedom; a Vigorous
Interpretation of the United Nations." 15 March
1953. Christian Century, 70 (22 April 1953), 479-
481.

SE263 _____. "Dreams and Realities." 8 April 1953.
In Man Thinking: Representative Phi Beta Kappa
Orations, 1915-1959. Ed. William T. Hastings.
Ithaca: Cornell Univ. Press, 1962. Pages 264-272.

SE264 _____. "Human Relations in World Perspective."
Spring 1954. In Foner, A74:882-892.

SE265 _____. "The Road to Peace: Learn To Live Together or Perish Together." 30 June 1954. Vital
Speeches, 20 (15 Aug. 1954), 654-657.

SE266 _____. "The Forward March of Democracy." 4
July 1954. In Hale, A90:153-161.

SE267 _____. "The United Nations in 1963." 23 Oct.
1963. In Williams and Williams, A175:25-35.

BUNCHE, RALPH J. See Phifer, HC1115.

SE268 Burleigh, A. A. "The Afro-American Press." 1890.
In Penn, A139:450-452.

SE269 Cain, Richard H. "Our Duty in the Crisis." c. 1865.
In Payne, HC1181:146-148.

SE270 _____. "The Rights of Colored Men and Women."
1865. In Payne, HC1181:150-152.

SE271 _____, et al. "Black Delegates to the South Carolina Constitutional Convention of 1868 Debate the Distribution of Lands to the Freedmen." 1868. In
Bracey, A21:235-247.

SE272 Cain, Richard H. "Civil Rights Bill." 10 Jan. 1874.
In Woodson, A177:328-338; and in Reconstruction,

1865-1877. Ed. Robert W. Johannsen. New York:
Free Press, 1970. Pages 163-172.

SE273 _____. "Speech on the Civil Rights Act." 3 Feb.
1875. In Fishel and Quarles, A72:283-289, abr.

CAIN, RICHARD H. See Christopher, HC24:87-96;
Simmons, HC163a:866-871 or HC163b:613-616;
Brown, HC445:544-545; and Woodson, HC1188:211-
212.

SE274 Campbell, J. P. "Give Us Equal Pay and We Will Go
to War." 29 Feb. 1864. In Foner, A74:301-303.

CAMPBELL, J. P. See Simmons, HC163a:1031-1034
or HC163b:741-742; and Brown, HC445:446-447.

SE275 Cardozo, Francis L. "Break Up the Plantation System." 1868. In Foner, A74:351-353.

SE276 _____, et al. "Black Delegates to the South Caro-
lina Constitutional Convention of 1868 Debate the
Distribution of Lands to the Freedmen." 1868. In
Bracey, A21:235-247.

CARDOZO, FRANCIS L. See Simmons, HC163a:428-
431 or HC163b:281-283; Sweat, HC171; and Brown,
HC445:463-465.

SE277 Carey, Archibald J., Jr. "An Address to the Republican National Convention." 8 July 1952. In Hill,
A93:149-154.

SE278 _____. "The Negro Methodist Churches in America." 18 Aug. 1961. In Williams and Williams,
A175:137-145.

CAREY, ARCHIBALD J., JR. See Boulware, HC1023:
165-169.

SE279 Carmichael, Stokely. "Statement to the Southern Students Organizing Committee Conference." 1965. In
Fishel and Quarles, A72:547-549.

SE280 _____. "Who Is Qualified?" 8 Jan. 1966. New
Republic, 8 Jan. 1966, pp. 20-22. Rpt. in Carmichael, A31:9-16.

SE281 _____. "Black Power: The Widening Dialogue."
13 July 1966. New South, 21 (Summer 1966), 65-80.

SE282 _____. "Black Power." 28 July 1966. In Bracey,
A21:740-744; in Bracey, A22:470-476; and in Osofsky, A135:629-636.

SE283 _____. "Black Power--Black Audience." 30 July
1966. In Scott and Brockriede, A154:85-95, abr.

SE284 _____. "What We Want," Sept. 1966. New York
Review of Books, 22 Sept. 1966, pp. 5-8. Rpt. in
Carmichael, A31:17-30; in Barbour, A8:61-71; and
in Rose, A151:237-246.

SE285 _____. "Toward Black Liberation." Sept. 1966.
Massachusetts Review, 7 (Sept. 1966), 639-651.
Rpt. in Carmichael, A31:31-43; in Jones and Neal,
A103:119-132; and in Littleton and Burger, A112:
442-448, abr.

SE286a _____. "Berkeley Speech." Oct. 1966. In Carmichael, A31:45-60. [Same as SE286b, substantially
rev. for publ.]

SE286b _____. "Black Power." Nov. 1966. In Lomas,
A116:137-151. [Same as SE286a before revision.
Note discrepancy in dates.]

SE287 _____. "Black Power." 19 Nov. 1966. In Foner,
A74:1034-1040; and in Grant, A84:459-466.

SE288 _____. "Speech at Morgan State College." 16
Jan. 1967. In Bosmajian and Bosmajian, A19:109-
125; and in Carmichael, A31:61-76. [Carmichael,
A31, text dated 28 Jan. 1967.]

SE289 _____. "Black Power--White Audience." 6 Feb.
1967. In Scott and Brockriede, A154:96-111.

SE290 _____. "Toward Black Liberation." 8 April 1967.
In Williams and Williams, A175:263-275.

SE291 _____. "The Dialectics of Liberation." 18 July
1967. In Carmichael, A31:77-100. Rpt. in To Free
a Generation: The Dialectics of Liberation. Ed.
David Cooper. [New York]: Collier [Macmillan],

1969. Pages 150-174.

SE292 _____. "Solidarity with Latin America." July
1967. In Carmichael, A31:101-110.

SE293 _____. "Stokely Carmichael Interviewed by Suce-
sos Magazine." c. Sept. 1967. In Golden and
Rieke, A82:523-535.

SE294 _____. "Free Huey." 17 Feb. 1968. In Carmichael, A31:111-130. Rpt. in The Movement Toward a New America. Ed. Mitchell Goodman.
Philadelphia: Pilgrim, 1970. Pages 180-184, excerpt.

SE295 _____. "The Black American and Palestinian
Revolutions." Aug. 1968. In Carmichael, A31:131-
143.

SE296 _____. "A New World To Build." 9 Dec. 1968.
In Carmichael, A31:145-164.

SE297 _____. "The Pitfalls of Liberalism." Jan. 1969.
In Carmichael, A31:165-173.

SE298 _____. "Message from Guinea." Oct. 1969. In
Carmichael, A31:175-182.

SE299 _____. "Pan-Africanism." April 1970. In Carmichael, A31:183-220.

SE300 _____. "From Black Power Back to Pan-Africanism." c. 1970. In Carmichael, A31:221-227.

SE301 _____. "Marxism-Leninism and Nkrumahism."
1973. Black Scholar, 4 (Feb. 1973), 41-43.

CARMICHAEL, STOKELY. See Stembridge, HC356;
Roberts, HC944; Brockriede and Scott, HC1048;
Campbell, HC1057; Jefferson, HC1092; Jefferson,
HC1093; Jefferson, HC1094; Phifer and Taylor,
HC1114; Pollock, HC1117; Richardson, HC1121;
Draper, HC1256:118-124; Baldwin, SE70; and
Cleaver, SE379.

SE302 Carter, R. A. "Whence and Whither." 30 May
1923. In Woodson, A177:626-636.

SE303 Carter, Robert L. "The United States Supreme Court and the Issue of Racial Discrimination Since 1940." March 1959. Presence Africaine, Nos. 24-25 (Feb.- May 1959), 177-195.

SE304 Carter, W. Justin. "The Duty and Responsibility of the Anglo-Saxon Idea of Citizenship." 16 Dec. 1904. In Dunbar, A70:265-276.

SE305 Carver, George W. "The Negro as a Farmer." 1902. In Culp, A46:388-394.

CARVER, GEORGE W. See Bullock, HC19:45-50.

SE306 Cashin, John. "Address to the Congress of African Peoples." Sept. 1970. In Jones, A101:12-17.

SE307 _____. "Public Office: Appointed or Elected (Major Premise)." Sept. 1970. In Jones, A101:150-153.

SE308 _____. "Challenging the White Bourbon Power Structure." 1972. In Wright, A180:165-177.

SE309 Chaney, Fannie Lee. "Ben Is Going To Take His Big Brother's Place." 1965. Freedomways, 5 (Spring 1965), 290-291. Rpt. in Foner, A74:1018-1019.

SE310 Charleston, S.C., Negroes. "Petition to the South Carolina State Legislature." Sept. 1865. JNH, 31 (Jan. 1946), 93-95.

SE311 Cheatham, Henry P. "How Can the Friendly Relations Now Existing Between the Two Races in the South Be Strengthened and Maintained?" 1902. In Culp, A46:57-62.

CHEATHAM, HENRY P. See Christopher, HC24:149-159.

SE312 Cheek, James. "From Weakness to Strength." 25 Oct. 1967. In Golden and Rieke, A82:129-134.

SE313 Cheek, King V., Jr. "Toward a Redefinition of the University." 10 Oct. 1969. In Golden and Rieke, A82:135-141.

SE314 _____. "On Black Studies and Black Youth." 22
       Oct. 1971. JNH, 57 (Jan. 1972), 72-82.

SE315 Chesnutt, Charles W. "The Disfranchisement of the
       Negro." 1903. In The Negro Problem, A133:79-
       124.

SE316 _____. "Women's Rights." Aug. 1915. In Apthe-
       ker, A2:100-101.

SE317 Chicago Conservator. "Blood, Brand, or Liberty."
       1880. In Barbour, A8:50-51.

SE318 Chicago Freedom Movement. "Program of the Chi-
       cago Freedom Movement." July 1966. In Bracey,
       A21:709-718.

SE319 Chisholm, Shirley. "It Is Time for a Change." 26
       March 1969. In Foner, A74:1153-1156.

SE320 _____. "Black Is an Attitude." 1969. In Little-
       ton and Burger, A112:348-353.

SE321 _____. "Racism and Anti-Feminism." 1969.
       Black Scholar, 1 (Jan.-Feb. 1970), 40-45.

SE322 _____. "Race, Revolution and Women." 1971.
       Black Scholar, 3 (Dec. 1971), 17-21.

SE323 _____. "Economic Justice for Women." 1971-
       1972. In Chisholm, A33:188-192.

SE324 _____. "The Cost of Care." 1971-1972. In
       Chisholm, A33:193-199.

SE325 _____. "'All We Are Saying Is.'" 20 April
       1972. Freedomways, 12 (2d Qrtr 1972), 118-123.

SE326 _____. "Coalitions--the Politics of the Future."
       1972. In Wright, A180:82-93.

SE327 _____. "The Politics of Coalition." 1972. Black
       Scholar, 4 (Sept. 1972), 30-32.

SE328 _____. "Equality of Commitment--Africa." 1972.
       In Chisholm, A33:165-168.

SE329 _____. "Foreign Aid." 1972. In Chisholm,
A33:169-173.

SE330 _____. "Justice in America: Gun Control, Drug
Abuse, Court, Police, Prison Reform, Political and
Civil Dissent." 1972. In Chisholm, A33:174-184.

SE331 _____. "The Economy." 1972. In Chisholm,
A33:185-186.

CHISHOLM, SHIRLEY. See Chisholm, A33; Chisholm,
HC23; Christopher, HC24:255-261; and Hicks, HC81.

SE332 Churchville, John E. "The Question of Discipline."
19 March 1969. In Wright, A179:183-185.

SE333 _____. "On Correct Black Education." 24 June
1969. In Wright, A179:177-182.

SE334 Clanton, S. T. "Baptists and Bible Work." 1890.
In Brawley, A25:188-199.

CLANTON, SOLOMON T. See Simmons, HC163a:419-
421 or HC163b:275-276.

SE335 Clark, Felton G. "Founder's Day Address." 9
March 1942. In Hill, A93:73-78.

SE336 Clark, Kenneth. "The Crisis of American Democracy
and the Negro." 19 Nov. 1955. In Hale, A90:56-
67.

SE337 _____. " 'The Wonder Is There Have Been So Few
Riots.' " Sept. 1965. New York Times Magazine,
5 Sept. 1965, pp. 10, 38, 45, 48. Rpt. in Meier
and Rudwick, A124:107-115.

SE338 _____. "The Present Dilemma of the Negro." 14
Oct. 1967. JNH, 53 (Jan. 1968), 1-11. Rpt. in
Foner, A74:1092-1101; and in Littleton and Burger,
A112:94-101, abr. [Cf. Patterson, HC942.]

SE339 _____. "The Present Dilemma." Fall 1969. New
South, 24 (Fall 1969), 74-80.

SE340 _____. "Fifteen Years of Deliberate Speed." Dec.
1969. Saturday Review, Dec. 1969, pp. 59-61.

Rpt. in Littleton and Burger, A112:189-197.

SE341 _____. "Public School Desegregation in the Seventies." Spring 1972. New South, 27 (Summer 1972),
21-28.

SE342 Clark, Molson M. "On Episcopal Ordination." May
1852. In Payne, HC1180:274-276.

SE343 Clark, Peter H. "Socialism: The Remedy for the
Evils of Society." 22 July 1877. In Foner, A74:
452-457, abr.

CLARK, PETER H. See Gutman, HC69; Simmons,
HC163a:374-383 or HC163b:244-249; and Brown,
HC445:522-524.

SE344 Clarke, John Henrik. "The Meaning of Black History." 15 Feb. 1969. In Foner, A74:1139-1145.

SE345 Cleage, Albert B., Jr. "Fear Is Gone." 1967. In
Cleage, A38:11-21.

SE346 _____. "A Sense of Urgency." 1967. In Cleage,
A38:22-34.

SE347 _____. "An Epistle to Stokely." 1967. In Cleage,
A38:35-47.

SE348 _____. " 'We Are God's Chosen People.' " 1967.
In Cleage, A38:48-59.

SE349 _____. " 'He Who Is Not With Me....' " 1967.
In Cleage, A38:60-70.

SE350 _____. " 'He Stirs Up the People.' " 1967. In
Cleage, A38:71-84.

SE351 _____. "The Resurrection of the Nation." 1967.
In Cleage, A38:85-99.

SE352 _____. "New-Time Religion." 1967. In Cleage,
A38:100-114.

SE353 _____. "No Halfway Revolution." 1967. In
Cleage, A38:115-129.

SE354 _____. "Grapes of Wrath." 1967. In Cleage,
A38:130-142.

SE355 _____. "But God Hardened Pharaoh's Heart."
1967. In Cleage, A38:143-155.

SE356 _____. " 'An Enemy Hath Done This.' " 1967.
In Cleage, A38:156-170.

SE357 _____. "Great Gettin' Up Morning." 1967. In
Cleage, A38:171-185.

SE358 _____. "Brother Malcolm." 1968. In Cleage,
A38:186-200.

SE359 _____. "Dr. King and Black Power." 1968. In
Cleage, A38:201-213.

SE360 _____. "Not Peace but a Sword." 1968. In
Cleage, A38:214-226.

SE361 _____. "Black Church, White School." 1968. In
Cleage, A38:227-240.

SE362 _____. "What Can We Give Our Youth?" In
Cleage, A38:241-253.

SE363 _____. "The Promised Land." 1968. In Cleage,
A38:254-265.

SE364 _____. "Coming In Out of the Wilderness." 1968.
In Cleage, A38:266-278.

SE365 Cleaver, Eldridge. "As Crinkly as Yours." March
1962. NHB, 25 (March 1962), 127-132. Rpt. in
Bracey, A22:429-445.

SE366 _____. "On Becoming." June 1965. Ramparts,
Aug. 1966, pp. 16, 18-20. Rpt. in Cleaver, A40:
3-17.

SE367 _____. "Initial Reactions on the Assassination of
Malcolm X." June 1965. Ramparts, Aug. 1966,
pp. 24-25. Rpt. in Cleaver, A40:50-61.

SE368 _____. "Four Vignettes." Aug.-Nov. 1965.
Ramparts, Aug. 1966, pp. 22-23. Rpt. in Cleaver,

A40:26-39, enl.

SE369 _____. "A Day in Folsom Prison." Sept. 1965.
In Cleaver, A40:40-49.

SE370 _____. "Soul on Ice." Oct. 1965. Ramparts,
Aug. 1966, pp. 23-24. Rpt. in Cleaver, A40:18-25.

SE371 _____. "The White Race and Its Heroes." c. 1965.
In Cleaver, A40:65-83; in Long and Collier, A118:
701-714; and in Littleton and Burger, A112:252-256,
excerpt.

SE372 _____. "Lazarus, Come Forth." c. 1965. In
Cleaver, A40:84-96.

SE373 _____. "Notes on a Native Son." June 1966.
Ramparts, June 1966, pp. 51-52, 54-56. Rpt. in
Cleaver, A40:97-111; and in Katope and Zolbrod,
A105:399-407. [See Addison Gayle, Jr., "A De-
fense of James Baldwin," CLA Journal, 10 (March
1967), 201-208.]

SE374 _____. "Rallying Round the Flag." c. 1966. In
Cleaver, A40:112-120.

SE375 _____. "The Black Man's Stake in Vietnam."
c. 1966. In Cleaver, A40:121-127.

SE376 _____. "Domestic Law and International Order."
c. 1966. In Cleaver, A40:128-137.

SE377 _____. "Psychology: The Black Bible." Jan.
1967. In Cleaver, A39:18-20.

SE378 _____. "The Decline of the Black Muslims." Feb.
1967. In Cleaver, A39:13-17.

SE379 _____. "My Father and Stokely Carmichael."
April 1967. Ramparts, April 1967, pp. 10-14. Rpt.
in Cleaver, A39:43-56.

SE380 _____. "Robert Kennedy's Prison." May 1967.
In Cleaver, A39:21-22.

SE381 _____. "White Woman, Black Man." 1968. In
Cleaver, A40:155-210.

SE382 _____. "Political Struggle in America." 11 Feb. 1968. In Smith, HC1246:166-174.

SE383 _____. "Revolution in the White Mother Country & National Liberation in the Black Colony." 16 March 1968. North American Review, NS 5 (July-Aug. 1968), 13-15. Rpt. in Foner, A74:1102-1108; and in Littleton and Burger, A112:437-441.

SE384 _____. "Affidavit #1: I Am 33 Years Old." April 1968. In Cleaver, A39:3-12.

SE385 _____. "The Land Question and Black Liberation." April 1968. Ramparts, May 1968, pp. 51-53. Rpt. in Cleaver, A39:57-72.

SE386 _____. "The Death of Martin Luther King: Requiem for Nonviolence." April 1968. Ramparts, May 1968, pp. 48-49. Rpt. in Cleaver, A39:73-79.

SE387 _____. "Affidavit #2: Shoot-Out in Oakland." April 1968. In Cleaver, A39:80-94.

SE388 _____. "Open Letter to Ronald Reagan." 13 May 1968. In Cleaver, A39:95-107.

SE389 _____. "The Courage To Kill: Meeting the Panthers." June 1968. In Cleaver, A39:23-39.

SE390 _____. "Stanford Speech." 1 Oct. 1968. In Cleaver, A39:113-146.

SE391 _____. "Introduction to the Biography of Huey P. Newton." Oct. 1968. Ramparts, 26 Oct. 1968, pp. 23-24. Rpt. in Cleaver, A39:40-42.

SE392 _____. "An Aside to Ronald Reagan." Oct. 1968. Ramparts, 26 Oct. 1968, p. 22. Rpt. in Cleaver, A39:108-112.

SE393 _____. "The Playboy Interview: Eldridge Cleaver." Oct. 1968. Playboy, Dec. 1968, pp. 90-92, 94-96, 98, 100, 102, 104, 106, 108, 238. Rpt. in Cleaver, A39:163-211.

SE394 _____. "Farewell Address." 22 Nov. 1968. Ramparts, 14-28 Dec. 1968, pp. 6, 8-10. Rpt. in

Cleaver, A39:147-160; and in Smith and Robb, A156:
286-295.

SE395 _____. "Tears for the Pigs." March 1969. Humanist, 29 (March-April 1969). Rpt. in Moss,
A130:87-91.

SE396 [_____.] Conversation with Eldridge Cleaver, Al-
giers. By Lee Lockwood. June 1969. New York:
Dell, 1970.

SE397 _____. "A Note to My Friends." July 1969.
Ramparts, Sept. 1969, pp. 29-30.

SE398 _____. "An Open Letter to Stokely Carmichael."
July 1969. Ramparts, Sept. 1969, pp. 31-32. Rpt.
in Foner, A73:104-108.

SE399 _____. "On Meeting the Needs of the People."
c. July 1969. Ramparts, Sept. 1969, pp. 34-35.

SE400 _____. "The Black Moochie: A Novella [Part
I]." Oct. 1969. Ramparts, Oct. 1969, pp. 21-24,
26-27.

SE401 _____. "The Black Moochie: A Novella [Part
II]." Nov. 1969. Ramparts, Nov. 1969, pp. 8,
12, 14-15.

SE402 _____. "Culture and Revolution: Their Synthesis
in Africa." 1971. Black Scholar, 3 (Oct. 1971),
33-39.

SE403 _____. "On Lumpen Ideology." 1972. Black
Scholar, 4 (Nov.-Dec. 1972), 2-10.

SE404 _____. "The Crisis of the Black Bourgeoisie."
1972. Black Scholar, 4 (Jan. 1973), 2-11.

CLEAVER, ELDRIDGE. See Swados, HC169; Swain,
HC170; Leary, HC247; Schanche, HC945; and Cleaver,
SE406.

SE405 Cleaver, Kathleen. "Liberation and Political Assassination." May 1968. In Foner, A73:146-150.

SE406 _____. "On Eldridge Cleaver." June 1969.

Ramparts, June 1969, pp. 4, 6, 8, 10-11.

SE407 Clement, George Clinton. "Boards for Life's Building." May 1921. In Woodson, A177:637-643.

SE408 Clement, Kenneth W. "Will the New Separatism
Work." April 1968. In Golden and Rieke, A82:
264-269. [Note: Golden and Rieke give April
1969 as date of delivery (p. 263), but attribute text
to an April 1968 source (p. 264n).]

SE409 Coker, Daniel. "A Dialogue Between a Virginian and
an African Minister." 1810. In Porter, A142:
orig. pag.

SE410 _____. "The Negro Church Achieves Independence."
21 Jan. 1816. In Aptheker, A1:68-69, excerpt.

SE411 Colored Advisory Committee of the Republican National Committee. "Address to the Colored Voters."
6 Oct. 1916. In Aptheker, A2:139-141.

SE412 Colored Baltimorean. "Letters on Colonization."
Nov. 1829-Jan. 1830. In Garrison, A77:52-57.

SE413 Colored Female of Philadelphia. "Emigration to Mex-
ico." 2 Jan. 1832. In Porter, A141:292-293.

SE414 Colored Philadelphian. "Colonization Hints." 3 Feb.
1831. In Woodson, A176:224-225.

SE415 Columbia University Students' Afro-American Society
and SDS. "What We Want." 24 April 1968. In
Wallerstein and Starr, A164:4-7.

SE416 Comer, James P. "The Social Power of the Negro."
Scientific American, 216 (April 1967), 21-27. Rpt.
in Barbour, A8:72-84.

[Condol, Daniel R., and Luther Wright. See Wright,
SE2371.]

SE417 Constitution of the American Society of Free Persons
of Colour, for Improving Their Condition in the
United States; for Purchasing Lands; and for the Establishment of a Settlement in Upper Canada, also
the Proceedings of the Convention, with Their

Address to the Free Persons of Colour in the United
States. 20-24 Sept. 1830. 1831; rpt. in Bell,
A10:orig. pag. ["Minutes" and "Address" rpt. in
Aptheker, A1:104-107.] [See "The First Colored
Convention," SE893.]

SE418 Conyers, John, Jr. "Politics and the Black Revolution." Aug. 1969. Ebony, Aug. 1969, pp. 162-166.
Rpt. in The Black Revolution, A12:223-234.

SE419 _____. "A Black Political Strategy for 1972."
1972. In Wright, A180:129-136.

SE420 _____. "Portugal Invades Guinea: The Failure of
U.S. Policy Toward Africa." 1972. In Wright,
A180:94-109.

CONYERS, JOHN, JR. See Christopher, HC24:237-
242.

SE421 Cook, Charles C. "A Comparative Study of the Negro
Problem." 1899. American Negro Academy, Occasional Papers No. 4. Washington: The Academy,
1899.

SE422 _____. "The Penning of the Negro." 1905. In
The Negro and the Elective Franchise, A132:15-50.

SE423 Cook, George William. "The Two Seals." 21 May
1912. In Dunbar, A70:379-388.

SE424 Cook, John Francis. "Remarks on the Subject of
Temperance." 16 Aug. 1837. In Porter, A141:
241-248.

COOK, JOHN FRANCIS. See Cromwell, HC447:228-
230.

SE425 Cook, Mary V. "The Work for Baptist Women."
1890. In Brawley, A25:271-286.

SE426 Cook, Samuel Du Bois. "Revolution and Responsibility." Feb. 1964. New South, 18 (Feb. 1964), 8-12,
15.

SE427 _____. "The Tragic Myth of Black Power." 1966.
New South, 21 (Summer 1966), 58-64.

SE428 _____. "Is Martin Luther King, Jr., Irrelevant?"
1971. New South, 26 (Spring 1971), 2-14.

SE429 Cooper, Arthur, and Edward J. Pompey. "Resolutions on Colonization." 5 Aug. 1831. In Garrison,
A77:33-34.

SE430 Coppin, Fanny Jackson. "A Plea for Industrial Opportunity." c. 1900? In Dunbar, A70:251-256.

COPPIN, FANNY MURIEL JACKSON. See Cromwell,
HC447:213-218.

SE431 Coppin, L. J. "The Afro-American Editor's Mission." 1890. In Penn, A139:483-487.

SE432 _____. "The Negro's Part in the Redemption of
Africa." Feb. 1902. In Dunbar, A70:243-250.

SE433 _____. "The A. M. E. Church in South Africa."
May 1904. In Smith, HC1183:228-229, excerpt.

SE434 _____. "Episcopal Address." 5 May 1916. In
Smith, HC1183:292-297, excerpt.

COPPIN, LEVI J. See Coppin, HC30.

SE435 Cork, Lewis, and Abner H. Francis. "Resolutions
on Colonization." 30 Nov. 1831. In Garrison, A77:
45-47.

[Cornish, James, et al. See Whipper, SE2309.]

SE436 Cornish, Samuel, and John B. Russwurm. "First Negro Newspaper's Opening Editorial." 16 March
1827. In Aptheker, A1:82-85.

CORNISH, SAMUEL ELI. See Pease and Pease,
HC532:140-161.

SE437 Corr, Joseph M. "Address Delivered Before the Humane Mechanics' Society." 4 July 1834. In Porter,
A141:146-154.

SE438 Costley, William. "A Plan for a Defense Movement."
Sept. 1902. In Foner, A74:640-642.

[Craw, Lentey, and William Bowler. See Bowler, SE190.]

SE439 Crockett, George W. , Jr. "Racism in the Law." 15
Oct. 1968. Science & Society, 33 (Spring 1969),
223-230. Rpt. in Foner, A74:1132-1138.

SE440 _____. "Paul Robeson: True Revolutionary."
16 Feb. 1973. Freedomways, 13 (1st Qrtr 1973),
10-13.

SE441 Crogman, William H. "The Negro, His Need and
Claims." 14 Oct. 1883. [Atlanta]: Judson, n.d.
Rpt. in Simmons, HC163a:696-697 or HC163b:481-
482, excerpt.

SE442 _____. "Negro Education: Its Helps and Hind-
rances." 16 July 1884. N.p. , [1884].

SE443 _____. "An Address on the Occasion of the Laying of the Corner-Stone." 21 Dec. 1888. Atlanta:
Clark Univ. Press, 1889.

SE444 _____. "Introduction." 1902. In Culp, A46:7-9.

SE445 _____. "Woman in the Ancient State." Aug. 1915.
In Aptheker, A2:99-100.

CROGMAN, WILLIAM H. See Simmons, HC163a:694-
698 or HC163b:480-482.

SE446 Cromwell, John W. "Religious, Political, and Civil
Rights Gained by the Negro in the Nineteenth Century." 1902. In Culp, A46:291-295.

SE447 _____. "The American Negro Bibliography of the
Year." Dec. 1915. In Papers of the American Negro Academy, A136:73-78.

SE448 _____. "The Challenge of the Disfranchised: A
Plea for the Enforcement of the 15th Amendment."
American Negro Academy, Occasional Papers No.
22. Washington: The Academy, 1924.

CROMWELL, JOHN WESLEY. See Penn, A139:154-
158, and Ferris, HC451:869-870.

SE449 Crosswaith, Frank R. "The Negro Labor Committee."
6 March 1952. In Foner, A74:857-860.

CROSSWAITH, FRANK R.   See Boulware, HC1023:115-116.

SE450 Crummell, Alexander. "Eulogium on the Life and Character of Thomas Clarkson, Esq. of England." 26 Dec. 1846. In Crummell, A43:201-267.

SE451 _____. "Hope for Africa: A Sermon on Behalf of the Ladies' Negro Education Society." 21 April 1852. In Crummell, A44:285-323. Rpt. in Brawley, A24:301-305, excerpt.

SE452 _____. "The Negro Race Not Under a Curse: An Examination of Genesis IX. 25." Sept. 1852. In Crummell, A44:327-354.

SE453 _____. "God and the Nation." 30 July 1854. In Crummell, A44:151-171.

SE454 _____. "The Duty of a Rising Christian State To Contribute to the World's Well-Being and Civilization, and the Means By Which It May Perform the Same." 26 July 1855. In Crummell, A44:57-102.

SE455 _____. "Address on Laying the Corner-Stone of St. Mark's Hospital." 24 April 1859. In Crummell, A44:195-211.

SE456 _____. "The Fitness of the Gospel for Its Own Work." 25 Dec. 1859. In Crummell, A44:175-191.

SE457 _____. "The English Language in Liberia." 26 July 1860 and Feb. 1861. In Crummell, A44:9-54.

SE458 _____. "The Relations and Duties of Free Colored Men in America to Africa." 1 Sept. 1860. In Crummell, A44:215-281. Rpt. in Hill and Kilson, A92a:87-93 or A92b:99-107, excerpt.

SE459 _____. "The Progress of Civilization Along the West Coast of Africa." 1861. In Crummell, A44:105-129.

SE460 _____. "The Progress and Prospects of the Republic of Liberia." 9 May 1861. In Crummell, A44:133-148.

SE461 _____. "Emigration, an Aid to the Evangelization
of Africa." 14 May 1863. In Crummell, A43:407-
429.

SE462 _____. "The Responsibility of the First Fathers
of a Country for Its Future Life and Character."
1 Dec. 1863. In Crummell, A43:129-163.

SE463 _____. "The Regeneration of Africa." Oct. 1865.
in Crummell, A43:433-453.

SE464 _____. "Our National Mistakes and the Remedy for
Them." 26 July 1870. In Crummell, A43:167-198.

SE465 _____. "The Social Principle Among a People;
and Its Bearing on Their Progress and Development."
Thanksgiving Day 1875. In Crummell, A45:285-311.
Rpt. in Bracey, A22:128-139, excerpt.

SE466 _____. "Address Before the American Geographi-
cal Society." 22 May 1877. In Crummell, A43:309-
323.

SE467 _____. "The Destined Superiority of the Negro:
A Thanksgiving Discourse." 1877. In Crummell,
A45:332-352.

SE468 _____. "The Assassination of President Garfield."
10 July 1881. In Crummell, A45:312-331.

SE469 _____. "The Dignity of Labour; and Its Value to a
New People." 1881. In Crummell, A43:381-404.

SE470 _____. "Eulogium on Henry Highland Garnet, D.D."
4 May 1882. In Crummell, A43:271-305.

SE471 _____. "A Defence of the Negro Race in America
from the Assaults and Charges of Rev. J. L. Tucker,
D.D., of Jackson, Mississippi." c. 1882. In Crummell, A43:85-125.

SE472 _____. "The Greatness of Christ." pre-1882. In
Crummell, A45:1-19.

SE473 _____. "The Family." pre-1882. In Crummell,
A45:20-36.

SE474 _____. "Marriage." pre-1882. In Crummell,
A45:37-54.

SE475 _____. "The Lamb of God." pre-1882. In Crummell, A45:55-70.

SE476 _____. "Rising with Christ." pre-1882. In
Crummell, A45:71-85.

SE477 _____. "Glorifying God." pre-1882. In Crummell, A45:86-99.

SE478 _____. "Unbelieving Nazareth." pre-1882. In
Crummell, A45:100-115.

SE479 _____. "The Rejection of Christ." pre-1882. In
Crummell, A45:116-133.

SE480 _____. "The Motives to Discipleship." pre-1882.
In Crummell, A45:134-149.

SE481 _____. "The Agencies to Saintly Sanctification."
pre-1882. In Crummell, A45:150-164.

SE482 _____. "Affluence and Receptivity." pre-1882.
In Crummell, A45:165-180.

SE483 _____. "Christ Receiving and Eating with Sinners."
pre-1882. In Crummell, A45:181-196.

SE484 _____. "The Discipline of Human Powers." pre-
1882. In Crummell, A45:197-215.

SE485 _____. "Joseph." pre-1882. In Crummell, A45:
216-232.

SE486 _____. "Influence." pre-1882. In Crummell,
A45:233-249.

SE487 _____. "Building Men." pre-1882. In Cummell,
A45:250-266.

SE488 _____. "Christian Conversation." pre-1882. In
Crummell, A45:267-284.

SE489 _____. "The Black Woman of the South: Her Neg-
lects and Her Needs." 15 Aug. 1883. In

Crummell, A43:61-82. Rpt. in Dunbar, A70:159-172, abr.; and in Foner, A74:480-490, abr.

SE490 _____. "Excellence, an End of the Trained Intellect." 6 June 1884. In Crummell, A43:345-354.

SE491 _____. "The Need of New Ideas and New Aims for a New Era." 30 May 1885. In Crummell, A43:13-36.

SE492 _____. "Common Sense in Common Schooling." 13 Sept. 1886. In Crummell, A43:327-341.

SE492a _____. "The Race-Problem in America." 20 Nov. 1888. In Crummell, A43:39-57. Rpt. in Brotz, A27:180-190; and in Golden and Rieke, A82:79-88.

SE493 _____. "Address at the Laying of the Corner Stone of the New St. Thomas Church, Philadelphia, Pa." 14 May 1890. In Crummell, A43:457-466.

SE494 _____. "The Absolute Need of an Indigenous Missionary Agency for the Evangelization of Africa." 14 Dec. 1895. In Bowen, A20:137-142.

SE495 _____. "Civilization as a Collateral and Indispensable Instrumentality in Planting the Christian Church in Africa." 14 Dec. 1895. In Bowen, A20:119-124.

SE496 _____. "Civilization, The Primal Need of the Race." 5 March 1897. American Negro Academy, Occasional Papers No. 3. Washington: The Academy, 1898. Pages 3-7.

SE497 _____. "The Attitude of the American Mind Toward the Negro Intellect." 28 Dec. 1897. American Negro Academy, Occasional Papers No. 3. Washington: The Academy, 1898. Pages 8-19. Rpt. in Fishel and Quarles, A72:352-355, excerpt; and in Long and Collier, A117:119-122, excerpt.

SE498 _____. "Right-Mindedness." N.d. In Crummell, A43:357-378. Rpt. in Cromwell, A42:258-272.

SE499 _____. "Sermon." N.d. In Golden and Rieke,

A82:288-298.

CRUMMELL, ALEXANDER.   See Du Bois, A65:215-
227; Brawley, HC13:101-105; Simmons, HC163a:530-
535 or HC163b:357-361; Wahle, HC181; Brown,
HC443:165-169; Brown, HC445:455-457; Cromwell,
HC447:130-138; Loggins, HC992:199-209; Woodson,
HC1188:155-156; Ferris, SE892; and Grimké, SE
1089.

SE500 Cruse, Harold.   "Revolutionary Nationalism and the
Afro-American."   1962.   In Jones and Neal, A103:
39-63.

SE501 _____.   "The Integrationist Ethic as a Basis for
Scholarly Endeavors."   May 1968.   In Robinson,
HC424:4-12.

SE502 Cuffee, Paul.   "A Brief Account of the Settlement and
Present Situation of the Colony of Sierra Leone in
Africa."   1812.   In Porter, A141:257-261; in Hill
and Kilson, A92a:14-19 or A926:17-23; and in Harris,
HC74:266-271.

CUFFEE, PAUL.   See Harris, HC74; and Sherwood,
HC162.

SE503 Cummings, Gwenna.   "Black Women--Often Discussed
but Never Understood."   c. 1968.   In Barbour, A8:
235-239.

SE504 Curtis, James L.   "Abraham Lincoln."   12 Feb. 1909.
In Dunbar, A70:321-324.

SE505 Dancy, John C.   "The Future of the Negro Church."
Sept. 1913.   In Dunbar, A70:475-482.

DANCY, JOHN C.   See Penn, A139:197-200; Dancy,
HC34; and Simmons, HC163a:1101-1104 or HC163b:
796-797.

SE506 Davis, Allison.   "What Does Negro Youth Think of
Present-Day Negro Leaders?"   1928.   In Cromwell,
A42:307-310.

SE507 Davis, Angela.   "I Am a Black Revolutionary Woman."   c. Dec. 1970.   In Foner, A74:1178-1181.

SE508 _____. "Address to the Marin County Court." 5
Jan. 1971. In Foner, A74:1181-1182.

SE509 _____. "Trials of Political Prisoners Today."
c. 1971. In Davis, A50:67-96.

SE510 _____. "Prison Interviews." c. 1971. In Davis,
A50:177-188.

SE511 _____. "Political Prisoners, Prisons and Black
Liberation." May 1971. In Davis, A50:19-36.

SE512 _____. "The Legacy of George Jackson." Aug.
1971. In Foner, A74:1192-1194.

SE513 _____. "The Soledad Brothers." 1971. Black
Scholar, 2 (Apr.-May 1971), 2-7.

SE514 _____. "Reflections on the Black Woman's Role in the
Community of Slaves." Black Scholar, 3 (Dec. 1971),
2-15. Rpt. in Massachusetts Review, 13 (Winter-Spring
1972), 81-100; and in Woman: An Issue. Ed. Lee R.
Edwards, Mary Heath, and Lisa Backin. Boston: Little,
1972. Pages 81-100. [See Johnetta Cole, "Affirmation
of Resistance: A Response to Angela Davis." Massachusetts Review, 13 (Winter-Spring 1972), 100-103.]

DAVIS, ANGELA. See Davis, A50; Nadelson, HC123;
Parker, HC129; Major, HC251; and Baldwin, SE72.

SE515 Davis, Arthur P. "Integration and Race Literature."
March 1959. In Chapman, A32:606-611.

SE516 Davis, Benjamin J. "The Path of Negro Literature."
Dec. 1946. New York: New Century, 1947.

SE517 _____. "Why I Am a Communist." 1947. Phylon,
8 (2d Qrtr 1947), 105-116.

SE518 _____. "The Negro People in the Struggle for
Peace and Freedom." Dec. 1950. New York: New
Century, 1951.

SE519 _____. "The Negro People on the March." June
1956. In Foner, A74:903-906.

SE520 Davis, D. Webster. "Achievements of the

Nineteenth-Century American Negro." 1902. In
Culp, A46:38-41.

SE521 _____. "The Sunday-School and Church as a Solution of the Negro Problem." 27 June 1905. In
Dunbar, A70:291-304.

SE522 Davis, Ossie. "Malcolm Was Our Manhood, Our Living Black Manhood." 27 Feb. 1965. In Clarke,
A35:xi-xii; and in Foner, A74:1011-1012.

SE523 Davis, Samuel H. "Address to the National Convention
of Colored Citizens." 15 Aug. 1843. In Minutes
of the National Convention of Colored Citizens,
SE1720:4-7, abr. Rpt. in Foner, A74:77-81, further abr.

SE524 Dawson, William L. "Race Is Not a Limitation."
14 June 1945. In Williams and Williams, A175:79-
86.

DAWSON, WILLIAM L. See Christopher, HC24:185-
193; Wilson, HC772; and Boulware, HC1023:153-155.

SE525 De Baptiste, Richard. "A Gospel Church." 1890.
In Brawley, A25:116-128.

DE BAPTISTE, RICHARD. See Penn, A139:262-264;
Simmons, HC163a:352-357 or HC163b:229-233; and
Woodson, HC1188:218-219.

SE526 DeGrass, Isiah G. "Essay." 21 Oct. 1828. In
Porter, A141:576-577.

SE527 Delany, Martin R. The Condition, Elevation, Emigra-
tion, and Destiny of the Colored People of the United
States, Politically Considered. 1852; rpt. New
York: Arno, 1968. [Conclusion, "A Glance at Our-
selves," pp. 197-208, rpt. in Golden and Rieke,
A82:352-357.]

SE528 _____. "Political Destiny of the Colored Race."
Aug. 1854. In Rollin, HC151:327-367. Rpt. in
Stuckey, A160:195-236; and in Bracey, A21:198-214,
excerpt.

SE529 _____. "Speech to the International Statistical

Congress, London." July 1860. In Rollin, HC151:
129-130.

SE530 _____. "Official Report of the Niger Valley Ex-
ploring Party." 1861. In Search for a Place:
Black Separatism and Africa, 1860. Ed. Howard
H. Bell. Ann Arbor: Univ. of Michigan Press,
1969. Pages 23-148. [Excerpt (of pp. 27-32, 107-
111) rpt. in Golden and Rieke, A82:317-323.]

SE531 _____. "The International Policy of the World towards the African Race." c. 1864. In Rollin,
HC151:313-327.

SE532 _____. "Advice to Ex-Slaves." July 1865. In
Foner, A74:320-325.

SE533 _____. "Reflections on the War." c. 1865. In
Rollin, HC151:309-313.

SE534 _____. "Prospects of the Freedmen of Hilton
Head." Sept.-Dec. 1865. In Rollin, HC151:230-241.

SE535 _____. "Letter to Downing, Whipper, Douglass,
et al." 22 Feb. 1866. In Rollin, HC151:281-283.

DELANY, MARTIN R. See Draper, HC41; Simmons,
HC163a:1007-1015 or HC163b:721-725; Sterling,
HC167; Ullmann, HC179; Brown, HC443:174-175;
Brown, HC445:460-461; Loggins, HC992:182-187;
Douglass, SE693; and Rollin, HC151.

SE536 DeLarge, R. C. "Speech on the Enforcement of the
Fourteenth Amendment." 6 April 1871. In Woodson, A177:295-299.

DELARGE, ROBERT C. See Christopher, HC24:97-
103.

SE537 Dellums, Ronald V. "The Coalition's the Thing." 30
Jan. 1972. Freedomways, 12 (1st Qrtr 1972), 7-16.

SE538 De Priest, Oscar. "Chicago and Woman's Suffrage."
Aug. 1915. In Aptheker, A2:95-96.

DE PRIEST, OSCAR. See Christopher, HC24:168-
175; and Gosnell, HC756:163-195.

SE539 Derrick, W. B. "Episcopal Address." May 1908.
In Smith, HC1183:247-251, excerpt.

DERRICK, W. B. See Simmons, HC163a:88-96 or
HC163b:37-42; and Woodson, HC1188:208-209.

SE540 Diggs, Charles C., Jr. "The Role of the American
Negro in American-African Relations." June 1959.
In Hill and Kilson, A92a:382-385 or A92b:448-452.

SE541 _____. "Address to the Mississippi NAACP Movement." 23 Aug. 1963. In Williams and Williams,
A175:159-166.

SE542 _____. "My Resignation from the United Nations
Delegation." 1972. Black Scholar, 3 (Feb. 1972),
2-6.

DIGGS, CHARLES C., JR. See Christopher, HC24:
209-214.

SE543 Domingo, W. A. "Socialism: The Negroes' Hope."
July 1919. In Aptheker, A2:260-262.

SE544 _____. "Restricted West Indian Immigration and
the American Negro." Oct. 1924. In Aptheker,
A2:466-470.

SE545 _____. "Gift of the Black Tropics." 1925. In
Locke, A113:341-349.

[Dorsey, Thomas, and Peter Spencer. See Spencer,
SE2119.]

SE546 Douglas, Roosevelt. "Address to the Congress of
African Peoples." Sept. 1970. In Jones, A101:82-
87.

SE547 _____. "The Pan-African Struggle in the Caribbean." Sept. 1970. In Jones, A101:154-156.

SE548 Douglass, Frederick. "Remarks at Hingham, Mass."
4 Nov. 1841. In Fulkerson, A76:442, 443, 443-444,
444-446. [Excerpt (of pp. 444-446) in Douglass,
A51:103-105.] [See "Observations of Parker Pillsbury," HC1111.]

SE549 _____. "Against the Liberty Party." 26 Jan.
       1842. In Fulkerson, A76:449-450.

SE550 _____. "The Slaveholder's Sermon." 28 Jan.
       1842. In Fulkerson, A76:453-454. [Cf. Quarles,
       HC143:363.]

SE551 _____. "In Defense of Abolitionism." 9 May
       1843. In Fulkerson, A76:458-459.

SE552 _____. "A Word About the Sunny South." 6 May
       1845. In Fulkerson, A76:463-466.

SE553 _____. "Slavery and the Question of Negro Inferi-
       ority." 20 Oct. 1845. In Fulkerson, A76:469-474.

SE554 _____. "Slavery and Texas." 3 Nov. 1845. In
       Fulkerson, A76:477-480.

SE555 _____. "The Folly of Our Opponents." 1845. In
       Douglass, A51:113-115.

       [_____. Narrative of the Life of Frederick Doug-
       lass, An American Slave (1845). See Douglass,
       HC40.]

SE556 _____. "The Golden Gift." 6 Jan. 1846. In
       Fulkerson, A76:483-485.

SE557 _____. "Send Back the Money!" 13 Feb. 1846.
       In Fulkerson, A76:488-493.

SE558 _____. "The Sinfulness of Slavery." 21 April
       1846. In Fulkerson, A76:496-501; in Douglass,
       A51:173-179; and in Woodson, A177:170-177.

SE559 _____. "American Slavery." 22 May 1846. In
       Fulkerson, A76:505-524; in Douglass, A51:154-165;
       in Smith and Robb, A156:32-45; and in Woodson,
       A177:158-170.

SE560 _____. "The Crime of the Free Church." 23
       Sept. 1846. In Fulkerson, A76:528-533.

SE561 _____. "Farewell Speech to the British People."
       30 March 1847. In Fulkerson, A76:538-560; and in
       Douglass, A51:206-233.

SE562 _____. "The Right of Invoking English Aid for the
Overthrow of American Slavery." 11 May 1847.
In Fulkerson, A76:567-574; in Bormann, A18:157-
165; in Douglass, A51:234-243; and in Long and Collier, A117:61-70.

SE563 _____. "Bibles for the Slaves." June 1847. In
Douglass, A51:253-255.

SE564 _____. "In Celebration of West India Emancipation." 2 Aug. 1847. In Fulkerson, A76:578-586.

SE565 _____. "The Churches and the Constitution: Sup-
porters of Slavery." 24 Sept. 1847. In Fulkerson,
A76:589-596; and in Douglass, A51:269-278.

SE566 _____. "The North and the Presidency." 17
March 1848. In Douglass, A51:296-299.

SE567 _____. "The Humanity of the Negro." 9 May 1848.
In Fulkerson, A76:601-606.

SE568 _____. "What Are the Colored People Doing for
Themselves." 14 July 1848. In Brotz, A27:203-
208; in Douglass, A51:314-320; and in Golden and
Rieke, A82:99-103.

SE569 _____. "The Struggle Between the Angel and the
Monster." 1 Aug. 1848. In Fulkerson, A76:609-
617; and in Douglass, A51:321-330.

SE570 _____. "Letter to Thomas Auld." 3 Sept. 1848.
In Douglass, A51:336-343; in Woodson, A176:202-
209; in Brown, A28:608-612, abr.; and in Katope and
Zolbrod, A105:370-374, abr.

SE571 _____, et al. "An Address to the Colored People of
the United States." 29 Sept. 1848. In Douglass,
A51:331-336; and in Brotz, A27:208-213.

SE572 Douglass, Frederick. "The Blood of the Slave on the
Skirts of the Northern People." 17 Nov. 1848. In
Douglass, A51:343-347.

SE573 _____. "Colonization." 26 Jan. 1849. In Douglass, A51:350-352.

SE574 _____. "The Address of Southern Delegates in
Congress to Their Constituents; or, the Address of
John C. Calhoun and Forty Other Thieves." 9 Feb.
1849. In Douglass, A51:353-360.

SE575 _____. "The Constitution and Slavery." 16 March
1849. In Douglass, A51:361-367.

SE576 _____. "The American Colonization Society: Our
Janus-Faced Enemy." 23 April 1849. In Fulkerson,
A76:621-627.

SE577 _____. "Great Britain and the Colonization of
American Negroes." 24 April 1849. In Fulkerson,
A76:631-635.

SE578 _____. "The State of American Morals." 8 May
1849. In Fulkerson, A76:638-640.

SE579 _____. "The Guilt of the Churches." 9 May 1849.
In Fulkerson, A76:643-653.

SE580 _____. "Colorphobia in New York!" 25 May 1849.
In Douglass, A51:384-387.

SE581 _____, and Henry Highland Garnet. "A Douglass-
Garnet Debate." May 1849. In Aptheker, A1:288-
290.

SE582 Douglass, Frederick. "Henry Clay and the American
Colonization Society." 31 May 1849. In Fulkerson,
A76:660-669; in Douglass, A51:387-399; in Brown,
A28:612-621; and in Woodson, A177:178-191.

SE583 _____. "Weekly Review of Congress." 15 March
1850. In Douglass, A52:109-115.

SE584 _____. "Am I a Man?" 7 May 1850. In Fulkerson, A76:675-678.

SE585 _____. "Shameful Abandonment of Principle." 30
May 1850. In Douglass, A52:121-125.

SE586 _____. "Prejudice Against Color." 13 June 1850.
In Douglass, A52:127-130.

SE587 _____. "The Power, Prevalence, and Nature of

Slavery." 1 Dec. 1850. In Fulkerson. A76:681-689; in Douglass, A52:132-139; and in Brotz, A27: 215-220.

SE588 _____. "The Guilt of the North." 8 Dec. 1850. In Fulkerson, A76:691-700; and in Douglass, A52: 139-149.

SE589 _____. "The North and the Fugitive Slave Law." 12 Jan. 1851. In Fulkerson, A76:702-711.

SE590 _____. "Change of Opinion Announced." 23 May 1851. In Douglass, A52:155-156.

SE591 _____. "Cuba and the United States." 4 Sept. 1851. In Douglass, A52:159-163.

SE592 _____. "Against Emigration from America." 18 Sept. 1851. In Fulkerson, A76:715-717.

SE593 _____. "What the Fourth of July Means to the Negro." 5 July 1852. In Fulkerson, A76:720-739; in Douglass, A52:181-204; in Foner, A74:106-129; in Golden and Rieke, A82:176-194; in Woodson, A177:197-223; and in Smith, HC1246:125-153.

SE594 _____. "The Platform of the Free Democracy: Popularity or Principle." 11 Aug. 1852. In Fulkerson, A76:742-745; and in Douglass, A52:206-209.

SE595 _____. "Agitation: The Grand Instrumentality." 23 Aug. 1852. In Fulkerson, A76:748-750.

SE596 _____. "Our Position in the Present Presidential Canvass." 10 Sept. 1852. In Douglass, A52:211-219.

SE597 _____. "Why Abolitionists Should Not Support Pierce or Scott." 14 Oct. 1852. In Fulkerson, A76:753-765.

SE598 _____. "Learn Trades or Starve!" 4 March 1853. In Douglass, A52:223-225.

SE599 _____. "To Harriet Beecher Stowe." 8 March 1853. In Douglass, A52:229-236; in Woodson, A176: 654-659, abr.; and in Douglass, HC38:284-290, abr.

SE600 _____. "A Few Words More About Learning
          Trades." 11 March 1853. In Douglass A52:236-238.

SE601 _____. "The Designs of the Slave Power." 11
          May 1853. In Fulkerson, A76:768-769.

SE602 _____. "The Present and Future of the Negro in
          America." 11 May 1853. In Fulkerson, A76:773-
          783; in Douglass, A52:243-254; in Griffiths, A87:
          251-255, abr.; in Woodson, A177-223-228, abr.;
          and in Douglass, HC39a:451-456 or HC39b:358-362,
          abr.

SE603 _____, et al. "The Claims of Our Common
          Cause." July 1853. In Douglass, A52:254-268.

SE604 Douglass, Frederick. "The Heroic Slave." 1853. In
          Griffiths, A86:174-239. Rpt. in Violence in the Black
          Imagination: Essays and Documents. Ed. Ronald T.
          Takaki. New York: Putnam's, 1972. Pages 37-77.

SE605 _____. "The Industrial College." 2 Jan. 1854.
          In Douglass, A52:272-275.

SE606 _____. "Slavery and the North." 24 Jan. 1854.
          In Fulkerson, A76:785-790.

SE607 _____. "Where Are We?" 10 May 1854. In Ful-
          kerson, A76:793-798.

SE608 _____. "Is It Right and Wise To Kill a Kidnapper?"
          2 June 1854. In Douglass, A52:284-289.

SE609 _____. "The Claims of the Negro Ethnologically
          Considered." 12 July 1854. In Fulkerson, A76:802-
          819; in Brotz, A27:226-244; in Golden and Rieke,
          A82:56-73; in Douglass, A52:289-309, abr.; and in
          Foner, A74:144-164, abr.

SE610 _____. "The Repeal of the Missouri Compromise."
          30 Oct. 1854. In Fulkerson, A76:823-837; and in
          Douglass, A52:316-332.

SE611 _____. "The Anti-Slavery Movement." 19 March
          1855. In Fulkerson, A76:841-864; and in Douglass,
          A52:333-359.

SE612 _____. "Self-Elevation--Rev. S. R. Ward." 13
April 1855. In Douglass, A52:359-362.

SE613 _____. "The Doom of the Black Power." 27 July
1855. In Douglass, A52:363-366; and in Brotz, A27:
244-247.

SE614 _____. "The True Ground Upon Which To Meet
Slavery." 24 Aug. 1855. In Douglass, A52:367-
369.

SE615 _____. "The New York Tribune--'Unpalatable
Counsel'--Our Political Rights and Duties." 28
Sept. 1855. In Douglass, A52:369-374.

SE616 _____. "The New York Tribune--'Its Unpalatable
Counsel'--'A Particular Kind of Effort.'" 5 Oct.
1855. In Douglass, A52:374-377.

SE617 _____. "The Republican Party--Our Position." 7
Dec. 1855. In Douglass, A52:379-383.

SE618 _____. "The Unholy Alliance of Negro Hate and
Anti-Slavery." 5 April 1856. In Douglass, A52:
385-387.

SE619 _____. "What Is My Duty as an Anti-Slavery
Voter?" 25 April 1856. In Douglass, A52:390-395.

SE620 _____. "The Danger of the Republican Movement."
28 May 1856. In Fulkerson, A76:869-873.

SE621 _____. "The Dred Scott Decision." 14 May 1857.
In Fulkerson, A76:876-891; in Douglass, A52:407-
424; and in Brotz, A27:247-262.

SE622 _____. "The True Significance of West India
Emancipation." 4 Aug. 1857. In Fulkerson, A76:
894-909; and in Douglass, A52:426-439, abr.

SE623 _____. "The Reproach and Shame of the American Government." 2 Aug. 1858. In Fulkerson,
A76:912-926.

SE624 _____. "African Civilization Society." Feb. 1859.
In Douglass, A52:441-447; and in Brotz, A27:262-
266.

SE625 _____. "Eulogy of William Jay." 12 May 1859.
In Fulkerson, A76:929-947.

SE626 _____. "Progress of Slavery." Aug. 1859. In
Douglass, A52:453-457.

SE627 _____. "The Ballot and the Bullet." Oct. 1859.
In Douglass, A52:457-458.

SE628 _____. "Capt. John Brown Not Insane." Nov.
1859. In Douglass, A52:458-460.

SE629 _____. "To My American Readers and Friends."
Nov. 1859. In Douglass, A52:463-467.

SE630 _____. "The Constitution: Pro-Slavery or Anti-
Slavery?" 26 March 1860. In Fulkerson, A76:
950-969; and in Douglass, A52:467-480, rev. and
abr.

SE631 _____. "The Chicago Nominations." June 1860.
In Douglass, A52:483-486.

SE632 _____. "The Republican Party." Aug. 1860. In
Douglass, A52:490-493.

SE633 _____. "The Democratic Party." Aug. 1860. In
Douglass, A52:493-494.

SE634 _____. "The Prospect in the Future." Aug. 1860.
In Douglass, A52:494-497.

SE635 _____. "Presidential Politics in the 1860 Campaign." 1 Aug. 1860. In Fulkerson, A76:972-984;
and in Douglass, A52:502-518.

SE636 _____. "Republican Opposition to the Right of Suffrage." Oct. 1860. In Douglass, A52:518-520.

SE637 _____. "The Abolition Movement Re-Organized."
Oct. 1860. In Douglass, A52:520-525.

SE638 _____. "The Late Election." Dec. 1860. In
Douglass, A52:526-530.

SE639 _____. "Equal Suffrage Defeated." Dec. 1860.
In Douglass, A52:530-532.

SE640 _____. "The John Brown Way." 3 Dec. 1860.
In Fulkerson, A76:988-992; and in Douglass, A52:
533-538.

SE641 _____. "A Plea for Free Speech in Boston." 10
Dec. 1860. In Douglass, A52:538-540; and in Foner,
A74:244-246.

SE642 _____. "Dissolution of the American Union." Jan.
1861. In Douglass, A53:57-62.

SE643 _____. "The Union and How To Save It." Feb.
1861. In Douglass, A53:62-65.

SE644 _____. "The Inaugural Address." April 1861. In
Douglass, A53:71-80.

SE645 _____. "The Future of the Abolition Crusade."
April 1861. In Douglass, A53:80-85.

SE646 _____. "Sudden Revolution in Northern Sentiment."
May 1861. In Douglass, A53:91-93.

SE647 _____. "How To End the War." May 1861. In
Douglass, A53:94-96.

SE648 _____. "Black Regiments Proposed." May 1861.
In Douglass, A53:96-98.

SE649 _____. "The Past and the Present." May 1861.
In Douglass, A53:100-104.

SE650 _____. "Position of the Government Toward Slavery." June 1861. In Douglass, A53:104-109.

SE651 _____. "Danger to the Abolition Cause." June
1861. In Douglass, A53:111-114.

SE652 _____. "The Decision of the Hour." 16 June
1861. In Douglass, A53:118-125.

SE653 _____. "The War and Slavery." Aug. 1961. In
Douglass, A53:125-130.

SE654 _____. "The Lessons of the Hour." 30 June
1861. In Douglass, A53:136-142.

SE655 _____. "Fighting Rebels with Only One Hand."
Sept. 1861. In Douglass, A53:151-154.

SE656 _____. "The Slave Power Still Omnipotent at
Washington." Jan. 1862. In Douglass, A53:185-
187.

SE657 _____. "The Reasons for Our Troubles." 14
Jan. 1862. In Douglass, A53:196-208.

SE658 _____. "The Future of the Negro People of the
Slave States." 12 Feb. 1862. In Douglass, A53:
210-225.

SE659 _____. "The Slaveholders' Rebellion." 4 July
1862. In Douglass, A53:242-259.

SE660 _____. "The Spirit of Colonization." Sept. 1862.
In Douglass, A53:260-266.

SE661 _____. "The President and His Speeches." Sept.
1862. In Douglass, A53:266-270.

SE662 _____. "Address to Our Readers and Friends in
Great Britain and Ireland." Oct. 1862. In Douglass, A53:278-281.

SE663 _____. "The Work of the Future." Nov. 1862.
In Douglass, A53:290-293.

SE664 _____. "What Shall Be Done with the Freed
Slaves?" Nov. 1862. In Douglass, A53:297-299.

SE665 _____. "A Day for Poetry and Song." 28 Dec.
1862. In Douglass, A53:310-312.

SE666 _____. "The Black Man, His Antecedents, His
Genius and His Achievements, by William Wells
Brown." Jan. 1863. In Douglass, A53:312-313.

SE667 _____. "The Proclamation and a Negro Army."
Feb. 1863. In Douglass, A53:321-337.

SE668 _____. " 'Men of Color, to Arms!' " 2 March
1863. In Woodson, A177:253-255; and in Douglass,
A53:317-319. [Note: A53 text dated 21 March
1865.]

SE669 _____. "Why Should a Colored Man Enlist?"
April 1863. In Douglass, A53:340-344.

SE670 _____. "Another Word to Colored Men." April
1863. In Douglass, A53:344-347.

SE671 _____. "The Present and Future of the Colored
Race in America." May 1863. In Douglass, A53:
347-359; in Brotz, A27:267-277; and in Littleton
and Burger, A112:40-48, abr.

SE672 _____. "Address for the Promotion of Colored
Enlistments." 6 July 1863. In Douglass, A53:361-
366; in Woodson, A177:247-253; and in Bracey, A21:
217-222.

SE673 _____. "The Commander-in-Chief and His Black
Soldiers." Aug. 1863. In Douglass, A53:369-372.

SE674 _____. "Our Work Is Not Done." Dec. 1863. In
Douglass, A53:378-386.

SE675 _____. "The Mission of the War." 13 Jan. 1864.
In Douglass, A53:386-403; and in Foner, A74:283-
300.

SE676 _____. "Statement to the National Convention of
Colored Men." 4 Oct. 1864. In Proceedings of the
National Convention of Colored Men, SE1877:8-9.

SE677 _____. "The Cause of the Negro People." Oct.
1864. In Douglass, A53:408-422.

SE678 _____. "What the Black Man Wants." April 1865.
In Douglass, A54:157-165; in Brotz, A27:277-284;
in Brawley, A24:208-215, abr.; and in Agitation for
Freedom: The Abolitionist Movement. Ed. Donald
G. Mathews. New York: Wiley, 1972. Pages 175-
183.

SE679 _____. "The Need for Continuing Anti-Slavery
Work." 10 May 1865. In Aptheker, A1:547-550;
and in Douglass, A54:166-169. [Note: A54 text
dated 9 May 1865.]

SE680 _____. "Address of Frederick Douglass at the
Inauguration of Douglass Institute." 1 Oct. 1865.

JNH, 54 (April 1969), 175-182; in Douglass, A54: 174-182; and in Foner, A74:327-333.

SE681 _____. "Address to President Johnson, with Interview." 7 Feb. 1866. In McPherson, HC692:52-55; in Douglass, A54:184-191; and in Cox and Cox, A41: 21-28. [See Lynch, SE1551.]

SE682 _____. "The Future of the Colored Race." May 1866. North American Review, 102 (May 1866), 437-440. Rpt. in Douglass, A54:193-196.

SE683 _____. "Reconstruction." Dec. 1866. Atlantic, 18 (Dec. 1866), 761-765. Rpt. in Douglass, A54: 198-204.

SE684 _____. "The Work Before Us." 27 Aug. 1868. In Douglass, A54:206-210.

SE685 _____. "My Son, Louis Douglass." Aug. 1869. In Douglass, A54:218-220.

SE686 _____. "Woman Suffrage Movement." 20 Oct. 1870. In Douglass, A54:231-233.

SE687 _____. "Howard University." 20 Oct. 1870. In Douglass, A54:233-235.

SE688 _____. "Woman and the Ballot." 27 Oct. 1870. In Douglass, A54:235-239.

SE689 _____. "Barbarism Against Civilization." 6 April 1871. In Douglass, A54:242-244.

SE690 _____. "Liberty of Speech South." 4 May 1871. In Douglass, A54:245-246.

SE691 _____. "The New Party Movement." 10 Aug. 1871. In Douglass, A54:254-257.

SE692 _____. "Politics an Evil to the Negro?" 24 Aug. 1871. In Douglass, A54:270-274.

SE693 _____. "Letter to Major Delany." 31 Aug. 1871. In Douglass, A54:276-281.

SE694 _____. "The Labor Question." 12 Oct. 1871.

In Douglass, A54:282-285.

SE695 _____. "Mixed Schools." 2 May 1872. In Douglass, A54:288-290.

SE696 _____. "Equality in Schools." 9 May 1872. In Douglass, A54:293-294.

SE697 _____. "U. S. Grant and the Colored People." 1872. Washington, 1872.

SE698 _____. "African Colonization." 19 Dec. 1872. In Douglass, A54:301-302.

SE699 _____. "Address Before the Tennessee Colored Agricultural and Mechanical Association." 18 Sept. 1873. In Brotz, A27:284-297.

SE700 _____. "Oration in Memory of Abraham Lincoln." 14 April 1876. In Douglass, A54:309-319; in Dunbar, A70:133-150; in Woodson, A177:516-527; and in Foner, A74:435-443, abr.

SE701 _____. "Speech on the Death of William Lloyd Garrison." 2 June 1879. In Cromwell, A42:251-258.

SE702 _____. "The Negro Exodus from the Gulf States." 12 Sept. 1879. In Douglass, A54:324-342; and in Woodson, A177:453-473. [See Greener, SE1040.]

SE703 _____. "The Color Line." June 1881. North American Review, 132 (June 1881), 567-577. Rpt. in Douglass, A54:342-352.

SE704 _____. "The United States Cannot Remain Half-Slave and Half-Free." 16 April 1883. In Douglass, A54:354-371; and in Golden and Rieke, A82: 220-233.

SE705 _____. "Address to the People of the United States." 24 Sept. 1883. In Douglass, A54:373-392; and in Foner, A74: 491-498, excerpt.

SE706 _____. "The Civil Rights Case." 22 Oct. 1883. In Douglass, A54:392-403; in Bracey, A21:335-344; in Brotz, A27:298-306; and in Cox and Cox, A41: 145-151, abr.

SE707 _____. "The Condition of the Freedmen." 8 Dec.
1883. Harper's Weekly, 27 (8 Dec. 1883), 782-783.
Rpt. in Douglass, A54:403-410.

SE708 _____. "The Future of the Negro." July 1884. In
Douglass, A54:411-413; and in Brotz, A27:307-308.

SE709 _____. "The Return of the Democratic Party to
Power." 1885. In Douglass, A54:413-426.

SE710 _____. "Southern Barbarism." April 1886. In
Douglass, A54:430-442.

SE711 _____. "The Future of the Colored Race." May
1886. In Brotz, A27:308-310.

SE712 _____. "The Woman's Suffrage Movement." April
1888. In Douglass, A54:448-454; and in Foner,
A74:518-520, excerpt.

SE713 _____. "The Nation's Problem." 16 April 1889.
In Brotz, A27:311-328; and in Foner, A74:521-536.

SE714 _____. "The Afro-American Press." 1890. In
Penn, A139:448-450. Rpt. in Douglass, A54:468-
469.

SE715 _____. "Lynch Law in the South." July 1892.
North American Review, 155 (July 1892), 17-24.

SE716 _____. "Introduction to the Reason Why the Colored American Is Not in the World's Columbian Exposition." 1892. In Douglass, A54:469-477.

SE717 _____. "Lecture on Haiti." 2 Jan. 1893. In
Douglass, A54:478-490.

SE718 _____. "The Lesson of the Hour ['Why Is the Negro Lynched?']." 9 Jan. 1894. In Douglass, A54:
491-523.

DOUGLASS, FREDERICK. See Fulkerson, A76; Braw-
ley, HC12:61-66; Brawley, HC13:51-58; Chesnutt,
HC22; Douglass, HC38; Douglass, HC39a or HC39b;
Douglass, HC40; Foner, HC54; Graham, HC64; Greg-
ory, HC67; Holland, HC83; Quarles, HC143; Quarles,
HC144; Simmons, HC163a:65-87 or HC163b:21-35;

Thompson, HC174; Washington, HC187; Himelhoch,
HC238; McClendon, HC250; Meier, HC253; Quarles,
HC259; Quarles, HC260; Shepperson, HC263; Walker,
HC269; Ruchkin, HC426; Bennett, HC437:66-74, 86-
89; Brown, HC443:180-187; Brown, HC445:435-440;
Cromwell, HC447:139-154; Quarles, HC534; Quarles,
HC592; Quarles, HC593:63-65; Loggins, HC992:134-
156; Fulkerson, HC1070; Hale, HC1078; Ladner,
HC1100; "Observations...," HC1111; Oliver, HC1112:
246-253; Du Bois, SE742; Grimké, SE1087; Grimké,
SE1121; Grimké, SE1122; Grimké, SE1173; and
Pickens, SE1818.

SE719 Douglass, H. Ford. "The Constitution Is Pro-Slavery."
Jan. 1851. In Aptheker, A1:316-318.

SE720 _____. "Address to the National Emigration Convention." 27 Aug. 1854. In Aptheker, A1:366-368.

SE721 _____. "Speech to a Mass Meeting of 'The Friends
of the Enslaved.'" 4 July 1860. In Foner, A74:232-
243; and in Fishel and Quarles, A72:211-213, excerpt.

DOUGLASS, H. FORD. See Hitchcock and Reynolds,
HC1088.

SE722 Douglass, Joseph H. "Some Significant Results of the
Emancipation, 1863-1963." 15 Feb. 1963. In Hill,
A93:327-332.

SE723 Douglass, William, and William Watkins. "Resolutions on Colonization." 21 March 1831. In Garrison, A77:21-22.

SE724 Douglass, William. "The God of Hope." pre-1854.
In Douglass, A55:9-27.

SE725 _____. "Pease in Christ." pre-1854. In Douglass, A55:29-52.

SE726 _____. "Spiritual Prosperity of Gaius." pre-1854.
In Douglass, A55:53-70.

SE727 _____. "Mutual Forbearance and Forgiveness."
pre-1854. In Douglass, A55:71-92.

SE728 _____. "The Sin of Grieving the Holy Spirit."

pre-1854. In Douglass, A55:93-110.

SE729 _____. "The Forbearance and Retributive Justice
of God." pre-1854. In Douglass, A55:111-132.

SE730 _____. "Price in Hand of the Foolish To Get Wisdom." pre-1854. In Douglass, A55:133-151.

SE731 _____. "The Shortness and Uncertainty of Time."
pre-1854. In Douglass, A55:153-171.

SE732 _____. "Admonition to Redeem the Time." pre-
1854. In Douglass, A55:173-192.

SE733 _____. "The Wisdom of Duly Considering the Lat-
ter End." pre-1854. In Douglass, A55:193-212.

SE734 _____. "A Sacred Nearness to God Recommended."
pre-1854. In Douglass, A55:213-230.

SE735 _____. "Happy End of the Servants of God." pre-
1854. In Douglass, A55:231-251.

DOUGLASS, WILLIAM. See Brown, HC443:271-272.

SE736 Downing, George T. "May Hungary Be Free." 9
Dec. 1851. In Foner, A74:102-104.

SE737 _____. "Address to a Convention of Colored Citizens." Aug. 1859. In Brown, HC443:250-253, excerpt.

SE738 _____. "Address to President Johnson." 7 Feb.
1866. In McPherson, HC692:52; in Douglass, A54:
183; and in Cox and Cox, A41:20-21.

SE739 _____, et al. "Reply of the Colored Delegation to
the President." 7 Feb. 1866. In McPherson,
HC692:55-56; in Douglass, A54:191-193; and in Cox
and Cox, A41:28-29. [See Lynch, SE1551.]

DOWNING, GEORGE T. See Simmons, HC163a:1003-
1006 or HC163b:718-719; Brown, HC443:250-253; and
Brown, HC445:474-475.

SE740 Drake, St. Clair. "The Responsibility of Men of Culture for Destroying the 'Hamitic' Myth." March

1959. <u>Presence Africaine</u>, Nos. 24-25 (Feb.-May 1959), 228-243.

[Drayton, Paul, and Henry Foster. See Foster, SE922.]

SE741 DRUM. "Constitution of the Dodge Revolutionary Union Movement." 1968. In Bracey, A22:551-555.

SE742 Du Bois, W. E. B. "Du Bois on Douglass." 1895. <u>JNH</u>, 49 (Oct. 1964), 264-268.

SE743 _____. "The Conservation of Races." 1897. American Negro Academy, Occasional Papers No. 2. Washington: The Academy, 1897. Rpt. in Du Bois, A67:19-31; and in Brotz, A27:483-492.

SE744 _____. "The Study of the Negro Problems." 19 Nov. 1897. In Du Bois, A63:229-247; and in Du Bois, A68:102-123.

SE745 _____. "Careers Open to College-Bred Negroes." June 1898. In Du Bois, A68:86-101.

SE746 _____. "To the Nations of the World" [Address of the Pan-African Congress]. 1900. In Du Bois, A68:125-127; and in Bracey, A21:388-390.

SE747 _____. "The Black North." Nov.-Dec. 1901. In Bracey, A21:520-534, abr.

SE748 _____. "Of Mr. Booker T. Washington and Others." 1903. In Du Bois, A65:42-54; in Du Bois, A63:354-366; in Bracey, A21:375-384; and in Brotz, A27:509-518.

SE749 _____. "The Talented Tenth." 1903. In <u>The Negro Problem</u>, A133:33-75. Rpt. in Du Bois, A67:31-51; and in Brotz, A27:518-533.

SE750 _____. "The Atlanta University Conferences." May 1903. <u>Charities</u>, 10 (2 May 1903), 435-439.

SE751 _____. "The Laboratory in Sociology at Atlanta University." May 1903. In Du Bois, A63:247-252.

SE752 _____. "Of the Training of Black Men." 1903.

In Du Bois, A65:88-109; and in Golden and Rieke, A82:117-127.

SE753 _____. "The Training of Negroes for Social Power." Oct. 1903. New York Outlook, 75 (17 Oct. 1903), 409-414. Rpt. in Dunbar, A70:491-504; and in Du Bois, A68:130-141.

SE754 _____. "The Joy of Living." 1904. Political Affairs, 44 (Feb. 1965), 35-44.

SE755 _____. "Credo." Oct. 1904. In Du Bois, A59:3-4; in Du Bois, A67:124-125; and in Du Bois, A68:142-143.

SE756 _____. "The Niagara Movement." 1905. In Du Bois, A68:144-150; and in Bracey, A21:384-388.

SE757 _____. "Declaration of Principles of the Niagara Movement." 1905. In Brotz, A27:533-537.

SE758 _____. "Atlanta University." 1905. In From Servitude to Service, A75:155-197.

SE759 _____. "St. Francis of Assisi." 15 June 1906. In Du Bois, A67:290-302; and in Cromwell, A42:273-284. [Note: A67 text dated June 1907.]

SE760 _____. "The Hampton Idea." 30 June 1906. In Du Bois, A60:6-15.

SE761 _____. "Resolutions of the Niagara Movement." 15 Aug. 1906. In Brotz, A27:537-539; in Du Bois, A68:170-173; and in Aptheker, A1:907-910. [Note: A68 text dated 16 Aug. 1906.]

SE762 _____. "The Economic Future of the Negro." 1906. In Du Bois, A68:150-169.

SE763 _____. "The Value of Agitation." March 1907. In Du Bois, A68:174-178; and in Foner, A74:665-668.

SE764 _____. "Is Race Separation Practicable?" Dec. 1907. American Journal of Sociology, 13 (May 1908), 834-838. Rpt. in Du Bois, A68:179-186.

SE765 _____. "The Economic Revolution in the South."

1907. In Washington and Du Bois, A171:79-122.

SE766 _____. "Religion in the South." 1907. In Washington and Du Bois, A171:125-191.

SE767 _____. "Galileo Galilei." June 1908. In Du Bois, A60:19-30.

SE768 _____. "Politics and Industry." 31 May 1909. In Proceedings of the National Negro Conference, 1909, A145:79-88. Rpt. in Du Bois, A68:187-195; and in Foner, A74:673-679.

SE769 _____. "Evolution of the Race Problem." 31 May 1909. In Proceedings of the National Negro Conference, 1909, A145:142-158. Rpt. in Du Bois, A68:196-210; and in Brotz, A27:539-549.

SE770 _____. "Race Prejudice." 5 March 1910. In Du Bois, A68:211-217; and in Golden and Rieke, A82:235-239.

SE771 _____. "The College-bred Community." 1910. In Du Bois, A60:31-40.

SE772 _____. "Starvation and Prejudice." June 1911. In Du Bois, A61:309-311.

SE773 _____. "The Negro Race in the United States of America." July 1911. In Spiller, A157:348-364.

SE774 _____. "How To Celebrate the Semicentennial of the Emancipation Proclamation." 2 Feb. 1912. In Du Bois, A68:226-229.

SE775 _____. "Divine Right." March 1912. In Aptheker, A2:53-54.

SE776 _____. "Votes for Women." Sept. 1912. In Aptheker, A2:56-57.

SE777 _____. "Disfranchisement." 1912. In Du Bois, A68:230-238.

SE778 _____. "Socialism and the Negro Problem." Jan. 1913. In Du Bois, A66:337-340; and in Du Bois, A68:239-243.

SE779 _____. "Negro in Literature and Art." 1913.
Annals of the American Academy of Political and
Social Science, 49 (Sept. 1913), 233-237. Rpt. in
Du Bois, A67:81-86.

SE780 _____. "The Immediate Program of the American
Negro." April 1915. In Littleton and Burger,
A112:54-58.

SE781 _____. "The African Roots of War." May 1915.
Atlantic, May 1915, pp. 707-714. Rpt. in Du Bois,
A66:360-371; and in Du Bois, A68:244-257. [Cf. Du
Bois, "The Hands of Ethiopia," in Du Bois, A59:56-
74, esp. 56-57, 74.]

SE782 _____. "Booker T. Washington." Dec. 1915. In
Du Bois, A61:311-312.

SE783 _____. "An Open Letter to Robert Russa Moton."
July 1916. In Du Bois, A61:312-314.

SE784 _____. "The Migration of Negroes." June 1917.
In Aptheker, A2:185-190.

SE785 _____. "The Problem of Problems." 27 Dec.
1917. In Du Bois, A68:258-267.

SE786 _____. "The Great Migration North." 1918. In
Du Bois, A68:268-271; and in Foner, A74:721-724.

SE787 _____. "The Future of Africa: A Platform." 6
Jan. 1919. In Du Bois, A68:273-275.

SE788 _____. "Marcus Garvey (I)." Dec. 1920. In Du
Bois, A61:318-321; in Du Bois, A64:173-176; in Du
Bois, A69:11-14; and in Clarke, A36:200-203.

SE789 _____. "Marcus Garvey (II)." Jan. 1921. In Du
Bois, A64:177-183; in Du Bois, A69:14-20; and in
Clarke, A36:203-209.

SE790 [_____.] "To the World: Manifesto of the Second
Pan-African Congress." Sept. 1921. In Du Bois,
A61:222-227; and in Aptheker, A2:337-342.

SE791 _____. "The U.N.I.A." Jan. 1923. In Du Bois,
A61:321-325.

SE792 _____. "Back to Africa." Feb. 1923. In Clarke,
A36:105-119.

SE793 _____. "A Lunatic or a Traitor." May 1924. In
Du Bois, A61:325-327; and in Du Bois, A64:184-186.

SE794 _____. "Diuturni Silenti." June 1924. In Du
Bois, A60:42-59.

SE795 _____. "Tuskegee and Moton." Sept. 1924. In
Du Bois, A61:317-318.

SE796 _____. "The Gentlemen's Agreement and the Negro Vote." Oct. 1924. In Aptheker, A2:461-466.

SE797 _____. "The Dilemma of the Negro." Oct. 1924.
American Mercury, 3 (Oct. 1924), 179-185. Rpt.
in Du Bois, A63:534-545.

SE798 _____. "The Amenia Conference: An Historic
Gathering." Sept. 1925. In Du Bois, A69:21-31.

SE799 _____. "Worlds of Color." 1925. Foreign Affairs, 3 (April 1925), 423-444. Rpt. in Locke,
A113:385-414.

SE800 _____. "Criteria of Negro Art." June 1926. In
Du Bois, A61:360-368; and in Du Bois, A67:86-96.

SE801 _____. "Marcus Garvey and the N.A.A.C.P."
Feb. 1928. In Aptheker, A2:570-572.

SE802 _____. "The Negro Citizen." 19 Dec. 1928. In
Du Bois, A69:32-42.

SE803 _____. "The Denial of Economic Justice to Negroes." Feb. 1929. In Du Bois, A69:44-46.

SE804 _____. "Shall the Negro Be Encouraged To Seek
Cultural Equality?" 17 March 1929. In Du Bois,
A69:47-54; and in Foner, A74:772-778.

SE805 _____. "Education and Work." 6 June 1930. In
Du Bois, A60:61-82; in Du Bois, A67:303-324; and
in Du Bois, A69:55-76.

SE806 _____. "Du Bois on James Weldon Johnson." 14

May 1931. JNH, 52 (July 1967), 224-227.

SE807 _____. "Beside the Still Waters." 1931. In Du
Bois, A61:371-375.

SE808 _____. "Where Do We Go From Here? (A Lecture on Negroes' Economic Plight)." May 1933. In
Du Bois, A67:146-163.

SE809 _____. "The Field and Function of the American
Negro College." June 1933. In Du Bois, A60:83-
102; in Du Bois, A67:51-69; and in Du Bois, A61:
145-153, excerpt.

SE810 _____. "On Being Ashamed of Oneself: An Essay
on Race Pride." Sept. 1933. In Du Bois, A61:64-
68.

SE811 _____. "William Monroe Trotter." May 1934. In
Du Bois, A61:350-351.

SE812 _____. "A Negro Nation Within the Nation." June
1935. In Du Bois, A67:69-78; and in Du Bois, A69:
77-86.

SE813 _____. "Does the Negro Need Separate Schools?"
1935. JNE, 4 (July 1935), 328-335. Rpt. in Du
Bois, A64:408-418; and in Du Bois, A66:278-288.

SE814 _____. "The Present Economic Problem of the
American Negro." Sept. 1935. In Du Bois, A67:
163-179.

SE815 _____. "Social Planning for the Negro, Past and
Present." 1936. JNE, 5 (Jan. 1936), 110-125.
Rpt. in Du Bois, A64:418-438.

SE816 _____. "What the Negro Has Done for the United
States and Texas." 1936. In Du Bois, A69:87-99.

SE817 _____. "On Discussion." 1936. In Du Bois, A67:
121-122.

SE818 _____. "The Revelation of Saint Orgne the Damned."
1938. In Du Bois, A60:103-126; in Du Bois, A67:
325-348; and in Du Bois, A69:100-123.

SE819 _____. "The Future of Wilberforce University."
13 June 1940. JNE, 9 (Oct. 1940), 553-570.

SE820 _____. "The Future of the Negro State University." 12 Jan. 1941. Wilberforce Univ. Quarterly,
2 (April 1941), 53-60. Rpt. in Du Bois, A60:129-
138.

SE821 _____. "The Vision of Phillis the Blessed (An Al-
legory of Negro American Literature in the Eighteenth and Nineteenth Centuries)." 1941. In Du
Bois, A67:96-115.

SE822 _____, and Ira De A. Reid. "Africa and World
Freedom." 1943. Phylon, 4 (2d Qrtr 1943, supplement), 8-12.

SE823 Du Bois, W. E. B. "Phylon: Science or Propaganda."
1944. Phylon, 5 (1st Qrtr 1944), 5-9.

SE824 _____. "Prospect of a World without Race Conflict." American Journal of Sociology, 49 (March
1944), 450-456. Rpt. in Du Bois, A64:526-537; in
Du Bois, A66:413-424; and in Du Bois, A69:124-136.

SE825 _____. "Jacob and Esau." 1944. In Du Bois,
A67:348-360; and in Du Bois, A69:137-149.

SE826 _____. "The Negro and Imperialism." 15 Nov.
1944. In Du Bois, A69:150-160.

SE827 _____. "My Evolving Program for Negro Freedom." 1944. In Logan, A115:31-70.

SE828 _____. "The Pan-African Movement." Oct. 1945.
In Du Bois, A69:161-178.

SE829 _____. "Human Rights for All Minorities." 7 Nov.
1945. In Du Bois, A69:179-191.

SE830 _____. "Bound by the Color Line." Feb. 1946.
In Du Bois, A69:192-194.

SE831 _____. "The Future and Function of the Private
Negro College." 10 June 1946. In Du Bois, A60:
139-148.

SE832 _____. "Behold the Land!" 20 Oct. 1946. Free-
domways, 4 (Winter 1964), 8-15. Rpt. in Du Bois,
A67:361-367; in Du Bois, A69:195-201; and in Foner,
A74:837-842.

SE833 _____. "An Appeal to the World." 1946. In Du
Bois, A69:202-221.

SE834 _____. "We Must Know the Truth." 26 June 1947.
In Du Bois, A69:222-227.

SE835 _____. "Race Relations in the United States, 1917-
1947." 1948. Phylon, 9 (3rd Qrtr 1948), 234-247.
Rpt. in Sternsher, A158:29-44.

SE836 _____. "The Nature of Intellectual Freedom."
March 1949. In Du Bois, A69:232-234; and in
Marxism and Art: Essays Classic and Contemporary.
Ed. Maynard Solomon. New York: Knopf, 1973.
Pages 259-260.

SE837 _____. "America's Pressing Problems." Aug.
1949. In Du Bois, A69:235-241; and in Du Bois,
HC44:351-355.

SE838 _____. "Senate Campaign Speech." 5 Oct. 1950.
In Du Bois, A64:601-608.

SE839 _____. "I Take My Stand." 29 April 1951. In
Du Bois, A69:242-249.

SE840 _____. "The Negro and the Warsaw Ghetto." 15
April 1952. In Du Bois, A69:250-255.

SE841 _____. "What Is Wrong with the United States?"
13 May 1952. In Du Bois, A58:202-205; and in Du
Bois, A69:256-258.

SE842 _____. In Battle for Peace: The Story of My
83rd Birthday. New York: Masses, 1952.

SE843 _____. "One Hundred Years of Negro Freedom."
Jan. 1953. In Du Bois, A69:259-267.

SE844 _____. "On the Future of the American Negro."
1953. In Du Bois, A69:268-277.

SE845 _____. "Save the Rosenbergs." c. 1953. In Du
Bois, A64:610-616.

SE846 _____. "Two Hundred Years of Segregated
Schools." Feb. 1955. In Du Bois, A69:278-284.

SE847 _____. "If Eugene Debs Returned." 28 Nov. 1955.
In Du Bois, A69:285-290.

SE848 _____. "The American Negro and the Darker
World." 30 April 1957. Freedomways, 8 (Summer
1968), 245-251.

SE849 _____. "Last Message to the World." 26 June
1957. In Du Bois, A69:326.

SE850 _____. "Advice to a Great-Grandson." March
1958. In Du Bois, A69:291-293.

SE851 _____. "Tribute to Paul Robeson." 9 April 1958.
In Du Bois, A69:294-296; and in Du Bois, HC44:
396-397.

SE852 _____. "The Negro and Socialism." 1958. In
Du Bois, A67:179-193; and in Du Bois, A69:297-311.

SE853 _____. "The Future of All Africa Lies in Socialism." 1958. In Du Bois, A64:657-661; in Du Bois,
A67:252-257; and in Du Bois, A69:312-315.

SE854 _____. "Hail Humankind!" 22 Feb. 1959. In Du
Bois, A69:316-321; and in Du Bois, HC44:405-408.

SE855 _____. "Whither Now and Why." 2 April 1960.
Qrtrly Rev. of Higher Education Among Negroes,
28 (July 1960), 135-141. Rpt. in Du Bois, A60:
149-158.

SE856 _____. "The United States and the Negro." 1961.
Freedomways, 1 (Spring 1961), 11-19.

SE857 _____. "Africa and the French Revolution." 1961.
Freedomways, 1 (Summer 1961), 136-151.

SE858 _____. "Conference of Encyclopedia Africana."
15 Dec. 1962. Freedomways, 3 (Winter 1963), 28-
30. Rpt. in Du Bois, A69:322-325.

DU BOIS, W. E. B.   See Aptheker, B1; Clarke, A37;
Logan, A114; Brawley, HC12:185-190; Brawley,
HC13:195-202; Broderick, HC16; Bullock, HC19:67-
71; Du Bois, HC43; Du Bois, HC44; Du Bois, HC45;
Du Bois, HC46; Lovett, HC103; McGill, HC108;
Rudwick, HC152; Shaw, HC161; Contee, HC218; De
Marco, HC220; Gilbert, HC230; Guzman, HC233;
Harding, HC235; Partington, HC257; Paschal, HC258;
Rogers, HC261; Troy, HC267; Wesley, HC273; Ben-
nett, HC437:115-133; Brisbane, HC442:44-63; Cruse,
HC448:39-43, 330-335; Ferris, HC451:910-920;
Thorpe, HC475:310-334; Newman, HC828; Rudwick,
HC830; Contee, HC840; Brodwin, HC1049; Chaffee,
HC1058; Rudwick, HC1124; Stuckey, HC1272; Bela-
fonte, SE80; Bond, SE175; Garvey, SE970; Garvey,
SE1011; King, SE1470; and see "The Problem of Col-
or in the Twentieth Century: A Memorial to W. E.
B. Du Bois." Journal of Human Relations, 14 (Fall
1966), 1-184.

SE859 Dumas, Alexander. "Alexander Dumas, Fils." 11
Feb. 1875. In Dunbar, A70:95-96.

SE860 Dunbar, Alice Moore. "The Life of Social Service as
Exemplified in David Livingstone." 7 March 1913.
In Dunbar, A70:425-444.

SE861 Dunbar, Paul Laurence. "Representative American
Negroes." 1903. In The Negro Problem, A133:
189-209.

DUNBAR, PAUL LAURENCE. See Brawley, HC12:
158-166; Bone, HC964:38-43; Gloster, HC981:46-56;
and Turner, HC1008.

SE862 Dunn, Oscar J. "We Ask an Equal Chance in the
Race of Life." 31 July 1868. In Foner, A74:356-
357.

SE863 Durham, J. J. "Harmony of the Law and the Gospel."
1890. In Brawley, A25:113-115.

DURHAM, J. J. See Simmons, HC163a:878-882 or
HC163b:622-624.

SE864 Duster, Troy. "The Third World College and the
Colonial Analogy." Feb. 1969. In Wallerstein and

Starr, A163:340-343.

SE865 Dymally, Mervyn M.   "The Rise of Black Political
        Leadership in California."   1972.   In Wright, A180:
        32-43.

SE866 Easton, Hosea.   "Address Delivered Before the Col-
        ored Population of Providence."   27 Nov. 1828.   In
        Garrison, A77:63-64, excerpt.

SE867 _____.   "A Treatise on the Intellectual Character,
        and Civil and Political Condition of the Colored
        People of the U. States; and the Prejudice Exer-
        cised towards Them."   1837.   In Porter, A142:
        orig. pag.; and in Osofsky, A135:66-71, excerpt.

SE868 [Edge, Elder.]   "Why We Come to Church."   9 Aug.
        1942.   In Pipes, HC1197:37-38.

SE869 Elliott, Robert B.   "The Civil Rights Bill."   6 Jan.
        1874.   In Foner, A74:385-398; in Golden and Rieke,
        A82:203-217; in Woodson, A177:309-328; and in Dun-
        bar, A70:67-88, abr.

SE870 _____.   "Eulogy of Charles Sumner."   14 April
        1874.   In Woodson, A177:502-516.

        ELLIOTT, ROBERT B.   See Brawley, HC12:133-138;
        Christopher, HC24:69-77; Simmons, HC163a:466-473
        or HC163b:310-314; Brown, HC445:503-504; and
        Cromwell, HC447:179-187.

SE871 Ellison, Ralph.   "Brave Words for a Startling Occa-
        sion."   27 Jan. 1853.   In Ellison, A71:102-106;
        and in Long and Collier, A118:603-606.

        ELLISON, RALPH.   See Brown, HC1052.

SE872 Ennals, Samuel, and Philip Bell.   "Resolutions of the
        People of Color ... with an Address to the Citizens
        of New York, in Answer to Those of the New York
        Colonization Society."   25 Jan. 1831.   In Garrison,
        A77:13-17; in Porter, A141:281-285; and in Aptheker,
        A1:109, excerpt.

SE873 Evers, Charles.   "Black Americans and the Press:
        Comment."   1968.   In Littleton and Burger, A112:

390-392; and in The Black American and the Press.
Ed. Jack Lyle. Los Angeles: Ward Ritchie, 1968.
Pages 68-70.

SE874 _____. "We Are Going To Make It Better for
Blacks and Whites." May 1969. In Foner, A74:
1167-1169; and in Littleton and Burger, A112:271-
273.

EVERS, CHARLES. See Berry, HC9; Evers, HC49;
and Rugaber, HC262.

SE875 Faduma, Orishatukeh. "Religious Beliefs of the Yo-
ruba People in West Africa." 13 Dec. 1895. In
Bowen, A20:31-36.

SE876 _____. "Success and Drawback of Missionary
Work in Africa by an Eye-Witness." 14 Dec. 1895.
In Bowen, A20:125-136.

SE877 _____. "The Defects of the Negro Church." 1904.
American Negro Academy, Occasional Papers No.
10. Washington: The Academy, 1904.

SE878 Fanon, Frantz. The Wretched of the Earth. Tr.
Constance Farrington. New York: Grove, 1966.

FANON, FRANTZ. See Zolberg and Zolberg, HC958.

SE879 Faris, Ellsworth. "The Natural History of Race
Prejudice." c. 1927. In Johnson, A100:89-94.

SE880 Farmer, James, and Malcolm X. "Separation or Integration" [debate]. 7 March 1962. In Golden and
Rieke, A82:422-439; and in Broderick and Meier,
A26:358-383. [Note: A26 text reverses order of
opening speeches.]

SE881 Farmer, James. "Message to the March on Washington." 28 Aug. 1963. In Speeches by the Leaders,
A131:n. pag.

SE882 _____. "Guilty Bystanders." 22 Sept. 1963.
Liberation, 8 (Oct. 1963), 9. Rpt. in Goodman,
A83:346-349.

SE883 _____. "If Not Now, When?" 26 Oct. 1964. In

Hale, A90:338-354.

SE884 _____. "Annual Report to the National CORE Convention." 1 July 1965. In Williams and Williams,
A175:169-177; and in Broderick and Meier, A26:
422-428.

SE885 _____. Freedom--When? New York: Random,
1965.
Contains: "A Southern Tale," pp. 3-22.
" '... But When Will the Demonstrations End?"
pp. 25-50.
"We Are Soldiers," pp. 53-82.
"Black Nationalists and White Liberals," pp. 85-
107.
"Integration or Desegregation," pp. 111-128.
"Africa Revisited," pp. 131-165.
"Freedom--When?" pp. 169-197.

SE886 _____. "The 'Movement' Now." 25 Feb. 1967.
In Foner, A74:1041-1048.

SE887 _____. "Are White Liberals Obsolete in the Black
Struggle?" Jan. 1968. Progressive, 22 (Jan. 1969),
13-16. Rpt. in Littleton and Burger, A112:85-92.

SE888 _____, and Algernon D. Black. "The Negro and
American Values" [conversation]. March 1968.
Humanist, 28 (March-April 1968), 7-9. Rpt. in
Moss, A130:42-50.

SE889 Farmer, James. "Education Is the Answer." April
1969. Today's Education, 58 (April 1969), 25-26.
Rpt. in Littleton and Burger, A112:205-207.

FARMER, JAMES. See Meier and Rudwick, HC886;
and Boulware, HC1023:220-222.

SE890 Farrakhan, Louis. "Address to the Congress of African Peoples." Sept. 1970. In Jones, A101:44-56.

SE891 Fauset, Jessie. "Some Notes on Color." March
1922. In Aptheker, A2:354-358.

SE892 Ferris, William H. "Alexander Crummell: An
Apostle of Negro Culture." 1920. American Negro
Academy, Occasional Papers No. 20. Washington:

The Academy, 1920.

SE893 "The First Colored Convention." Oct. 1859. In Bell,
A10:n. pag.; and in Aptheker, A1:98-102, abr.
[See SE417.]

SE894 Fisk University Students. "Basic Concepts of the
Black University." Feb. 1970. In Wallerstein and
Starr, A163:360-361.

SE895 Fleetwood, Christian A. "The Negro as a Soldier."
Nov. 1895. In Dunbar, A70:187-204.

SE896 Flipper, J. S. "Is the Young Negro an Improvement,
Morally, on His Father?" 1902. In Culp, A46:257-
259.

SE897 _____. "Episcopal Address." May 1920. In
Smith, HC1183:317-321, excerpt.

SE898 Florence, Franklin. "The Meaning of Black Power."
10 Sept. 1967. In Smith, HC1246:161-165.

SE899 Fontaine, William. "Segregation and Desegregation in
the United States: A Philosophical Analysis." 20
Sept. 1956. Presence Africaine, Nos. 8-10 (June-
Nov. 1956), 154-176.

SE900 _____. "Toward a Philosophy of the American Negro Literature." March 1959. Presence Africaine,
Nos. 24-25 (Feb.-May 1959), 165-176.

SE901 Ford, James W. "The Bankruptcy of Capitalism and
Capitalist Education." 4 Aug. 1932. In Aptheker,
A2:726-733, abr.

SE902 _____. "The Right of Revolution for the Negro
People." Aug. 1935. In Foner, A74:801-807.

SE903 _____. "The Vital Problem of the Right of Trade
Unions in Countries in Africa." 1947. JNE, 16
(Spring 1947), 251-256. Rpt. in Hill and Kilson,
A92a:369-375 or A92b:433-440.

SE904 Forman, James. "Black Manifesto." 26 April 1969.
In Lecky and Wright, A110:114-126; in Golden and
Rieke, A82:537-545; in Littleton and Burger, A112:

394-400; and in O'Neill, A134:235-245.

SE905 _____. "Control, Conflict and Change: The Under-
lying Concepts of the Black Manifesto." 1969. In
Lecky and Wright, A110:34-51.

FORMAN, JAMES. See Lecky and Wright, A110.

SE906 Forten, James. "A Late Bill Before the Senate of
Pennsylvania." 1813. In Woodson, A177:42-51; and
in Aptheker, A1:60-66, abr.

SE907 _____, and Russell Parrott. "Resolutions on Colonization." Jan. 1817. In Garrison, A77:9-10; and
in Aptheker, A1:71-72.

SE908 _____. "An Address to the Humane and Benevo-
lent Inhabitants of the City and County of Philadelphia." 10 Aug. 1817. In Porter, A141:265-268;
in Garrison, A77:10-13; and in Woodson, A177:52-55.
[Note: A141 text dated (p. 268) 10 Dec. 1818.]

SE909 Forten, James, William Whipper, and Robert Purvis.
"To the Honorable the Senate and House of Repre-
sentatives of the Commonwealth of Pennsylvania."
Jan. 1832. In Aptheker, A1:126-133.

FORTEN, JAMES. See Billington, HC11; and Purvis,
SE1883.

SE910 Forten, James, Jr. "An Address Delivered Before the
Ladies' Anti-Slavery Society of Philadelphia." 14 April 1836. In Fishel and Quarles, A72:191-193, excerpt.

SE911 _____. "An Address Delivered Before the American Moral Reform Society." 17 Aug. 1837. In
Porter, A141:225-241.

SE912 Fortune, T. Thomas. "The Colored Man as an Independent Force in Our Politics." 27 June 1882. In
Fortune, HC783a:112-130 or HC783b:67-78.

SE913 _____. "Condition of the Colored Population,
1883." 17 Sept. 1883. In Cox and Cox, A41:364-
373.

[_____. See Fortune, HC783a or HC783b.]

SE914 _____. "The Present Relations of Labor and Capital." 20 April 1886. In Foner, A74:507-510.

SE915 _____. "Address to the Afro-American League."
Jan. 1890. In Bracey, A22:212-222; in Foner,
A74:557-561, excerpt; and in Aptheker, A1:703-705,
excerpt.

SE916 _____. "The Afro-American Editor's Mission."
1890. In Penn, A139:479-483.

SE917 _____. "The Agitator and His Mission." c. 1890.
In Golden and Rieke, A82:492.

SE918 _____. "The Logic of Revolutions." c.1890.
In Golden and Rieke, A82:491-492.

SE919 _____. "The Nationalization of Africa." 14 Dec.
1895. In Bowen, A20:199-204; and in Hill and Kilson, A92a:304-309 or A92b:352-359.

SE920 _____. "What Should Be the Negro's Attitude in
Politics?" 1902. In Culp, A46:227-231.

SE921 _____. "The Negro's Place in American Life at
the Present Day." 1903. In The Negro Problem,
A133:213-234.

FORTUNE, T. THOMAS. See Penn, A139:133-138;
Simmons, HC163a:785-791 or HC163b:549-554;
Thornbrough, HC175; and Drake, HC222.

SE922 Foster, Henry, and Paul Drayton. "Resolutions on
Colonization." 14 July 1831. In Garrison, A77:28-
29.

[Francis, Abner H., and Lewis Cork. See Cork,
SE435.]

SE923 Franklin, John Hope. "Desegregation--The South's
Newest Dilemma." 8 Sept. 1955. JNE, 25 (Spring
1956), 95-100.

SE924 _____. "The New Negro History." 1957. JNH,
43 (April 1957), 89-97.

SE925 _____. " 'Legal' Disfranchisement of the Negro."

1957. JNE, 26 (Summer 1957), 241-248.

SE926 _____. "America's Window to the World: Her
Race Problem." 26 Oct. 1958. In Hill, A93:201-
211; and in Foner, A74:907-916, abr.

SE927 _____. "Booker T. Washington, the Man and the
Educator." 22 April 1959. In Hill, A93:212-219.

SE928 _____. "A Century of Civil War Observance."
12 Oct. 1961. JNH, 47 (April 1962), 97-107.

SE929 _____. "Civil Rights in American History." Dec.
1962. Progressive, 26 (Dec. 1962), 6-9.

SE930 _____. "George Washington Williams and Africa."
1971. [Washington]: Dept. of History, Howard
Univ., 1971.

SE931 Frazier, E. Franklin. "The Negro and Non-Resistance." March 1924. In Aptheker, A2:449-451.

SE932 _____. "Durham: Capital of the Black Middle
Class." 1925. In Locke, A113:333-340.

SE933 _____. "The Pathology of Race Prejudice." June
1927. Forum, 70 (June 1927), 856-862. Rpt. in
Brown, A28:904-909.

SE934 _____. "Racial Self-Expression." c. 1927. In
Johnson, A100:119-121.

FRAZIER, E. FRANKLIN. See Edwards, B8.

SE935 "A Free Negro." "Slavery." 1789. American Museum, 6 (July 1789), 77-80. Rpt. in Woodson, A177:
25-30.

SE936 Fuller, Howard, "Address to the Congress of African
Peoples." Sept. 1970. In Jones, A101:57-63.

SE937 Fuller, Hoyt. "Identity, Reality and Responsibility:
Elusive Poles in the World of Black Literature."
23 Oct. 1971. JNH, 57 (Jan. 1972), 83-98.

SE938 Fuller, Thomas O. "Post-Election Speech." 1898.
In Aptheker, A1:815-816.

FULLER, THOMAS O. See Fuller, HC59.

SE939 [Fulse, Elder.] "Elijah, the Man of God." 9 Aug.
       1942. In Pipes, HC1197:44-45.

SE940 Gaines, W. J. "An Appeal to Our Brothers in
       White." 1897. In Gaines, SE941:213-218. Rpt. in
       Dunbar, A70:257-262.

SE941 _____. The Negro and the White Man. 1897; rpt.
       New York: Negro Universities Press, 1969.

SE942 Galamison, Milton A. "Integration Must Work--Noth-
       ing Else Can." 27 March 1963. Freedomways, 3
       (Spring 1963), 215-217. Rpt. in Foner, A74:960-
       961.

SE943 Garnet, Henry Highland. "An Address." May 1840.
       In Golden and Rieke, A82:169-174; and in Ofari,
       HC126:127-135.

SE944 _____. "Speech Delivered at the Liberty Party
       Convention." Feb. 1842. In Ofari, HC126:138-144.

SE945 _____. "An Address to the Slaves of the United
       States of America." 16 Aug. 1843. In Barbour,
       A8:34-41; in Bracey, A21:192-198; in Foner, A74:
       82-89; in Golden and Rieke, A82:478-483; in Robin-
       son, A149:85-92; in Smith and Robb, A156:22-30; in
       Stuckey, A160:165-173; in Woodson, A177:150-157;
       and in Ofari, HC126:144-153. [See Minutes of the
       National Convention, SE1720.]

SE946 _____. "The Past and the Present Condition, and
       the Destiny, of the Colored Race: A Discourse De-
       livered at the Fifteenth Anniversary of the Female
       Benevolent Society of Troy, N.Y." 14 Feb. 1848.
       1848; rpt. Miami: Mnemosyne, 1969. Rpt. in
       Ofari, HC126:160-183; and in Brotz, A27:199-202,
       excerpt.

       [_____, and Frederick Douglass. See Douglass,
        SE581.]

SE947 Garnet, Henry Highland. "Speech at an Enthusiastic
       Meeting of the Colored Citizens of Boston." 29
       Aug. 1859. In Stuckey, A160:177-193.

SE948 _____. "Eulogy of John Brown." 1859. In Ofari,
HC126:186-187.

SE949 _____. "Speech Delivered at Cooper's Institute."
1860. In Ofari, HC126:183-185.

SE950 _____. "A Memorial Discourse." 12 Feb. 1865.
In Dunbar, A70:107-124; in Foner, A74:308-316; in
Ofari, HC126:187-203; and in Fishel and Quarles,
A72:255-256, excerpt.

SE951 _____. "A Plea in Behalf of the Cuban Revolution." 13 Dec. 1872. In Foner, A74:381-384.

GARNET, HENRY HIGHLAND. See Brawley, HC13:
47-50; Brewer, HC14; Ofari, HC126; Simmons,
HC163a:656-661 or HC163b:453-456; Brown, HC443:
149-151; Brown, HC445:457-459; Cromwell, HC447:
126-129; Pease and Pease, HC532:162-190; Loggins,
HC992:191-195; Mann, HC1103; Shiffrin, HC1133;
Smith, HC1136; Woodson, HC1188:153-155; and Crummell, SE470.

SE952 Garvey, Marcus. "The British West Indies in the
Mirror of Civilization: History Making by American Negroes." Oct. 1913. In Clarke, A36:77-82.

SE953 _____. "A Talk with Afro-West Indians: The Negro Race and Its Problems." c. Jan. 1916. In
Clarke, A36:83-87.

SE954 _____. "West Indies in the Mirror of Truth."
Jan. 1917. In Clarke, A36:88-91.

SE955 _____, et al. "Declaration of Rights of the Negro
Peoples of the World." 15 Aug. 1920. In Garvey,
A79:135-143; in Clarke, A36:443-451; and in Osofsky,
A135:296-304.

SE956 Garvey, Marcus. "Second International Convention of
Negroes." Aug. 1921. In Garvey, A78a:93-97 or
A78b:71-74; in Bracey, A21:424-427; and in Golden
and Rieke, A82:395-398.

SE957 _____. "Disarmament." 6 Nov. 1921. In Garvey,
A79:110-115.

SE958 _____. "Emancipation Day Address." 1 Jan. 1922.
In Garvey, A78a:79-82 or A78b:59-61.

SE959 _____. "The Resurrection of the Negro." 16
April 1922. In Garvey, A78a:87-92 or A78b:66-70.

SE960 _____. "The Principles of the Universal Negro
Improvement Association." 25 Nov. 1922. In Garvey, A79:93-100; in Foner, A74:749-757; in Long
and Collier, A118:357-364; and in Smith and Robb,
A156:101-109.

SE961 _____. "Christ the Greatest Reformer." 24 Dec.
1922. In Garvey, A79:27-33.

SE962 _____. "Race Assimilation." c. 1922. In Garvey,
A78a:26 or A78b:21-22; in Brotz, A27:553-554; and
in Golden and Rieke, A82:391-392.

SE963 _____. "Man Know Thyself." c. 1922. In Garvey, A78a:38-39 or A78b:30-31; and in Golden and
Rieke, A82:393-394.

SE964 _____. "The True Solution of the Negro Problem."
c. 1922. In Garvey, A78a:52-53 or A78b:38-39; and
in Brotz, A27:554-555.

SE965 _____. "Shall the Negro Be Exterminated?"
c. 1922. In Garvey, A78a:63-67 or A78b:46-49.

SE966 _____. "Africa for the Africans." c. 1922. In
Garvey, A78a:68-72 or A78b:50-53.

SE967 _____. "The Future as I See It." c. 1922. In
Garvey, A78a:73-78 or A78b:54-58; and in Barbour,
A8:54-58.

SE968 _____. "An Answer to His Many Critics." Jan.
1923. In Golden and Rieke, A82:381-386; and in
Clarke, A36:247-252, abr.

SE969 _____. "Who and What Is a Negro?" 16 Jan.
1923. In Garvey, A79:18-21; and in Brotz, A27:560-
562.

SE970 _____. "W. E. Burghardt Du Bois as a Hater of
Dark People." Feb. 1923. In Garvey, A79:310-320.

SE971 _____. "The Negro's Place in World Reorganization." 24 March 1923. In Garvey, A79:34-36; in Brotz, A27:566-568; in Brown, A28:677-681; in Clarke, A36:312-313, abr.; and in Hill, A93:50-54. [Note: A36 text dated 1 Feb. 1930; A93 text includes (pp. 53-54) opening paragraphs of Garvey, SE987:37-38.]

SE972 _____. "Will Negroes Succumb to the White Man's Plan of Economic Starvation?" 31 March 1923. In Garvey, A79:44-50.

SE973 _____. "Africa's Wealth." 18 April 1923. In Garvey, A79:63-68.

SE974 _____. "Last Speech Before Imprisonment." 17 June 1923. In Garvey, A79:180-183; and in Clarke, A36:150-151, excerpt.

SE975 _____. "Address to Jury at Close of Trial." June 1923. In Garvey, A79:184-216.

SE976 _____. "An Analysis of Warren G. Harding." c. July 1923. In Garvey, A79:51-54.

SE977 _____. "The Crime of Injustice." 2 Aug. 1923. In Garvey, A79:11-14.

SE978 _____. "An Exposé of the Caste System Among Negroes." 31 Aug. 1923. In Garvey, A79:55-61.

SE979 _____. "The Negro's Greatest Enemy." Sept. 1923. In Garvey, A79:124-134; and in Aptheker, A2:393-403.

SE980 _____. "Statement to Press on Release on Bail." 10 Sept. 1923. In Garvey, A79:228-230.

SE981 _____. "First Speech After Release from Prison." 13 Sept. 1923. In Garvey, A79:231-235.

SE982 _____. "A Journey of Self-Discovery." Sept. 1923. In Clarke, A36:71-76.

SE983 _____. "An Appeal to the Soul of White America." 2 Oct. 1923. In Garvey, A79:1-6; in Aptheker, A2:403-408; in Brotz, A27:555-559; and in Golden and Rieke, A82:377-381.

SE984 _____. "Racial Reforms and Reformers."
c. 1923. In Garvey, A79:7-10; and in Brotz, A27:
559-560.

SE985 _____. "World Materialism." c. 1923. In Garvey, A79:15-17.

SE986 _____. "An Appeal to the Conscience of the Black
Race To See Itself." c. 1923. In Garvey, A79:
22-26; in Brotz, A27:562-566; in Littleton and Burger, A112:62-66; in Long and Collier, A118:365-369;
and in Osofsky, A135:291-295.

SE987 _____. "Aims and Objects of Movement for Solution of Negro Problem." c. 1923. In Garvey,
A79:37-43; and in Brotz, A27:568-572, abr.

SE988 _____. "The Negro, Communism, Trade Unionism and His (?) Friend: 'Beware of Greeks Bearing Gifts.' " c. 1923. In Garvey, A79:69-71.

SE989 _____. "Capitalism and the State." c. 1923. In
Garvey, A79:72-73.

SE990 _____. "Governing the Ideal State." c. 1923. In
Garvey, A79:74-76.

SE991 _____. "The 'Colored' or Negro Press." c. 1923.
In Garvey, A79:77-80.

SE992 _____. "History of the Negro." c. 1923. In
Garvey, A79:82-83.

SE993 _____. "What We Believe." 1 Jan. 1924. In
Garvey, A79:81.

SE994 _____. "Letter to Guy M. Walker." 10 March
1924. In Clarke, A36:152-155.

SE995 _____. "Racial Ideals." 16 March 1924. In
Garvey, A79:118-123; and in Brotz, A27:572-576.

SE996 _____. "Fourth International Convention of the
Negro Peoples of the World." 1 Aug. 1924. In
Garvey, A79:101-109.

SE997 _____. "African Fundamentalism." 1925. In
Clarke, A36:156-159.

SE998 _____. "First Message to the Negroes of the
World from Atlanta Prison." 10 Feb. 1925. In
Garvey, A79:237-239; and in Clarke, A36:189-190.

SE999 _____. "Message from Atlanta Prison." 1 Aug.
1925. In Garvey, A79:324-328; and in Long and
Collier, A118:369-373.

SE1000 _____. "The Internal Prejudices of Negroes."
c. 1925. In Garvey, A79:84-87; rpt. in Clarke,
A36:309-311, abr. [Note: A36 text dated 31 Jan.
1930.]

SE1001 _____. "The Case of the Negro for International
Racial Adjustment." 6 June 1928. In Clarke, A36:
284-299.

SE1002 _____. "Negro Progress Postulates Negro Government." April 1929. In Clarke, A36:300-301.

SE1003 _____. "One Mr. Sparks and His Anthropology"
and "South Africa and the Natives." May 1929. In
Clarke, A36:302-303.

SE1004 _____. "A Brutal Man." May 1929. In Clarke,
A36:304-306.

SE1005 _____. "Insulting Negro Womanhood." May 1929.
In Clarke, A36:307-308.

SE1006 _____. "Why the Black Star Line Failed." Feb.
1930-May 1931. In Clarke, A36:139-149.

SE1007 _____. "In Prison in Atlanta." May 1930. In
Clarke, A36:191-192.

SE1008 _____. "An Apostrophe to Miss Nancy Cunard."
July 1932. In Clarke, A36:314-316.

SE1009 _____. "The Communists and the Negro." Sept.
1932. In Clarke, A36:317-321.

SE1010 _____. "Let the Negro Accumulate Wealth: It
Will Bring Him Power." July 1935. In Clarke,
A36:345-346.

SE1011 _____. "A Barefaced Colored Leader." July
1935. In Clarke, A36:253-255.

SE1012 _____. "We Are Mostly Subject Peoples All Over
the World." Aug. 1935. In Foner, A74:790-800.

SE1013 _____. "The World as It Is." Oct. 1935. In
Clarke, A36:347-351.

SE1014 _____. "The War." Oct. 1935. In Clarke, A36:
352-353.

SE1015 _____. "Lest We Forget." Oct. 1935. In Clarke,
A36:354-356.

SE1016 _____. "The American Mind and the War." Dec.
1935. In Clarke, A36:357-358.

SE1017 _____. "Unpreparedness a Crime: The Negro Is
Guilty." March 1936. In Clarke, A36:359-362.

SE1018 _____. "Italy's Conquest?" Aug. 1936. In
Clarke, A36:363-365.

SE1019 _____. "The Rise of African Sentiment." July
1938. In Clarke, A36:366-368.

SE1020 _____. "The Negro's Fullest Part." Aug. 1938.
Black Images, 1 (Summer 1972), 22-24.

GARVEY, MARCUS. See Williams, B36; Clarke,
A36; Cronon, HC32; Davis, HC35; Edwards, HC48;
Fax, HC52; Frazier, HC58; Garvey, HC60; Harris,
HC73; Lynch, HC105; Reid, HC149; Brisbane,
HC211; Essien-Udom, HC225; Rogers, HC261; Sun-
diata, HC264; Record, HC377; Bennett, HC437:145-
149; Bontemps and Conroy, HC439:162-174, 185-186;
Brisbane, HC442:81-99; Cruse, HC448:117-135;
Foster, HC452:442-451; Peeks, HC469:180-200;
Aron, HC835; Brisbane, HC839; Elkins, HC845; El-
kins, HC846; Fierce, HC847; Frazier, HC849;
Frazier, HC850; James, HC851; Moses, HC855;
Zickefoose, HC861; Vincent, HC953; Boulware,
HC1023:54-62; Rudwick, HC1124; Essien-Udom,
HC1207; Draper, HC1256:50-56; Weisbord, HC1274;
Bruce, SE243; Bruce, SE246; Bruce, SE248; Du
Bois, SE788; Du Bois, SE789; Du Bois, SE791; Du

Bois, SE792; Du Bois, SE793; Du Bois, SE801; Johnson, SE1362; McKay, SE1564; Miller, SE1710; Pickens, SE1837; and "A Symposium on Garvey," SE2152.

SE1021 Gibbs, Jonathan C. "Freedom's Joyful Day." 1 Jan. 1863. In Foner, A74:263-265.

SE1022 Gibson, Kenneth A. "Address to the Congress of African Peoples." Sept. 1970. In Jones, A101:18-21.

SE1023 _____. "Newark and We." 1972. In Wright, A180:110-125.

SE1024 Gilbert, Joseph, and Amos G. Beman. "Resolution on Colonization." 15 July 1831. In Garrison, A77:30.

SE1025 Gilbert, M. W. "Baptism." 1890. In Brawley, A25:129-142.

SE1026 Gordon, Eugene. "A New Religion for the Negro." Oct. 1928. In Aptheker, A2:572-579.

SE1027 Gothard, Louis J. "A Report on Racism in the United Service Organization." Sept. 1970. In Jones, A101:371-380.

SE1028 Graham, D. A. "Some Facts About Southern Lynchings." 4 June 1899. In Foner, A74:613-616.

SE1029 Granger, Lester B. "The Negro--Friend or Foe of Organized Labor?" May 1935. In Grant, A84:234-239.

SE1030 _____. "Some Tactics Which Should Supplement Resort to the Courts in Achieving Racial Integration in Education." 17 April 1952. JNE, 21 (Summer 1952), 344-349.

SE1031 _____. "American Teamwork--Today and in the Years Ahead." 4 Sept. 1961. In Williams and Williams, A175:5-12.

SE1032 Grant, Abram. "Quadrennial Sermon." May 1900. In Smith, HC1183:205-206, excerpt.

SE1033 Gray, Alfred. "We'll Carry This Constitution." 3
Feb. 1868. In Allen, HC623:124-125.

SE1034 Gray, William H. "Justice Should Recognize No Color." 1868. In Foner, A74:354-355.

SE1035 Gray, William H., Jr. "Broaden Our Horizons for
Correctional Service." 23 May 1952. In Hill,
A93:140-148.

SE1036 Green, Alfred M. "Let Us Take Up the Sword." 20
April 1861. In Foner, A74:249-250.

SE1037 Green, John P. "These Evils Call Loudly for Redress." May 1884. In Foner, A74:499-504, abr.;
and in Fishel and Quarles, A72:322-325, further
abr.

SE1038 _____. "Should the Ignorant and Non-Property-
Holding Negro Be Allowed To Vote?" 1902. In
Culp, A46:89-91.

SE1039 Greener, Richard T. "Young Men, To the Front!"
c. 1870 (?). In Dunbar, A70:63-66.

SE1040 _____. "The Emigration of Colored Citizens from
the Southern States." 12 Sept. 1879. In Golden and
Rieke, A82:365-375; in Woodson, A177:473-487; and
in Foner, A74:467-471, abr. [See Douglass,
SE702.]

GREENER, RICHARD T. See Simmons, HC163a:
327-335 or HC163b:211-216; and Brown, HC445:542-
543.

SE1041 Gregory, Dick. "Let Your Son Fight for Freedom."
Sept. 1963. In Foner, A74:981-984.

SE1042 _____. "You Will Know the Truth." 1968. In
Gregory, A85:39-59.

SE1043 _____. "America Is My Momma." 1968. In
Gregory, A85:63-78.

SE1044 _____. "Who's the Nigger Today?" 1968. In
Gregory, A85:81-103.

SE1045 _____. "If You Cut Me, I Am Going To Bleed."
1968. In Gregory, A85:107-117.

SE1046 _____. "America's Caesar." 1968. In Gregory,
A85:121-134.

SE1047 _____. "Nonviolent Protest or Eyetooth Revolution?" 1968. In Gregory, A85:137-151.

SE1048 _____. "Windy Cities." 1968. In Gregory, A85:
155-168.

SE1049 _____. "The Shoe's Too Tight." 1968. In
Gregory, A85:171-176.

SE1050 _____. "The Name Game." 1968. In Gregory,
A85:179-195.

SE1051 _____. "The City of Chaos." 1968. In Gregory,
A85:199-210.

SE1052 _____. Write Me In! Ed. James R. McGraw.
New York: Bantam, 1968.
Contains: "Why I Want To Be President," pp. 15-20.
"How I Want To Be President," pp. 23-28.
"This Nation Is Insane," pp. 31-58.
"Moral Fallout," pp. 61-75.
"The Gregory Report on Civil Disorders," pp. 79-
96.
"The Gregory Accords," pp. 101-117.
"Life in These United States," pp. 121-124.
"Crisis in Town and Country," pp. 127-136.
"The Gregorian Court Calendar," pp. 139-153.
"Pencil Power," pp. 157-158.

SE1053 _____. "Black Politics." Sept. 1968. Humanist, 28 (Sept.-Oct. 1968), 11-12. Rpt. in Moss,
A130:91-96.

SE1054 _____. "Divine Libel." 1969. In Lecky and
Wright, A110:105-113; and in Littleton and Burger,
A112:401-408.

SE1055 _____. No More Lies: The Myth and the Reality of American History. Ed. James R. McGraw.
New York: Harper, 1971.
Contains: "Introduction: For White Only,"
pp. xi-xxii.

"The Myth of the Puritan Pilgrim," pp. 1-30.
"The Myth of the Savage," pp. 31-63.
"The Myth of the Founding Fathers," pp. 64-100.
"The Myth of Black Content," pp. 101-138.
"The Myth of the Courageous White Settler and
   the Free Frontier," pp. 139-156.
"The Myth of the Mason-Dixon Line," pp. 157-167.
"The Myth of Free Enterprise," pp. 168-177.
"The Myth of Emancipation," pp. 178-197.
"The Myth of the Bootstrap," pp. 198-212.
"The Myth of the Good Neighbor," pp. 213-223.
"The Myth of American Rhetoric," pp. 224-243.
"The Myth of Free Elections," pp. 244-252.
"From Myth to Reality," pp. 253-279.

SE1056 _____. "From Poverty to President." 1972.
In Wright, A180:71-81.

SE1057 _____. Dick Gregory's Political Primer. Ed.
James R. McGraw. New York: Harper, 1972.
   Contains: "Bicentennial Breakthrough," pp. 3-28.
   "That Long, Hot Summer--1787," pp. 31-47.
   "Parties Prevail," pp. 51-77.
   "The Primary Objective," pp. 83-90.
   "Politics on Parade," pp. 93-106.
   "Pounding Out Platforms," pp. 109-131.
   "Promises, Promises," pp. 135-142.
   "The High Cost of Conviction," pp. 147-155.
   "Power to What People?" pp. 159-166.
   "Missing the Party," pp. 169-182.
   "The Constitution's Institutions," pp. 185-205.
   "Now That Voting Has Caught Up with the Draft,"
      pp. 209-220.
   "Techniques of Persuasion," pp. 223-228.
   "Studying War No More," pp. 231-247.
   "A Turnip in Every Plot," pp. 251-273.
   "Citizen Surveillance," pp. 277-295.
   "Planetary Politics," pp. 299-306.
   "How To Evaluate a Candidate," pp. 309-315.
   "Dick Gregory's Do-It-Yourself Acceptance
      Speech," p. 317.

GREGORY, DICK. See Gregory, HC66; and Asinof,
HC1036.

SE1058 Gregory, James Francis. "The Social Bearings of
the Fifth Commandment." c. 1910 (?). In Dunbar,
A70:397-402.

SE1059 [Griffin, E. G.] "Elijah, the Man of God." 9 Aug.
1942. In Pipes, HC1197:39-43.

SE1060 Grimké, Archibald H. "Right on the Scaffold, or
the Martyrs of 1822." 1901. American Negro
Academy, Occasional Papers No. 7. Washington:
The Academy, 1901.

SE1061 _____. "Why Disfranchisement Is Bad." July
1904. Atlantic, July 1904, pp. 72-81.

SE1062 _____. "The Meaning and Need of the Movement
To Reduce Southern Representation." 1905. In
The Negro and the Elective Franchise, A132:3-14.

SE1063 _____. "Modern Industrialism and the Negroes
of the United States." 1908. American Negro
Academy, Occasional Papers No. 12. Washington:
The Academy, 1908. Rpt. in Brotz, A27:464-480.

SE1064 _____. "Address on the Occasion of the Presentation of a Loving Cup to Hon. Joseph Benson For-
aker, United States Senator." 6 March 1909. In
Dunbar, A70:337-346.

SE1065 _____. "Charles Sumner Centenary: Historical
Address." 6 Jan. 1911. American Negro Acad-
emy, Occasional Papers No. 14. Washington: The
Academy, 1911.

SE1066 _____. "The Ballotless Victim of One-Party Gov-
ernments: Annual Address." 1913. American Negro Academy, Occasional Papers No. 16. Washington: The Academy, 1913.

SE1067 _____. "The Ultimate Criminal: Annual Address." 1915. American Negro Academy, Occasional Papers No. 17. Washington: The Academy,
1915.

SE1068 _____. "The Sex Question and Race Segregation."
Dec. 1915. In Papers of the American Negro Academy, A136:3-24.

SE1069 _____. "The Shame of America, or, The Negro's Case Against the Republic." 1924. American Negro Academy, Occasional Papers No. 21.

Washington: The Academy, 1924. Rpt. in Woodson,
A177:671-689; and in Foner, A74:764-771, excerpt.

GRIMKE, ARCHIBALD H. See Brawley, HC13:165-
167; Grimké, HC68; Ferris, HC451:892-897; and
Grimké, SE1170.

SE1070 Grimké, Francis J. "Sermon on Considerations of
Age, Relation, and Support in Marriage." 29 Jan.
1888, 2 May 1897, and 22 April 1917. In Grimké,
A89:132-141.

SE1071 _____. "Sermon on the Duties of Parents." 22
July 1888 and 16 Nov. 1919. In Grimké, A89:1-12.

SE1072 _____. "Sermon on Heredity and the Development
of Children." 29 July 1888 and 18 Jan. 1920. In
Grimké, A89:12-22.

SE1073 _____. "The Afro-American Pulpit in Relation to
Race Elevation." 1892. In Grimké, A88:223-234.

SE1074 _____. "Bishop Daniel A. Payne." 10 Dec.
1893 and 17 Dec. 1893. In Grimké, A88:1-28.

SE1075 _____. "Pride." 29 March 1896. In Grimké,
A89:539-550.

SE1076 _____. "Sermon on the Marriage Relation as Divine, Monogamous, and Affective." 25 April 1897.
In Grimké, A89:121-131.

        [_____. 2 May 1897. Same as SE1070.]

SE1077 _____. "Sermon on Inter-Faith Marriage and
Marriage To Beget Children." 9 May 1897 and 29
April 1917. In Grimké, A89:141-153.

SE1078 _____. "Sermon on the Benefits of Marriage:
Prolongation of Life, Loving Companionship, Support
in Life's Work, Counseling during Perplexity, Incen-
tive to Industry and Virtue." 16 May 1897 and 6
May 1917. In Grimké, A89:153-163.

SE1079 _____. "Sermon on the Benefits of Marriage--
Care during Sickness and Life's Greatest Happiness
--and on the Duties of Marriage." 23 May 1897

and 20 May 1917. In Grimké, A89:163-172.

SE1080 _____. "Sermon on the Duties of the Husband."
30 May 1897 and 27 May 1917. In Grimké, A89:
173-185.

SE1081 _____. "Sermon on the Duties of the Wife." 30
May 1897 and 3 June 1917. In Grimké, A89:185-
198.

SE1082 _____. "Sermon on How To Keep the Home Hap-
py--The Wife's Part." 6 June 1897 and 17 June
1917. In Grimké, A89:198-208.

SE1083 _____. "Sermon on How To Keep the Home
Happy--The Husband's Part." 6 June 1897 and 24
June 1917. In Grimké, A89:208-219.

SE1084 _____. "Sermon on How the Happiness of the
Home May Be Destroyed, or, on Some of the
Causes of Domestic Infelicity: Lack of True Love,
Spirit of Jealousy, and Neglect of the Wife by the
Husband." 13 June 1897 and 1 July 1917. In
Grimké A89:219-230.

SE1085 _____. "Sermon on Bad Housekeeping and on
Sustaining Love." 27 June 1897 and 15 July 1917.
In Grimké, A89:230-238.

SE1086 _____. "Some Things That Lie Across the Path-
way of Our Progress." July 1897. In Grimké,
A89:550-566.

SE1087 _____. "Frederick Douglass." 10 March 1898.
In Grimké, A88:34-54.

SE1088 _____. "Temperance and the Negro Race." 20
July 1898. In Grimké, A89:482-494.

[_____. 16 Oct. 1898. Same as SE1088.]

[_____. 27 Nov. 1898. Same as SE1088.]

SE1089 _____. "Rev. Alexander Crummell." 17 Dec.
1898. In Grimké, A88:28-34.

SE1090 _____. "Sermon on the Parable of the Prodigal

Son--II." 12 Feb. 1899. In Grimké, A89:289-299.

SE1091 _____. "Sermon on the Parable of the Prodigal
Son--III." 19 Feb. 1899 and 25 Feb. 1923. In
Grimké, A89:299-310.

[_____. 18 March 1899. Same as SE1088.]

[_____. 19 March 1899. Same as SE1088.]

SE1092 _____. "Sermon on the Parable of the Prodigal
Son--VIII." 8 April 1899. In Grimké, A89:354-364.

SE1093 _____. "Its [Lynching's] Causes: A Low State
of Civilization and Race Hatred." 4 June 1899. In
Grimké, A88:291-303.

SE1094 _____. "Its [Lynching's] Causes: The Crimes of
the Negro." 18 June 1899. In Grimké, A88:303-
316.

SE1095 _____. "The Remedy for the Present Strained Relations between the Races in the South." 25 June
1899. In Grimké, A88:317-333.

[_____. 23 July 1899. Same as SE1088.]

SE1096 _____. "Sources from Which No Help May Be
Expected--The General Government, Political Parties." 27 Nov. 1900. In Grimké, A88:247-260.

SE1097 _____. "Signs of a Brighter Future." 4 Dec.
1900. In Grimké, A88:260-273; and in Culp, A46:
427-433, excerpt.

SE1098 _____. "God and Prayer as Factors in the Struggle." 11 Dec. 1900. In Grimké, A88:274-290.

SE1099 _____. "Sermon on the Environment and the Development of Children." 14 April 1901 and 19 Sept.
1920. In Grimké, A89:32-42.

SE1100 _____. "Sermon on the Character and Conduct of
the Community in the Development of Children." 21
April 1901 and 16 Jan. 1921. In Grimké, A89:52-
62.

SE1101 _____. "Sermon on the Ideal of Truthfulness and the Training of Children." 28 April 1901 and 15 May 1921. In Grimké, A89:62-73.

SE1102 _____. "Sermon on the Ideals of Justice, Purity, and Industry in the Training of Children." 28 April 1901, 17 July 1921, and 18 Sept. 1921. In Grimké, A89:73-84.

SE1103 _____. "Sermon on the Ideals of Sympathy, Politeness, and Neatness in the Training of Children." 19 May 1901 and 21 May 1922. In Grimké, A89: 84-94.

SE1104 _____. "Sermon on the Ideals of Punctuality, Unselfishness and Thoroughness in the Training of Children." 19 May 1901 and 17 Sept. 1922. In Grimké, A89:94-104.

SE1105 _____. "The Roosevelt-Washington Episode, or Race Prejudice." 27 Oct. 1901. In Grimké, A88: 334-347.

[_____. 27 March 1902. Same as SE1088.]

[_____. 14 May 1902. Same as SE1088.]

SE1106 _____. "A Resemblance and a Contrast Between the American Negro and the Children of Israel in Egypt." 12 Oct. 1902. In Grimké, A88:347-364.

SE1107 _____. "Things of Paramount Importance in the Development of the Negro Race." 29 March 1903. In Grimké, A88:378-391.

SE1108 _____. "God and the Race Problem." 3 May 1903. In Grimké, A88:364-378.

SE1109 _____. "Temperance Sermon." 22 Nov. 1903 and 6 Nov. 1910. In Grimké, A89:494-506.

SE1110 _____. "Mrs. Helen Pitts Douglass." 5 Dec. 1903. In Grimké, A88:71-81.

SE1111 _____. "Sermon on Some Qualities of an Ideal Woman." 17 Jan. 1904. In Grimké, A89:412-423.

SE1112 _____. "Sermon on the Ideal Woman as Pious, God-Fearing." 24 Jan. 1904. In Grimké, A89:423-434.

SE1113 _____. "Sermon on the Ideal Woman as Wife." 31 Jan. 1904. In Grimké, A89:434-446.

SE1114 _____. "Sermon on the Ideal Woman as Mother." 7 Feb. 1904. In Grimké, A89:446-460.

SE1115 _____. "The Negro and His Citizenship." 1905. In The Negro and the Elective Franchise, A132:72-85. Rpt. in Grimké, A88:391-406.

SE1116 _____. "William Lloyd Garrison." 10 Dec. 1905. In Grimké, A88:81-101.

SE1117 _____. "Religion and Race Elevation." 11 Feb. 1906, 17 Nov. 1909, and 25 April 1910. In Grimké, A89:566-588.

SE1118 _____. "The Attitude of the Home on the Temperance Question." 21 Sept. 1906 and 21 Sept. 1913. In Grimké, A89:471-482.

SE1119 _____. "The Atlanta Riot." 7 Oct. 1906. In Grimké, A88:406-418.

SE1120 _____. "Centennial of John Greenleaf Whittier." 15 Dec. 1907 and 5 Jan. 1908. In Grimké, A88:101-122.

SE1121 _____. "Frederick Douglass." 14 Feb. 1907. In Grimké, A88:55-63.

SE1122 _____. "Frederick Douglass." 14 Feb. 1908. In Grimké, A88:63-71.

SE1123 _____. "The Message of the Studio to the Home." 17 May 1908 and 25 May 1930. In Grimké, A89:588-600.

SE1124 _____. "Equality of Rights for All Citizens, Black and White Alike." 7 March 1909. In Grimké, A88:418-440; in Dunbar, A70:347-356, abr.; and in Foner, A74:669-673, excerpt. [Note: A88 text dated 27 March 1909.]

[_____.   17 Nov. 1909.   Same as SE1117.]

SE1125 _____.   "Discouragements, Hostility of the Press,
Silence and Cowardice of the Pulpit."   20 Nov.
1909.   In Grimké, A88:234-247.

SE1126 _____.   "John Brown."   5 Dec. 1909.   In Grimké, A88:122-141.

SE1127 _____.   "Thanks to Mr. Andrew Carnegie on Behalf of the Trustees of Howard University."   25
April 1910.   In Grimké, A88:440-442.

[_____.   25 April 1910.   Same as SE1117.]

SE1128 _____.   "Christianity and Race Prejudice."   29
May 1910.   In Grimké, A88:442-454.

SE1129 _____.   "Christianity and Race Prejudice."   5
June 1910.   In Grimké, A88:454-473.

[_____.   6 Nov. 1910.   Same as SE1109.]

SE1130 _____.   "Remarks at the Semi-centennial of the
Ordination to the Ministry of the Reverend John B.
Reeve."   4 June 1911.   In Grimké, A88:141-146.

SE1131 _____.   "The Paramount Importance of Character,
or Character, the True Standard By Which To Esti-
mate Individuals and Races."   27 Oct. 1911.   In
Grimké, A88:473-489.

SE1132 _____.   "George F. T. Cook."   10 Aug. 1912.
In Grimké, A88:158-169.

[_____.   21 Sept. 1913.   Same as SE1118.]

SE1133 _____.   "Fifty Years of Freedom, with Matters
of Importance to Both the White and Colored People
of the United States."   26 Oct. 1913.   In Grimké,
A88:489-516.

SE1134 _____.   "Temperance Sermon."   23 Oct. 1914.
In Grimké, A89:506-516.

SE1135 _____.   "Excerpts from a Thanksgiving Sermon
and Two Letters Addressed to Woodrow Wilson."

26 Nov. 1914.   In Grimké, A88:516-523.

SE1136 _____.   "The Logic of Woman Suffrage."   Aug.
1915.   In Aptheker, A2:94-95.

SE1137 _____.   "Rev. John B. Reeve."   20 Jan. 1916.
In Grimké, A88:146-153.

SE1138 _____.   "Lincoln University Alone of Negro Institutions Shuts Colored Men Out of Its Trustee Board
and Out of Its Professorships."   18 March 1916.
In Grimké, A88:528-531.

SE1139 _____.   "Anniversary Address on the Occasion
of the Seventy-Fifth Anniversary of the Fifteenth
Street Presbyterian Church, Washington, D.C."   19
Nov. 1916.   In Grimké, A88:531-554.

SE1140 _____.   "Evangelism and Institutes of Evangelism."   1916.   In Grimké, A88:523-528.

[_____.   22 April 1917.   Same as SE1070.]

[_____.   29 April 1917.   Same as SE1077.]

[_____.   6 May 1917.   Same as SE1078.]

[_____.   20 May 1917.   Same as SE1079.]

[_____.   27 May 1917.   Same as SE1080.]

[_____.   3 June 1917.   Same as SE1081.]

[_____.   17 June 1917.   Same as SE1082.]

[_____.   24 June 1917.   Same as SE1083.]

[_____.   1 July 1917.   Same as SE1084.]

[_____.   15 July 1917.   Same as SE1085.]

SE1141 _____.   "The Home as a Training School."   26
Oct. 1917.   In Grimké, A89:461-471.

SE1142 _____.   "Sermon on Divorce."   2 Dec. 1917.   In
Grimké, A89:238-248.

SE1142a _____. " 'Billy' Sunday's Campaign in Washington, D.C." March 1918. In Grimké, A88:554-559.

SE1143 _____. "James E. Walker." 12 April 1918. In Grimké, A88:169-174.

SE1143a _____. "Victory for the Allies and the United States a Ground of Rejoicing, of Thanksgiving." 24 Nov. 1918. In Grimké, A88:559-577; and in Woodson, A177:690-708.

SE1144 _____. "A Special Christmas Message in View of Present World Conditions." 22 Dec. 1918. In Grimké, A88:577-589.

SE1145 _____. "Theodore Roosevelt." 9 Feb. 1919. In Grimké, A88:174-189.

SE1146 _____. "Address of Welcome Given at a Reception Tendered to the Men Who Have Returned from the Battlefront." 24 April 1919. In Grimké, A88:589-591; and in Aptheker, A2:242-243.

SE1147 _____. "Sermon on the Laws of Divorce." 29 June 1919. In Grimké, A89:249-259.

SE1148 _____. "The Race Problem--Two Suggestions as to Its Solution." c. July 1919. In Grimké, A88:591-599.

[_____. 16 Nov. 1919. Same as SE1071.]

SE1149 _____. "The Race Problem as It Respects the Colored People and the Christian Church in the Light of the Developments of the Last Year." 27 Nov. 1919. In Grimké, A88:600-618.

[_____. 18 Jan. 1920. Same as SE1072.]

SE1150 _____. "Sermon on the Home and the Development of Children." 16 May 1920. In Grimké, A89:22-32.

[_____. 19 Sept. 1920. Same as SE1099.]

SE1151 _____. "Sermon on the Relation of the Home to Outside Influences in the Development of Children."

21 Nov. 1920. In Grimké, A89:42-52.

[_____. 16 Jan. 1921. Same as SE1100.]

SE1152 _____. "The National Association for the Advancement of Colored People, Its Value--Its Aims--Its Claims." 24 April 1921. In Grimké, A88:618-627.

[_____. 15 May 1921. Same as SE1101.]

[_____. 17 July 1921. Same as SE1102.]

[_____. 18 Sept. 1921. Same as SE1102.]

SE1153 _____. "Temperance Sermon." 30 Oct. 1921. In Grimké, A89:516-528.

[_____. 21 May 1922. Same as SE1103.]

SE1154 _____. "Sermon on the Ideals of a Thorough Knowledge of Housekeeping for Girls, and Economy for All Children." 19 Nov. 1922. In Grimké, A89:104-112.

SE1155 _____. "The Pharisees and Scribes Murmured." 28 Jan. 1923. In Grimké, A89:260-269.

SE1156 _____. "The Parable of the Lost Sheep." 4 Feb. 1923. In Grimké, A89:269-279.

SE1157 _____. "Sermon on the Parable of the Prodigal Son--I." 11 Feb. 1923. In Grimké, A89:279-289.

[_____. 25 Feb. 1923. Same as SE1091.]

SE1158 _____. "Sermon on the Parable of the Prodigal Son--IV." 4 March 1923. In Grimké, A89:311-321.

SE1159 _____. "Sermon on the Parable of the Prodigal Son--V." 18 March 1923. In Grimké, A89:321-332.

SE1160 _____. "Sermon on the Parable of the Prodigal Son--VI." 25 March 1923. In Grimké, A89:332-343.

SE1161 _____. "Sermon on the Parable of the Prodigal Son--VII." 1 April 1923. In Grimké, A89:343-354.

SE1162 _____. "Sermon on the Parable of the Prodigal Son--VIII." 8 April 1923. In Grimké, A89:354-364.

SE1163 _____. "Sermon on the Parable of the Prodigal Son--IX." 15 April 1923. In Grimké, A89:364-374.

SE1164 _____. "Sermon on the Parable of the Prodigal Son--X." 22 April 1923. In Grimké, A89:374-386.

SE1165 _____. "Sermon on the Things Not Necessary to a True Womanhood." 29 April 1923. In Grimké, A89:387-399.

SE1166 _____. "Sermon on the Things Necessary to a True Womahood." 8 May 1923. In Grimké, A89:399-411.

SE1167 _____. "Hugh M. Browne." 2 Nov. 1923. In Grimké, A88:189-200.

SE1168 _____. "Sermon on the Ideals of Self-Reliance, Conscientiousness, and Racial Pride in the Training of Children." 18 Nov. 1923. In Grimké, A89:112-120.

SE1169 _____. "James Henry Nelson Waring." 2 Jan. 1924. In Grimké, A88:200-212.

SE1170 _____. "Archibald H. Grimké." Feb. 1930. In Grimké, A88:212-218.

[_____. 25 May 1930. Same as SE1123.]

SE1171 _____. "A Short Address Delivered ... in Connection with the Presentation of a Portrait of the Rev. John B. Reeve." 11 Nov. 1930. In Grimké, A88:153-158.

SE1172 _____. "The Repeal of the Eighteenth Amendment." 14 Jan. 1934 and 4 Nov. 1934. In Grimké, A89:528-538.

SE1173 _____. "The Second Marriage of Frederick

Douglass." 1934. JNH, 19 (July 1934), 324-329.

[_____. 4 Nov. 1934. Same as SE1172.]

SE1174 _____. "Thomas Walker." 21 May 1935. In
Grimké, A88:220-222.

SE1175 _____. "Mrs. Rosetta Lawson." 24 May 1936.
In Grimké, A88:218-220.

GRIMKE, FRANCIS J. See Simmons, HC163a:608-
612 or HC613b:416-419; and Ferris, HC451:888-892.

SE1176 Grisham, G. N. "The Functions of the Negro Scholar." 28 Dec. 1897. In Foner, A74:600-603.

SE1177 Hall, Prince, et al. "Petition to the Senate and
House of Representatives of the Commonwealth of
Massachusetts." 27 Feb. 1788. In Aptheker, A1:
20-21.

SE1178 Hall, Prince. "A Charge Delivered to the Brethren of
the African Lodge." 25 June 1792. In Porter,
A141:63-69; and in Robinson, A149:47-50, abr.

SE1179 _____. "A Charge Delivered to the African
Lodge." 24 June 1797. In Porter, A141:70-78; and
in Foner, A74:14-15, excerpt.

HALL, PRINCE. See Greene, HC65.

SE1180 Hamer, Fannie Lou. "If the Name of the Game Is
Survive, Survive." 1972. In Wright, A180:44-50.

SE1181 Hamilton, Charles V. "An Advocate of Black Power
Defines It." New York Times Magazine, 14 April
1968, pp. 22-23, 79-83. Rpt. in Meier and Rudwick, A124:154-168; and in Scott and Brockriede,
A154:179-193.

SE1182 _____. "The Black Revolution: A Primer for
White Liberals." Jan. 1969. Progressive, 33
(Jan. 1969), 29-31. Rpt. in Moss, A130:155-161.

SE1183 _____. "An Address to the New York African
Society." 2 Jan. 1809. In Porter, A141:34-41;
and in Foner, A74:26-27, excerpt.

SE1184 _____. "An Oration on the Abolition of the Slave
Trade." 2 Jan. 1815. In Porter, A141:391-399.

SE1185 _____. "An Oration ... in Commemoration of the
Abolition of Domestic Slavery in This State [New
York]." 4 July 1827. In Porter, A141:96-104.

SE1186 _____. "Address to the Fourth Annual Convention of the Free People of Color of the United States."
2 June 1834. In Porter, A142:orig. pag.; in Aptheker, A1:154-157; in Foner, A74:57-60; and in Minutes of the Fourth Annual Convention, SE1719:3-7.

SE1187 Hammon, Briton. "A Narrative of the Uncommon
Sufferings, and Surprising Deliverance of Briton Hammon, a Negro Man." 1760. In Porter, A141:522-
528; and in Robinson, A149:109-114.

SE1188 Hammon, Jupiter. "An Address to the Negroes in
the State of New York." 1786. In Porter, A141:
314-323; in Robinson, A149:37-46; and in Woodson,
A176:vii-xvi.

SE1189 Hammond, E. W. S. "Africa in Its Relation to Christian Civilization." 15 Dec. 1895. In Bowen, A20:
205-210.

SE1190 Hampton, Fred. "You Can Murder a Liberator, But
You Can't Murder Liberation." 27 April 1969. In
Foner, A73:138-144.

SE1191 _____. "The Illinois Black Panthers" [interview].
May 1969. Riots, Civil and Criminal Disorders:
Hearings Before the Permanent Sub-Committee on
Government Operations, U.S. Senate, 91st Congress,
First Session, June 26, 30, 1969, Part 20, pp. 4436-
4438. Rpt. in Bracey, A21:746-751.

SE1192 Hancock, Gordon B. "Race Relations in the United
States: A Summary." 1944. In Logan, A115:217-
247.

SE1193 Handy, Arthur W. "Nat Turner." Dec. 1889. In
Foner, A74:539-540.

SE1194 Handy, J. A. "Episcopal Address." May 1904. In
Smith, HC1183:232-234, excerpt.

SE1195 Hansberry, Lorraine. "A Challenge to Artists." 27
Oct. 1962. Freedomways, 3 (Winter 1963), 31-35.
Rpt. in Foner, A74:954-959.

SE1196 _____. The Movement: Documentary of a Struggle for Equality. 1964. New York: Simon, 1964.

HANSBERRY, LORRAINE. See Bigsby, HC963:156-
173.

SE1197 Harding, Vincent. "Where Have All the Lovers
Gone?" 1966. New South, 21 (Winter 1966), 27-
38.

SE1198 _____. "Black Power and the American Christ."
Jan. 1967. Christian Century, 84 (4 Jan. 1967),
10-13. Rpt. in Barbour, A8:85-93.

SE1199 Hare, Nathan. "Brainwashing of Black Men's
Minds." 1966. In Jones and Neal, A103:178-186.

SE1200 _____. " 'Black Power'--Its Goals and Methods."
May 1967. U.S. News and World Report, 22 May
1967, pp. 64-66, 68. Rpt. in Littleton and Burger,
A112:103-111.

SE1201 _____. "A Radical Perspective on Social Science
Curricula." May 1968. In Robinson, HC424:104-
117.

SE1202 _____. "How White Power Whitewashes Black
Power." 1968. In Barbour, A8:182-188.

SE1203 _____. "The Case for Separatism: 'Black Perspective.' " Feb. 1969. Newsweek, 10 Feb. 1969,
p. 56. Rpt. in Littleton and Burger, A112:202-204;
and in Black Power and Student Rebellion. Ed.
James McEvoy and Abraham Miller. Belmont, Cal.:
Wadsworth, 1969. Pages 233-235. [See Wilkins,
SE2349.]

SE1204 _____. "The Battle for Black Studies." 1972.
Black Scholar, 3 (May 1972), 32-47.

SE1205 _____. "The Revolutionary Role of the Black
Bourgeoisie." 1972. Black Scholar, 4 (Jan. 1973),
32-35.

SE1206 Harper, Frances Ellen Watkins. "An Address at the Centennial Anniversary of the Pennsylvania Society for Promoting the Abolition of Slavery." 14 April 1875. In Dunbar, A70:101-106; and in Foner, A74:431-434.

HARPER, FRANCES ELLEN WATKINS. See Brawley, HC13:116-120; Penn, A139:420-422; Brown, HC443:160-162; Brown, HC445:524-525; Still, HC598a:755-780; Brawley, HC968; and Montgomery, HC1107.

SE1207 Harris, Abram L. "The Prospects of Black Bourgeoisie." c. 1927. In Johnson, A100:131-134.

SE1208 Harris, Patricia Roberts. "The Law and Moral Issues." Fall 1963. In Williams and Williams, A175:15-22.

SE1209 Harrison, Hubert H. "What Socialism Means To Us." c. 1912. In Foner, A74:699-702.

SE1210 Harrison, Linda. "On Cultural Nationalism." Feb. 1969. In Foner, A73:151-154.

SE1211 Hatcher, Richard Gordon. "Which Is the Path of Change?" May 1968. In Foner, A74:1110-1120.

SE1212 _____. "The Age of a New Humanity." 22 Feb. 1969. Freedomways, 9 (2d Qrtr 1969), 105-119.

SE1213 _____. "Address to the Congress of African Peoples." Sept. 1970. In Jones, A101:64-72.

SE1214 _____. "Art and Liberation: Culture and Freedom." 20 Sept. 1970. Freedomways, 10 (4th Qrtr 1970), 319-325.

SE1215 _____. "History Will Be Our Judge." 11 March 1972. Freedomways, 12 (2d Qrtr 1972), 134-142.

SE1216 _____. "Black Politics in the '70's." 1972. Black Scholar, 4 (Sept. 1972), 17-22.

SE1217 Hawkins, Lawrence. "Urban Schoolteaching: The Personal Touch." March 1969. In Wright, A179:43-47.

SE1218 Hawkins, W. Ashbie. "The Negro Lawyer: His Opportunity, His Duty." 1 Oct. 1913. In Dunbar, A70:483-490.

SE1219 Hayden, Lewis. "Deliver Us from Such a Moses." 27 Dec. 1865. In Foner, A74:335-336, excerpt.

SE1220 Hayne, William A. "On Outrages in Edgefield County, S.C." 1 March 1876. JNH, 7 (July 1922), 330-333.

HAYNE, WILLIAM. See Work, HC202.

SE1221 Haynes, Lemuel. "Universal Salvation, a Very Ancient Doctrine." June 1805. In Porter, A141:449-454.

SE1222 _____. Six Letters. May 1818-July 1833. In Robinson, A149:20-23.

HAYNES, LEMUEL. See Cooley, HC29; Haynes, HC78; Morse, HC121; Simmons, HC163a:677-678 or HC163b:467; Loggins, HC992:117-126; and Woodson, HC1188:52-56.

SE1223 "Haytian Advertisements." 3 Nov. 1860. And "Haytian Bureau of Emigration." 31 Aug. 1861. In Golden and Rieke, A82:359-363.

SE1224 Hemsley, Hubert. "A Black Perspective of the Health Crisis." Sept. 1970. In Jones, A101:228-234.

SE1225 Henderson, James M. "On the Present and Future of the Afro-American." May 1904. In Smith, HC1183:230-232, excerpt.

SE1226 Henry, Hayward. "Address to the Congress of African Peoples." Sept. 1970. In Jones, A101:3-8.

SE1227 Henry, Milton R. "The Republic of New Africa." 29 May 1968. In Golden and Rieke, A82:441.

SE1228 _____. "The Republic of New Africa" [interview]. Jan. 1969. In Bracey, A22:518-523.

SE1229 Henry, Oliver. "A Negro Student's Observations on

Blacks." March 1969. In Wallerstein and Starr, A163:365-369. [See Sales, SE2061.]

SE1230 Henson, Josiah. Truth Stranger than Fiction: Father Henson's Story of His Own Life. 1858; rpt. Williamstown, Mass.: Corner House, 1973.

HENSON, JOSIAH. See Hartgrove, HC76; and Tanser, HC172.

SE1231 Herndon, Angelo. "Speech to the Jury." Jan. 1933. In Herndon, HC79:342-348. Rpt. in Foner, A74: 780-785.

SE1232 _____. "You Cannot Kill the Working Class." c. 1934. In Grant, A84:226-233.

SE1233 _____. "Speech at Emergency Conference." Oct. 1935. In Herndon, HC79:404-407.

HERNDON, ANGELO. See Herndon, HC79.

SE1234 Hernton, Calvin C. "Dynamite Growing Out of Their Skulls." c. 1968. In Jones and Neal, A103:78-104.

SE1235 Hershaw, L. M. "Disfranchisement in the District of Columbia." Aug. 1915. In Aptheker, A2:102-103.

SE1236 _____. "Peonage." 1915. American Negro Academy, Occasional Papers No. 15. Washington: The Academy, 1915.

SE1237 _____. "The Status of the Free Negro Prior to 1860." Dec. 1915. In Papers of the American Negro Academy, A136:39-47.

SE1238 Hewitt, Ray "Masai." "The Black Panther Party and Revolutionary Trade Unionism." c. May 1969. In Foner, A73:249-252.

SE1239 Hicks, George. "The New Well: 'Operation Coat Puller.'" Sept. 1970. In Jones, A101:398-409.

SE1240 Hill, Adelaide Cromwell. "What Is Africa to Us?" 1967. In Barbour, A8:127-135.

SE1241 _____. "Black Education in the Seventies: A
Lesson from the Past." 1970. In Barbour, A9:
51-67.

SE1242 Hill, Leslie Pinckney. "What the Negro Wants and
How To Get It: The Inward Power of the Masses."
1944. In Logan, A115:71-89.

SE1243 Hill, Roy L. "I Am Somebody." 15 Feb. 1961.
In Hill, A93:333-344.

SE1244 Hill, T. Arnold. "Phantom Color Lines." c. 1927.
In Johnson, A100:100-102.

SE1245 Hilliard, David. "If You Want Peace You Got To
Fight for It." 15 Nov. 1969. In Foner, A73:128-
130.

SE1246 _____. "Black Student Unions." c. Dec. 1969.
In Foner, A73:124-127.

[Hinton, Frederick A., et al. See Whipper, SE2309.]

SE1247 Hobson, Julius W. "Black Power: Right or Left?"
c. 1968. In Barbour, A8:199-203.

[Hogarth, George, and Henry C. Thompson. See
Thompson, SE2172.]

SE1248 Hogarth, George. "Address Delivered Before a Colored Association in Brooklyn." 5 Aug. 1831. In
Garrison, A77:69-70.

SE1249 Holly, James Theodore. "A Vindication of the Capacity of the Negro Race for Self-Government, and
Civilized Progress, as Demonstrated by Historical
Events of the Haytian Revolution; and the Subsequent
Acts of That People Since Their National Independence: A Lecture." 1855-1856. In Black Separatism
and the Caribbean 1860. Ed. Howard H. Bell.
Ann Arbor: Univ. of Michigan Press, 1970. Pages
21-66. In Brotz, A27:141-170; in Foner, A74:170-
197; and in Woodson, A177:242-246, excerpt.

HOLLY, JAMES THEODORE. See Brown, HC443:
274-276; Cromwell, HC447: 241-242; Loggins,
HC992:198-199; and Woodson, HC1188:158-159.

SE1250 Holsey, L. H. "Man an Ideal Empire in Miniature." pre-1898. In Holsey, A94:33-42.

SE1251 _____. "The Irrepressible Conflict." pre-1898. In Holsey, A94:43-56.

SE1252 _____. "The Fatherhood of God and the Brotherhood of Man." pre-1898. In Holsey, A94:57-66.

SE1253 _____. "Christianity Shiloh's Empire." pre-1898. In Holsey, A94:67-78.

SE1254 _____. "The Song of Believers." pre-1898. In Holsey, A94:79-90.

SE1255 _____. "The Rich and the Poor." pre-1898. In Holsey, A94:91-100.

SE1256 _____. "The Perpetuity of the Name of Christ." pre-1898. In Holsey, A94:101-110.

SE1257 _____. "From Repentance to Final Restitution." pre-1898. In Holsey, A94:111-123.

SE1258 _____. "Deep Concern for the Welfare of Zion." pre-1898. In Holsey, A94:124-135.

SE1259 _____. "Life and Death." pre-1898. In Holsey, A94:136-145.

SE1260 _____. "The Insufficiency of the Wisdom of Man." pre-1898. In Holsey, A94:146-158.

SE1261 _____. "Why We Should Love God." pre-1898. In Holsey, A94:159-171.

SE1262 _____. "The Work of an Enemy." pre-1898. In Holsey, A94:172-180.

SE1263 _____. "Holiness and Peace." pre-1898. In Holsey, A94:181-191.

SE1264 _____. "The Unity of Christianity." pre-1898. In Holsey, A94:192-202.

SE1265 _____. "The Christmas." pre-1898. In Holsey, A94:203-209.

SE1266 _____. "The Unity of Force." pre-1898. In
Holsey, A94:210-213.

SE1267 _____. "The Colored Methodist Episcopal
Church." March 1891. In Holsey, A94:214-219.

SE1268 _____. "The Origin and Place of Religion in
Civilization." pre-1898. In Holsey, A94:220-232.

SE1269 _____. "Amalgamation or Miscegenation." pre-
1898. In Holsey, A94:233-238.

SE1270 _____. "Speech Delivered Before Several Conferences of the M. E. Church, South." pre-1898. In
Holsey, A94:239-248.

SE1271 _____. "Religion." pre-1898. In Holsey, A94:
249-252.

SE1272 _____. "Southern Methodism and the Slaves."
pre-1898. In Holsey, A94:253-256.

SE1273 _____. "The Papacy." pre-1898. In Holsey,
A94:257-265.

SE1274 _____. "The Image of God in Man." pre-1898.
In Holsey, A94:266-272.

SE1275 _____. "The Trend of Civilization." pre-1898.
In Holsey, A94:273-278.

SE1276 _____. "The Great Presence." pre-1898. In
Holsey, A94:279-282.

SE1277 _____. "The Connection of the Spirit and Body."
pre-1898. In Holsey, A94:283-288.

SE1278 _____. "Will It Be Possible for the Negro To
Attain the American Type of Civilization?" 1902.
In Culp, A46:46-48.

HOLSEY, L. H. See Holsey, HC85; and Woodson,
HC1188:216-217.

SE1279 Hood, J. W. "The Claims of the Gospel Message."
pre-1884. In Hood, A95:13-19.

SE1280 _____. "Personal Consecration." pre-1884. In
Hood, A95:20-32.

SE1281 _____. "Exemplified Attachment to Christ and the
Reward." pre-1884. In Hood, A95:33-48.

SE1282 _____. "Divine Sonship the Sequence of Wondrous
Love." pre-1884. In Hood, A95:49-60.

SE1283 _____. "Why Was the Rich Man in Torment."
pre-1884. In Hood, A95:61-78.

SE1284 _____. "The Marvelous Vitality of the Church."
pre-1884. In Hood, A95:79-89.

SE1285 _____. "On Easter." pre-1884. In Hood, A95:
90-104.

SE1286 _____. "Creation's First-born, or the Earliest
Symbol of the Gospel." pre-1884. In Hood, A95:
105-121.

SE1287 _____. "The Soul's Anchor." pre-1884. In
Hood, A95:122-135.

SE1288 _____. "The Loss of the Soul." pre-1884. In
Hood, A95:136-147.

SE1289 _____. "The Two Characters and Two Destinies."
pre-1884. In Hood, A95:148-164.

SE1290 _____. "Man's Natural Disinclination To Turn in
His Distress to His Maker." pre-1884. In Hood,
A95:165-177.

SE1291 _____. "The Streams Which Gladden God's City."
pre-1884. In Hood, A95:178-189.

SE1292 _____. "The Perfect Felicity of the Resurrected
Saints a Result of Conformity to the Divine Like-
ness." pre-1884. In Hood, A95:190-204.

SE1293 _____. "The Doom of the Hypocrite's Hope."
pre-1884. In Hood, A95:205-221.

SE1294 _____. "The Glory Revealed in the Christian
Character." pre-1884. In Hood, A95:222-235.

SE1295 _____. "A Desirable Consummation." pre-1884. In Hood, A95:236-246.

SE1296 _____. "Loss of First Love." pre-1884. In Hood, A95:247-261.

SE1297 _____. "The Helplessness of Human Nature." pre-1884. In Hood, A95:262-277.

SE1298 _____. "The Christian Characteristics." pre-1884. In Hood, A95:278-289.

SE1299 _____. "David's Root and Offspring, or Venus in the Apocalypse." pre-1884. In Hood, A95:290-303.

SE1300 _____. "Will It Be Possible for the Negro To Attain the American Type of Civilization?" 1902. In Culp, A46:51-56.

HOOD, J. W.   See Simmons, HC163a:133-143 or HC163b:70-76.

SE1301 Hood, William R. "Uncle Tom Is Dead!" 27 Oct. 1951. In Foner, A74:843-849.

SE1302 Hope, John. "We Are Struggling for Equality." 1896. In Torrence, HC176:114-115; and in Foner, A74:595.

SE1303 _____. "Negro Suffrage in the States Whose Constitutions Have Not Been Specifically Revised." 1905. In The Negro and the Elective Franchise, A132:51-60.

SE1304 _____, et al. "Memorial to the Atlanta Board of Education." April 1917. In Aptheker, A2:170-176.

HOPE, JOHN.   See Bullock, HC19:73-77; Du Bois, HC44:300-302; and Torrence, HC176.

SE1305 Howard University Students. "Demands." Feb. 1968. In Wallerstein and Starr, A164:485-486.

SE1306 Hughes, Langston. "The Negro Artist and the Racial Mountain." June 1926. Nation, 23 June 1926, pp. 692-694. Rpt. in Aptheker, A2:526-530.

SE1307 _____. "Southern Gentlemen, White Prostitutes,
Mill-Owners, and Negroes." Dec. 1931. In
Hughes, A96:49.

SE1308 _____. "Brown America in Jail: Kilby." June
1932. In Hughes, A96:50-51.

SE1309 _____. "Moscow and Me." 1933. In Hughes,
A96:67-75.

SE1310 _____. "Going South in Russia." June 1934. In
Hughes, A96:75-80.

SE1311 _____. "Negroes Speak of War." July 1934. In
Foner, A74:788-789.

SE1312 _____. "Cowards from the Colleges." Aug.
1934. In Hughes, A96:55-63.

SE1313 _____. "To Negro Writers." April 1935.
American Writers' Congress. Ed. Henry Hart.
New York: International, 1935. Pages 139-141.
Rpt. in Hughes, A96:125-126.

SE1314 _____. "Too Much of Race." July 1937. In
Hughes, A96:97-98.

SE1315 _____. "Negroes in Spain." Sept. 1937. In
Hughes, A96:102-104.

SE1316 _____. "Franco and the Moors." Oct. 1937.
In Hughes, A96:99-102.

SE1317 _____. "Laughter in Madrid." Jan. 1938. In
Hughes, A96:106-110.

SE1318 _____. "Democracy and Me." June 1939. In
Hughes, A96:127-130; and in Fighting Words. Ed.
Donald Ogden Stewart. New York: Harcourt, 1940.
Pages 58-63, abr.

SE1319 _____. "Harlem Literati of the Twenties."
Saturday Review of Literature, 22 June 1940, pp.
13-14.

SE1320 _____. "My America." 1944. In Logan A115:
299-307.

SE1321 _____. "My Most Humiliating Jim Crow Experience." May 1945. In Hughes, A97:488-489.

SE1322 _____. "Simple and Me." 1945. Phylon, 6 (4th Qrtr 1945), 349-353.

SE1323 _____. "The Soviet Union." June 1946. In Hughes, A96:80-82.

SE1324 _____. "The Soviet Union and Jews." June 1946. In Hughes, A96:82-84.

SE1325 _____. "The Soviet Union and Color." June 1946. In Hughes, A96:84-86.

SE1326 _____. "The Soviet Union and Women." June 1946. In Hughes, A96:86-88.

SE1327 _____. "The Soviet Union and Health." July 1946. In Hughes, A96:88-90.

SE1328 _____. "Faults of the Soviet Union." Aug. 1946. In Hughes, A96:90-92.

SE1329 _____. "Light and the Soviet Union." Aug. 1946. In Hughes, A96:92-94.

SE1330 _____. "My Adventures as a Social Poet." 1947. Phylon, 8 (3rd Qrtr 1947), 205-212. Rpt. in Hughes, A96:135-143.

SE1331 _____. "The Revolutionary Armies in China-- 1949." Oct. 1949. In Hughes, A96:117-118.

SE1332 _____. "Langston Hughes Speaks." 26 March 1953. In Hughes, A96:143-145.

SE1333 _____. "Concerning the Future of Asia." Aug. 1953. In Hughes, A96:120-122.

SE1334 _____. "The Glory of Negro History: A Pageant." 1955. In Highes, A97:465-480.

SE1335 _____. "The Writer's Position in America." 7 May 1957. In Hughes, A97:483-485; and in Foner, A74:916-918.

SE1336 _____. "Jazz as Communication." 1958. In
Hughes, A97:492-494.

SE1337 _____. "The Fun of Being Black." 1958. In
Hughes, A97:498-500.

SE1338 _____. "Writers: Black and White." 28 Feb.
1959. In Chapman, A32:618-622; in Hill, A93:274-
278; and in The American Negro Writer and His
Roots. New York: American Society of African
Culture, 1960. Pages 41-45.

SE1339 _____. "The Glory." 1 March 1959. In Hill,
A93:266-273.

HUGHES, LANGSTON. See Brawley, HC13:246-250;
Dickinson, HC37; Hughes, HC90; Hughes, HC91;
Meltzer, HC115; Bone, HC964:75-77; Gloster,
HC981:184-187, 219-222; MacLeod, HC993; and Rus-
tin, SE2023.

SE1340 Hulett, John. "We've Decided To Stop Begging." 22
May 1966. In Grant, A84:402-407; and in Foner,
A74:1020-1026.

SE1341 Hurst, Charles G., Jr. "The African Heritage."
19 May 1971. In Hurst, HC410:13-22.

SE1342 Hurst, John. "Christianity and Woman." Aug. 1915.
In Aptheker, A2:97.

SE1343 Innis, Roy. "When Negro Leaders Look Ahead."
Nov. 1968. U.S. News and World Report, 25 Nov.
1968, pp. 59-61. Rpt. in Littleton and Burger,
A112:324-328.

SE1344 _____. "Separatist Economics: A New Social
Contract." 1969. In Littleton and Burger, A112:
160-169.

SE1345 Ivy, James W. "The National Association for the
Advancement of Colored People as an Instrument of
Social Change." 21 Sept. 1956. Presence Afri-
caine, Nos. 8-10 (June-Nov. 1956), 337-343.

SE1346 _____. "The Semantics of Being Negro in the
Americas." March 1959. Presence Africaine,

Nos. 24-25 (Feb.-May 1959), 133-141.

SE1347 Jackson, G. H. "The Christian Sabbath." 1890.
In Brawley, A25:157-165.

SE1348 Jackson, George. "Towards the United Front."
c. 1971. In Davis, A50:141-147.

SE1349 _____. "Letters to Jonathan Jackson." c. 1971.
In Davis, A50:148-151.

SE1350 Jackson, Jesse L. "Black Power and White
Churches." 1968. Church in Metropolis, No. 16
(Spring 1968), 7-9. Rpt. in Littleton and Burger,
A112:355-359.

SE1351 _____. "Address to the Congress of African
Peoples." Sept. 1970. In Jones, A101:22-34.

SE1352 _____. "Three Challenges to Organized Labor."
9 Aug. 1972. Freedomways, 12 (4th Qrtr 1972),
307-315.

SE1353 _____. "The New Spirit of '76." 1972. In
Wright, A180:51-67.

JACKSON, JESSE. See "Jesse Jackson," HC94.

SE1354 Jason, William C. "Life's Morn." c. 1900 (?). In
Dunbar, A70:403-408.

SE1355 Jasper, John. "Dem Sebun Wimmin." c.1884 (?).
In Hatcher, HC77:89-93.

SE1356 _____. "The Stone Cut Out of the Mountain." 20
July 1884. In Hatcher, HC77:108-120.

SE1357 _____. "De Sun Do Move." c. 1884 (?). In
Hatcher, HC77:133-149; and in The Book of Negro
Folklore. Ed. Langston Hughes and Arna W. Bon-
temps. New York: Dodd, 1958. Pages 225-233.

SE1358 _____. "Whar Sin Kum Frum?" c. 1884 (?).
In Hatcher, HC77:49-56.

JASPER, JOHN. See Brawley, HC12:80-87; Harlin,
HC72; Hatcher, HC77; Simmons, HC163a:1064-1072

or HC163b:767-774; Brown, HC444:203-207; and Honan, HC1089.

SE1359 Jelinek, Donald A. "The Problem Is Poverty." 12
Feb. 1967. In Grant, A84:493-498.

SE1360 Jenkins, Martin D. "The Function of Morgan State
College as a State Institution of Higher Education."
17 Dec. 1948. In Hill, A93:94-107.

SE1361 John, Vernon S. "Civilized Interiors." c. 1950.
In Hill, A93:70-72.

SE1362 Johnson, Charles S. "After Garvey--What?" Aug.
1923. Opportunity, 1 (Aug. 1923), 231-233. Rpt.
in Fishel and Quarles, A72:433-436, abr.

SE1363 _____. "The New Frontage on American Life."
1925. In Locke, A113:278-298.

SE1364 _____. "A Southern Negro's View of the South."
Sept. 1956. New York Times Magazine, 23 Sept.
1956, pp. 15, 64, 66-67. Rpt. in JNE, 26 (Winter
1957), 4-9.

SE1365 Johnson, Edwina C. "An Alternative to Miseducation for the Afro-American People." 13 Dec. 1968.
In Wright, A179:198-205.

SE1366 Johnson, Harvey. "The Righteous and the Wicked."
1890. In Brawley, A25:166-174.

JOHNSON, HARVEY. See Simmons, HC163a:729-732
or HC163b:509-511.

SE1367 Johnson, Henry. "Introductory Address" [for Sipkins, SE2097]. 2 Jan. 1809. In Porter, A141:366.

SE1368 _____, and A. Lawrence. "Resolutions on Colonization." Oct. 1831. In Garrison, A77:43-44.

SE1369 Johnson, James Weldon. "Should the Negro Be Given
an Education Different from That Given to the
Whites?" 1902. In Culp, A46:72-75.

SE1370 _____. " 'About Aunties.' " Aug. 1915. In
Aptheker, A2:97-98.

SE1371 _____. "Organizing in the South." March 1917.
In Aptheker, A2:169-170.

SE1372 _____. "Africa at the Peace Table and the Descendants of Africans in Our American Democracy."
1919. In Foner, A74:731-740; and in Hill and Kilson, A92a:329-335 or A92b:384-392.

SE1373 _____. "Our Democracy and the Ballot." 10
March 1923. In Woodson, A177:663-671; and in
Foner, A74:757-763, abr.

SE1374 _____. "Lynching--America's National Disgrace."
1924. Current History, 19 (Jan. 1924), 596-601.

SE1375 _____. "Harlem: The Culture Capital." 1925.
In Locke, A113:301-311.

SE1376 _____. "Detroit." July 1926. In Aptheker, A2:
517-522.

SE1377 _____. "Practice of Lynching." 1927. Century,
115 (Nov. 1927), 65-70.

SE1378 _____. "Race Prejudice and the Negro Artist."
Nov. 1928. Harper's, Nov. 1928, pp. 769-776.
Rpt. in Aptheker, A2:585-596.

SE1379 _____. "The Dilemma of the Negro Author."
Dec. 1928. American Mercury, 15 (Dec. 1928),
477-481.

SE1380 _____. "Negro Authors and White Publishers."
July 1929. Crisis, July 1929, pp. 228-229.

SE1381 _____. "The Shining Life: An Appreciation of
Julius Rosenwald Delivered at a Memorial Service
in Fisk Memorial Chapel." 14 Feb. 1932. Fisk
Univ. Bulletin, Vol. 8, No. 1.

SE1382 _____. Negro Americans, What Now? New
York: Viking, 1934.
    Contains: "Choices," pp. 3-18.
    "Forces and Resources," pp. 19-40.
    "Techniques and Policies," pp. 41-97.
    "Conclusion," pp. 98-103.

SE1383 _____. "Letters to a Friend: Correspondence from James Weldon Johnson to George A. Towns." Phylon, 29 (2d Qrtr 1968), 182-198.

JOHNSON, JAMES WELDON. See Adelman, HC1; Brawley, HC13:206-214; Bullock, HC19:97-100; Johnson, HC95; Levy, HC99; Collier, HC216; Cruse, HC448:33-38; Hughes, HC459:70-74; Bone, HC964: 45-49; Bronz, HC969:18-46; Gloster, HC981:79-83; Boulware, HC1023:81-86; Du Bois, SE806; Crisis, 45 (Aug. 1938), 265; and Phylon, 32 (4th Qrtr 1971), 333-402.

SE1384 Johnson, Jesse J. "The Black Psychologist: Pawn or Professional?" 11 April 1969. In Wright, A179:31-35.

SE1385 Johnson, John E., Jr. "Super Black Man." c. 1968. In Barbour, A8:224-226.

SE1386 Johnson, Mordecai Wyatt. "The Faith of the American Negro." 22 June 1922. In Brown, A28:681-685; in Foner, A74:743-748; and in Woodson, A177: 658-663.

SE1387 _____. "Welcome Address and Explanation of the General Purposes of the Conference [on 'The Courts and Racial Integration in Education']." 16 April 1952. JNE, 21 (Summer 1952), 233-241.

SE1388 _____. "Speech to the Atlantic Congress." 6 June 1959. In Hale, A90:97-108; and in Hill, A93: 245-257.

JOHNSON, MORDECAI WYATT. See Bullock, HC19: 7-13; and Boulware, HC1023:70-77.

SE1389 Johnson, Richard, and R. G. Overing. "Resolutions on Colonization." 23 Jan. 1832. In Garrison, A77:50-51.

SE1390 [Johnson, S. J.] "John the Baptist--A Voice Crying in the Wilderness." 28 June 1942. In Pipes, HC1197:22-30.

SE1391 [_____.] "Pray!" 26 July 1942. In Pipes, HC1197:46-52.

SE1392 Johnson, William H. "The Afro-American Press."
1890. In Penn, A139:439-442.

[Johnston, Martin, and Samuel Johnston. See Johnston, SE1393.]

SE1393 Johnston, Samuel, and Martin Johnston. "Resolutions on Colonization." 9 Jan. 1832. In Garrison,
A77:49.

SE1394 Johnstone, Abraham. "Address to the People of
Color." 1797. In Foner, A74:17-19.

SE1395 Jones, Absalom, and Richard Allen. "A Narrative
of the Proceedings of the Black People, during the Late
Awful Calamity in Philadelphia, in the Year, 1793:
and a Refutation of Some Censures, Thrown upon
Them in Some Late Publications." 1794. In Porter,
A142:orig. pag.; in Allen, HC2:48-65; in Aptheker,
A1:32-38, abr.; and in Brawley, A24:89-95, abr.

SE1396 Jones, Absalom, et al. "Petition ... to the President, Senate, and House of Representatives." 30
Dec. 1799. In Porter, A141:330-332.

SE1397 Jones, Absalom. "A Thanksgiving Sermon, Preached
... on Account of the Abolition of the African Slave
Trade." 1 Jan. 1808. In Porter, A141:335-342.

SE1398 Jones, Eugene Kinckle. "Some Observations on the
American Race Problem." c. 1927. In Johnson,
A100:96-99.

SE1399 Jones, LeRoi. "Tokenism: 300 Years for Five
Cents." 1962. In Jones, A102:68-81; and in Littleton and Burger, A112:80-83, excerpt.

SE1400 _____. "Street Protest." 1962. In Jones, A102:
97-100.

SE1401 _____. "The Myth of a 'Negro Literature.' "
14 March 1962. Saturday Review, 20 April 1963,
pp. 20-21. Rpt. in Jones, A102:105-115.

SE1402 _____. "What Does Nonviolence Mean?" 1963.
In Jones, A102:133-154.

SE1403 _____. "Expressive Language." 1963. In
Jones, A102:166-172; and in Smith, A155:323-328.

SE1404 _____. "LeRoi Jones Talking." 1964. In Jones,
A102:179-188.

SE1405 _____. "The Last Days of the American Empire
(Including Some Instructions for Black People)."
1964. In Jones, A102:189-209.

[_____. "The Revolutionary Theatre." See
HC988.]

SE1406 _____. "Blackhope." 1965. In Jones, A102:
234-237.

SE1407 _____. "The Legacy of Malcolm X, and the
Coming of the Black Nation." 1965. In Jones,
A102:238-250; and in Littleton and Burger, A112:
414-421.

SE1408 _____. "The Need for a Cultural Base to Civil
Rites & Bpower Mooments [sic]." 1967. In Barbour, A8:119-126.

SE1409 [_____.] Imamu Amiri Baraka. "A Black Value
System." 1969. Black Scholar, 1 (Nov. 1969).
Rpt. [as a pamphlet] Newark: Jihad, 1969.

SE1410 [_____.] Imamu Amiri Baraka. "Address to the
Congress of African Peoples." Sept. 1970. In
Jones, A101:92-103.

SE1411 [_____.] Imamu Amiri Baraka. "Political Liberation: Coordinator's Statement." Sept. 1970.
In Jones, A101:115-122.

SE1412 [_____.] Imamu Amiri Baraka. "The Pan African Party and the Black Nation." 1971. Black
Scholar, 2 (March 1971), 24-32.

SE1413 [_____.] Imamu Amiri Baraka. "Black Nationalism: 1972." 1972. Black Scholar, 4 (Sept. 1972),
23-29.

JONES, LEROI. See Hudson, HC239; Cruse, HC448:
355-368, 484-487, 530-532, 538-541; Bigsby,

HC963:138-155; and Llorens, HC991.

SE1414 Jones, Paul W. L. "Negro Biography." 23 Nov.
1922. JNH, 8 (April 1923), 128-133.

SE1415 Jones, Robert E. "A Few Remarks on Making a
Life." 29 May 1913. In Dunbar, A70:455-460.

SE1416 Jones, S. J. "A Farewell, Delivered Before the
Kentucky Conference." pre-1884. In Hood, A95:
335-351.

SE1417 _____. "The Good Samaritan." pre-1884. In
Hood, A95:353-363.

SE1418 Jones, William N. "Why Negroes Should Support the
Communists." 2 Oct. 1932. In Foner, A74:786-
787.

SE1419 Joseph, James A. "Has Black Religion Lost Its
Soul?" 1970. In Barbour, A9:69-83.

SE1420 Karenga, Maulana Ron. "From the Quotable Karenga." 1967. In Barbour, A8:162-170.

SE1421 _____. "The Black Community and the University: A Community Organizer's Perspective."
May 1968. In Robinson, HC424:37-54; and in Littleton and Burger, A112:209-217, abr.

SE1422 _____. "Overturning Ourselves: From Mystifi-
cation to Meaningful Struggle." 1972. Black Scholar, 4 (Oct. 1972), 6-14.

SE1423 Kawanza, Evelyn. "Address to the Congress of African Peoples." Sept. 1970. In Jones, A101:74-
75.

SE1424 Kealing, H. T. "The Characteristics of the Negro
People." 1903. In The Negro Problem, A133:163-
185.

SE1425 Killens, John O. "White Liberals and the Black
Revolution." 15 June 1964. In Foner, A74:1002-
1004.

SE1426 Kilson, Martin, Jr. "The Intellectual Validity of

Studying the Black Experience." May 1968. In Robinson, HC424:13-16.

SE1427 _____. "The Black Experience at Harvard." Sept. 1973. New York Times Magazine, 2 Sept. 1973, pp. 13, 31-32, 34, 37. [See Williams, SE 2351.]

SE1428 King, Coretta Scott. "We Need To Be United." 22 April 1970. In Foner, A74:1169-1172.

SE1429 King, Martin Luther, Jr. "Our Struggle." April 1956. In Goodman, A83:262-269; and in Bracey, A21:672-677.

SE1430 _____. "Walk for Freedom." May 1956. Fellowship, 22 (May 1956), 5-7. Rpt. in Bracey, A21: 677-680.

SE1431 _____. "Facing the Challenge of a New Age." Dec. 1956. Phylon, 18 (1st Qrtr 1957), 25-34. Rpt. in Golden and Rieke, A82:248-257; and in Long and Collier, A118:641-652.

SE1432 _____. "Nonviolence and Racial Justice." Feb. 1957. Christian Century, 74 (6 Feb. 1957), 165-167. Rpt. in Osofsky, A135:523-526.

SE1433 _____. "Give Us the Ballot--We will Transform the South." 17 May 1957. In Foner, A74:920-924.

SE1434 _____. "The Social Organization of Nonviolence (A Reply to Robert F. Williams)." 1959. In Goodman, A83:282-286; and in Williams, SE2359:11-15. [See Williams, SE2358.]

SE1435 _____. "The American Dream." 6 June 1961. In Foner, A74:933-943.

SE1436 _____. "Love, Law and Civil Disobedience." 16 Nov. 1961. In Hill, A93:345-356; in Boulware, HC1023:258-270; in Foner, A74:943-953, abr.; and in Contemporary American Speeches: A Sourcebook of Speech Forms and Principles. Ed. Wil A. Linkugel, R. R. Allen, and Richard L. Johannesen. Belmont, Cal.: Wadsworth, 1965. Pages 53-63.

SE1437 _____. "The Luminous Promise." Dec. 1962.
Progressive, 26 (Dec. 1962), 34-37.

SE1438 _____. "Letter from Birmingham Jail." 16
April 1963. In King, SE1459:77-100; and in Daniel,
A48:62-80. [See Bosmajian, HC1042.]

SE1439 _____. "I Have a Dream." 28 Aug. 1963. In
Speeches by the Leaders, A131:n. pag.; in Foner,
A74:971-975; in Golden and Rieke, A82:258-261; in
Hill, A93:371-375; in Smith and Robb, A156:184-188;
etc.

SE1440 _____. "Interview with Kenneth B. Clark."
1963. In Clark, A34:35-46.

SE1441 _____. "A Tough Mind and a Tender Heart."
c. 1963. In King, A106:1-7.

SE1442 _____. "Transformed Nonconformist." c. 1963.
In King, A106:8-15.

SE1443 _____. "On Being a Good Neighbor." c. 1963.
In King, A106:16-24.

SE1444 _____. "Love in Action." c. 1963. In King,
A106:25-33.

SE1445 _____. "Loving Your Enemies." c. 1963. In
King, A106:34-41.

SE1446 _____. "A Knock at Midnight." c. 1963. In
King, A106:42-50.

SE1447 _____. "The Man Who Was a Fool." c. 1963.
In King, A106:51-57.

SE1448 _____. "The Death of Evil Upon the Seashore."
c. 1963. In King, A106:58-66.

SE1449 _____. "Three Dimensions of a Complete Life."
c. 1963. In King, A106:67-77; and as "The Dimensions of a Complete Life" in King. The Measure
of a Man. [2d edn.] Philadelphia: Pilgrim, 1968.
Pages 41-59, rev.

SE1450 _____. "Shattered Dreams." c. 1963. In King,
A106:78-86.

SE1451 _____. "What Is Man?" c. 1963. In King,
A106:87-92; and in King. The Measure of a Man.
[2d edn.] Philadelphia: Pilgrim, 1968. Pages 17-
37, rev.

SE1452 _____. "How Should a Christian View Communism?" c. 1963. In King, A106:93-100.

SE1453 _____. "Our God Is Able." c. 1963. In King,
A106:101-107.

SE1454 _____. "Antidotes for Fear." c. 1963. In King,
A106:108-117.

SE1455 _____. "The Answer to a Perplexing Question."
c. 1963. In King, A106:118-126.

SE1456 _____. "Paul's Letter to American Christians."
c. 1963. In King, A106:127-134.

SE1457 _____. "Pilgrimage to Nonviolence." c. 1963.
In King, A106:135-142.

SE1458 _____. "Nobel Peace Prize Acceptance Statement." 10 Dec. 1964. In Hale, A90:374-377.

SE1459 _____. Why We Can't Wait. New York: Harper,
1964.
Contains: "The Negro Revolution--Why 1963?"
pp. 1-14.
"The Sword That Heals," pp. 15-38.
"Bull Connor's Birmingham," pp. 39-53.
"New Day in Birmingham," pp. 55-75.
"Letter from Birmingham Jail" [SE1438], pp. 77-
100.
"Black and White Together," pp. 101-117.
"The Summer of Our Discontent," pp. 119-136.
"The Days To Come," pp. 137-169.

SE1460 _____. "A Long Way To Go." 1965. In Smith
and Robb, A156:188-204.

SE1461 _____. "A Time To Break Silence." 4 April
1967. Freedomways, 7 (Spring 1967), 103-117.
Rpt. in Ramparts, May 1967, pp. 33-37; in Foner,
A74:1048-1058, abr.; in Grant, A84:418-425, abr.;
and in Readings in Speech. 2d edn. Ed. Haig A.
Bosmajian. New York: Harper, 1971. Pages 426-442.

SE1462 _____. "The President's Address to SCLC." 16
Aug. 1967. In Scott and Brockriede, A154:146-165;
and in Foner, A74:1069-1077.

SE1463 _____. "The Role of the Behavioral Scientist in
the Civil Rights Movement." 1 Sept. 1967. Journal of Social Issues, 24 (April 1968), 1-12. Rpt. in
Blacks in the United States. Ed. Norval D. Glenn
and Charles M. Bonjeau. San Francisco: Chandler,
1969. Pages 3-12.

SE1464 _____. Where Do We Go from Here: Chaos or
Community? New York: Harper, 1967.
Contains: "Where Are We?" pp. 1-22.
"Black Power," pp. 23-66.
"Racism and the White Backlash," pp. 67-101.
"The Dilemma of Negro Americans," pp. 102-134.
"Where We Are Going," pp. 135-166.
"The World House," pp. 167-191.
"Appendix: Programs and Prospects," pp. 193-
202.

SE1465 _____. "Impasse in Race Relations." 1967. In
King, A107:3-17.

SE1466 _____. "Conscience and the Vietnam War."
1967. In King, A107:21-34.

SE1467 _____. "Youth and Social Action." 1967. In
King, A107:37-50.

SE1468 _____. "Nonviolence and Social Change." 1967.
In King, A107:53-64.

SE1469 _____. "A Christmas Sermon on Peace." 24
Dec. 1967. In King, A107:67-78.

SE1470 _____. "Honoring Dr. Du Bois." 23 Feb. 1968.
Freedomways, 8 (Spring 1968), 104-111. Rpt. in
Clarke, A37:176-183; in Du Bois, A68:12-20; and in
Smith and Robb, A156:204-212.

SE1471 _____. "The Future of Integration." March 1968.
Humanist, 28 (March-April 1968), 2-6. Rpt. in
Moss, A130:31-42.

SE1471a _____. "Showdown for Non-Violence." April

1968. <u>Look</u>, 16 April 1968, pp. 23-25. Rpt. in
Littleton and Burger, A112:332-341.

SE1472 _____ . "I See the Promised Land." 3 April
1968. In Gregory, SE1055:280-287, abr.; and in
Foner, A74:1109, excerpt.

KING, MARTIN LUTHER, JR. See Williams, B35;
Bennett, HC7; King, HC96; Lewis, HC101; Lokos,
HC102; Miller, HC119; Reddick, HC148; Sharma,
HC160; Preston, HC141; Lomax, HC249; Meier,
HC254; Walton, HC270; Walton, HC271; Yglesias,
HC274; HC437:229-247; King, HC898; Valien, HC908;
Andrews, HC1020:41-48; Boulware, HC1023:243-258;
Anatol and Bittner, HC1035; Black, HC1039; Bos-
majian, HC1042; Scott, HC1126; Smith, HC1143;
Smith, HC1144; Steinkraus, HC1149; Wander, HC
1157; Baldwin, SE59; Belafonte, SE80; Boggs, SE143;
Cleage, SE359; Cleaver, SE386; Cook, SE428; Mays,
SE1629; Rustin, SE2006; Rustin, SE2021; Rustin,
SE2032; and <u>Martin Luther King, Jr.: A Profile</u>.
Ed. C. Eric Lincoln. New York: Hill, 1970.

SE1473 Koontz, Elizabeth Duncan. "Where Do We Go from
Here?" 12 June 1969. In Wright, A179:121-125.

SE1474 "L. H." "Duty of Females." May 1832. In Porter,
A141:123-126.

SE1475 Labrie, Peter. "The New Breed." 1966. In Jones,
and Neal, A103:64-77.

SE1476 Ladner, Joyce. "Tanzanian Women and Nation Building." Dec. 1971. <u>Black Scholar</u>, 3 (Dec. 1971),
22-28.

SE1477 Langford, Anna R. "How I 'Whupped' the Tar Out
of the Daley Machine." 1972. In Wright, A180:3-
31.

SE1478 Langston, Charles H. "The Constitution Is Pro-
Slavery." Jan. 1851. In Aptheker, A1:319-320.

SE1479 _____ . "Should Colored Men Be Subject to the
Pains and Penalties of the Fugitive Slave Law?"
12 May 1859. In Dunbar, A70:49-62; in Foner,
A74:209-215; and in Brown, A28:642-647, abr.

LANGSTON, CHARLES H.   See Guthrie, HC1077;
and Langston, SE1483.

SE1480 Langston, John Mercer. "The Intellectual, Moral,
and Spiritual Condition of the Slave."   27 Aug. 1853.
In Griffiths, A87:147-150.

SE1481 _____.   "Speech to the American Anti-Slavery
Society."   9 May 1855. In Langston, HC97:151-155.

SE1482 _____.   "The World's Anti-Slavery Movement: Its
Heroes and Its Triumphs."   2-3 Aug. 1858.   In
Langston, A109:41-67.

SE1483 _____.   "The Oberlin-Wellington Rescue Case."
July 1859. In Aptheker, A1:423-433.

SE1484 _____.   "Citizenship and the Ballot."   25 Oct.
1865. In Langston, A109:99-122.

SE1485 _____.   "The Passage of the Fifteenth Amendment."   May 1870. In Golden and Rieke, A82:198-
201.

SE1486 _____.   "Our Patriot Dead."   30 May 1873.   In
Langston, A109:180-187.

SE1487 _____.   "Eulogy on Charles Sumner."   24 April
1874. In Langston, A109:162-179.

SE1488 _____.   "Equality Before the Law."   17 May
1874. In Langston, A109:141-161; in Woodson,
A177:436-451; and in Foner, A74:410-418, abr.

SE1489 _____.   "Daniel O'Connell."   28 Dec. 1874.   In
Langston, A109:68-98.

SE1490 _____.   "An Address Delivered at the Centennial
Anniversary of the Pennsylvania Society for Promot-
ing the Abolition of Slavery."   14 April 1875.   In
Dunbar, A70:97-100.

SE1491 _____.   "Future of the Colored American."   25
Nov. 1875. In Langston, A109:259-286.

SE1492 _____.   "Our Political Parties."   1 April 1876.
In Langston, A109:188-208.

SE1493 _____. "Bishop Richard Allen." 17 Dec. 1876.
In Langston, A109:123-140.

SE1494 _____. "Pacific Reconstruction." 17 April 1877.
In Langston, A109:209-213; in Smith and Robb,
A156:47-65; and in Woodson, A177:417-435.

SE1495 _____. "The Exodus." 7 Oct. 1879. In Langston, A109:233-258; and in Brown, A28:667-672, excerpt.

SE1496 _____. "The Afro-American Press." 1890. In
Penn, A139:434-438.

SE1497 _____. "A Speech Laudatory of the Negro." 16
Jan. 1891. In Woodson, A177:387-403.

LANGSTON, JOHN MERCER. See Brawley, HC12:
139-146; Cheek, HC21; Christopher, HC24:137-148;
Langston, HC97; Rankin, HC145; Simmons, HC163a:
510-523 or HC163b:345-352; Blodgett, HC209; Cheek,
HC214; Brown, HC443:235-237; Brown, HC445:447-
448; Cromwell, HC447:155-163; Foner, HC573; and
Loggins, HC992:293-294.

[Lawrence, A., and Henry Johnson. See Johnson,
SE1368.]

SE1498 Lawrence, George. "Oration on the Abolition of the
Slave Trade." 1 Jan. 1813. In Porter, A141:375-
382.

SE1499 Lawson, J. H. "The Afro-American Press." 1890.
In Penn, A139:475-477.

SE1500 Lawson, James. "A Nonviolent Endorsement." 1969.
In Lecky and Wright, A110:78-91.

SE1501 Lawson, Jesse. "I Protest Against Hayes's Southern
Policy." Aug. 1877. In Foner, A74:458-459.

SE1502 _____. "The Remedy for Anarchy." 5 Feb. 1902.
In Foner, A74:639-640.

SE1503 Lee, B. F. "Episcopal Address." May 1900. In
Smith, HC1183:210-213, excerpt.

LEE, B. F.   See Simmons, HC163a:922-927 or
HC163b:655-657.

SE1504 Lee, Canada.   "Africa and a New World A-Coming."
c. 1945.   In Hill and Kilson, A92a:358-361 or A92b:
419-423.

SE1505 Lee, Don L.   "Dynamite Voices: Black Poets of the
1970's."   Sept. 1970, In Jones, A101:200-211.

SE1506 Lester, Julius.   "From the Other Side of the
Tracks."   1 July 1968.   In Golden and Rieke, A82:
494-496.

SE1507 _____.   Look Out, Whitey! Black Power's Gon'
Get Your Mama!   New York: Dial, 1968.
         Contains: " 'We Shall Overcome,' " pp. 3-30.
         "Bang! Bang! Mr. Moynihan," pp. 33-54.
         "Black Pawns in a White Game," pp. 57-68.
         " 'Tear This Building Down,' " pp. 71-80.
         "Cultural Nationalism," pp. 83-93.
         "Beep! Beep! Bang! Bang! Umgawa! BLACK
            POWER!" pp. 97-107.
         "The Rhetoric and the Reality," pp. 111-122.
         "White Power," pp. 125-134.
         "Look Out, Whitey! Black Power's Gon' Get
            Your Mama!" pp. 137-143.

SE1508 Lewis, John.   "March on Washington Speech [Origi-
nal Version]."   28 Aug. 1963.   Liberation, 8 (Sept.
1963), 8.   Rpt. in Foner, A74:975-977; and in
Grant, A84:375-377.

SE1509 _____.   "March on Washington Speech [Delivered
Version]."   28 Aug. 1963.   In Speeches by the
Leaders, A131:n. pag.

SE1510 _____.   "Religion and Human Rights: A Final
Appeal to the Church."   3 May 1968.   New South,
23 (Spring 1968), 57-61.

SE1511 _____.   "Barriers to the Dream."   Summer 1968.
New South, 23 (Summer 1968), 56-58.

LEWIS, JOHN.   See Allen, HC207; Good, HC232;
and Zinn, HC911.

SE1512 Lewis, W. Arthur.   "The Road to the Top Is Through

Higher Education--Not Black Studies." May 1969.
In Wallerstein and Starr," A163:343-347.

SE1513 Lewis, William H. "Address Before the Massachusetts House of Representatives." 12 Feb. 1913. In
Woodson, A177:562-572.

SE1514 _____. "Booker T. Washington--A Lover of His
Fellow-Men." 11 Feb. 1916. In Woodson, A177:
596-601.

SE1515 Lincoln, C. Eric. "Anxiety, Fear and Integration."
1960. Phylon, 21 (3rd Qrtr 1960), 278-285. Rpt.
in Lincoln, A111:13-31.

SE1516 _____. "Extremist Attitudes in the Black Muslim
Movement." 1963. New South, 18 (Jan. 1963), 3-
10. Rpt. in Lincoln, A111:62-75.

SE1517 _____. "The Meaning of the Negro Experience."
1963. In Lincoln, A111:76-89.

SE1518 _____. My Face Is Black. Boston: Beacon,
1964.
    Contains: "The American Tragedy: A Christian
    Dilemma," pp. 1-30.
    "The Fight for Freedom: Protest and Communi-
    cation," pp. 31-71.
    "Mood Ebony: The Acceptance of Being Black,"
    pp. 72-90.
    "Mood Ebony: The Meaning of Malcolm X," pp.
    pp. 91-117.
    "Black Chauvinism: The Armageddon Complex,"
    pp. 118-133.

SE1519 _____. "Breakers Ahead!" 1964. In Lincoln,
A111:100-112.

SE1520 _____. "Patterns of Protest." 1964. Christian
Century, 81 (3 June 1964), 733-736. Rpt. in Lincoln, A111:113-122.

SE1521 _____. "The Negro's Middle-Class Dream."
1964. New York Times Magazine, 25 Oct. 1964,
pp. 35, 91-92, 94, 96, 99-100. Rpt. in Lincoln,
A111:133-145.

SE1522 _____. "The Meaning of Malcolm X." 1965.
Christian Century, 82 (7 April 1965), 431-433. Rpt.
in Lincoln, A111:146-152. [Cf. Lincoln, SE1518:91-
117.]

SE1523 _____. "The British Say They Aren't Prejudiced."
1965. New York Times Magazine, 14 Nov. 1965,
pp. 64-65, 107-110, 112. Rpt. in Lincoln, A111:
153-162.

SE1524 _____. "The Absent Father Haunts the Negro Family." 1965. New York Times Magazine, 28 Nov.
1965, pp. 60, 172-176. Rpt. in Lincoln, A111:163-
172.

SE1525 _____. "The Race Problem and International Relations." 1966. New South, 21 (Fall 1966), 2-14.

SE1526 _____. "Thirty-Four Million Poor: Right Here
in Affluent America." 1967. In Lincoln, A111:173-
187.

SE1527 _____. "Some Theological and Ethical Implications of the Black Ghetto." March 1967. Christian
Century, 84 (1 March 1967), 264-267. Rpt. in Lincoln, A111:188-200.

SE1528 _____. "Color and Group Identity in the United
States." 1967. In Lincoln, A111:201-220.

SE1529 _____. "The Black Ghetto as an Urban Phenomenon." 1967. In Lincoln, A111:221-238.

SE1530 _____. "A Last Admonition." 1967. In Lincoln,
A111:239-245.

SE1531 _____. "The New Blacks in Search of a Self."
1970. Boston University Journal, 19 (Spring 1971),
53-60.

SE1532 Llorens, David. "The Fellah, The Chosen Ones, The
Guardian." 1966. In Jones and Neal, A103:169-177.

SE1533 Locke, Alain. "Apropos of Africa." Feb. 1924. In
Long and Collier, A118:335-343; and in Hill and Kilson, A92a:350-357, abr., or A92b:411-418, abr.

SE1534 _____. "Our Little Renaissance." c. 1927. In
Johnson, A100:117-118; and in Cromwell, A42:206-
209.

SE1535 _____. "The Negro in the Three Americas."
May 1943. JNE, 13 (Winter 1944), 7-18.

SE1536 Logan, Rayford W. "The Negro Wants First-Class
Citizenship." 1944. In Logan, A115:1-30.

SE1537 _____. "Carter G. Woodson: Mirror and Molder
of His Time, 1875-1950." 21 Oct. 1972. JNH, 58
(Jan. 1973), 1-17.

SE1538 Loguen, J. W. "I Won't Obey the Fugitive Slave
Law." 4 Oct. 1850. In Foner, A74:98-100.

LOGUEN, J. W. See Brown, HC445:531-532.

SE1539 Lomax, Louis E. The Negro Revolt. New York:
Harper, 1962.
        Contains: "A Negro View of American History,"
        pp. 3-63.
        "The Negro Revolt," pp. 67-206.
        "The Way Ahead," pp. 209-247.

SE1540 _____. "I Am Somebody." 1963. In Lomas,
A116:121-135.

SE1541 _____. "The Black Goldwater." 1964. Ramparts, Nov. 1964, pp. 31-34.

SE1542 _____. "Interview with Pierre Berton." c. 1966.
Voices from the Sixties: Twenty-Two Views of a
Revolutionary Decade. Ed. Pierre Berton. Garden
City, N.Y.: Doubleday, 1967. Pages 12-21.

SE1543 Lomax, Thomas H. "The Love of God--Its Objects,
Gift and Design." pre-1884. In Hood, A95:322-334.

SE1544 Long, Jefferson F. "Speech on Disorders in the
South." 1 Feb. 1871. In Aptheker, A1:607-608;
and Woodson, A177:294-295.

LONG, JEFFERSON F. See Christopher, HC24:25-
37.

SE1545 Love, E. K. "Regeneration." 1890. In Brawley,
A25:64-80.

LOVE, E. K. See Simmons, HC163a:481-483 or
HC163b:321-322.

SE1546 Love, John L. "The Disfranchisement of the Negro."
1899. American Negro Academy, Occasional Papers
No. 6. Washington: The Academy, 1899.

SE1547 _____. "The Potentiality of the Negro Vote in
the North and West." 1905. In The Negro and the
Elective Franchise, A132:61-67.

SE1548 Lynch, Acklyn. "Education." Sept. 1970. In Jones,
A101:287-297.

SE1549 Lynch, James. "Reflections." 1862. In Payne,
HC1181:126-129.

SE1550 _____. "Colored Men Standing in the Way of
Their Own Race." May 1865. In Foner, A74:317-
318.

SE1551 _____. "The President and the Colored Delegation." 1866. In Payne, HC1181:159-160. [See
Douglass, SE681; and Downing, SE739.]

SE1552 _____. "Trying Moment for the Colored People."
1866. In Payne, HC1181:162-164.

SE1553 _____. "The Jew and the Black Gentile." 1866.
In Payne, HC1181:167-170.

SE1554 _____. "The Greatest Folly of White Americans."
1866. In Payne, HC1181:170-172.

LYNCH, JAMES. See Brown, HC445:519-520.

SE1555 Lynch, John R. "Speech on the Civil-Rights Bill."
3 Feb. 1875. In Woodson, A177:356-377; and in
Dunbar, A70:89-94, excerpt.

SE1556 _____. "Speech in the Case of His Contested
Election." 27 April 1882. In Woodson, A177:273-
285; and in Aptheker, A1:730-731, excerpt.

SE1557 _____. "The Afro-American Press." 1890. In
Penn, A139:438-439.

SE1558 _____. "States' Rights and the Suffrage." Aug.
1915. In Aptheker, A2:101-102.

LYNCH, JOHN R. See Christopher, HC24:55-68;
Lynch, HC106a or HC106b; Lynch, HC107; Mann,
HC111; Simmons, HC163a:1042-1045 or HC163b:749-
751; and Brown, HC445:491-493.

SE1559 Lyon, Ernest. "Emancipation and Racial Advancement." 30 May 1913. In Dunbar, A70:461-474.

SE1560 McCoy, Rhody. "Why Have an Ocean Hill-Browns-
ville?" 1969. In Wright, A179:251-260.

SE1561 McElwee, Robert. "A Plea for Universal Education
in the South." 23 Jan. 1883. In Foner, A74:478-
479, abr.

SE1562 McElwee, Samuel Allen. "Mobs." Feb. 1887. In
Simmons, HC163a:502-505, abr., or HC163b:339-
341, abr.

McELWEE, SAMUEL ALLEN. See Simmons, HC163a:
498-505 or HC163b:335-341.

SE1563 McGowan, Edward D. "Stop the Foes of Negro
Freedom." 30 April 1953. In Foner, A74:861-866.

SE1564 McKay, Claude. "Garvey as a Negro Moses."
April 1922. In Aptheker, A2:367-370.

SE1565 _____. "Soviet Russia and the Negro." Dec.
1923. In Aptheker, A2:433-444.

McKAY, CLAUDE. See Bone, HC964:67-75; and
Gloster, HC981:163-168.

SE1566 McKissick, Floyd B. "Speech at the National Conference on Black Power." 21 July 1967. In Bosmajian and Bosmajian, A19:127-141; and in Foner, A74:
1066-1068, excerpt.

SE1567 _____. "Programs for Black Power." 1968.
In Barbour, A8:179-181.

SE1568 _____. Three-Fifths of a Man. New York: Mac-
millan, 1969.
Contains: "What Is Happening Now?" pp. 23-47.
"The Constitution and Social Change," pp. 53-96.
"Program and Peoplehood," pp. 101-165.

SE1569 _____. "The Student and the Ghetto." May 1969.
In O'Neill, A134:216-226.

SE1570 _____. "A Proposal for Planning Funds to De-
velop Soul City, a New Town in North Carolina."
Aug. 1969. In Littleton and Burger, A112:145-149,
abr.

SE1571 McWorter, Gerald A. "Deck the Ivy Racist Halls:
The Case of Black Studies." May 1968. In Robinson, HC424:55-74.

SE1572 Malcolm X. "Unity." 1960. In Lomax, HC1218:
150-158; in Bracey, A22:413-420; and in Rich and
Smith, HC1120:260-268.

SE1573 _____. "Yale Address." Oct. 1960. In Hill,
A93:304-317; and in Lomax, HC1218:180-195.
[Note: HC1218 text dated 1962.]

SE1574 _____. "The Harvard Law School Forum." 24
March 1961. In Malcolm X, A122:115-131; and in
Lomax, HC1218:131-148. [Note: HC1218 text dated
1960.]

SE1575 _____. " 'University Speech.' " 1961-1962. In
Lomax, HC1218:160-171.

[_____, and James Farmer. See Farmer, SE
880.]

SE1576 Malcolm X. "Black Man's History." Dec. 1962.
In Malcolm X, A120:23-66.

SE1577 _____. "Address at Queens College." April 1963.
In Lomax, HC1218:174-178.

SE1578 _____. "The Black Revolution." June 1963. In
Malcolm X, A120:67-80.

SE1579 _____. "Malcolm X Talks with Kenneth B. Clark."

June 1963. In Clark, A34:18-32; in Clarke, A35:
168-181; and in Golden and Rieke, A82:412-421.

SE1580 _____. "The Old Negro and the New Negro."
Fall 1963. In Malcolm X, A120:82-120.

SE1581 _____. "Message to the Grass Roots." 10 Nov.
1963. In Malcolm X, A121:4-17, abr.; and in Littleton and Burger, A112:121-132, abr.

SE1582 _____. "God's Judgment of White America." 1
Dec. 1963. In Malcolm X, A120:121-148; and in
Clarke, A35:282-287, excerpt. [Note: A120 text
dated 4 Dec. 1963; and Epps, A122:32 gives date as
22 Nov. 1963.]

SE1583 _____. "A Declaration of Independence." 12
March 1964. In Malcolm X, A121:20-22; and in
Malcolm X, A123:3-4.

SE1584 _____. "The Leverett House Forum." 18 March
1964. In Malcolm X, A122:131-160.

SE1585 _____. "The Ballot or the Bullet." 3 April 1964.
In Malcolm X, A121:23-44; in Foner, A74:986-1001;
in Smith and Robb, A156:214-235; in Andrews,
HC1020:135-153; in Rich and Smith, HC1120:269-293;
and in Readings in Speech. 2d edn. Ed. Haig A.
Bosmajian. New York: Harper, 1971. Pages 405-
425.

SE1586 _____. "The Black Revolution." 8 April 1964.
In Malcolm X, A121:45-57; in Malcolm X, A123:5-14;
and in Smith and Robb, A156:235-250.

SE1587 _____. "Answers to Questions at the Militant
Labor Forum." 8 April 1964. In Malcolm X, A119:
15-32.

SE1588 _____. "Speech at the University of Ghana."
May 1964. In Smith, HC1271:211-220.

SE1589 _____. "The Harlem 'Hate-Gang' Scare." 29
May 1964. In Malcolm X, A121:64-71; and in Malcolm X, A123:15-18.

SE1590 _____. "The Founding Rally of the OAAU." 28

June 1964. In Malcolm X, A119:35-67.

SE1591 _____. "The Second Rally of the OAAU." 5
July 1964. In Malcolm X, A119:76-107.

SE1592 _____. "Appeal to African Heads of State." 17
July 1964. In Malcolm X, A121:72-77; and in
Clarke, A35:288-298.

SE1593 _____. "The Second African Summit Conference."
21 Aug. 1964. In Clarke, A35:294-301.

SE1594 _____. "The Homecoming Rally of the OAAU."
29 Nov. 1964. In Malcolm X, A119:133-156.

SE1595 _____. "Communication and Reality." 12 Dec.
1964. In Clarke, A35:307-320.

SE1596 _____. "At the Audubon." 13 Dec. 1964. In
Malcolm X, A121:97-112.

SE1597 _____. "The Harvard Law School Forum." 16
Dec. 1964. In Malcolm X, A122:161-182.

SE1598 _____. "With Mrs. Fannie Lou Hamer." 20
Dec. 1964. In Malcolm X, A121:113-122.

SE1599 _____. "At the Audubon." 20 Dec. 1964. In
Malcolm X, A121:123-144.

SE1600 _____. "To Mississippi Youth." 31 Dec. 1964.
In Malcolm X, A121:145-154; in Foner, A74:1005-
1010, abr.; and in Malcolm X. Malcolm X Talks
to Young People. New York: Young Socialist
Alliance, 1965. Pages 4-12.

SE1601 _____. "Prospects for Freedom in 1965." 7
Jan. 1965. In Malcolm X, A121:155-164; in Malcolm X, A123:18-27; and in Smith and Robb, A156:
250-263. [Note: A123 text includes excerpts from
question and discussion period.]

SE1602 _____. "Interview with Malcolm X." 18 Jan.
1965. In Malcolm X, A119:158-166; and in Malcolm X. Malcolm X Talks to Young People. New
York: Young Socialist Alliance, 1965. Pages 15-
24.

SE1603 _____. "Interview with Pierre Berton." 19 Jan.
1965. Voices from the Sixties: Twenty-Two Views
of a Revolutionary Decade. Ed. Pierre Berton.
Garden City, N. Y.: Doubleday, 1967. Pages 33-
41.

SE1604 _____. "On Afro-American History." 24 Jan.
1965. Malcolm X on Afro-American History. New
York: Merit, 1967. Pages 3-48. Rpt. in Clarke,
A35:321-332, excerpt. [Note: A35 text dated 25
Jan. 1965; Malcolm X on Afro-American History
text includes question-answer period.]

SE1605 _____. "After the Bombing." 14 Feb. 1965. In
Malcolm X, A121:165-170, 179-193.

MALCOLM X. See Clarke, A35; Goldman, HC62;
Jamal, HC93; Malcolm X, HC110; Steiner, HC166;
Warren, HC186; Breitman, HC210; Diamond, HC221;
Harper, HC236; Kahn and Rustin, HC242; Lomax,
HC249; Bennett, HC437:211-213; Lokos, HC934:41-
72; Andrews, HC1020:128-134; Boulware, HC1023:
233-238; Boulware, HC1044; Campbell, HC1056;
Campbell, HC1057; Epps, HC1065; Hurst, HC1090;
Illo, HC1091; Reynolds, HC1119; Rich and Smith,
HC1120:143-212; Weiss, HC1161; Lincoln, HC1213;
Lomax, HC1218; Draper, HC1256:86-96; Jones,
HC1265; Boggs, SE143; Cleage, SE358; Cleaver,
SE367; Lincoln, SE1518:91-117; Lincoln, SE1522;
Rustin, SE2017; and White, SE2318.

SE1606 Man of Color. "The Cause of Liberty." Feb. 1831.
In Woodson, A176:225-227.

SE1607 Marrant, John. "A Sermon Preached on the ...
Festival of St. John the Baptist." 24 June 1789.
Boston: Bible and Heart, n.d. [Available on micro-
film, New York Public Library, Film 1845.]

MARRANT, JOHN. See Marrant, HC112; Schomburg,
HC156; and Whitchurch, HC198.

SE1608 Marshall, Thurgood. "The Legal Attack to Secure
Civil Rights." 13 July 1944. In Broderick and
Meier, A26:228-238.

SE1609 _____. "An Evaluation of Recent Efforts to

Achieve Racial Integration in Education Through Resort to the Courts." 17 April 1952. JNE, 21
(Summer 1952), 316-327.

SE1610 _____. "Oral Argument on Behalf of the Appel-
lants." 7 Dec. 1953. In Golden and Rieke, A82:
243-244. [Outline of speech.]

SE1611 _____. "Rebuttal Argument." 8 Dec. 1953. In
Golden and Rieke, A82:244-246, excerpt.

SE1612 _____. "Segregation and Desegregation." Spring
1954. In Foner, A74:867-882.

SE1613 _____. "Special Message to the 48th Annual
NAACP Convention." 30 June 1957. In Williams
and Williams, A175:127-134.

SE1614 _____. "The Rise and Collapse of the 'White
Democratic Primary.'" 1957. JNE, 26 (Summer
1957), 249-254.

SE1615 _____. "The Cry for Freedom." 20 March 1960.
In Hill, A93:318-320, abr.; and in Foner, A74:931-
933, abr.

MARSHALL, THURGOOD. See Bennett, HC437:215-
221.

SE1616 Martin, J. Sella. "Speech Before the Paris Anti-
slavery Conference." 27 Aug. 1867. In Woodson,
A177:256-261.

MARTIN, J. SELLA. See Brown, HC443:241-245;
and Brown, HC445:535-536.

SE1617 Mason, M. C. B. "The Methodist Episcopal Church
and the Evangelization of Africa." 15 Dec. 1895.
In Bowen, A20:143-148.

SE1618 _____. "Achievements of the Nineteenth-Century
American Negro." 1902. In Culp, A46:34-37.

SE1619 _____. "Lincoln, the Man of the Hour." 12 Feb.
1909. In Woodson, A177:541-554.

SE1620 Mason, James E. "Joseph Charles Price." c. 1894.

In Ferris, HC451:771-773.

SE1621 Matthews, Connie. "The Struggle Is a World Struggle." 15 Oct. 1969. In Foner, A73:154-159.

SE1622 Mayfield, Julian. "The Cuban Challenge." 1961.
Freedomways, 1 (Summer 1961), 185-189.

SE1623 Mays, Benjamin E. "Democratizing and Christianiz-
ing America in This Generation." 8 June 1945.
JNE, 14 (Fall 1945), 527-534.

SE1624 _____. "The Christian Race Relations." 16
April 1952. In Hill, A93:120-139.

SE1625 _____. "The Present Status of and Future Outlook for Racial Integration in the Church Related
White Colleges in the South." 18 April 1952. JNE,
21 (Summer 1952), 350-352.

SE1626 _____. "The Moral Aspects of Segregation."
1954. In Daniel, A48:170-176.

SE1627 _____. "Desegregate and Integrate to What End?"
11 Feb. 1964. In Hale, A90:109-117; and in Williams and Williams, A175:89-98, abr.

SE1628 _____. "Higher Education and the American Negro." June 1967. In Wright, A179:104-113.

SE1629 _____. "Eulogy of Dr. Martin Luther King, Jr."
9 April 1968. In Hale, A90:117-122; in Smith and
Robb, A156:297-302; in King, HC96:352-359; and in
Representative American Speeches: 1967-1968. Ed.
Lester Thonssen. New York: Wilson, 1968. Pages
161-168.

MAYS, BENJAMIN E. See Boulware, HC1023:187-
191.

SE1630 Mbala, Raymond. "Address to the Congress of African Peoples." Sept. 1970. In Jones, A101:76-81.

SE1631 Member of the African Society in Boston. "The
Sons of Africans: An Essay on Freedom, with Ob-
servations on the Origin of Slavery." 1808. In
Porter, A141:13-27.

SE1632 "A Memorial from the Free People of Colour to the
Citizens of Baltimore." 1827. In Hill and Kilson,
A92a:33-37 or 92b:38-43.

SE1633 Menard, John Willis. "The Negro's First Speech in
Congress." 27 Feb. 1869. In Woodson, A177:263-
267.

MENARD, JOHN WILLIS. See Menard, HC116; and
Menard, HC117.

[Merriman, Henry N., and Henry Berrian. See Berrian, SE83.]

SE1634 Miller, George F. "They Are All Heroes." 14
May 1918. In Foner, A74:720-721.

SE1635 Miller, Kelly. "What Walt Whitman Means to the
Negro." 31 May 1895. In Miller, A129:199-210.

SE1636 _____. "A Review of Hoffman's Race Traits and
Tendencies of the American Negro." 1897. Amer-
ican Negro Academy, Occasional Papers No. 1.
Washington: The Academy, 1897. [See Hoffman,
HC288.]

SE1637 _____. "Address to the Graduating Class of the
College Department, Howard University." 1 June
1898. Washington, D.C., 1898.

SE1638 _____. " 'The Primary Needs of the Negro Race.' "
14 June 1899. Washington: Howard Univ. Press,
1899.

SE1639 _____. "The Negro as a Religious, Social and
Political Factor." 1900. Philadelphia, 1900.

SE1640 _____. "The Land of Goshen." 1900. In Miller,
A129:154-167.

SE1641 _____. "Rise of the Professional Class." c. 1900.
In Miller, A129:179-185.

SE1642 _____. "The Negro and Education." Feb. 1901.
Forum, 30 (Feb. 1901), 693-700.

SE1643 _____. "Will the Education of the Negro Solve

the Race Problem?" 1902. In Culp, A46:158-162.

SE1644 _____. "The Expansion of the Negro Population."
Feb. 1902. Forum, 32 (Feb. 1902), 671-679.

SE1645 _____. "Function of the Negro College."
April 1902. Dial, 32 (16 April 1902), 267-270.

SE1646 _____. "The City Negro." 1902-1903. In Miller, A129:119-132.

SE1647 _____. "Religion as a Solvent of the Race Problem." 26 May 1903. In Miller, A129:133-151.

SE1648 _____. "Washington's Policy." Sept. 1903. In
Meier and Rudwick, A126:119-124.

SE1649 _____. "The Negro's Part in the Negro Problem." 1904. In Miller, A129:88-108.

SE1650 _____. "Social Equality." c. 1904. In Miller,
A129:109-118.

SE1651 _____. "Howard University." 1905. In From
Servitude to Service, A75:3-47.

SE1652 _____. "As to the Leopard's Spots: An Open
Letter to Thomas Dixon, Jr." Sept. 1905. In Miller, A129:28-56; and in Osofsky, A135:229-233, excerpt; and in Brown, A28:885-895, excerpt.

SE1653 _____. "Surplus Negro Women." 1905. In Miller, A129:168-178.

SE1654 _____. "Migration and Distribution of the Negro
Population as Affecting the Elective Franchise."
1905. In The Negro and the Elective Franchise,
A132:68-71.

SE1655 _____. "Frederick Douglass." c. 1905 (?). In
Miller, A129:211-220.

SE1656 _____. "Jefferson and the Negro." c. 1905 (?).
In Miller, A129:221-231.

SE1657 _____. "The Early Struggle for Education."
c. 1905 (?). In Miller, A129:244-256.

SE1658 _____. "A Brief for the Higher Education of the
Negro." c. 1905. In Miller, A129:257-274.

SE1659 _____. "An Appeal to Reason on the Race Problem." Oct. 1906. In Miller, A129:57-87.

SE1660 _____. "The Artistic Gifts of the Negro." 1906.
In Miller, A129:232-243.

SE1661 _____. "Radicals and Conservatives." c. 1907.
In Miller, A129:11-27.

SE1662 _____. "Eminent Negroes." c. 1907. In Miller,
A129:186-198.

SE1663 _____. "Roosevelt and the Negro." 1907. In
Miller, A129:275-306; and in Foner, A74:654-663,
excerpt.

SE1664 _____. "Forty Years of Negro Education." Dec.
1908. Educational Review, 36 (Dec. 1908), 484-498.

SE1665 _____. "The Ultimate Race Problem." April
1909. Atlantic, April 1909, pp. 536-542. Rpt. in
Miller, A128:218-239.

SE1666 _____. "The American Negro as a Political Factor." Aug. 1910. Nineteenth Century, 68 (Aug.
1910), 285-302. Rpt. in Miller, A128:103-141.

SE1667 _____. "Crime Among Negroes." c. 1910 (?).
In Miller, A128:95-102.

SE1668 _____. "Negroes in Professional Pursuits."
c. 1910 (?). In Miller, A128:168-185.

SE1669 _____. " 'The Negro in the New World' and
'The Conflict of Color.' " c. 1910. In Miller,
A128:186-195.

SE1670 _____. "The Ministry." c. 1910 (?). In Miller, A128:196-217.

SE1671 _____. "The Physical Destiny of the American
Negro." c. 1911. In Miller, A128:42-59.

SE1672 _____. "Education for Manhood." April 1913.

In Miller, A128:60-94; and in Dunbar, A70:445-454, excerpt.

SE1673 _____. "I See and Am Satisfied." Aug. 1913. Independent, 75 (Aug. 1913), 319. Rpt. in Miller, A128:240-242.

SE1674 _____. "Professional and Skilled Occupations." Sept. 1913. Annals of the American Academy, 49 (Sept. 1913), 10-18.

SE1675 _____. "Out of the House of Bondage." Oct. 1913. In Miller, A128:13-41.

SE1676 _____. "Fifty Years of Negro Education." c. 1914. In Miller, A128:142-167.

SE1677 _____. "Practical Value of the Higher Education of the Negro." Dec. 1915. Educational Review, 36 (Dec. 1915), 234-240. Rpt. in Miller, A127: 194-205.

SE1678 _____. "The Historic Background of the Negro Physician." 1916. JNH, 1 (April 1916), 99-109.

SE1679 _____. "Disgrace of Democracy (Open Letter to President Wilson)." 4 Aug. 1917. In Miller, A127:136-160; and in Calverton, A30:363-378.

SE1680 _____. An Appeal to Conscience: America's Code of Caste a Disgrace to Democracy. New York: Macmillan, 1918.
    Contains: "Race Contact," pp. 13-28.
    "Lawlessness," pp. 29-51.
    "Segregation," pp. 52-67.
    "Negro Patriotism and Devotion," pp. 68-86 (rpt. in Cromwell, A42:199-206).
    "Righteousness," pp. 87-108.

SE1681 _____. "National Responsibility for the Education of the Negro." June 1919. Educational Review, 58 (June 1919), 31-38. Rpt. in Miller, A127:181-193.

SE1682 _____. "The Negro in the New World Order." 1919. In Miller, A127:44-86.

SE1683 _____. "Radicalism and the Negro." 1920. In

Miller, A127:5-43.

SE1684 _____. "The Negro and the Japanese." c. 1920.
In Miller, A127:161-168.

SE1685 _____. "Education of the Negro in the North."
Oct. 1921. Educational Review, 62 (Oct. 1921),
232-238. Rpt. in Miller, A127:169-180.

SE1686 _____. "Race Differences ... (Open Letter to
President Harding and Reply)." 30 Nov. 1921. In
Miller, A127:104-135.

SE1687 _____. "Unrest Among Weaker Races." c. 1921.
In Miller, A127:87-103.

SE1688 _____. "The Negro Balance of Power." c. 1921.
In Miller, A127:206-218.

SE1689 _____. "The Haitian Mission." c. 1921. In
Miller, A127:219-224.

SE1690 _____. "Booker T. Washington Five Years After." 1921. In Miller, A127:253-270.

SE1691 _____. "The Negro's Place in the Labor Struggle." c. 1921. In Miller, A127:279-289.

SE1692 _____. "Lloyd George on Methodism." c. 1921.
In Miller, A127:299-303.

SE1693 _____. "Enumeration Errors in Negro Population." Feb. 1922. Scientific Monthly, 14 (Feb.
1922), 168-177. Rpt. in Miller, A127:225-252.

SE1694 _____. "Christianity and Backward Races."
c. 1922. In Miller, A127:290-294.

SE1695 _____. "Tagore." c. 1922. In Miller, A127:
295-298.

SE1696 _____. "The Order of Melchisedech." 1922.
In Miller, A127:304-308.

SE1697 _____. "The College Bred Negro and the
Church." c. 1922. In Miller, A127:309-313.

SE1698 _____. "The Sport of the Ghouls." c. 1922.
In Miller, A127:314-332.

SE1699 _____. "Abraham Lincoln--A Moral Genius."
c. 1922. In Miller, A127:333-338.

SE1700 _____. "Jubilee and Jazz." c. 1922. In Miller,
A127:339-345.

SE1701 _____. "Pessimism of the Negro." c. 1922.
In Miller, A127:346-350.

SE1702 _____. " 'Awake, Arise, or Be Forever Fallen."
c. 1922. In Miller, A127:351-352.

SE1703 _____. "The Everlasting Stain." c. 1923. In
Miller, A127:1-4.

SE1704 _____. "Race Cooperation." c. 1923. In Miller, A127:271-278.

SE1705 _____. "Howard: The National Negro University." 1925. In Locke, A113:312-322.

SE1706 _____. "The Negro as a Workingman." 1925.
American Mercury, 6 (Nov. 1925), 310-313.

SE1707 _____. "Is the American Negro to Remain Black
or Become Bleached?" July 1926. South Atlantic
Quarterly, 25 (July 1926), 240-252.

SE1708 _____. "The Higher Education of the Negro Is at
the Crossroads." Dec. 1926. Educational Review,
72 (Dec. 1926), 272-278.

SE1709 _____. "Causes of Segregation." March 1927.
Current History, 25 (March 1927), 827-831.

SE1710 _____. "After Marcus Garvey--What of the Negro?" April 1927. Contemporary Review, 131
(April 1927), 492-500. Rpt. in Clarke, A36:242-
246, abr.

SE1711 _____. "Negro Education and the Depression."
Jan. 1933. JNE, 2 (Jan. 1933), 1-4.

SE1712 _____. "The Past, Present and Future of the

Negro College." July 1933. JNE, 2 (July 1933), 411-422.

MILLER, KELLY. See Holmes, HC84; Eisenberg, HC224; Meier, HC255; and Ferris, HC451:383-389.

SE1713 Miller, Thomas E. "A Plea Against the Disfranchisement of the Negro." 26 Oct. 1895. In Foner, A74: 584-594; in Du Bois, HC450:242-248, excerpt; and in Love, SE1546:11-13, excerpt.

MILLER, THOMAS E. See Christopher, HC24:113-122.

SE1714 Minutes and Proceedings of the First Annual Convention of the People of Colour. 6-11 June 1831. In Bell, A10:orig. pag.; in Bracey, A21:159-170; and in Aptheker, A1:115-118, excerpt.

SE1715 Minutes and Proceedings of the Second Annual Convention, for the Improvement of the Free People of Color in These United States. 4-13 June 1832. In Bell, A10:orig. pag.; and in Aptheker, A1:133-137, excerpt.

SE1716 Minutes and Proceedings of the Third Annual Convention, for the Improvement of the Free People of Colour in These United States. 3-13 June 1833. In Bell, A10:orig. pag.; and in Aptheker, A1:142-146, excerpt.

SE1717 Minutes of the Albany Convention of Colored Citizens. 1840. In Stuckey, A160:237-251.

SE1718 Minutes of the Fifth Annual Convention for the Improvement of the Free People of Colour in the United States. 1-5 June 1835. In Bell, A10:orig. pag.

SE1719 Minutes of the Fourth Annual Convention, for the Improvement of the Free People of Colour, in the United States. 2-12 June 1834. In Bell, A10:orig. pag.

SE1720 Minutes of the National Convention of Colored Citizens. 15-19 Aug. 1843. In Bell, A10:orig. pag.

SE1721 Montgomery, M. Lee. "Community Building and

Learning Centers." 14 Jan. 1968. In Wright,
A179:278-282.

SE1722 _____. "The Education of Black Children." 20
Aug. 1968. In Wright, A179:48-52.

SE1723 _____. "Our Changing School and Community."
17 Oct. 1968. In Wright, A179:272-277.

SE1724 Moore, J. J. "The Unpardonable Sin." pre-1884.
In Hood, A95:307-314.

SE1725 Moorland, Jesse E. "The Demand and the Supply of
Increased Efficiency in the Negro Ministry." 1909.
American Negro Academy, Occasional Papers No.
13. Washington: The Academy, 1909.

SE1726 Moorman, Elliot Duane. "The Benefit of Anger."
June 1969. Saturday Review, 21 June 1969, pp.
72-73, 84-85. Rpt. in Wallerstein and Starr, A163:
336-339.

[Morel, Junius C., et al. See Whipper, SE2309.]

SE1727 Morris, Charles S. "The Wilmington Massacre."
Jan. 1899. In Aptheker, A1:813-815; and in Foner,
A74:605-607.

SE1728 Morris, Robert. "Speech to the Prince Hall Grand
Lodge of Boston." c. 1861. In Brown, HC443:
228-230, excerpt.

MORRIS, ROBERT. See Brown, HC443:227-230.

SE1729 Mossell, Mrs. N. F. "The Afro-American Editor's
Mission." 1890. In Penn, A139:487-491.

MOSSELL, MRS. N. F. See Penn, A139:405-407.

SE1730 Mossell, Nathan F. "The Teachings of History Considered in Relation to Race Problems in America."
1898. In Dunbar, A70:227-232.

SE1731 Motley, Constance Baker. "Keynote Address to the
Annual Convention of the SCLC." 9 Aug. 1965.
In Williams and Williams, A175:193-200.

SE1732 Moton, Robert Russa. "Some Elements Necessary
to Race Development." May 1912. In Dunbar, A70:
367-378; and in Foner, A74:692-698.

SE1733 _____. "A Life of Achievement." 11 Feb. 1916.
In Woodson, A177:602-607.

SE1734 _____. "Installation Address at Tuskegee." 25
May 1916. In Aptheker, A2:123-130.

SE1735 _____. "The American Negro and the World
War." May 1918. In Aptheker, A2:208-215.

SE1736 _____. "The Negro's Debt to Lincoln." 30 May
1922. In Woodson, A177:573-578.

SE1737 _____. "Hampton-Tuskegee: Missioners of the
Mass." 1925. In Locke, A113:323-332.

SE1738 _____. "Special Report of the Principal to the
Board of Trustees, the Tuskegee Normal and Industrial Institute." 1 April 1930. In Aptheker, A2:
643-652.

SE1739 _____. What the Negro Thinks. Garden City,
N.Y.: Garden City, 1942.
        Contains: " 'I Know the Negro,' " pp. 1-13.
        "Knowing the White Man," pp. 14-28.
        "The Advancing Negro," pp. 29-46.
        "Solving the Negro Problem Without the Negro,"
            pp. 47-68.
        "The Negro and the Law: Common Carriers,"
            pp. 69-99.
        "The Negro and the Law: Schools--Housing,"
            pp. 100-126.
        "The Negro and the Government: The Ballot--
            The Courts," pp. 127-157.
        "The Negro and the Government: Public Office--
            Public Policy," pp. 158-183.
        "The Negro and Public Sentiment," pp. 184-215.
        "The Negro's Reaction," pp. 216-239.
        "The Outlook," pp. 240-267.

    MOTON, ROBERT RUSSA. See Bullock, HC19:15-20;
    Hughes and Patterson, HC92; Moton, HC122; Du
    Bois, HC223; Du Bois, SE783; and Du Bois, SE795.

SE1740 Muhammad, Elijah. "Atlanta Speech." 1961. In
Lomax, HC1218:111-129.

SE1741 _____. "We Must Have Justice." 21 June 1963.
In Hill, A93:292-293, abr.; and in Foner, A74:969-
971, abr.

SE1742 _____. Message to the Blackman in America.
Chicago: Muhammad Mosque of Islam No. 2, 1965.
Contains: "Allah Is God," pp. 1-30.
"Original Man," pp. 31-67.
"Islam," pp. 68-85.
"The Bible and Holy Qur-an," pp. 86-99.
"The Devil," pp. 100-134.
"Prayer Service," pp. 135-160.
"Program and Position," pp. 161-191.
"Economic Program," pp. 192-205.
"The Persecution of the Righteous," pp. 206-219.
"Land of Our Own and Qualifications," pp. 220-
247.
"Hypocrites, Disbelievers and Obedience," pp.
248-264.
"The Judgment," pp. 265-305.
"Answer to Critics," pp. 306-341.

SE1743 _____. "Separation Is a Must." 25 April 1969.
In Golden and Rieke, A82:400.

SE1744 _____. "Negro." 25 April 1969. In Golden and
Rieke, A82:401-402.

SE1745 _____. "Why Black Man Should Be Called by the
Names of God." 25 April 1969. In Golden and
Rieke, A82:403-404.

SE1746 _____. "Accusations of Teaching Hate." 4 April
1969. In Golden and Rieke, A82:404-406.

SE1747 _____. "Are We the Black Muslims?" 25 April
1969. In Golden and Rieke, A82:406-407.

SE1748 _____. "The Muslim Program: What the Mus-
lims Want." 25 April 1969. In Golden and Rieke,
A82:408-410; and in Bracey, A22:404-407. [Note:
A22 text dated 31 July 1962; cf. SE1742:161-164.]

MUHAMMAD, ELIJAH. See Haley, HC234; and

various authors, HC1200-HC1227.

SE1749 Murray, George Mason. "Black Panther Leader
Calls for Armed Struggle." Aug. 1968. In Golden
and Rieke, A82:506-513.

SE1750 Murray, George W. "What Should Be the Negro's Attitude in Politics?" 1902. In Culp, A46:231-235.

MURRAY, GEORGE W. See Christopher, HC24:113-
122.

SE1751 Myers, Isaac. "Finish the Good Work of Uniting
Colored and White Workingmen." 18 Aug. 1869.
In Foner, A74:367-371.

SE1752 N.A.A.C.P., District of Columbia Branch. "What
Will the Negro Get Out of War?" 11 Dec. 1918.
In Aptheker, A2:235-237.

SE1753 N.A.A.C.P. "Resolutions." June 1919. In Aptheker, A2:244-247.

SE1754 _____. "The Negro and the Labor Union: An
N.A.A.C.P. Report." Sept. 1919. In Aptheker,
A2:267-271.

SE1755 National Committee of Negro Churchmen. "Black
Power." 31 July 1966. In Barbour, A8:264-272;
and in Wright, A178:187-194.

SE1756 National Conference of the Colored Men of the United
States. "National Negro Convention Urges Negroes
to Leave the South." 1879. In Bracey, A21:303-
321.

SE1757 National Liberty Congress. " 'Hear Our Grievances.' "
June 1918. In Aptheker, A2:215-218.

SE1758 National Negro Committee. "The National Negro
Committee on Mr. Washington." 26 Oct. 1910.
In Aptheker, A1:884-886; and in Grant, A84:203-206.

SE1759 National Negro Congress. "The Call." 1935. In
Grant, A84:240-243.

NATIONAL NEGRO CONGRESS. See Cruse, HC448:
171-180.

SE1760 National Negro Convention. "Call for the Convention." 1853. In Aptheker, A1:342-344.

SE1761 _____. "Address ... to the People of the United
States." July 1853. In Aptheker, A1:344-350.

SE1762 Neal, Lawrence P. "Black Power in the International Context." 1968. In Barbour, A8:136-145.

SE1763 _____. "New Space/The Growth of Black Con-
sciousness in the Sixties." 1970. In Barbour, A9:
9-31.

SE1764 _____. "Creativity: Coordinator's Statement."
Sept. 1970. In Jones, A101:191-193.

SE1765 Nell, William C. "The Triumph of Equal School
Rights in Boston." 17 Dec. 1855. In Foner, A74:
165-168.

NELL, WILLIAM C. See Smith, HC164; Brown,
HC445:485-486; and Loggins, HC992:177-179.

SE1766 New Pittsburgh Courier. "Is Black Power Ebbing?"
3 March 1969. In Fishel and Quarles, A72:588.

SE1767 Newton, Huey P. "Black Panther Party Platform
and Program: What We Want, What We Believe."
Oct. 1966. In Foner, A73:2-4.

SE1768 _____. "Rules of the Black Panther Party."
1966. In Foner, A73:4-6.

SE1769 _____. "Interview." c. 1967. In Foner, A73:
50-66.

SE1770 _____. "In Defense of Self Defense." June 1967.
In Littleton and Burger, A112:424-427.

SE1771 _____. "In Defense of Self Defense." March
1968. In Bracey, A22:534-551.

SE1772 _____. "Prison, Where Is Thy Victory?" July
1969. In Littleton and Burger, A112:428-430; and
in Davis, A50:50-56.

SE1773 _____. "The Black Panthers." Aug. 1969.
Ebony, Aug. 1969, pp. 107-108, 110-112. Rpt. in

The Black Revolution, A12:125-135.

SE1774 _____, and Erik H. Erikson. In Search of Common Ground: Conversations with Erik H. Erikson and Huey P. Newton. Feb.-April 1971. New York: Norton, 1973.

SE1775 Newton, Huey P. "The Transformation of the Black Panther Party." 19 May 1971. In Foner, A74: 1183-1191.

NEWTON, HUEY P. See Newton, HC125; Keating, HC243; Marine, HC937; Seale, HC946; and Cleaver, SE391.

SE1776 Nicholson, Jacob, et al. "Petition to Congress." Jan. 1797. In Aptheker, A1:40-44.

SE1777 Nickens, David. "An Address to the People of Color in Chillicothe." 5 July 1832. In Bracey, A22:34-37.

[Niger, Alfred, and George C. Willis. See Willis, SE2360.]

SE1778 Northup, Solomon. Twelve Years a Slave: Narrative of Solomon Northup [1853]. In Osofsky, HC1017: 225-406.

SE1779 Northwestern University Black Students. "Black Student Demands." 22 April 1968. In Wallerstein and Starr, A163:297-298.

SE1780 _____. "Revised Demands of the Black Students." 2 May 1968. In Bracey, A22:476-485; and in Wallerstein and Starr, A163:302-306, A164:486-488, abr.

SE1781 Osborne, Peter. "The American Negro's Fourth of July." 5 July 1832. In Aptheker, A1:137-138; and in Foner, A74:48-49.

SE1782 "Othello." "Negro Slavery." May 1788. American Museum, 4 (Nov. 1788), 414-417, and 4 (Dec. 1788), 509-512. Rpt. in Woodson, A177:14-25.

SE1783 Parker, Annie. "Passages in the Life of a Slave Woman." 1853. In Griffiths, A86:85-94.

SE1784 Parks, H. B.   "The Miracle of Continuance." 3
       May 1916. In Smith, HC1183:291-292, excerpt.

SE1785 Parks, W. G.   "The Freeness of Salvation." 1890.
       In Brawley, A25:60-63.

SE1786 Parris, Robert (Moses).   "Questions Raised by
       Moses."   April 1965. In Jacobs and Landau, A99:
       120-123.

SE1787 Parrish, C. H. "Sanctification." 1890. In Brawley,
       A25:91-103.

       PARRISH, C. H.   See Simmons, HC163a:1059-1063
       or HC163b:763-766.

SE1788 Parrott, Russell. "An Oration on the Abolition of
       the Slave Trade." 1 Jan. 1814. In Porter, A141:
       383-390.

       [_____, and James Forten. See Forten, SE907.]

       [_____. See Forten, SE908.]

SE1789 Patterson, Frederick D. "The Negro Wants Full
       Participation in the American Democracy." 1944.
       In Logan, A115:259-280.

SE1790 Patterson, William L.   " 'Free by '63.' " 1960. In
       Foner, A74:925-930.

SE1791 _____. "The Negro Citizen and the Government."
       1961. Freedomways, 1 (Summer 1961), 190-200.

       PATTERSON, WILLIAM L. See Patterson, HC130.

SE1792 Paul, Nathaniel. "An Address, Delivered on the
       Celebration of the Abolition of Slavery in the State
       of New York." 5 July 1827. In Porter, A142:orig.
       pag.; in Woodson, A177:64-77; and in Foner, A74:
       38-42, abr.

SE1793 _____. "Letter." 10 April 1833. In Woodson,
       A176:165-167.

SE1794 _____. "Speech Delivered at the Anti-Coloniza-
       tion Meeting in Exeter Hall, London." 13 July 1833.

In Porter, A141:286-291.

SE1795 Paul, Thomas. "On the Advantages of the Island of
Hayti." 1 July 1824. In Porter, A141:279-280.

PAUL, THOMAS. See Woodson, HC1188:76-79.

SE1796 Payne, Daniel A. "American Slavery Brutalizes
Man." June 1839. JNH, 52 (Jan. 1967), 60-64.
Rpt. in Foner, A74:67-72.

SE1797 _____. "Essay on the Education of the Ministry."
1845. In Payne, A137:orig. pag.; and in Payne,
HC1180:195-196.

SE1798 _____. "Opening Sermon Preached Before the
A. M. E. General Conference." 3 May 1852. In
Payne, A137:orig. pag.; and in Payne, HC1180:268-
271.

SE1799 _____. "On the Education of the Ministry." May
1852. In Payne, A137:orig. pag.; and in Payne,
HC1180:276-277.

SE1800 _____. "First Annual Address to the Philadelphia
Annual Conference of the A. M. E. Church." 16 May
1853. In Payne, A137:orig. pag.

SE1801 _____. "The Christian Ministry: Its Moral and
Intellectual Character." c. Jan. 1859. In Payne,
A137:orig. pag.

SE1802 _____. "God." Jan. 1859. In Payne, A137:orig.
pag.

SE1803 _____. "Welcome to the Ransomed; or, Duties of
the Colored Inhabitants of the District of Columbia."
13 April 1862. In Payne, A137:orig. pag.

SE1804 _____. "Appeal to the Colored People of the
United States." 1862. In Payne, HC1181:129-131.

[_____. The Semi-Centenary and the Retrospection of the African Meth(odist) Episcopal Church in
the United States of America. See Payne, HC1181.]

SE1805 _____. "The Relations of This Conference with

the African Methodist Church." 1868. In Payne,
A137:orig. pag.

SE1806 _____. "Annual Report and Retrospection of the
First Decade of Wilberforce University." 18 June
1873. In Payne, A137:orig. pag.

SE1807 _____. "Semi-Centennial Sermon." 1874. In
Payne, A137:orig. pag.

SE1808 _____. "The Quadrennial Sermon." 10 May 1888.
In Payne, A138:5-41. Rpt. in Payne, A137:orig.
pag.

SE1809 _____. "The Ordination Sermon." 24 May 1888.
In Payne, A138:43-64. Rpt. in Payne, A137:orig.
pag.

SE1810 _____. "Organization Essential to Success."
1890. In Payne, A137:orig. pag.

PAYNE, DANIEL A. See Brawley, HC13:74-80;
Coan, HC27; Payne, HC132; Simmons, HC163a:1078-
1085 or HC163b:779-783; Brown, HC443:207-211;
Brown, HC445:454-455; Cromwell, HC447:115-125;
Woodson, HC1188:150-151; Grimké, SE1074; and
Ward, SE2222.

SE1811 Penn, William F. "Negro Mortality." 1902. In
Culp, A46:221-223.

SE1812 Pennington, J. W. C. "The Destiny of the Colored
Race in the United States." July 1852. In Payne,
HC1180:299-300.

SE1813 _____. "The Position and Duties of the Colored
People." 24 Aug. 1863. In Foner, A74:272-281.

PENNINGTON, J. W. C. See Pennington, HC134;
Simmons, HC163a:913-915 or HC163b:648-649;
Brown, HC443:276-278; Brown, HC445:461-463; Log-
gins, HC992:195-197; and Woodson, HC1188:156-158.

SE1814 Perkins, Eugene. "The Black Arts Movement: Its
Challenge and Responsibility." 1970. In Barbour,
A9:85-97.

SE1815 Perry, Rufus L. "The Scriptures." 1890. In
Brawley, A25:28-38.

PERRY, RUFUS L. See Simmons, HC163a:620-625
or HC163b:425-429; and Brown, HC445:533.

SE1816 Peters, Sampson, et al. "Address on Colonization."
30 Nov. 1831. In Garrison, A77:47-48.

SE1817 Pickens, William. "Abraham Lincoln." 1910. In
Pickens, A140:119-147.

SE1818 _____. "Frederick Douglass." 1912. In Pickens,
A140:71-102.

SE1819 _____. "Fifty Years After Emancipation." 1913.
In Pickens, A140:44-60.

SE1820 _____. "The Ultimate Effects of Segregation."
1915. In Pickens, A140:206-223; and in Aptheker,
A2:79-87.

SE1821 _____. "The Constitutional Status of the Negro
from 1860 to 1870." Dec. 1915. In Papers of the
American Negro Academy, A136:63-72. Rpt. in
Pickens, A140:16-29.

SE1822 _____. "The Renaissance of the Negro Race."
1916. In Pickens, A140:9-15.

SE1823 _____. "The Negro a Test for Our Civilization."
1916. In Pickens, A140:30-43.

SE1824 _____. "Grounds of Hope." 1916. In Pickens,
A140:61-70.

SE1825 _____. "Alexander Hamilton." 1916. In Pickens,
A140:103-118; and in Cromwell, A42:224-234.

SE1826 _____. "Industry." 1916. In Pickens, A140:148-
154.

SE1827 _____. "Education." 1916. In Pickens, A140:
155-175.

SE1828 _____. "From the Christian Viewpoint." 1916.
In Pickens, A140:176-189.

SE1829 _____. "Lynching." 1916. In Pickens, A140: 190-205.

SE1830 _____. "The New Negro." 1916. In Pickens, A140:224-239.

SE1831 _____. "The Kind of Democracy the Negro Race Expects." c. 1917. In Foner, A74:715-719; and in Woodson, A177:654-658.

SE1832 _____. "Injustice Makes Bolsheviks." 1920. In Aptheker, A2:298-301.

SE1833 _____. "The Woman Voter Hits the Color Line." Oct. 1920. Nation, 6 Oct. 1920, pp. 372-373. Rpt. in Aptheker, A2:305-309.

SE1834 _____. "The American Congo--Burning of Henry Lowry." March 1921. Nation, 23 March 1921, pp. 426-428.

SE1835 _____. "Lynching and Debt-Slavery." May 1921. In Aptheker, A2:318-327.

SE1836 _____. "Jim Crow in Texas." Aug. 1923. Nation, 15 Aug. 1923, pp. 155-156.

SE1837 _____. "The Emperor of Africa: The Psychology of Garveyism." Aug. 1923. In Aptheker, A2: 379-386.

SE1838 _____. "Youth Attacks the 'Color Line.'" June 1926. Nation, 2 June 1926, pp. 607-608.

SE1839 _____. "Suffrage." c. 1927. In Johnson, A100: 111-114.

PICKENS, WILLIAM. See Pickens, HC135.

SE1840 Pinchback, Pinckney Benton Stewart. "Address During the Presidential Campaign of 1880." 1880. In Dunbar, A70:151-158.

SE1841 _____. "The Afro-American Press." 1890. In Penn, A139:454-456.

SE1842 _____. "The Whole Race Must Protest." c. 1897.

In Foner, A74:597-599.

PINCHBACK, PINCKNEY BENTON STEWART. See
Christopher, HC24:104-112; Simmons, HC163a:759-
781 or HC163b:533-546; Brown, HC445:517-519; and
Bennett, HC628:235-240, 260-272.

SE1843 Pledger, W. A. "Speech to the Founding Convention
of the Afro-American League." Jan. 1890. In
Aptheker, A1:706-707.

SE1844 Pollard, R. T. "Baptists and Colportage." 1890.
In Brawley, A25:211-220.

[Pompey, Edward J., and Arthur Cooper. See
Cooper, SE429.]

SE1845 Poussaint, Alvin F. "The Negro American: His
Self-Image and Integration." 1966. In Barbour,
A8:94-102.

SE1846 _____. "A Negro Psychiatrist Explains the Negro
Psyche." New York Times Magazine, 20 Aug. 1967,
pp. 52-53, 55-56, 58, 73, 75-76, 78, 80. Rpt. in
Meier and Rudwick, A124:129-138.

SE1847 _____. "The Role of Education in Providing a
Basis for Honest Self-Identification." May 1968. In
Robinson, HC424:194-201.

SE1848 Powell, A. Clayton, Sr. "A Plea for Strong Manhood." June 1924 and May 1939. In Powell, A144:
180-195.

SE1849 _____. "Saints in Caesar's Household." Sept.
1928. In Powell, A144:209-217.

SE1850 _____. "The Source of All Power." 24 Oct.
1932. In Powell, A144:138-150.

SE1851 _____. "The Significance of the Hour." c. 1933.
In Powell, A144:97-109.

SE1852 _____. "The Valley of Dry Bones." c. 1939 (?).
In Powell, A144:110-128.

SE1853 _____. "A Model Church." c. 1939 (?). In

Powell, A144:129-137.

SE1854 _____. "The Value of an Ideal." c. 1939 (?).
In Powell, A144:151-162.

SE1855 _____. "The Fool's Motto." c. 1939 (?). In
Powell, A144:163-171.

[_____. May 1939. Same as SE1848.]

SE1856 _____. "The Molding Influence of Woman." May
1939. In Powell, A144:172-179.

SE1857 _____. "The Transforming Power of the Word of
God." c. 1939 (?). In Powell, A144:196-208.

POWELL, A. CLAYTON, SR. See Powell, HC140.

SE1858 Powell, Adam Clayton, Jr. "A Sermon for a Crisis."
3 Dec. 1950. In Powell, A143:211-219.

SE1859 _____. "Walking Under a Cloud." 13 Dec. 1953.
In Powell, A143:151-153.

SE1860 _____. "Do You Really Believe in God?" 23 Jan.
1955. In Powell, A143:285-287.

SE1861 _____. "Why I Am a Christian." 2 Oct. 1955.
In Powell, A143:107-117.

SE1862 _____. "Brotherhood and Freedom." 1959. In
Powell, A143:229-238.

SE1863 _____. "What We Must Do about Africa." 3
April 1960. In Powell, A143:51-55.

SE1864 _____. "The Injustice of Justice." 23 May 1960.
In Powell, A143:161-167.

SE1865 _____. "Let's Give Up Our Own Prejudices." 3
July 1960. In Powell, A143:77-80.

SE1866 _____. "A New Frontier of Faith." c. Dec.
1960. In Powell, A143:83-86.

SE1867 _____. "The Imperishable Dream." 7 Jan. 1962.
In Powell, A143:43-47.

SE1868 _____. "Facing the Future." Nov. 1963. In
Powell, A143:279-282.

SE1869 _____. "Marching Blacks, 1965: Black Position
Paper for America's 20,000,000 Negroes." 28 May
1965. In Hale, A90:221-227; and in Williams and
Williams, A175:101-109.

SE1870 _____. "Can There Any Good Thing Come Out
of Nazareth?" 29 May 1966. In Foner, A74:1028-
1033; in Littleton and Burger, A112:219-224; in
O'Neill, A134:193-198; and in Smith, HC1246:154-160.

SE1871 _____. "My Black Position Paper." 6 June 1966.
In Barbour, A8:257-260.

SE1872 _____. "Black Power in the Church." Dec. 1970.
Black Scholar, 2 (Dec. 1970), 32-34.

POWELL, ADAM CLAYTON, JR. See Chapman and
Chapman, HC20; Christopher, HC24:194-208; Clarke,
HC25; Hickey and Edwin, HC80; Lewis, HC100;
Powell, HC139; Wilson, HC772; Boulware, HC1023:
169-176; and Kane, HC1095.

SE1873 Price, Joseph C. "The Race Problem Stated."
1890. In Woodson, A177:488-501; and in Smith and
Robb, A156:79-93.

SE1874 _____. "The Afro-American Press." 1890. In
Penn, A139:459-460.

PRICE, JOSEPH C. See Du Bois, HC47; Simmons,
HC163a:754-758 or HC163b:529-531; Walls, HC182;
Cromwell, HC447:171-178; Loggins, HC992:294-295;
and Mason, SE1620.

SE1875 Proceedings of the Colored National Convention. 6-
8 July 1853. In Bell, A10:orig. pag.

SE1876 _____. 16-18 Oct. 1855. In Bell, A10:orig. pag.

SE1877 Proceedings of the National Convention of Colored
Men. 4-7 Oct. 1864. In Bell, A10:orig. pag.; and
in Aptheker, A1:511-525, excerpt.

SE1878 Proceedings of the National Convention of Colored

People, and Their Friends. 6-9 Oct. 1847. In
Bell, A10:orig. pag.

SE1879 Proctor, Samuel D. "An Address." 12 April 1959.
In Hill, A93:225-230.

SE1880 Prout, John W., and Arthur Waring. "Resolutions
on Colonization." 4 May 1831. In Garrison, A77:
22-23.

SE1881 Puller, A. W. "Final Perseverance of the Saints."
1890. In Brawley, A25:104-112.

SE1882 "A Puritan." "The Abrogation of the Seventh Commandment, by the American Churches." 4 May
1835. In Porter, A141:478-493.

[Purvis, Robert, et al. See Whipper, SE2309.]

[Purvis, Robert, James Forten, and William Whipper.
See Forten, SE909.]

SE1883 Purvis Robert. "Remarks on the Life and Character of James Forten." 30 March 1842. Philadelphia: Merrihew and Thompson, 1842.

SE1884 _____. "Speech at the Twenty-Fourth Anniversary
of the American Anti-Slavery Society." 12 May
1857. In Robert C. Dick. Black Protest: Issues
and Tactics. Westport, Conn.: Greenwood, 1974.
Pages 257-260.

SE1885 _____. "American 'Democracy' and the Negro."
8 May 1860. In Aptheker, A1:451-454; In Foner,
A74:227-231; and in Barbour, A8:47-50, abr.

SE1886 _____. "The Good Time Is at Hand." 12 May
1863. In Foner, A74:266-267.

PURVIS, ROBERT. See Brown, HC443:253-259;
Brown, HC445:468-469; Borome, HC567; and Still,
HC598a:711.

SE1887 Putnam, Frank. "The Negro's Part in New National
Problems." May 1900. In Foner, A74:630-635.

SE1888 Quinn, William Paul. "The Origin, Horrors, and

Results of Slavery." 1834. In Porter, A141:614-
636.

SE1889 _____. "The Bishop's Address." 3 May 1852.
In Payne, A137:orig. pag.; and in Payne, HC1180:
271-273.

QUINN, WILLIAM PAUL. See Brown, HC445:432-
433.

SE1890 Raiford, G. W. "Repentance and Faith." 1890. In
Brawley, A25:81-86.

SE1891 Rainey, Joseph H. "The Southern Situation." 1
April 1871. In Woodson, A177:300-308.

SE1892 _____. "Speech on Education." 3 Feb. 1872.
In Woodson, A177:380-387.

SE1893 _____. "Reply to Representative Cox." 5 March
1872. In Woodson, A177:378-380.

SE1894 _____. "Eulogy on Charles Sumner." 27 April
1874. In Foner, A74:404-409.

RAINEY, JOSEPH H. See Christopher, HC24:25-37;
and Brown, HC445:507-508.

SE1895 Randolph, A. Philip, and Chandler Owen. "The
Hanging of the Negro Soldiers." Jan. 1918. In
Aptheker, A2:196-197.

SE1896 _____. "The Bolsheviki." Jan. 1918. In Aptheker, A2:197-198.

SE1897 _____. "How to Stop Lynching." Aug. 1919. In
Aptheker, A2:255-259.

SE1898 _____. "Our Reason for Being." Aug. 1919. In
Aptheker, A2:263-267.

SE1899 Randolph, A. Philip. "The Political Situation and the
Negro: Coolidge, Davis or La Follette." Oct. 1924.
In Aptheker, A2:471-483.

SE1900 _____. "Negro Labor and the Church." 1929.
In Aptheker, A2:630-636.

SE1901 _____. "Defense of Resolution Urging AFL to End the Color Line in Organized Labor." In Bracey, A21:476-500.

SE1902 _____. "The Trade Union Movement and the Negro. 1936. JNE, 5 (Jan. 1936), 54-58.

SE1903 _____. "The Task of the Negro People." Feb. 1936. In Foner, A74:808-815.

SE1904 _____. "The Crisis of the Negro and the Constitution." 1937. In Broderick and Meier, A26:180-189; and in Foner, A74:816-822, abr.

SE1905 _____. " 'Let the Negro Masses Speak!' " March 1941. In Osofsky, A135:392-396.

SE1906 _____. "Call to the March on Washington." May 1941. In Bracey, A21:611-614.

SE1907 _____. "Keynote Address to the Policy Conference of the March on Washington Movement." Sept. 1942. In Broderick and Meier, A26:201-210, abr.; in Foner, A74:823-829, abr.; and in Smith and Robb, A156:111-119, abr.

SE1908 _____. "March on Washington Movement Presents Program for the Negro." 1944. In Logan, A115:133-162.

SE1909 _____. "Labor and the Struggle for a Better Tomorrow." 2 Sept. 1956. In Hill, A93:175-184.

SE1910 _____. "A Program for World Peace and Freedom." 11 Dec. 1957. In Hill and Kilson, A92a:376-381 or A92b:442-447.

SE1911 _____. "The Struggle for the Liberation of the Black Laboring Masses." Nov. 1961. In Grant, A84:487-493.

SE1912 _____. "The Unfinished Revolution." Dec. 1962. Progressive, 26 (Dec. 1962), 20-25.

SE1913 _____. "Address at the March on Washington." 28 Aug. 1963. In Speeches By the Leaders, A131: n. pag.; and in Williams and Williams, A175:205-208.

SE1914 _____. "Opening Remarks." 30 Jan. 1965. In
Bennett, HC437:vii-x, excerpt.

RANDOLPH, A. PHILIP. See Anderson, HC4; Bennett, HC873; Garfinkle, HC877; Boulware, HC1023:
118-123; Bruce, SE244; and Rustin, SE2043.

SE1915 Randolph, P. B. "Address to the National Convention of Colored Men." 6 Oct. 1864. In Proceedings of the National Convention of Colored Men,
SE1877:20-22.

SE1916 Ransier, A. J. "Speech Delivered at Charleston,
S.C." 9 March 1871. In Woodson, A177:411-417.

RANSIER, A. J. See Christopher, HC24:97-103; and
Brown, HC445:510-512.

SE1917 Ransier, H. P. "Petition to the South Carolina State
Legislature." 25 Nov. 1865. JNH, 31 (Jan. 1946),
96-97.

SE1918 Ransom, Reverdy C. "Fifteenth Amendment." 14
Feb. 1893. In Ransom, A147:146-153.

SE1919 _____. "Heredity and Environment." 1898. In
Ransom, A147:160-163.

SE1920 _____. "Work of the Methodist Churches in the
Twentieth Century." 4 Sept. 1901. In Ransom,
HC146:98-99, excerpt.

SE1921 _____. "Duty and Destiny: A Union Thanksgiving Service Address." 24 Nov. 1904. In Ransom,
A147:169-175.

SE1922 _____. "William Lloyd Garrison: A Centennial
Oration." 11 Dec. 1905. In Ransom, A147:5-14;
in Woodson, A177:531-541; in Dunbar, A70:305-320;
in Smith and Robb, A156:67-77. [See Ransom,
HC146:169-171.]

SE1923 _____. "Race Problem in Christian State."
April 1906. In Ransom, A147:128-137.

SE1924 _____. "The Spirit of John Brown." 17 Aug.
1906. In Ransom, A147:16-25. [See W. E. B. Du

Bois, "A Word," 29 Aug. 1935, in Ransom, A146:
n. pag.]

SE1925 _____. "The Atlanta Riot." 28 Sept. 1906. In
Ransom, A147:117-121.

SE1926 _____. "John Greenleaf Whittier: Plea for Political Equality." 17 Dec. 1907. In Ransom, A147:
31-41.

SE1927 _____. "Thanksgiving Sermon: The American
Tower of Babel or the Confusion of Tongues." 25
Nov. 1909. In Ransom, A147:62-70.

SE1928 _____. "Martyrdom of John Brown: Oration at
Celebration of the Fiftieth Anniversary of the Hang-
ing of John Brown." 2 Dec. 1909. In Ransom,
A147:104-112.

SE1929 _____. "Democracy, Disfranchisement and the
Negro." 12 May 1910. In Ransom, A147:42-50.

SE1930 _____. "Crossing the Color Line." c. 1910.
In Ransom, A147:84-87.

SE1931 _____. "The Negro as a National Business As-
set." c. 1910. In Ransom, A147:113-116.

SE1932 _____. "The Reno Prize Fight." c. 1910. In
Ransom, A147:122-127.

SE1933 _____. "Charles Sumner: Centennial Oration
Plea." 6 Jan. 1911. In Ransom, A147:51-61.

SE1934 _____. "Wendell Phillips." 29 Nov. 1911. In
Ransom, A147:72-83.

SE1935 _____. "Abraham Lincoln." Feb. 1912. In Ransom, A147:26-30.

SE1936 _____. "The Mission of the Religious Press."
16 May 1912. In Ransom, A147:88-97.

SE1937 _____. "The National Republic Convention." 17
June 1912. In Ransom, A147:98-103.

SE1938 _____. "Aftermath of the Republican National

Convention." Sept. 1912. In Ransom, A147:142-145.

SE1939 _____. "Lynching and American Public Opinion."
c. 1912. In Ransom, A147:138-141.

SE1940 _____. "Reply to Prof. William Starr Myers."
March 1913. In Ransom, A147:154-159.

SE1941 _____. "Future Influence of Negro Scholarship in
America." 27 Dec. 1925. In Ransom, A147:165-
168.

SE1942 _____. "Crispus Attucks." 6 March 1930. In
Ransom, A146:78-87.

SE1943 _____. "The Negro, The Hope or the Despair of
Christianity." 1933. In Ransom, A146:1-7.

SE1944 _____. "Afro-Americans Seek to Share in Freedom, Culture, and Good Will." 15 Feb. 1935. In
Ransom, A146:57-63.

SE1945 _____. "The Race Problem in a Christian State."
15 Feb. 1935. In Ransom, A146:64-77.

SE1946 _____. "The Negro Family and Home." c. 1935
(?). In Ransom, A146:9-19.

SE1947 _____. "The Negro Church." c. 1935 (?). In
Ransom, A146:21-28.

SE1948 _____. "Negro Schools." c. 1935 (?). In Ransom, A146:29-40.

SE1949 _____. "The Pulpit and the American Negro."
c. 1935 (?). In Ransom, A146:41-47.

SE1950 _____. "The Economic and Industrial Plight of
the Negro." c. 1935 (?). In Ransom, A146:49-54.

SE1951 _____. "The Future of the Negro in the United
States." c. 1935 (?). In Ransom, A146:88-98.

RANSOM, REVERDY C. See Ransom, HC146.

SE1952 Rapier, James T. "Civil Rights Bill." 9 June
1874. In Woodson, A177:338-356; in Foner,

A74:419-430; and in Feldman, HC53:46-69.

RAPIER, JAMES T.   See Christopher, HC24:123-136;
Feldman, HC53; and Walton, HC769.

SE1953 Reason, Charles L.   "The Colored People's 'Industrial College.' "   1854.   In Griffiths, A87:11-15.

SE1954 Redding, J. Saunders.   "The Negro Writer and His
Relationship to His Roots."   March 1959.   In Chapman, A32:612-618.

SE1955 _____.   "The Sanctions of the American Negro's
Literary Art."   March 1959.   In Hill, A93:279-285.

SE1956 [Reeves, A. M.]   "The Danger of Neglect."   2 Aug.
1942.   In Pipes, HC1197:31-36.

[Reid, Ira De A., and W. E. B. Du Bois.   See Du
Bois, SE822.]

SE1957 Reid, Ira De A.   "Social Change, Social Relations,
and Social Work."   May 1955.   In Hill, A93:165-
174.

SE1958 Remond, Charles Lenox.   "Slavery As It Concerns
the British."   14 May 1841.   In Woodson, A177:127-
130; and in Smith and Robb, A156:17-20.

SE1959 _____.   "Slavery and the Irish."   1841.   In Woodson, A177:131-143; in Golden and Rieke, A82:154-
163; and in Smith, HC1246:110-124.

SE1960 _____.   "The Rights of Colored Citizens in Travel-
ing."   c. Feb. 1842.   In Woodson, A177:144-149; in
Golden and Rieke, A82:164-168; in Foner, A74:72-77,
abr.; and in Aptheker, A1:215-219, abr.

SE1961 _____.   "Speech Before the New England Anti-
Slavery Convention."   30 May 1854.   In Woodson,
A177:229-237; and in Bormann, A18:166-173.

SE1962 _____.   "An Anti-Slavery Discourse."   4 July 1857.
In Woodson, A177:237-241.

REMOND, CHARLES LENOX.   See Brown, HC443:
246-250; Brown, HC445:459-460; Quarles,

HC593:131-133; and Loggins, HC992:132-134.

SE1963 Remond, Sarah P. "The Negroes in the United
States of America." 1862. JNH, 27 (April
1942), 216-218.

REMOND, SARAH P. See Porter, HC138.

SE1964 Report of the Proceedings of the Colored National
Convention. 6 Sept. 1848. In Bell, A10:orig. pag.

SE1965 Reuter, E. B. "The Changing Status of the Mulatto."
c. 1927. In Johnson, A100:107-110.

SE1966 Revels, Hiram R. "Speech on the Georgia Bill."
16 March 1870. In Woodson, A177:286-293.

SE1967 _____. "A Plea for Desegregated Schools." 8
Feb. 1871. In Foner, A74:372-378; and in Fishel
and Quarles, A72:297-298, excerpt.

REVELS, HIRAM R. See Christopher, HC24:1-14;
Lawson, HC98; Simmons, HC163a:948-950 or
HC163b:672-673; Wheeler, HC197; Brown, HC445:
500-503; Bennett, HC628:211-214; "Three Negro Senators...," HC764; and Woodson, HC1188:162-163.

[Richards, James, and Stephen Smith. See Smith,
SE2109.]

SE1968 Richardson, Harry V. "Claflin Yesterday, Today
and Tomorrow." 30 April 1958. In Hill, A93:193-
200.

SE1969 Richardson, Jacob D., and Jacob G. Williams.
"Resolutions on Colonization." Oct. 1831. In Garrison, A77:40-43.

SE1970 Roberts, Robert, and James G. Barbadoes. "Resolutions on Colonization." 12 March 1831. In Garrison, A77:17-21.

SE1971 Robeson, Paul. "African Culture." March 1935.
In Hill and Kilson, A92a:133-135 or A92b:153-156.

SE1972 _____. "American Negroes in the War." 16
Nov. 1943. Freedomways, 11 (1st Qrtr 1971), 107-
109.

SE1973 _____. "Anti-Imperialists Must Defend Africa."
6 June 1946. In Foner, A74:833-836.

SE1974 _____. "Negro-Labor Unity for Peace." 10 June
1950. Freedomways, 11 (1st Qrtr 1971), 109-116.

SE1975 _____. "The Negro Artist Looks Ahead." Dec.
1951. In Foner, A74:849-857.

SE1976 _____. "The Battleground Is Here." 21 Nov.
1952. Freedomways, 11 (1st Qrtr 1971), 116-119.

SE1977 _____. "Playing Catch-Up." Oct. 1953. Freedomways, 11 (1st Qrtr 1971), 119-120.

ROBESON, PAUL. See Kaiser, B13; Brawley,
HC13:294-296; Graham, HC63; Hoyt, HC89; Robeson,
HC150; Fishman, HC228; Cruse, HC448:285-301;
Crockett, SE440; Du Bois, SE851; and Freedomways,
11 (1st Qrtr 1971), passim.

SE1978 Robinson, Armstead L. "A Concluding Statement."
May 1968. In Robinson, HC424:207-214.

SE1979 Rock, John S. "Comparing White and Negro Americans." 5 March 1858. In Aptheker, A1:402-405;
in Barbour, A8:43-47; and in Foner, A74:204-208.

SE1980 _____. "Address to the Massachusetts Anti-
Slavery Society." 23 Jan. 1862. In Aptheker, A1:
465-469, abr.; and in Foner, A74:251-256, abr.

SE1981 _____. "We Ask for Our Rights." 1 Aug. 1862.
In Foner, A74:257-259.

SE1982 _____. "Address to the National Convention of
Colored Men." 6 Oct. 1864. In Proceedings of the
National Convention of Colored Men, SE1877:23-25.

ROCK, JOHN S. See Link, HC248; and Brown,
HC443:266-270.

SE1983 Roman, C. V. "Is Church Money Wasted?" 1904.
In Roman A150:40-41.

SE1984 _____. "The Study of the Eye." 29 Jan. 1909.
In Roman, A150:42-47.

SE1985 _____. "A Knowledge of History Is Conducive to Racial Solidarity." 24 Feb. 1911. In Roman, A150: 11-36; and Woodson, A177:643-652.

SE1986 _____. "Correct Ideals." c. 1911 (?). In Roman A150:37-39.

SE1987 _____. "Faith in God Is an Inspiration to a Useful Life." c. 1911 (?). In Roman, A150:48-54.

SE1988 Roper, Moses. A Narrative of the Adventures and Escape of Moses Roper from American Slavery. 2d edn. 1838; rpt. New York: Negro Universities Press, 1970. [1st edn. (1837) rpt. in Robinson, A149:115-121, excerpt.]

SE1989 Rowan, Carl T. "An Address." 17 May 1947. In Hill, A93:108-119.

SE1990 _____. "Our Contemporary World." 14 Oct. 1965. In Williams and Williams, A175:39-47.

SE1991 _____. "New Frontiers in Racial Relations." 24 Oct. 1968. In O'Neill, A134:201-213.

SE1992 Ruffin, George L. "Crispus Attucks." 7 March 1876. In Dunbar, A70:125-132.

RUFFIN, GEORGE L. See Simmons, HC163a:740-743 or HC163b:518-520; and Brown, HC445:540-542.

SE1993 Ruffin, Josephine St. Pierre. "An Open Letter to the Educational League of Georgia." June 1889. In Dunbar, A70:173-176.

SE1994 _____. " 'Trust the Women!' " Aug. 1915. In Aptheker, A2:110-111.

SE1955 Ruggles, David. "The 'Extinguisher' Extinguished, or David M. Reese, M.D., Used Up." 1834. In Brown, A28:595-600, excerpt.

SE1996 _____. "Appeals to the Colored Citizens of New York and Elsewhere in Behalf of the Press." Jan.-Feb. 1835. In Porter, A141:637-655.

SE1997 _____ ["A Puritan"]. "The Abrogation of the

Seventh Commandment by the American Churches."
4 May 1835. In Porter, A141:478-493.

SE1998 _____. "On the Question of Negro Disunity." 8
Sept. 1841. In Aptheker, A1:211.

RUGGLES, DAVID. See Porter, HC137; and Brown,
HC445:434-435.

SE1999 Rushing, Byron. "I Was Born." c. 1968. In Barbour, A8:227-234.

SE2000 Russwurm, John B. "The Condition and Prospects of
Hayti." 6 Sept. 1826. JNH, 54 (Oct. 1969), 395-
397. Rpt. in Foner, A74:35-37; and in Fishel and
Quarles, A72:157-158, excerpt.

[_____, and Samuel Cornish. See Cornish,
SE436.]

RUSSWURM, JOHN B. See Brewer, HC15.

SE2001 Rustin, Bayard. "Nonviolence vs. Jim Crow." July
1942. In Rustin, A153:5-7.

SE2002 _____. "The Negro and Nonviolence." Oct. 1942.
In Rustin, A153:8-12.

SE2003 _____. "We Challenged Jim Crow." April 1947.
In Rustin, A153:13-25.

SE2004 _____. "Twenty-Two Days on a Chain Gang."
1947. In Rustin, A153:26-49.

SE2005 _____. "Civil Disobedience, Jim Crow, and the
Armed Forces." 11 April 1948. In Rustin, A153:
50-52.

SE2006 _____. "Montgomery Diary." Feb. 1956. In
Rustin, A153:55-61.

SE2007 _____. "Getting on with the White Folks." Sept.
1956. In Rustin, A153:88-91.

SE2008 _____. "Fear in the Delta." Oct. 1956. In
Rustin, A153:62-87.

SE2009 _____. "New South ... Old Politics." Oct.
1956. In Rustin, A153:92-98.

SE2010 _____. " 'Even in the Face of Death.' " Feb.
1957. In Rustin, A153:99-103.

SE2011 _____, and A. J. Muste. "Struggle for Integra-
tion--1960." 1960. In Goodman, A83:287-299.

SE2012 Rustin, Bayard. "The Meaning of Birmingham."
June 1963. In Rustin, A153:107-108; and in Goodman, A83:317-324.

SE2013 _____. "In Answer to Senator Thurmond." 12
Aug. 1963. In Rustin, A153:109-110.

SE2014 _____. "The Meaning of the March on Washington." Oct. 1963. Liberation, 8 (Oct. 1963), 11-
13.

SE2015 _____. "From Protest to Politics: The Future
of the Civil Rights Movement." Feb. 1964. Commentary, Feb. 1964, pp. 25-31. Rpt. in Rustin,
A153:111-122; in Jacobs and Landau, A99:296-310;
and in Littleton and Burger, A112:367-380.

SE2016 _____. "The Influence of the Right and Left in
the Civil Rights Movement." Jan. 1965. In Rustin,
A153:123-131.

SE2017 _____. "Making His Mark." Nov. 1965. In
Rustin, A153:132-139.

SE2018 _____. "The Watts 'Manifesto' and the McCone
Report." March 1966. Commentary, March 1966,
pp. 29-35. Rpt. in Rustin, A153:140-153.

SE2019 _____. " 'Black Power' and Coalition Politics."
Sept. 1966, Commentary, Sept. 1966, pp. 35-40.
Rpt. in Rustin, A153:154-165; and in Grant, A84:
466-472.

SE2020 _____. "Guns, Bread, and Butter." March 1967.
War/Peace Report, 7 (March 1967), 12-14. Rpt.
in Rustin, A153:166-168.

SE2021 _____. "Dr. King's Painful Dilemma." March

1967. In Rustin, A153:169-170.

SE2022 _____. "The Premise of the Stereotype." April
1967. In Rustin, A153:171-173.

SE2023 _____. "On Langston Hughes." May 1967. In
Rustin, A153:174-175.

SE2024 _____. "In Defense of Muhammad Ali." June
1967. In Rustin, A153:176-177.

SE2025 _____. "The Mind of the Black Militant." 10
July 1967. In Rustin, A153:206-212.

SE2026 _____. "A Way Out of the Exploding Ghetto."
Aug. 1967. New York Times Magazine, 13 Aug.
1967, pp. 16-17, 54, 59-60, 62, 64-65. Rpt. in
Rustin, A153:178-186; and in Foner, A74:1078-1088.

SE2027 _____. "The Lessons of the Long Hot Summer."
Oct. 1967. Commentary, Oct. 1967, pp. 39-45.
Rpt. in Rustin, A153:187-199.

SE2028 _____. "The Southern Negro Vote and the 1968
Elections." 1967. New South, 22 (Fall 1967), 48-
53.

SE2029 _____. "Minorities: The War Amidst Poverty."
Dec. 1967. In Rustin, A153:200-201.

SE2030 _____. "Memo on the Spring Protest in Washington, D.C." 1 Jan. 1968. In Rustin, A153:202-205.

SE2031 _____. "Integration within Decentralization." 6
April 1968. In Rustin, A153:213-221.

SE2032 _____. "Reflections on the Death of Martin Luther
King, Jr." May 1968. In Rustin, A153:222-229.

SE2033 _____. "The Anatomy of Frustration." 6 May
1968. In Rustin, A153:230-237.

SE2034 _____. "Soul Searching vs. Social Change."
May 1968. In Rustin, A153:238-239.

SE2035 _____. "Now Kennedy: The Bill Mounts Higher."
June 1968. In Rustin, A153:240-241.

SE2036 _____. "The Choice Is Clear." Sept. 1968. In
Rustin, A153:242-243.

SE2037 _____. "Where Is the Negro Movement Now?"
Nov. 1968. In Moss, A130:61-84.

SE2038 _____. "Negroes and the 1968 Elections." Dec.
1968. In Rustin, A153:244-252.

SE2039 _____. "Towards Integration as a Goal." Jan.
1969. American Federationist, 76 (Jan. 1969), 5-7.
Rpt. in Littleton and Burger, A112:275-280.

SE2040 _____. "Separate Is Not Equal." Feb. 1969. In
Rustin, A153:253-254.

SE2041 _____. "How Black Americans See Black Afri-
cans--and Vice Versa." March 1969. War/Peace
Report, 9 (March 1969), 14-15. Rpt. in Rustin,
A153:255-258.

SE2042 _____. "What About Black Capitalism?" March
1969. In Rustin, A153:259-260.

SE2043 _____. "The Total Vision of A. Philip Randolph."
April 1969. In Rustin, A153:261-266.

SE2044 _____. "No More Guns." April 1969. In Rustin,
A153:267-268.

SE2045 _____. "Fear, Demagogues, and Reaction."
June 1969. In Rustin, A153:269-270.

SE2046 _____. "The Role of the Negro Middle Class."
June 1969. In Rustin, A153:271-276.

SE2047 _____. "The Ballot Box and the Union Card."
July 1969. New Leader, 21 July 1969, pp. 8-10.

SE2048 _____. "An Exchange with Daniel Moynihan and
Thomas A. Billings." Aug. 1969. In Rustin,
A153:280-287.

SE2049 _____. "The Myths of Black Revolt." Aug. 1969.
Ebony, Aug. 1969, pp. 96-98, 101-102, 104. Rpt.
in The Black Revolution, A12:109-123.

SE2050 _____. "Nature, Nurture, or Nonsense?" Oct. 1969. In Rustin, A153:277-279.

SE2051 _____. "The Failure of Black Separatism." Jan. 1970. Harper's Magazine, Jan. 1970, pp. 25-32, 34. Rpt. in Rustin, A153:291-308.

SE2052 _____. "Benign Neglect: A Reply to Daniel Moynihan." March 1970. In Rustin, A153:309-315.

SE2053 _____. "Violence and the Southern Strategy." April 1970. In Rustin, A153:316-317.

SE2054 _____. "Death in Black and White." May 1970. In Rustin, A153:318-319.

SE2055 _____. "A Word to Black Students." 31 May 1970. Dissent, 17 (Nov.-Dec. 1970), 496, 581-585. Rpt. in Rustin, A153:327-334.

SE2056 _____. "A West Side Story." July 1970. In Rustin, A153:320-322.

SE2057 _____. "The Story of a Black Youth." July 1970. In Rustin, A153:323-324.

SE2058 _____. "Feminism and Equality." Aug. 1970. In Rustin, A153:325-326.

SE2059 _____. "The Blacks and the Unions." May 1971. Harper's Magazine, May 1971, pp. 73-76, 78-81. Rpt. in Rustin, A153:335-349.

SE2060 _____. "Nixon, the Great Society, and the Future of Social Policy." May 1973. Commentary, May 1973, pp. 51-53.

RUSTIN, BAYARD. See Brooks, HC212.

SE2061 Sales, William W., Jr. "Response to a 'Negro Negative.'" March 1969. In Wallerstein and Starr, A163:369-374. [See Henry, SE1229.]

SE2062 Sampson, B. K. "To My White Fellow Citizens." Nov. 1867. In Foner, A74:347-349.

SE2063 Sampson, Edith S. "Jane Addams' Unfinished

Business." 28 April 1960. In Hill, A93:294-303.

SE2064 _____. "Choose One of Five." 30 May 1965. In
Williams and Williams, A175:221-230.

SE2065 San Francisco State College Black Students. "Demands." 6 Nov. 1968. In Wallerstein and Starr,
A164:489-490.

SE2066 Saunders, Prince. "An Address ... Before the
Pennsylvania Augustine Society, for the Education of
People of Colour." 30 Sept. 1818. In Porter,
A141:88-92.

SE2067 _____. "A Memoir Presented to the American
Convention for Promoting the Abolition of Slavery,
and Improving the Condition of the African Race."
11 Dec. 1818. In Porter, A141:270-278; in Woodson, A177:56-63; and in Dunbar, A70:13-18, abr.

SE2068 Scarborough, W. S. "The Afro-American Press."
1890. In Penn, A139:431-434.

SE2069 _____. "The Ethics of the Hawaiian Question."
March 1894. In Foner, A74:571-577.

SE2070 _____. "The Party of Freedom and the Freed-
men--A Reciprocal Duty." 11 Feb. 1899. In Dunbar, A70:219-226.

SE2071 _____. "What the Omen?" 1902. In Culp, A46:
414-417.

SE2072 _____. "The Negro and Higher Learning." May
1902. Forum, 33 (May 1902), 349-355.

SE2073 _____. "The Educated Negro and His Mission."
1903. American Negro Academy, Occasional Papers
No. 8. Washington: The Academy, 1903. Rpt. in
Cromwell, A42:291-302.

SE2074 _____. "Address at the Unveiling of the Monument to Dunbar." 26 June 1909. In Ferris, HC451:
886-888.

SCARBOROUGH, W. S. See Simmons, HC163a:410-
418 or HC163b:269-274; Weisenburger, HC193;

Weisenburger, HC194; and Ferris, HC451:883-888.

SE2075 Schomburg, Arthur A. "The Economic Contribution by the Negro to America." Dec. 1915. In Papers of the American Negro Academy, A136:49-62.

SCHOMBURG, ARTHUR A. See Ferris, HC451:866-867.

SE2076 Schuyler, George S. "From Job to Job: A Personal Narrative." May 1923. In Aptheker, A2:428-430.

SE2077 _____. "Negro-Art Hokum." June 1926. Nation, 16 June 1926, pp. 662-663.

SE2078 _____. "Our Greatest Gift to America." c. 1927. In Johnson, A100:122-124; and in Calverton, A30: 405-412.

SE2079 _____. "The Caucasian Problem." 1944. In Logan, A115:281-298.

SCHUYLER, GEORGE S. See Schuyler, HC157; Bone, HC964:89-92; and Gloster, HC981:155-157, 188-190.

SE2080 Scott, Benjamin. "Scientific Technology in Black Community Development." Sept. 1970. In Jones, A101:225-227.

SE2081 Scott, Emmett J. "Is Liberia Worth Saving?" 1911. Journal of Race Developments, 1 (Jan. 1911), 277-301.

SE2082 _____. "Memorial Address." 16 Aug. 1916. In Woodson, A177:607-616.

SE2083 _____. "The Negro and the War Department." Dec. 1917. In Aptheker, A2:194-195.

SE2084 _____. "Twenty Years After: An Appraisal of Booker T. Washington." 5 April 1936. JNE, 5 (Oct. 1936), 543-554.

SE2085 Seale, Bobby. "Free Huey." 17 Feb. 1968. In Smith, HC1246:175-186.

SE2086 _____. "Other Voices, Other Strategies." April
1970. Time, 6 April 1970, pp. 23-24, 27. Rpt.
in Littleton and Burger, A112:432-436.

SE2087 _____. "Interview." 1972. Black Scholar, 4
(Sept. 1972), 7-16.

SE2088 Settle, Josiah T. "The Afro-American Press."
1890. In Penn, A139:463-467.

SE2089 Shadd, Abraham D., et al. "Address of the Free
People of Color of the Borough of Wilmington, Del."
12 July 1831. In Garrison, A77:36-40.

SE2090 Shepard, James E. "Is the Game Worth the Candle?"
pre-1913. In Dunbar, A70:357-366.

SE2091 Shuttlesworth, Fred L. "Birmingham Shall Be Free
Some Day." 1964. Freedomways, 4 (Winter 1964),
16-19.

SE2092 Sidney, Joseph. "An Oration Commemorative of the
Abolition of the Slave Trade." 2 Jan. 1809. In
Porter, A141:356-363.

SE2093 "Sidney." Four Letters. Feb.-March 1841. In
Stuckey, A160:149-164.

SE2094 Simmons, William J. "The Lord's Supper." 1890.
In Brawley, A25:143-156.

SIMMONS, WILLIAM J. See Turner, HC178.

SE2095 Sims, Harold R. "Which Way Black History?" 21
Oct. 1971. JNH, 57 (Jan. 1972), 65-74.

SE2096 Sipkins, Henry. "The Introductory Address" [for
Williams, SE2355]. 1 Jan. 1808. In Porter, A141:
344.

SE2097 _____. "An Oration on the Abolition of the Slave
Trade." 2 Jan. 1809. In Porter, A141:366-373.
[See Johnson, SE1367.]

SE2098 Smalls, Robert. "On the Hamburgh, S. C., Massacre." 15 July 1876. In Aptheker, A1:610-614.

SMALLS, ROBERT. See Christopher, HC24:38-54;
Simmons, HC163a:165-179 or HC163b:93-104; Uya,
HC180; Brown, HC443:175-180; and Cromwell,
HC447:242-245.

SE2099 Smith, C. S. "The Fallacy of Industrial Education
as the Solution of the Race Problem." 28 Jan.
1899. In Foner, A74:608-611.

SE2100 _____. "Episcopal Address." May 1912. In
Smith, HC1183:266-272, excerpt.

SE2101 Smith, J. G., et al. "Address on Colonization." 9
Jan. 1832. In Garrison, A77:49-50.

SE2102 Smith, James McCune. "The Abolition of Slavery
and the Slave Trade." c. June 1838. In Woodson,
A177:119-124.

SE2103 _____. "Toussaint L'Ouverture and the Haytian
Revolutions." 26 Feb. 1841. In Dunbar, A70:19-
32.

SE2104 _____. "John Murray of Glasgow." 25 Sept.
1852. In Griffiths, A86:62-67.

SE2105 _____. "Freedom--Liberty." 22 Nov. 1853. In
Griffiths, A87:241.

SE2106 [_____.] "An Address to the People of the
United States." Oct. 1855. In Proceedings of the
Colored National Convention, SE1876:30-33.

SE2107 _____. "On the Fourteenth Query of Thomas
Jefferson's Notes on Virginia." 1859. In Foner,
A74:216-226.

SMITH, JAMES McCUNE. See Brawley, HC13:44-
46; Brown, HC443:205-207; Brown, HC445:453-454;
Loggins, HC992:179-182.

SE2108 Smith, Jean. "I Learned to Feel Black." Aug.
1967. In Barbour, A8:207-218.

SE2109 Smith, Stephen, and James Richards. "Resolutions
on Colonization." 5 Aug. 1831. In Garrison, A77:
31-33.

SE2110 Smith, Venture. "A Narrative of the Life and Ad-
        ventures of Venture, a Native of Africa." 1798.
        In Porter, A141:538-558.

SE2111 Smith, Wilford H. "The Negro and the Law." 1903.
        In The Negro Problem, A133:127-159.

SE2112 Smyth, John H. "The Color Line in Ohio." c. 1895.
        In Golden and Rieke, A82:305-309.

SE2113 _____. "The African in Africa and the African
        in America." 13 Dec. 1895. In Bowen, A20:69-83;
        and in Hill and Kilson, A92a:49-58 or A92b:56-67.

SE2114 _____. "Negro Criminality." 1902. In Culp,
        A46:434-441.

        SMYTH, JOHN H. See Simmons, HC163a:872-877 or
        HC163b:617-621.

SE2115 SNCC. "Statement of Purpose." 14 May 1960. In
        Grant, A84:289-290. [Note: SE2115 drafted by
        James Lawson.]

SE2116 _____. "Black Body, White Mind." 1967. In
        Wallerstein and Starr, A163:349-355.

SE2117 South Carolinian. "Opinions of a Freeman of Colour
        in Charleston." 1832. In Porter, A141:303-307.

SE2118 Spaulding, Asa T. "Wanted! More George Leigh-
        Mallorys: There Are So Many Mount Everests."
        1 June 1959. In Hill, A93:231-244.

SE2119 Spencer, Peter, and Thomas Dorsey. "Resolutions
        on Colonization." 12 July 1831. In Garrison, A77:
        36.

SE2120 Spingarn, Arthur B. "Collecting a Library of Negro
        Literature." 12 Feb. 1937. JNE, 7 (Jan. 1938),
        12-18.

SE2121 Spottswood, Stephen G. "The Nixon Administration's
        Anti-Negro Policy." 19 June 1970. In Foner, A74:
        1173-1177.

SE2122 Stanford, Max. "Towards Revolutionary Action

Movement [RAM] Manifesto." March 1964. In
Bracey, A22:508-513.

SE2123 _____. "Black Guerilla Warfare: Strategy and Tactics." Nov. 1970. Black Scholar, 2 (Nov. 1970), 30ff.

SE2124 _____. "The Pan-African Party." Feb. 1971.
Black Scholar, 2 (Feb. 1971), 26-30.

SE2125 _____. "Black Nationalism and the Afro-American Student." June 1971. Black Scholar, 2 (June
1971), 27-31.

SE2126 [_____.] Muhammad Ahmad. "The Roots of the
Pan-African Revolution." May 1972. Black Scholar,
3 (May 1972), 48-55.

SE2127 [_____.] Muhammad Ahmad. "We Are All Prisoners of War." Oct. 1972. Black Scholar, 4 (Oct.
1972), 3-5.

SE2128 Stanley, J. "Tribute to a Fallen Black Soldier." 8
Sept. 1863. In Foner, A74:269-271.

SE2129 Stephens, George E. "The Afro-American Press."
1890. In Penn, A139:460-463.

SE2130 Steward, Theophilus G. "The Afro-American Press."
1890. In Penn, A139:471-475.

SE2131 _____. "How the Black St. Domingo Legion
Saved the Patriot Army in the Siege of Savannah,
1779." 1899. American Negro Academy, Occasional Papers No. 5. Washington: The Academy, 1899.

SE2132 _____. "The Army as a Trained Force." 1904.
In Dunbar, A70:277-290.

SE2133 _____. "The Message of San Domingo to the African Race." Dec. 1915. In Papers of the American Negro Academy, A136:25-37.

SE2134 Steward, William H. "Colored Baptists and Journal-
ism." 1890. In Brawley, A25:233-236.

STEWARD, WILLIAM H. See Simmons, HC163a:
603-607 or HC163b:413-415.

SE2135 Stewart, James T. "The Development of the Black
Revolutionary Artist." 1966. In Jones and Neal,
A103:3-10.

SE2136 Stewart, John. "An Address to the Wyandott Nation
and Accompanying Letter to William Walker." 25
May 1817. In Porter, A141:455-459; and in JNH,
21 (Oct. 1936), 406-410. [Note: JNH text is of
"Address" only.]

STEWART, JOHN. See Schomburg, HC156.

SE2137 Stewart, Maria W. "Religion and the Pure Principles
of Morality." Oct. 1831. In Porter, A141:460-471.

SE2138 _____. "An Address Delivered Before the Afric-
American Female Intelligence Society of Boston."
April 1832. In Golden and Rieke, A82:300-303.

SE2139 _____. "Lecture Delivered at the Franklin Hall,
Boston." 21 Sept. 1832. In Porter, A141:136-140.

SE2140 _____. "An Address Delivered at the African
Masonic Hall in Boston." 27 Feb. 1833. In Porter,
A141:129-135; and in Bormann, A18:177-183.

SE2141 Still, James T. "The Afro-American Press."
1890. In Penn, A139:452-454.

SE2142 Still, William. "A Defense of Independent Voting."
10 March 1874. In Foner, A74:399-403.

STILL, WILLIAM. See Simmons, HC163a:149-161
or HC163b:81-90; Brown, HC443:211-214; Brown,
HC445:520-522; and Gara, HC580.

SE2143 Stokes, Andrew J. "Justification." 1890. In Brawley, A25:87-90.

SE2144 Stokes, Carl B. "Testimony Before the U.S. Commission on Civil Rights." April 1966. In Fishel
and Quarles, A72:554-556.

SE2145 _____. "Rebuilding the Cities." March 1969.
In Moss, A130:54-61.

SE2146 _____. "Black Political Action in 1972." 1971.

Freedomways, 11 (4th Qrtr 1971), 384-392.

SE2147 Straker, D. Augustus. "Citizenship, Its Rights and Duties,--Woman Suffrage, A Lecture." 13 and 14 April 1874. Washington: New National Era Print., 1874. Pages 5-22.

SE2148 _____. "The New South Investigated." 1888. In Cox and Cox, A41:396-408, excerpt.

SE2149 _____. "The Afro-American Press." 1890. In Penn, A139:444-446.

SE2150 Sullivan, Leon Howard. "Building Black Economic Emancipation with Ten-Dollar Building Blocks." 1968. In Wright, A179:261-268.

SE2151 Sutton, Percy. "Black Communications--Black Power: A New Strategy for Black Liberation." 1972. In Wright, A180:144-164.

SE2152 "A Symposium on Garvey." Dec. 1922. In Aptheker, A2:371-377.

SE2153 Talbert, Mary B. "Women and Colored Women." Aug. 1915. In Aptheker, A2:103-104.

SE2154 Tanner, Benjamin T. "Life of St. Cyprian." 1863. In Payne, HC1181:131-134.

SE2155 _____. "The African Methodist Episcopal Church: Its Duty and Its Destiny." c. 1864. In Payne, HC1181:143-146.

SE2156 _____. "The Sioux's Revenge." 13 July 1876. In Foner, A74:444-445.

SE2157 _____. "The Church the Right Hand of God." 4 May 1896. In Smith, HC1183:187-189, excerpt.

TANNER, BENJAMIN T. See Simmons, HC163a: 985-988 or HC1636:705-708; and Brown, HC445:530-531.

SE2158 Taylor, George Edwin. "Revolution by the Ballot." 5 July 1904. In Foner, A74:648-652; and in Aptheker, A1:853-856.

SE2159 Teague, Hilary. "Liberia: Its Struggles and Its
Promises." 1846. In Dunbar, A70:33-40.

SE2160 Teer, Barbara Ann. "Needed: A New Image."
c. 1968. In Barbour, A8:219-223.

SE2161 Temple, R. J. "Baptists and Publication Work."
1890. In Brawley, A25:200-210.

SE2162 Terrell, Mary Church. "The Progress of the Colored Women." 18 Feb. 1898. Washington: Smith,
1898.

SE2163 _____. "What Role Is the Educated Negro Woman to Play in the Uplifting of Her Race?" 1902.
In Culp, A46:172-177.

SE2164 _____. "Lynching from a Negro's Point of View."
June 1904. North American Review, 178 (June
1904), 863-868.

SE2165 _____. "The Progress of Colored Women." July
1904. In Foner, A74:643-647.

SE2166 _____. "Plea for the White South by a Colored
Woman." July 1906. Nineteenth Century, 60 (July
1906), 70-84.

SE2167 _____. "Harriet Beecher Stowe: An Appreciation." 1911. Washington: Murray, 1911.

SE2168 _____. "Woman Suffrage and the Fifteenth
Amendment." Aug. 1915. In Aptheker, A2:115-116.

SE2169 _____. "The History of the High School for Negroes in Washington." July 1917. JNH, 2 (July
1917), 252-266.

TERRELL, MARY CHURCH. See Terrell, HC173

SE2170 Terrell, Robert H. "A Glance at the Past and Present of the Negro." 22 Sept. 1903. Washington:
Pendleton, 1903.

SE2171 _____. "Our Debt to Suffragists." Aug. 1915.
In Aptheker, A2:98-99.

SE2172 Thompson, Henry C., and George Hogarth. "Reso-
lutions on Colonization and Address to the Colored
Citizens of Brooklyn." 3 June 1831. In Garrison,
A77:23-28.

SE2173 Thompson, J. P. "The First Pair Banished." pre-
1884. In Hood, A95:315-321.

SE2174 Thurman, Howard. "Good News for the Underprivi-
leged." 26 May 1959. In Golden and Rieke, A82:
90-95; and in Hill, A93:258-265.

SE2175 _____. "An Interpretation of the Significance of
Higher Education in a Segregated Society." 15 Feb.
1967. In Williams and Williams, A175:233-239.

THURMAN, HOWARD. See Massey, B18; Yates,
HC206; and Boulware, HC1023:184-187.

SE2176 Tobias, Channing H. "Building for Tomorrow's Better Living." 9 Sept. 1954. In Hill, A93:159-164.

TOBIAS, CHANNING H. See Boulware, HC1023:192-
194.

SE2177 Touré, El Hajj Abdoulaye. "Address to the Congress
of African Peoples." Sept. 1970. In Jones, A101:
73.

SE2178 Townsend, Willard S. "One American Problem and
a Possible Solution." 1944. In Logan, A115:163-
192.

SE2179 Trigg, Frank. "The Afro-American Press." 1890.
In Penn, A139:442-444.

SE2180 Trotter, William M. "Why Be Silent?" 1902. In
Long and Collier, A117:195-197.

SE2181 _____. "Address to President Wilson." 12 Nov.
1914. In Aptheker, A2:74-76; and in Foner, A74:
703-706.

SE2182 _____. "How I Managed to Reach the Peace Conference." July 1919. In Foner, A74:741-742.

TROTTER, WILLIAM M. See Fox, HC56; Harrison,

HC75; Puttkamer and Worthy, HC142; Worthy, HC203; Brisbane, HC442:35-44; Du Bois, SE811; and Grimké, SE1135.

SE2183 Troup, C. V. "Two Kinds of Vision." 4 Oct. 1953. In Hill, A93:155-158.

SE2184 Truth, Sojourner. "Woman's Rights." 1851. In Foner, A74:101.

SE2185 _____. "When Woman Gets Her Rights Man Will Be Right." May 1867. In Foner, A74:345-347.

TRUTH, SOJOURNER. See Bernard, HC8; Brawley, HC12:73-79; Fauset, HC51; Pauli, HC131; Truth, HC177a or HC177b; Wyman, HC205; Brawley, HC441: 167-171; Cromwell, HC447:104-114; Montgomery, HC1107; and Wagner, HC1155.

SE2186 Turner, Darwin T. "The Afro-American College in American Higher Education." Aug. 1968. In Wright, A179:94-103.

SE2187 Turner, Henry McNeal. "On the Anniversary of Emancipation." 1 Jan. 1866. In Turner, A162:5-12.

SE2188 _____. "On the Eligibility of Colored Members to Seats in the Georgia Legislature." 3 Sept. 1868. In Turner, A162:14-28; in Bracey, A21:281-296; in Foner, A74:358-366; and in Aptheker, A1:569-571, excerpt.

SE2189 _____. "Testimony on the KKK." 3 Nov. 1871. In Cox and Cox, A41:279-285.

SE2190 _____. "How Long? How Long, O Heaven?" 5 Aug. 1876. In Foner, A74:446-447.

SE2191 _____. "The Barbarous Decision of the Supreme Court." 1883-1889. In Turner, A162:60-69.

[_____. The Genius and Theory of Methodist Polity, or the Machinery of Methodism. See Turner, HC1186.]

SE2192 _____. "Reasons for a New Political Party."

12 Feb. 1886. In Foner, A74:505-506.

SE2193 _____. "Episcopal Address." May 1892. In
Smith, HC1183:164-166, excerpt.

SE2194 _____. "African Emigration Excitement." 1892.
In Turner, A162:135-138.

SE2195 _____. "Justice or Emigration Should Be Our
Watchword." Nov. 1893. In Foner, A74:562-570.

SE2196 _____. "Critique of 'The Atlanta Compromise.' "
Oct. 1895. In Turner, A162:165-166.

SE2197 _____. "The American Negro and His Father-
land." 13 Dec. 1895. In Bowen, A20:195-198; and
in Turner, A162:167-171.

SE2198 _____. "The Black Man's Doom." 1896. In
Osofsky, A135:227-229.

SE2199 _____. "Will It Be Possible for the Negro to Attain the American Type of Civilization?" 1902. In
Culp, A46:42-45; and in Hill and Kilson, A92a:44-47.

TURNER, HENRY McNEAL. See Penn, A139:356-
360; Batten, HC6; Coulter, HC31; Simmons, HC163a:
805-819 or HC163b:567-576; Brown, HC445:506-507;
Woodson, HC1188:209-211; Redkey, HC1267; Redkey,
HC1268:24-46, 170-194, and passim; and Redkey,
HC1269.

SE2200 Turner, James M. "Eulogy of Dred Scott." 18
April 1882. JNH, 26 (Jan. 1941), 6-10.

SE2201 Turner, Nat. "The Confessions of Nat Turner."
1831. In Aptheker, HC499:127-151; in Robinson,
A149:68-82; and in Golden and Rieke, A82:461-465,
excerpt.

SE2202 Tuskegee Negro Conference. "Declarations." Jan.
1917. In Aptheker, A2:164-165.

SE2203 Universal Negro Improvement Association. "Constitution." Aug. 1922. In Hill and Kilson, A92a:184-
206 or A92b:214-239.

SE2204 _____. "Agenda for the Sixth Annual Convention."
Aug. 1929. In Hill and Kilson, A92a:207-208 or
A92b:240-241.

SE2205 Vance, J. Madison. "In the Wake of the Coming
Ages." 4 Oct. 1894. In Dunbar, A70:177-180.

SE2206 Vandervall, R. B. "The Way of Salvation." 1890.
In Brawley, A25:56-59.

VANDERVALL, R. B. See Simmons, HC163a:572-
578 or HC163b:387-391.

SE2207 Vann, Albert. "The Agency Shop." 6 May 1969.
In Wright, A179:234-235.

SE2208 _____. " 'Community Involvement' in Schools."
June 1969. In Wright, A179:231-233.

SE2209 Vann, M. "Baptists and Home Missions." 1890.
In Brawley, A25:251-255.

SE2210 Vashon, J. B., and R. Bryan. "Resolutions on Colonization." 1 Sept. 1831. In Garrison, A77:34-35.

SE2211 Vashon, J. B. "Sentiments of a Man of Color." 16
March 1832. In Woodson, A176:244-246.

SE2212 Vernon, W. T. " 'A Plea for a Suspension of Judgment.' " 1905. In Woodson, A177:618-626.

SE2213 Waldron, J. Milton. "The Problem's Solution." 31
May 1909. In Proceedings of the National Negro
Conference, 1909, A145:159-166; and in Dunbar,
A70:389-396, abr. [Note: A70 text dated 1912.]

SE2214 Walker, David. "We Must Have Unity." 1828. In
Bracey, A22:29-34; and in Smith and Robb, A156:
11-15.

SE2215 _____. Appeal to the Colored Citizens of the
World. 1829-1830. In Aptheker, HC558:61-147; and
in Stuckey, A160:39-117.
         Contains (HC558 pagination): "Preamble," pp. 63-
         68.
         "Our Wretchedness in Consequence of Slavery,"
         pp. 69-81 (rpt. in Golden and Rieke, A82:468-
         475).

"Our Wretchedness in Consequence of Ignorance,"
pp. 82-98.
"Our Wretchedness in Consequence of the
Preachers of the Religion of Jesus Christ,"
pp. 99-108.
"Our Wretchedness in Consequence of the Colon-
izing Plan," pp. 109-147.

WALKER, DAVID. See Brawley, HC13:40-44; Brawley, HC441:155-159; and Aptheker, HC558.

SE2216 Walker, Wyatt Tee. "Albany, Failure or First
Step?" June 1963. New South, 18 (June 1963), 3-8.

SE2217 Walrond, Eric D. "Imperator Africanus; Marcus
Garvey: Menace or Promise?" Jan. 1925. In
Aptheker, A2:386-393.

SE2218 Walters, Alexander. "Nothing But Manly Resistance."
April 1899. In Foner, A74:612, excerpt.

SE2219 _____. "Abraham Lincoln and Fifty Years of
Freedom." 12 Feb. 1909. In Woodson, A177:554-
561.

SE2220 _____. "Civil and Political Status of the Negro."
1 June 1909. In Proceedings of the National Negro
Conference, 1909, A145:167-173.

WALTERS, ALEXANDER. See Clement, HC26; Simmons, HC163a:340-343 or HC163b:221-223; and
Walters, HC183.

SE2221 Ward, Samuel R. "Speech at the Anti-Webster Meet-
ing in Faneuil Hall." 25 March 1850. In Woodson,
A177:193-196; in Brown, A28:622-625; in Foner,
A74:94-97; and in Golden and Rieke, A82:485-487.

WARD, SAMUEL R. See Ward, HC184a or HC184b;
Brown, HC443:284-285; Loggins, HC992:173-175;
Woodson, HC1188:160-162; Douglass, SE585; and
Douglass, SE612.

SE2222 Ward, T. M. D. "On Bishop Payne." May 1892.
In Smith, HC1183:167-169.

[Waring, Arthur, and John W. Prout. See Prout, SE
1880.]

SE2223 Washington, Booker T. "Industrial Education." 7
April 1882. In Washington, A167:191-195.

SE2224 _____. "The Educational Outlook in the South."
16 July 1884. In Washington, A167:255-262; in
Washington, A170:1-11; in Brotz, A27:351-356; and
in Golden and Rieke, A82:107-112.

SE2225 _____. "Our Opportunity Through the South."
21 Sept. 1886. In Washington, A167:308-312.

SE2226 _____. "Some Lessons from Socrates." 1887.
In Washington, A167:397-400.

SE2227 _____. "Opening Address [before the Alabama
State Teachers' Association]." 11 April 1888. In
Washington, A167:427-434; and in Washington, A170:
12-22.

SE2228 _____. "The South as an Opening for a Career."
26 April 1888. In Washington, A167:439-450.

SE2229 _____. "A Speech Before the Boston Unitarian
Club." 1888. In Washington, A167:497-505.

SE2230 _____. "An Excerpt from a Speech in Montgomery." 17 Jan. 1890. In Washington, A168:24.

SE2231 _____. "A Speech Delivered Before the Women's
New England Club." 27 Jan. 1890. In Washington,
A168:25-32.

SE2232 _____. "Reading a Means of Growth." 26 Oct.
1890. In Washington, A168:91-94.

SE2233 _____. "The Afro-American Press." 1890. In
Penn, A139:446-448.

SE2234 _____. "Self Denial." 8 Feb. 1891. In Washington, A168:129-132.

SE2235 _____. "Sowing and Reaping." 19 April 1891.
In Washington, A168:138-146.

SE2236 _____. "A Commencement Address to the Class
of 1891." 28 May 1891. In Washington, A168:154-
155.

SE2237 _____. "The South as an Opening for a Business
Career." 20 Nov. 1891. In Washington, A168:184-
194.

SE2238 _____. "A Speech at Old South Meeting House,
Boston." 15 Dec. 1891. In Washington, A168:199-
201.

SE2239 _____. "The Declarations of the First Tuskegee
Negro Conference." 23 Feb. 1892. In Washington,
A168:217-219.

SE2240 _____. "An Address to the Graduating Class of
Tuskegee Institute." 26 May 1892. In Washington,
A168:229-230.

SE2241 _____. "Aims and Results of Teaching." 8 June
1892. In Washington, A168:234-236.

SE2242 _____. "The Progress of the Negro." 16 Jan.
1893. In Washington, A168:279-288.

SE2243 _____. "A Speech at the Memorial Service for
Samuel Chapman Armstrong." 25 May 1893. In
Washington, A168:317-321; and in Washington, A170:
23-30.

SE2244 _____. "An Account of a Speech Before the Labor Congress, Chicago." 2 Sept. 1893. In Washington, A168:364-366.

SE2245 [_____.] "A Negro Who Has Sense: An Account
of a Speech in Washington, D.C." 7 April 1894.
In Washington, A168:397-402.

SE2246 _____. "A Speech Before the National Unitarian
Association." 26 Sept. 1894. In Washington,
A168:476-479.

SE2247 _____. "The Starting of the Calhoun School."
Oct. 1894. In Washington, A168:481-484.

SE2248 [_____.] "A Newspaper Report of an Emancipation Day Address." 1 Jan. 1895. In Washington,
A168:496.

SE2249 _____. "Unimproved Opportunities." 10 Feb.

1895. In Washington, A168:508-515; and in Washington, A169:119-131.

SE2250 _____. "The Work to Be Done By Tuskegee Graduates." 28 April 1895. In Washington, A168: 548-553.

SE2251 _____. "Growth." 12 May 1895. In Washington, A168:554-556; and in Washington, A169:277-282.

SE2252 _____. "The Manuscript Version of the Atlanta Exposition Address." 18 Sept. 1895. In Washington, A168:578-582.

SE2253 _____. "The Standard Printed Version of the Atlanta Exposition Address." 18 Sept. 1895. In Washington, A168:583-587; in Dunbar, A70:181-186; in Woodson, A177:580-583; in Golden and Rieke, A82: 112-115; etc.

SE2254 _____. "Extracts from Address." 1895. In Washington, A170:37-41.

SE2255 _____. "Our New Citizen." 31 Jan. 1896. In Washington, A170:46-50; and in Brotz, A27:359-362.

SE2256 _____. "Address Delivered at the Harvard Alumni Dinner." 24 June 1896. In Washington, A170: 51-53; in Woodson, A177:584-585; and in Hill, A93: 43-44.

SE2257 _____. "Democracy and Education." 30 Sept. 1896. In Washington, A170:60-77; and in Brotz, A27:362-371.

SE2258 _____. "Extracts from Address." 18 Nov. 1896. In Washington, A170:42-45; and in Brotz, A27:371- 372.

SE2259 _____. "Address Delivered at the Dedication of the Robert Gould Shaw Monument in Boston." 31 May 1897. In Washington, A170:54-59; in Dunbar, A70:205-210; in Woodson, A177:527-531; and in Cromwell, A42:285-288.

SE2260 _____. "Letter to the Louisiana State Constitutional Convention." 19 Feb. 1898. In Brotz, A27: 373-375.

SE2261 _____. "The Negro and His Relation to the Economic Progress of the South." 12 Oct. 1899. In Washington, A170:78-86.

SE2262 _____. "First Annual Address as President." 24 Aug. 1900. In Washington, A170:87-91.

SE2263 _____. "An Interview on the Hardwick Bill." 1900. In Brotz, A27:376-379.

SE2264 _____. "Will the Education of the Negro Solve the Race Problem?" 1902. In Culp, A46:142-153.

SE2265 _____. "The Educational and Industrial Emancipation of the Negro." 22 Feb. 1903. In Washington, A170:100-117.

SE2266 _____. "The Rights and Duties of the Negro." 2 June 1903. In Washington, A170:92-99.

SE2267 _____. "Industrial Education for the Negro." 1903. In The Negro Problem, A133:9-29.

SE2268 _____. "Negro Education Not a Failure." 12 Feb. 1904. In Washington, A170:118-134.

SE2269 _____. "The Education of the Southern Negro." June 1904. In Washington, A170:135-147.

SE2270 _____. "We Must Be a Law-Abiding and Law-Respecting People." 11 Oct. 1906. In Foner, A74:653-654.

SE2271 _____. "The Economic Development of the Negro Race in Slavery." 1907. In Washington and Du Bois, A171:9-41.

SE2272 _____. "The Economic Development of the Negro Race Since Its Emancipation." 1907. In Washington and Du Bois, A171:45-75.

SE2273 _____. "The Higher and the Lower Life." 16 Aug. 1907. In Washington, A170:148-153.

SE2274 _____. "Extracts from Address." 13 Sept. 1907. In Washington, A170:154-159.

SE2275 _____. "An Address to the Theological Department of Vanderbilt University." 29 March 1907.
In Washington, A170:160-189.

SE2276 _____. "An Address on Abraham Lincoln." 12
Feb. 1909. In Washington, A170:190-199.

SE2277 _____. "An Address Delivered Before the National Colored Teachers' Association." 30 July
1911. In Washington, A170:200-207.

SE2278 _____. "Extracts from Address Delivered Before
the A. M. E. Zion Conference." 14 May 1912. In
Washington, A170:208-212; and in Smith, HC1183:
275-276, excerpt. [Note: A170 text dated 9 May
1912.]

SE2279 _____. "Is the Negro Having a Fair Chance?"
Nov. 1912. In Brotz, A27:445-460.

SE2280 _____. "Extracts from Address Delivered to the
Fourth American Peace Congress." 1 May 1913.
In Washington, A170:213-217.

SE2281 _____. "An Address on the Negro Race." Jan.
1914. In Washington, A170:218-234.

SE2282 _____. "The Southern Sociological Congress as a
Factor for Social Welfare." 8 May 1914. In Washington, A170:235-242.

SE2283 _____. "What Coöperation Can Accomplish." 12
Nov. 1914. In Washington, A170:243-250.

SE2284 _____. "Last Annual Address as President." 19
Aug. 1915. In Washington, A170:251-270.

SE2285 _____. "My View of Segregation Laws." 13
Sept. 1915. New Republic, 4 Dec. 1915, pp. 113-
114. Rpt. in Aptheker, A2:117-120.

SE2286 _____. "Teamwork." 17 Oct. 1915. In Washington, A170:271-276; and in Hill, A93:45-49.

SE2287 _____. "Last Address." 25 Oct. 1915. In
Washington, A170:277-283; and in Foner, A74:707-
711.

WASHINGTON, BOOKER T.   See Williams, B31;
Brawley, HC12:147-157; Brawley, HC13:161-165;
Drinker, HC42; Harlan, HC71; Mathews, HC113;
Scott and Stowe, HC159; Simmons, HC163a:1027-
1030 or HC163b:737-739; Spencer, HC165; Washing-
ton, HC188; Washington, HC189; Washington, HC190;
Washington, HC191; Calista, HC213; Cook, HC219;
Flynn, HC229; Meier, HC252; Meier, HC256; Thorn-
brough, HC265; Thornbrough, HC266; Bond, HC381:
116-126; Brawley, HC441:303-307; Cromwell,
HC447:195-212; Ferris, HC451:898-909; Thorpe,
HC475:310-334; Newman, HC828; Walden, HC833;
Loggins, HC992:295-298; Boulware, HC1023:39-53;
Delaney, HC1062; Gottschalk, HC1073; Harris and
Kennicott, HC1082; Oliver, HC1112:353-356; Wallace,
HC1156; Du Bois, SE748; Du Bois, SE772; Franklin,
SE927; Grimké, SE1105; Lewis, SE1514; Miller,
SE1648; Moton, SE1733; Scott, SE2082; Scott, SE
2084; and Turner, SE2196.

SE2288 Waters, Hayden.   "An Address to the Gentlemen and
Ladies of the County of Otsego, N.Y."   30 Sept.
1830.   In Garrison, A77:61-63, excerpt.

[Watkins, William, and William Douglass.   See Douglass, SE723.]

SE2289 Watkins, William.   "Address Delivered Before the
Moral Reform Society in Philadelphia."   8 Aug.
1836.   In Porter, A141:156-166.

SE2290 _____.   "Our Rights as Men: An Address Delivered in Boston, Before the Legislative Committee
on the Militia."   24 Feb. 1853.   In Porter, A142:
orig. pag.; and in Foner, A74:131-143.

SE2291 _____.   "The Evils of Colonization."   31 Oct.
1853.   In Griffiths, A87:198-200.

SE2292 _____.   " 'The Work Goes Bravely On.' "   1854.
In Griffiths, A87:156-157.

SE2293 Wears, Isaiah C.   "Lincoln's Colonization Is Anti-
Christian."   15 Aug. 1862.   In Foner, A74:260-262.

SE2294 _____.   "The Ku Klux of the North."   Nov. 1871.
In Foner, A74:378-380.

SE2295 Weaver, Robert C. "Whither Northern Race Relations Committees?" 1944. Phylon, 5 (3rd Qrtr 1944), 205-218.

SE2296 _____. "Some Basic Issues in Desegregation." 1955. JNE, 25 (Spring 1956), 101-108.

SE2297 _____. "The Negro as an American." 13 June 1963. In Williams and Williams, A175:65-73; in Smith and Robb, A156:130-142; and in Voices of Crisis: Vital Speeches on Contemporary Issues. Ed. Floyd W. Matson. New York: Odyssey, 1967. Pages 163-174.

SE2298 Wells-Barnett, Ida B. "A Red Record: Tabulated Statistics and Alleged Causes of Lynchings in the United States, 1892-94." 1895. Chicago: The Author, 1895.

SE2299 _____. "Lynch Law in America." 1900. Arena, 23 (Jan. 1900), 15-24.

SE2300 _____. "Lynching Our National Crime." 1 June 1909. In Proceedings of the National Negro Conference, 1909, A145:174-179; and in Foner, A74:687-691.

SE2301 _____. "Our Country's Lynching Record." 1913. Survey, 29 (1 Feb. 1913), 573-574.

WELLS-BARNETT, IDA B. See Penn, A139:407-410; Wells, HC195; and Tucker, HC268.

SE2302 Wesley, Charles H. "Education for Citizenship in a Democracy." 31 May 1939. In Hill, A93:55-69.

SE2303 _____. "The Negro Has Always Wanted the Four Freedoms." 1944. In Logan, A115:90-112.

SE2304 _____. "The Dilemma of the Rights of Man." 26 Oct. 1952. JNH, 38 (Jan. 1953), 10-26.

SE2305 _____. "Creating and Maintaining an Historical Tradition." 17 Oct. 1963. JNH, 49 (Jan. 1964), 13-33.

SE2306 _____. "The Great Man Theory of Emancipation."

1965. <u>NHB</u>, 28 (Feb. 1965), 101-102, 111-113, 115, 119.

WESLEY, CHARLES H.   See Boulware, HC1023:133-137.

SE2307 Whipper, W. J., et al.   "Black Delegates to the South Carolina Constitutional Convention of 1868 Debate the Distribution of Lands to the Freedmen." 1868. In Bracey, A21:235-247.

SE2308 Whipper, William.   "An Address Delivered ... Before the Colored Reading Society of Philadelphia." 12 June 1828. In Porter, A141:106-119.

SE2309 _____, Robert Purvis, Junius C. Morel, Frederick A. Hinton, and James Cornish.   "Meeting in Philadelphia." 1 March 1831. <u>Liberator,</u> 12 March 1831, p. 43.

[_____, James Forten, and Robert Purvis. See Forten, SE909.]

SE2310 Whipper, William.   "Eulogy on William Wilberforce." 6 Dec. 1833. In Foner, A74:50-56.

SE2311 _____.   "Declaration of Sentiment" and "To the American People." Aug. 1837. In Porter, A141: 200-209.

SE2312 _____.   "Non-Resistance to Offensive Aggression." 16 Aug. 1837. In Woodson, A177:104-118.

SE2313 _____.   Three Letters. 3-17 Jan. 1841. In Stuckey, A160:252-260.

WHIPPER, WILLIAM.   See Brown, HC445:493-495; and Still, HC598a:735-740.

SE2314 White, George H.   "The Injustice to the Colored Voter." Jan. 1900. In Aptheker, A1:816-817.

SE2315 _____.   "I Raise My Voice Against One of the Most Dangerous Evils in Our Country." 20 Jan. 1900. In Foner, A74:625-628, excerpt.

SE2316 _____.   "A Speech in Defense of the Negro

Race." 29 Jan. 1901. In Woodson, A177:403-410; in Brown, A28:660-666; in Dunbar, A70:233-242, abr.; and in Foner, A74:636-639, abr.

SE2317 _____. "What Should Be the Negro's Attitude in Politics?" 1902. In Culp, A46:224-227.

WHITE, GEORGE H. See Christopher, HC24:160-167; Simmons, HC163a:536-537 or HC163b:362-363; and Katz, HC758.

SE2318 White, Milton. "Malcolm X in the Military." Sept. 1970. In Jones, A101:364-370.

SE2319 _____. "Self-Determination for Black Soldiers." Nov. 1970. Black Scholar, 2 (Nov. 1970), 40-46.

SE2320 White, Walter F. "Double Sessions in Atlanta Schools." Oct. 1917. In Aptheker, A2:192-194.

SE2321 _____. "The Work of a Mob." Sept. 1918. In Aptheker, A2:227-232.

SE2322 _____. " 'Work or Fight' in the South." March 1919. New Republic, 1 March 1919, pp. 144-146. Rpt. in Aptheker, A2:237-241; and in Foner, A74: 725-729.

SE2323 _____. "Chicago and Its Eight Reasons." Oct. 1919. In Aptheker, A2:272-278.

SE2324 _____. "The Race Conflict in Arkansas." Dec. 1919. In Aptheker, A2:279-282.

SE2325 _____. "Election Day in Florida." 1920. In Aptheker, A2:310-314.

SE2326 _____. "The Eruption of Tulsa." June 1921. In Aptheker, A2:327-332.

SE2327 _____. "The Defeat of Arkansas Lynch Law." April 1923. In Aptheker, A2:420-425.

SE2328 _____. "The Paradox of Color." 1925. In Locke, A113:361-368.

SE2329 _____. "I Investigate Lynchings." Jan. 1929.

American Mercury, 16 (Jan. 1929), 77-84. Rpt.
in Brown, A28:1005-1017; and in Calverton, A30:
389-404.

SE2330 _____. Rope and Faggot. 1929; rpt. New York:
Arno, 1969.

SE2331 _____. "Address to the Writers' Congress." 1
Oct. 1943. Writers' Congress. Berkeley: Univ.
of California Press, 1944. Pages 14-18.

SE2332 _____. A Rising Wind. Garden City, N.Y.:
Doubleday, 1945.

SE2333 _____. "Some Tactics Which Should Supplement
Resort to the Courts in Achieving Racial Integration
in Education." 17 April 1952. JNE, 21 (Summer
1952), 340-344.

SE2334 _____. How Far the Promised Land? New York:
Viking, 1955.
   Contains: "Why This Book?" pp. 3-28.
   "Decision Monday," pp. 29-64.
   "The Negro Votes," pp. 65-86.
   "The Fight for the Right to Fight," pp. 87-103.
   "Work to Do," pp. 104-121.
   "A Home of His Own," pp. 122-148.
   "The Negro Seeks Health," pp. 149-162.
   "Jim Crow on the Run," pp. 163-186.
   "Labor Unions and the Fight for Racial Equality,"
      pp. 187-193.
   "Sunday at Eleven," pp. 194-202.
   "The Negro in the Public Eye," pp. 203-211.
   "Why Has the Negro Rejected Communism?" pp.
      212-227.
   " 'Aye, But It Does Move!' " pp. 228-233.

WHITE, WALTER F. See Brawley, HC13:221-222;
White, HC199; Hughes, HC459:56-64; and Boulware,
HC1023:86-91.

SE2335 Wilcox, Preston. "Principal Concerns: Education
and Black Students." Sept. 1970. In Jones, A101:
279-286.

SE2336 _____. "Education for Black Humanism: A Way
of Approaching It." 1970. In Wright, A179:3-17.

SE2337 Wilkerson, Doxey A. "Freedom--Through Victory in
War and Peace." 1944. In Logan, A115:193-216.

SE2338 Wilkins, Roy. "The Bonuseers Ban Jim Crow."
Oct. 1932. In Aptheker, A2:734-739.

SE2339 _____. "An Interview with Louisiana's Kingfish."
1935. In Fishel and Quarles, A72:469-473.

SE2340 _____. "Next Steps in Education for Racial Understanding." 1944. JNE, 13 (Summer 1944), 432-
440.

SE2341 _____. "The Negro Wants Full Equality." 1944.
In Logan, A115:113-132.

SE2342 _____. "The Conspiracy to Deny Equality."
1955. In Foner, A74:893-902; in Broderick and
Meier, A26:255-262, abr.; and in Smith and Robb,
A156:121-128, abr.

SE2343 _____. "Deep South Crisis." 1 Nov. 1957.
Contemporary Forum: American Speeches on Twen-
tieth-Century Issues. Ed. Ernest J. Wrage and
Barnet Baskerville. New York: Harper, 1962.
Pages 344-351. Rpt. in Williams and Williams,
A175:53-62, abr.

SE2344 _____. " 'Shock Troops' and 'Solid Legal
Moves.' " 7 June 1961. In Broderick and Meier,
A26:282-287, abr.

SE2345 _____. "Address to the March on Washington."
28 Aug. 1963. In Speeches by the Leaders, A131:
n. pag.

SE2346 _____. "Freedom Tactics for 18,000,000." 29
Nov. 1963. New South, 18 (Feb. 1964), 3-5, abr.

SE2347 _____. "Keynote Address to the NAACP Annual
Convention, Los Angeles." 5 July 1966. In Bos-
majian and Bosmajian, A19:89-100; in O'Neill,
A134:166-174; and in Andrews, HC1020:101-109.

SE2348 _____. "When Negro Leaders Look Ahead." Nov.
1968. U.S. News and World Report, 25 Nov. 1968,
p. 61. Rpt. in Littleton and Burger, A112:329-331.

SE2349 _____. "The Case Against Separatism: 'Black
Jim Crow.' " Feb. 1969. Newsweek, 10 Feb.
1969, p. 57. Rpt. in Littleton and Burger, A112:
199-201; and in Wallerstein and Starr, A163:317-
319. [See Hare, SE1203.]

SE2350 _____. "Steady as She Goes." 1969. In Littleton and Burger, A112:294-303.

WILKINS, ROY. See Arnold, HC208; Hughes, HC459:
168-171; Andrews, HC1020:91-99; Boulware, HC1023:
92-97; and Ferris, HC1067.

SE2351 Williams, Eddie, Jr. "A Black Undergraduate Replies." Sept. 1973. New York Times Magazine,
2 Sept. 1973, p. 34. [See Kilson, SE1427.]

SE2352 Williams, Eric. "The Political Leader Considered
as a Man of Culture." March 1959. Presence Africaine, Nos. 24-25 (Feb.-May 1959), 98-111.

SE2353 Williams, Francis. "Duty of Colored Men in the
Present National Crisis." c. April 1864. In Foner,
A74:281-283.

SE2354 Williams, Franklin H. "The Black Crisis on Campus." 18 April 1969. In Wright, A179:150-165.

[Williams, Jacob G., and Jacob D. Richardson. See
Richardson, SE1969.]

SE2355 Williams, Peter. "An Oration on the Abolition of
the Slave Trade." 1 Jan. 1808. In Porter, A141:
345-353; in Woodson, A177:32-41; and in Foner,
A74:20-25, excerpt. [See Sipkins, SE2096.]

SE2356 _____. "A Discourse on the Death of Captain
Paul Cuffe." 21 Oct. 1817. In Foner, A74:28-33;
in Brawley, A24:101-109, abr.; and in Fishel and
Quarles, A72:75-78.

SE2357 _____. "A Discourse Delivered in St. Philip's
Church, for the Benefit of the Coloured Community
of Wilberforce, in Upper Canada." 4 July 1830.
In Porter, A141:295-302; in Woodson, A177:77-85;
in Foner, A74:43-47, excerpt; and in Garrison, A77:
64-67, excerpt.

WILLIAMS, PETER. See Woodson, HC1188:67-68.

SE2358 Williams, Robert F. "Can Negroes Afford to Be
Pacifists?" Sept. 1959. In Goodman, A83:270-277.
[See King, SE1434.]

SE2359 _____. Negroes with Guns. Ed. Marc Schleifer.
New York: Marzani, 1962.
Contains: "Self-Defense Prevents Bloodshed,"
pp. 42-49.
"An NAACP Chapter Is Reborn in Militancy," pp.
50-64.
"The Struggle for Militancy in the NAACP," pp.
65-74.
"Non-Violence Emboldens the Racists: A Week
of Terror," pp. 75-82.
"Self-Defense Prevents a Pogrom: Racists Engi-
neer a Kidnapping Frameup," pp. 83-90.
"The Monroe Case: Conspiracy Against the Ne-
gro," pp. 91-109.
"Self-Defense: An American Tradition," pp. 110-
124; rpt. in Barbour, A8:149-161; in Grant,
A84:340-344, excerpt; and in Katope and
Zolbrod, A105:395-398, excerpt.

WILLIAMS, ROBERT F. See Cohen, HC28; Mayfield,
HC901; Clarke, HC918:103-106; Boulware, HC1023:
217-220; Boulware, HC1043; and Bell, HC1229:53-57.

SE2360 Willis, George C., and Alfred Niger. "Resolutions
on Colonization." 1 Nov. 1831. In Garrison, A77:
44-45.

SE2361 Wilson, C. E. "The Screens." c. 1968. In Jones
and Neal, A103:133-143.

SE2362 [Wilson, Joseph.] "Life Among the Higher Classes
of Negro Society in Philadelphia." 1841. In Bracey,
A21:121-130.

SE2363 [Woodson, A. J.] "God's Mysteries upon the Mountain." 21 June 1942. In Pipes, HC1197:17-21.

SE2364 Woodson, Carter G. "Some Things Negroes Need
to Do." Jan. 1922. In Aptheker, A2:348-351.

SE2365 _____. Fifty Years of Negro Citizenship as

Qualified by the United States Supreme Court.
1924. Washington: Associated, 1924. Rpt. in Calverton, A30:413-435, excerpt.

SE2366 _____. "History and Propaganda." 10 Feb. 1926.
In Cromwell, A42:303-307.

SE2367 _____. "The Miseducation of the Negro." Aug.
1931. In Aptheker, A2:686-691.

WOODSON, CARTER G. See Bullock, HC19:121-128;
Klingberg, HC244; Wesley, HC272; and Logan, SE
1537.

SE2368 [Woodson, Lewis]. "Augustine." Letters, 3 Nov.
1837-26 Feb. 1841. In Stuckey, A160:118-148.

SE2369 _____. "Emigration." 1851. In Payne, HC1181:
85-90.

WOODSON, LEWIS. See Miller, HC118.

SE2370 Woodson, Sarah J. "Address to the Youth." 1863.
In Payne, HC1181:134-139.

SE2371 Wright, Luther, and Daniel R. Condol. "Resolutions
on Colonization." 9 Jan. 1832. In Garrison, A77:
48-49.

SE2372 Wright, Nathan, Jr. "A National Necessity." Oct.
1966. In Wright, A178:13-23. [Rev. of "Black
Power: A Creative Necessity." Catholic World,
204 (Oct. 1966), 46-51; rpt. in Littleton and Burger,
A112:381-389.]

SE2373 _____. "Self-Development and Self-Respect." 23
Oct. 1966. In Wright, A178:58-69.

SE2374 _____. "The Economics of Race." Jan. 1967.
American Journal of Economics, 26 (Jan. 1967), 1-
12. Rpt. as "Race Economics" in Wright, A178:46-
57; and in Littleton and Burger, A112:305-313.

SE2375 _____. "Is Brotherhood Enough?" Jan. 1967.
Catholic World, 204 (Jan. 1967), 234-238. Rpt. in
Wright, A178:174-185.

SE2376 _____. "Power and Conscience." 1967. In
Wright, A178:1-12.

SE2377 _____. "The Creative Use of Black Power."
1967. In Wright, A178:24-45.

SE2378 _____. "The Public Education Battleground."
1967. In Wright, A178:70-88.

SE2379 _____. "Race-Related Problems." 1967. In
Wright, A178:89-115.

SE2380 _____. "Black Leadership and American Goals."
1967. In Wright, A178:116-134.

SE2381 _____. "A Religious Opportunity." 1967. In
Wright, A178:135-155.

SE2382 _____. "The Difficulties of Self-Awareness."
1967. In Wright, A178:156-173.

SE2383 _____. Let's Work Together. 1968. New York:
Hawthorn, 1968.
        Contains: "Are We Really Together?" pp. 9-24.
        "Setting the Record Straight," pp. 25-38.
        "The Need for Helping Hands," pp. 39-52.
        "Making Educational Changes," pp. 53-76.
        "Twenty Tasks for White People," pp. 77-116.
        "Knowing the Beauty of What We Are," pp. 117-
        143.
        "The Need to Organize," pp. 144-176.
        "Healing the Sick," pp. 177-202.
        "Getting the Pitch," pp. 203-237.
        "Urgent Responsibilities," pp. 238-258.

SE2384 _____. "The Ethics of Power in the Black Revolution." 1969. In Moss, A130:13-23.

SE2385 _____. "Black Studies--Forecast from Hindsight."
19 April 1970. In Wright, A179:206-216.

SE2386 _____. "The Social Arena of Black Political Action." 1972. In Wright, A180:181-210.

SE2387 Wright, Richard. "The Ethics of Living Jim Crow."
1937. Uncle Tom's Children. New York: Harper,
1940. Pages 3-15. Rpt. in Brown, A28:1050-1060;

and in Chapman, A32:288-298.

SE2388 _____. "How Bigger Was Born." 7 March 1940.
Saturday Review of Literature, 1 June 1940, pp. 3-
4, 17-20. Rpt., enl., in Native Son. New York:
Harper, n.d. Pages vii-xxxiv. And in Chapman,
A32:538-563.

SE2389 _____. "I Tried to Be a Communist." 1944.
Atlantic Monthly, Aug. 1944, pp. 61-70; and Sept.
1944, pp. 48-56. Rpt. in The God That Failed.
Ed. Richard Crossman. New York: Harper, 1949.
Pages 115-162.

SE2390 _____. "Tradition and Industrialization: The
Plight of the Tragic Elite in Africa." 21 Sept.
1956. Presence Africaine, Nos. 8-10 (June-Nov.
1956), 355-369. Rpt. in Wright, A181:44-68.

SE2391 _____. "The Psychological Reactions of Op-
pressed People." 1957. In Wright, A181:1-43.

SE2392 _____. "The Miracle of Nationalism in the African Gold Coast." 1957. In Wright, A181:106-137.

WRIGHT, RICHARD. See Webb, HC192; Wright,
HC204; Cruse, HC448:181-189; Bone, HC964:140-
152; Gibson, HC980; Gloster, HC981:222-234;
Gloster, HC982; Baldwin, SE62; and CLA Journal,
12 (June 1969), passim.

SE2393 Wright, Richard R., Jr. "What Does the Negro
Want in Our Democracy?" June 1919. In Aptheker, A2:285-293.

SE2394 Wright, Stephen J. "The Price of Excellence." 9
Feb. 1963. In Hill, A93:321-326.

SE2395 Wright, Theodore S. "A Pastoral Letter." 20 June
1832. In Porter, A141:473-477.

SE2396 _____. "The Progress of the Antislavery Cause."
20 Sept. 1837. In Woodson, A177:86-92; in Aptheker,
A1:169-173; and in Foner, A74:61-63, excerpt.

SE2397 _____. "Prejudice Against the Colored Man."
20 Sept. 1837. In Woodson, A177:92-95; and in
Foner, A74:63-66.

SE2398 [Wynn, E. L.] "Thou Shalt Love the Lord Thy
God." 14 June 1942. In Pipes, HC1197:9-16.

SE2399 Young, Robert Alexander. "The Ethiopian Manifesto,
Issued in Defence of the Black Man's Rights in the
Scale of Universal Freedom." 13 Feb. 1829. In
Stuckey, A160:30-38.

SE2400 Young, Whitney M., Jr. "What Price Prejudice?--
On the Economics of Discrimination." 1962. Freedomways, 2 (Summer 1962), 237-242.

SE2401 _____. "Address to the March on Washington."
28 Aug. 1963. In Speeches by the Leaders, A131:
n. pag.

SE2402 _____. "The Social Revolution." 1963. In Broderick and Meier, A26:288-296, abr.; and in Foner,
A74:962-969, abr.

SE2403 _____. To Be Equal. 1964. New York: Mc-
Graw-Hill, 1964.
       Contains: "Introduction," pp. 10-20.
       "Needed Now: A Special Effort," pp. 22-33 (rpt.
          in Littleton, A112:287-293).
       "A Nation Governed by Law," pp. 36-50.
       "Help Wanted: New Jobs for Negroes," pp. 52-
          99.
       "Education: Last, Best Hope?" pp. 102-137.
       "Decent Housing: Whose Responsibility?" pp.
          140-162.
       "The Welfare of All," pp. 164-180.
       "Poor Health in the Richest Nation," pp. 182-211.
       "Leadership: The Responsibilities of Citizenship,"
          pp. 214-230.
       "The Social Revolution and the American Dream,"
          pp. 232-254.

SE2404 _____. "Agenda for the Future." 1 Aug. 1965.
In Williams and Williams, A175:181-189.

SE2405 _____. "The Crisis of the Cities: The Danger of
the Ghetto." 28 Feb. 1967. In Smith and Robb,
A156:161-181.

SE2406 _____. "When Negro Leaders Look Ahead." Nov.
1968. U.S. News and World Report, 25 Nov. 1968,

pp. 58-59.   Rpt. in Littleton and Burger, A112:320-323.

SE2407 _____. "Is America a Civilized Nation?" 1968. In Moss, A130:23-28.

SE2408 _____. "Crisis--Challenge--Change." April 1969. Parks and Recreation, 4 (April 1969), 42-43, 61-67. Rpt. in Littleton and Burger, A112:258-269.

SE2409 _____. Beyond Racism: Building an Open Society. 1969. New York: McGraw Hill, 1969. Contains: "The Open Society," pp. 3-13. "Black America," pp. 17-70. "White America," pp. 73-147. "Building an Open Society," pp. 151-202. "Responsibility for Change," pp. 205-265.

SE2410 _____. "Other Voices, Other Strategies." April 1970. Time, 6 April 1970, pp. 23-24, 27. Rpt. in Littleton and Burger, A112:432-436.

SE2411 _____. "Address to the Congress of African Peoples." Sept. 1970. In Jones, A101:35-43.

YOUNG, WHITNEY M., JR. See Boulware, HC1023: 238-242; and Lomax, SE1539:209-220.

CHRONOLOGICAL INDEX OF SE ITEMS

1760	1794	1809	1816	1827	429
					435
1187	1395	1183	410	436	723
		1367		1185	872
		2092		1632	922
1786	1797	2097	1817	1792	1024
					1248
1188	1179		190		1368
	1394	1810	907	1828	1606
	1776		908		1714
1788		409	2136	11	1816
			2356	526	1880
1177	1798			866	1969
1782		1812		2214	1970
	2110		1818	2308	2089
		502			2109
1789			1222		2119
	1799		2066	1829	2137
935		1813	2067		2172
1607	1396			412	2201
		906		2215	2210
		1498	1824	2399	2309
1791	1805				2360
			1795		
75	1221	1814		1830	
					1832
		1788	1825	28	
1792	1808			417	8
			78	2288	413
1178	13	1815		2357	909
	1397				1389
	1631	1184	1826		1393
1793	2096			1831	1474
	2355		2000		1715
12				83	1777
				414	1781

2101	424	_1843_	_1848_	592	1875
2117	867			719	2105
2138	911	523	566	736	2290
2139	2311	551	567	1478	2291
2211	2312	945	568	2184	
2371	2396	1720	569	2369	
2395	2397		570		_1854_
			571		
		_1844_	572	_1852_	220
_1833_	_1838_		946		453
		214	1964	19	528
14	34			20	605
15	1988			342	606
1716	2102	_1845_	_1849_	451	607
1793				452	608
1794		552	17	527	609
2140	_1839_	553	94	593	610
2310		554	573	594	720
	1796	555	574	595	724
		1797	575	596	725
_1834_			576	597	726
	_1840_		577	1798	727
437		_1846_	578	1799	728
1186	943		579	1812	729
1719	1717	450	580	1889	730
1888		556	581	2104	731
1995		557	582		732
	_1841_	558			733
		559		_1853_	734
_1835_	548	560	_1850_		735
	1958	2159		21	1953
1718	1959		583	22	1961
1882	1998		584	23	2292
1996	2093	_1847_	585	598	
1997	2103		586	599	
	2313	218	587	600	_1855_
	2362	219	588	601	
_1836_	2368	561	1538	602	221
		562	2221	603	454
910		563		604	611
2289	_1842_	564		871	612
		565	_1851_	1480	613
	549	1878		1760	614
_1837_	550		18	1761	615
	944		589	1778	616
24	1883		590	1783	617
25	1960		591	1800	1249

1487	**1878**	482	1290	**1888**	863
1488		483	1291		915
1489	112	484	1292	209	916
1807	113	485	1293	443	917
1894		486	1294	492a	918
1952		487	1295	712	1025
2142	**1879**	488	1296	1070	1347
2147		912	1297	1071	1366
	76	1556	1298	1072	1392
	701	2200	1299	1808	1496
1875	702	2223	1355	1809	1499
	1040		1356	2148	1545
108	1495		1357	2227	1557
273	1756	**1883**	1358	2228	1729
465			1416	2229	1785
859		117	1417		1787
1206	**1880**	230	1543		1810
1490		231	1724	**1889**	1815
1491	114	441	2173		1841
1555	228	489	2224	232	1843
	317	704		713	1844
	1840	705		1193	1873
1876		706	**1885**	1993	1874
		707			1881
109	**1881**	913	491		1890
110		1561	709	**1890**	2068
111	115	2191			2088
226	468			32	2094
227	469		**1886**	35	2129
700	703	**1884**		122	2130
1220			492	123	2134
1492		118	710	187	2141
1493	**1882**	442	711	193	2143
1992		490	914	194	2149
2098	116	708	2192	195	2161
2156	470	1037	2225	196	2179
2190	471	1279		198	2206
	472	1280		204	2209
	473	1281	**1887**	213	2230
1877	474	1282		233	2231
	475	1283	119	268	2232
229	476	1284	120	334	2233
343	477	1285	121	425	
466	478	1286	252	431	
467	479	1287	1562	493	**1891**
1494	480	1288	2226	525	
1501	481	1289		714	1497

<u>1904</u>	1658	1063	1930	505	1068
	1922	1122	1931	778	1136
304	2212	1123	1932	779	1235
433		1664		860	1236
754				952	1237
755	<u>1906</u>		<u>1911</u>	1066	1342
877		<u>1909</u>		1133	1370
1061	759		772	1218	1558
1111	760	235	773	1415	1677
1112	761	253	1065	1513	1820
1113	762	504	1130	1559	1821
1114	1117	768	1131	1672	1994
1194	1118	769	1671	1673	2075
1225	1119	1064	1933	1674	2133
1649	1659	1124	1934	1675	2153
1650	1660	1125	1985	1819	2168
1921	1923	1126	1986	1940	2171
1983	1924	1619	1987	2090	2284
2132	1925	1665	2081	2280	2285
2158	2166	1725	2167	2301	2286
2164	2270	1927	2277		2287
2165		1928			
2268		1984		<u>1914</u>	
2269	<u>1907</u>	2074	<u>1912</u>		<u>1916</u>
		2213		1134	
	763	2219	423	1135	239
<u>1905</u>	764	2220	774	1676	411
	765	2276	775	2181	434
250	766	2300	776	2281	783
251	1120		777	2282	953
422	1121		1132	2283	1137
521	1661	<u>1910</u>	1209		1138
756	1662		1732		1139
757	1663	770	1818	<u>1915</u>	1140
758	1926	771	1935		1514
1062	2271	1058	1936	191	1678
1115	2272	1127	1937	192	1733
1116	2273	1128	1938	237	1734
1303	2274	1129	1939	238	1784
1547	2275	1666	2100	316	1822
1651		1667	2278	445	1823
1652		1668	2279	447	1824
1653	<u>1908</u>	1669		538	1825
1654		1670		780	1826
1655	133	1758	<u>1913</u>	781	1827
1656	539	1817		782	1828
1657	767	1929	236	1067	1829

1026	1009	1174	1019	2398	1504
1378	1308	1233	1020		1623
1379	1381	1313	1317		2332
1849	1418	1759		_1943_	
	1850	1901			
	2338	1944	_1939_	186	_1946_
_1929_		1945		206	
		1946	1318	822	153
803	_1933_	1947	1852	1535	516
804		1948	1853	1972	830
1002	808	1949	1854	2331	831
1003	809	1950	1855		832
1004	810	1951	1856		833
1005	1231	1971	1857	_1944_	1323
1380	1309	2339	2302		1324
1900	1711			89	1325
2204	1712			216	1326
2329	1851	_1936_	_1940_	823	1327
2330	1943			824	1328
		254	255	825	1329
		815	819	826	1973
_1930_	_1934_	816	1319	827	
		817	2388	1192	
27	811	1017		1242	_1947_
805	1172	1018		1320	
1006	1173	1175	_1941_	1536	517
1007	1232	1902		1608	834
1170	1310	1903	820	1789	903
1171	1311	2084	821	1908	1330
1738	1312		1905	2079	1989
1942	1382		1906	2178	2003
		_1937_		2295	2004
				2303	
_1931_	_1935_	86	_1942_	2337	
		1314		2340	_1948_
1	812	1315	335	2341	
151	813	1316	868	2389	39
806	814	1904	939		40
807	902	2120	1059		835
1307	1010	2387	1390	_1945_	1360
2367	1011		1391		2005
	1012		1739	152	
	1013	_1938_	1907	524	
_1932_	1014		1956	828	_1949_
	1015	87	2001	829	
901	1016	88	2002	1321	41
1008	1029	818	2363	1322	90

1451	1520	1522	1542	378	2377
1452	1521	1523	1755	379	2378
1453	1541	1524	1767	380	2379
1454	1583	1601	1768	416	2380
1455	1584	1602	1845	886	2381
1456	1585	1603	1870	898	2382
1457	1586	1604	1871	1198	2405
1508	1587	1605	2018	1200	
1509	1588	1731	2019	1240	
1516	1589	1742	2135	1359	1968
1517	1590	1786	2144	1408	
1540	1591	1869	2347	1420	16
1577	1592	1914	2372	1461	70
1578	1593	1990	2373	1462	71
1579	1594	2016		1463	72
1580	1595	2017		1464	79
1581	1596	2064	1967	1465	134
1582	1597	2306		1466	140
1741	1598	2404	137	1467	141
1868	1599		138	1468	142
1913	1600		139	1469	143
2012	1627	1966	202	1526	144
2013	2015		203	1527	161
2014	2091	199	210	1528	223
2216	2122	200	211	1529	224
2297	2403	201	288	1530	294
2305		280	289	1566	295
2345		281	290	1628	296
2346	1965	282	291	1769	358
2394		283	292	1770	359
2401	69	284	293	1846	360
2402	279	285	312	2020	361
	309	286	338	2021	362
	337	287	345	2022	363
1964	366	318	346	2023	364
	367	373	347	2024	381
136	368	374	348	2025	382
426	369	375	349	2026	383
883	370	376	350	2027	384
1196	371	427	351	2028	385
1404	372	878	352	2029	386
1405	522	1197	353	2108	387
1425	884	1199	354	2116	388
1458	885	1340	355	2175	389
1459	1406	1475	356	2374	390
1518	1407	1525	357	2375	391
1519	1460	1532	377	2376	392

1972	2127
	2151
73	2386
80	
149	
174	1973
175	
176	301
177	440
178	1427
179	2060
180	2351
181	
182	
183	
308	
325	
326	
327	
328	
329	
330	
331	
341	
403	
404	
419	
420	
537	
542	
865	
1023	
1056	
1057	
1180	
1204	
1205	
1215	
1216	
1352	
1353	
1413	
1422	
1477	
1537	
2087	
2126	

AUTHOR INDEX
(Sections I-III)

Abbott, Martin, HC619,
HC620
Abrahams, Roger D., HC330
Abramowitz, Jack, HC775,
HC812, HC813
Abramson, Doris, HC959
Abzug, Robert H., HC497
Adams, Alice Dana, HC484
Adelman, Lynn, HC1
Aiello, John R., HC376
Alexander, Thomas B.,
HC621, HC622
Allen, Archie E., HC207
Allen, James S., HC623,
HC862
Allen, Richard, HC2, HC3
Allen, Robert L., HC912
American Negro Academy,
A132, A136
Anatol, Karl W., HC1035
Anderson, Jervis, HC4
Andrews, James R., HC1020
Andrews, Norman P., HC743
Anthony, Earl, HC913
Aptheker, Herbert, B1; A1,
A2, A3, A60, A157,
A171; HC44, HC485,
HC498, HC499, HC558,
HC624, HC887
Arnold, Martin, HC208
Aron, Birgit, HC835
Asinof, Eliot, HC1036
Auer, J. Jeffery, A4, A5

Bacote, Clarence A., HC5,

HC744
Bailey, Harry A., Jr., HC
1228
Bailey, Peter, HC960
Baird, A. Craig, HC1033
Baker, David N., HC961
Baldwin, James, A6, A7;
HC1200
Bancroft, Frederic, HC713
Banninga, Jerald L., HC1037
Baraka, Imamu Amiri, A101,
A102, A103; HC988,
HC1265
Baratz, Joan C., HC331
Barbour, Floyd B., A8, A9
Barksdale, Ethelbert, HC625
Barnes, Gilbert Hobbs, HC500
Barrett, Harold, HC1038
Barrows, Isabel C., HC776
Bartlett, Irving H., HC501
Batten, J. Minton, HC6
Baxandall, Lee, B2
Bell, Howard Holman, A10;
HC559, HC560, HC561, HC
562, HC563, HC564, HC1254
Bell, Inge Powell, HC914,
HC1229, HC1255
Belz, Herman, HC626
Bennett, Lerone, Jr., A11;
HC7, HC436, HC437, HC565,
HC566, HC604, HC627,
HC628, HC629, HC745,
HC777, HC778, HC814,
HC815, HC836, HC837,
HC863, HC873, HC881,

361